Anglo-Saxon Studies 29

REPRESENTING BEASTS IN EARLY MEDIEVAL
ENGLAND AND SCANDINAVIA

Anglo-Saxon Studies

ISSN 1475-2468

GENERAL EDITORS
John Hines
Catherine Cubitt

'Anglo-Saxon Studies' aims to provide a forum for the best scholarship on the Anglo-Saxon peoples in the period from the end of Roman Britain to the Norman Conquest, including comparative studies involving adjacent populations and periods; both new research and major re-assessments of central topics are welcomed.

Books in the series may be based in any one of the principal disciplines of archaeology, art history, history, language and literature, and inter- or multi-disciplinary studies are encouraged.

Proposals or enquiries may be sent directly to the editors or the publisher at the addresses given below; all submissions will receive prompt and informed consideration.

Professor John Hines, School of History, Archaeology and Religion, Cardiff University, John Percival Building, Colum Drive, Cardiff, Wales, CF10 3EU, UK

Professor Catherine Cubitt, Centre for Medieval Studies, University of York, The King's Manor, York, England, YO1 7EP, UK

Boydell & Brewer, PO Box 9, Woodbridge, Suffolk, England, IP12 3DF, UK

Previously published volumes in the series are listed at the back of this book

REPRESENTING BEASTS IN EARLY MEDIEVAL ENGLAND AND SCANDINAVIA

Edited by
Michael D. J. Bintley and Thomas J. T. Williams

THE BOYDELL PRESS

© Contributors 2015

All Rights Reserved. Except as permitted under current legislation no part of this work may be photocopied, stored in a retrieval system, published, performed in public, adapted, broadcast, transmitted, recorded or reproduced in any form or by any means, without the prior permission of the copyright owner

First published 2015
The Boydell Press, Woodbridge
Paperback edition 2019

ISBN 978 1 78327 008 8 hardback
ISBN 978 1 78327 369 0 paperback

The Boydell Press is an imprint of Boydell & Brewer Ltd
PO Box 9, Woodbridge, Suffolk IP12 3DF, UK
and of Boydell & Brewer Inc.
668 Mt Hope Avenue, Rochester, NY 14620–2731, USA
website: www.boydellandbrewer.com

The publisher has no responsibility for the continued existence or accuracy of URLs for external or third-party internet websites referred to in this book, and does not guarantee that any content on such websites is, or will remain, accurate or appropriate

A CIP catalogue record for this book is available
from the British Library

Contents

List of Figures and Tables	vii
Acknowledgements	x
List of Contributors	xi
List of Abbreviations	xii

Introduction
Michael D. J. Bintley and Thomas J. T. Williams — 1

1 Between Myth and Reality: Hunter and Prey in Early Anglo-Saxon Art
  Noël Adams — 13

2 '(Swinger of) the Serpent of Wounds': Swords and Snakes in the Viking Mind
  Sue Brunning — 53

3 *Wreopenhilt ond wyrmfah*: Confronting Serpents in *Beowulf* and Beyond
  Victoria Symons — 73

4 The Ravens on the Lejre Throne: Avian Identifiers, Odin at Home, Farm Ravens
  Marijane Osborn — 94

5 *Beowulf's* Blithe-Hearted Raven
  Eric Lacey — 113

6 Do Anglo-Saxons Dream of Exotic Sheep?
  László Sándor Chardonnens — 131

7 You Sexy Beast: The Pig in a Villa in Vandalic North Africa, and Boar-Cults in Old Germanic Heathendom
  Richard North — 151

8 'For the Sake of Bravado in the Wilderness': Confronting the Bestial in Anglo-Saxon Warfare
  Thomas J. T. Williams — 176

9 Where the Wild Things Are in Old English Poetry
  Michael D. J. Bintley — 205

10 Entomological Etymologies: Creepy-Crawlies in English
    Place-Names
    John Baker 229

11 Beasts, Birds and Other Creatures in Pre-Conquest Charters
    and Place-Names in England
    Della Hooke 253

    Index 283

Figures and Tables

Figures

1.1 Late Roman glass bowl from Wint Hill, Somerset; AN1957.186 © Ashmolean Museum, University of Oxford; Diam: 190 mm 23

1.2 Bucket mounts from Giberville, Calvados; after Christian Pilet, Luc Buchet, Jacqueline Pilet-Lemière *et al.*, 'L'apport de l'archéologie funéraire à l'étude de la présence militaire sur le limes saxon, le long des côtes de l'actuelle Basse-Normandie', *L'Armée romaine et les barbares du IIIe au VIIe siècle*, ed. Françoise Vallet and Michel Kazanski, AFAM, Musée des Antiquités Nationales (Saint-Germain, 1993), pl. 9 25

1.3 Bracelets 11 and 21 from Hoxne, Suffolk; British Museum P&E 1994,0408.11 and 21; after Catherine M. Johns, *The Hoxne Late Roman Treasure: Gold Jewellery and Silver Plate* (London, 2010), figs. 3.25 and 3.28(c); Diam of both: 62 mm 26

1.4 Strap end from Furfooz, Namur, grave 3; after Bernhard Salin, *Die altgermanische Tierornamentik* (Stockholm, 1904), fig. 332; L: 76 mm 28

1.5 *Stutzarmfibel* in private collection, London; photograph © Noël Adams; W: 50 mm 28

1.6 Nesse Type 1 brooch from Maidenhead, Berkshire; FASW-948D00 © Stuart Laidlaw; W: 78 mm 28

1.7 Scabbard mount from Cheriton, Hampshire; PAS SUR-029B13 © PAS and Surrey County Council; W: 50 mm 29

1.8 Fragmentary quoit brooch from Howletts grave 13; P&E 1935,1029.11 © Trustees of the British Museum; L: 47 mm 30

1.9 Quoit brooch from Sarre Grave 1; P&E 1893,0601.219 © Trustees of the British Museum; Diam: 77 mm 30

1.10 Enamelled disc from St Mary Bourne, Basingstoke, and Dean, Hampshire; PAS HAMP-FFCDF4 © Winchester Museums Service; Diam: 78.5 mm 31

1.11 Bow brooch; CANCM 2634, courtesy of Canterbury Museum; photograph: Andrew Richardson; L: 84.5 mm 31

1.12 Strap end from Sarre, Kent; P&E 1893,0601.237 © Trustees of the British Museum; L: 55 mm 33

1.13 Harness fitting from Long Marston, Harrogate, Yorkshire; PAS YORYM-A74BF7 © York Museums Trust; L: 58 mm 33

1.14 Saucer brooch from Long Wittenham grave 46 (Berkshire); after Nils Åberg, *The Anglo-Saxons in England during the Early Centuries after the Invasion* (Uppsala, 1926), fig. 23; Diam: 41 mm   33

1.15 Headplate of great-square-headed brooch from Ruskington, Lincolnshire; after John Hines, *A New Corpus of Anglo-Saxon Great Square-Headed Brooches* (Woodbridge, 1997), fig. 25e; W of headplate: 49 mm   35

1.16 Great square-headed brooch; Thaw Collection, The Pierpont Morgan Library, New York 2012.2:68; H: 133 mm   35

1.17 Shield mounts from Bromeswell, Suffolk; P&E 2001,0103.3.e and 2001,0103.3.f.1 © Trustees of the British Museum; W: 45 mm and L: 95 mm   37

1.18 Bird and snake mount from Dean and Shelton, Bedfordshire; PAS WMID-E4F0C5 © Birmingham Museum and Art Gallery; L: 16 mm   37

1.19 Panels of *Spangenhelm* from Montepagano, Teramo, Italy; after Volker Bierbrauer, *Die Ostgotischen Grab- und Schatzfunde in Italien*, Centro Italiano di Studi sull'alto Medioevo (Spoleto, 1975), fig. 28   41

1.20 Purse lid from Mound 1, Sutton Hoo, Suffolk; P&E 1933,1010.2 © Trustees of the British Museum; L: 190 mm   44

1.21 Sasanian bowl in private collection, London; photograph © Noël Adams; Diam: 75 mm   45

1.22 Detail of eleventh-century Saljūq sabre blade, R-249; The Furusiyya Art Foundation; photograph © Noël Adams; L: 752 mm   51

1.23 Dagger and scabbard from Outremer, R-937; The Furusiyya Art Foundation; photograph © Noël Adams; L: 385 mm   52

2.1 The characteristic diamond-shaped markings of the adder (*Vipera berus*)   60

2.2 Type D sword hilt from Trælnes, Norway; photograph: Ole Bjørn Pedersen © Museum of Natural History and Archaeology, NTNU, Trondheim, Norway   61

2.3 Type H sword hilt of unknown provenance; photograph: Christer Åhlin © Statens Historiska Museum, Stockholm, Sweden   62

4.1 The Lejre Raven Throne; drawing by Gilli Allan (2014)   95

4.2 Enthroned Zeus with his eagle; drawing by Gilli Allan (2014)   99

4.3 Gold bracteate from Várpalóta, Hungary; drawing by Herbert Lange, reproduced with permission   102

4.4	The Clonmacnoise Plaque; drawing by Gilli Allan (2014)	103
4.5	Seventh-century Vendel helmet plate; drawing by Gilli Allan (2014)	105
8.1	Predominant landscape attributes of conflict sites, AD 429–866 (graph)	189
8.2	The Neolithic long-barrow known as Adam's Grave (formerly *Woddesbeorg*), Wiltshire; photograph: Thomas J. T. Williams	192
11.1	A dragon depicted on an early ninth-century cross at Cropthorne, Worcestershire	255
11.2	Domestic animals noted in charters and early place-names in the West Midlands (map)	260
11.3	Pigs being used by conservators to clear woodland above an early enclosure in the Wyre Forest, Worcestershire; photograph: © Adam Mindykowski	261
11.4	Wild animals noted in charters and early place-names in the West Midlands (map)	270
11.5	Birds noted in charters and early place-names in the West Midlands (map)	273
11.6	The boundary landmarks of Bishop's Cleeve and adjacent lands, Gloucestershire, in a charter of AD 768×79 (S 141) and an undated boundary clause (S 1549) (map)	281

Tables

2.1	Sword kennings incorporating references to snakes	58
8.1	The toponymy of early medieval battles in English sources to AD 860	182–7
10.1	OE *wifel* place-names attested in the medieval period, excluding those with habitative generics	238–41
10.2	OE *wicga* place-names attested in the medieval period, excluding those with habitative generics	242–4

The editors, contributors and publishers are grateful to all the institutions and persons listed for permission to reproduce the materials in which they hold copyright. Every effort has been made to trace the copyright holders; apologies are offered for any omission, and the publishers will be pleased to add any necessary acknowledgement in subsequent editions.

Acknowledgements

The editors are grateful to the Institute of Archaeology and the English Department at UCL, and in particular to Professors Andrew Reynolds and Richard North, for helping to foster the spirit of cross-disciplinary engagement which has made both this book, and the 2011 conference from which it sprang, possible and fruitful. Several long-term collaborations and friendships have resulted from the enlightened attitude taken to medieval studies within that institution, to which end we would also like to thank Eric Lacey, Tina Paphitis, Michael Shapland, and Vicky Symons. Mike Bintley would also like to thank Canterbury Christ Church University for providing funding towards the research time necessary for the preparation of this volume. Thanks are also due to Caroline Palmer at Boydell & Brewer for her enthusiasm and patience, and also to the anonymous reader whose positive attention ensured that this book was taken up for publication. We are also, of course, grateful to all the contributors to this volume who have invested great time and energy in the project and whose lively and thought-provoking essays have helped significantly to lighten the burden of editorial duties.

Contributors

Noël Adams	Independent Scholar
John Baker	Institute for Name-Studies, University of Nottingham
Michael D. J. Bintley	Canterbury Christ Church University
Sue Brunning	The British Museum and University College London
László Sándor Chardonnens	Radboud University Nijmegen
Della Hooke	University of Birmingham
Eric Lacey	University of Winchester
Richard North	University College London
Marijane Osborn	University of California, Davis
Victoria Symons	University College London
Thomas J. T. Williams	University College London and The British Museum

Abbreviations

ASD	J. Bosworth and T. Toller, *An Anglo-Saxon Dictionary* (Oxford, 1898)
ASE	*Anglo-Saxon England*
ASPR	The Anglo-Saxon Poetic Records
ASSAH	*Anglo-Saxon Studies in Archaeology and History*
BAR	British Archaeological Reports
CDEPN	*The Cambridge Dictionary of English Place-Names, Based on the Collections of the English Place-Name Society*, ed. Victor Watts (Cambridge, 2004)
CSASE	Cambridge Studies in Anglo-Saxon England
DOE	*Dictionary of Old English: A to G Online*, ed. Angus Cameron, Ashley Crandell Amos, Antonette diPaolo Healey *et al.* (Toronto, 2007)
EETS	Early English Text Society
	es extra series
	os original series
	ss supplementary series
EPNS	English Place-Name Society
ES	*English Studies*
JEGP	*Journal of English and Germanic Philology*
JEPNS	*Journal of the English Place-Name Society*
LSE	*Leeds Studies in English*
ME	Middle English
MedArch	*Medieval Archaeology*
NM	*Neuphilologische Mitteilungen*
OE	Old English
OED	Oxford English Dictionary Online, accessed at http://www.oed.com/
OFr	Old French
ON	Old Norse
PDE	Present Day English
PL	*Patrologia Latina*

Introduction

Michael D. J. Bintley and Thomas J. T. Williams

A man stands with arms raised, brandishing spears in both hands; he appears to be naked apart from a belt and a sheathed sword slung from a baldrick over one shoulder. His head is adorned by a helmet – or it might be a head-dress – from which rise two horn-like projections, each one terminating with the head of a bird, clearly delineated with eye and beak. The birds (the curl of their beaks suggests they are intended to be understood as raptors) face each other, curving inward until they overlap and form a circle above the spearman's clean-shaven face. To the right of this figure stands another apparition. He too holds a spear, thrust seemingly into the earth – or perhaps into the foot of his companion. He is drawing a sword with his right hand. This figure is clothed, perhaps even in armour, but a tail hangs down at his rear and his features are inhuman. He has the head of a beast.

Various overlapping interpretations have been offered for this striking image – it is Óðinn/Woden leading an ecstatic dance; a warrior in ritual transformation from man to wolf; a shaman enacting an initiatory rite; the dramatisation of a mythological scene.[1] We will almost certainly never understand what message this image was truly intended to convey. What is clear, however, is that in this image the categories of beast and human are inextricably blurred, confused, confounded. Who here is the human? Which is the god, the animal, the hybrid? Does the naked spearman wear birds upon his head or do divine raptors control the body of a human puppet? Does a man wear a wolf's clothing, or does a wolf wear a man's? It is precisely this sort of ambiguity in the representation of beasts and beast-identities that lies at the heart of this collection of papers.

The image on the cover of this book is a matrix of seventh-century date, found at Torslunda in Sweden, and designed for the production of panels of decorated metal ultimately destined for the ostentatious helmets of an élite warrior aristocracy. Objects bearing this style of iconographic display are exemplified by finds from the Swedish cemeteries of Vendel and Valsgärde, and also in similar objects from English contexts: the famous helmet from mound 1 at the Sutton

---

[1] A. Margaret Arent, 'The Heroic Pattern: Old Germanic Helmets, *Beowulf*, and *Grettis Saga*', in *Old Norse Literature and Mythology: A Symposium*, ed. Edgar C. Polome (Austin, TX, 1969), pp. 130–99; Terry Gunnell, *The Origins of Drama in Scandinavia* (Cambridge, 1995), pp. 66–72; Neil Price, *The Viking Way* (Uppsala, 2003), pp. 372–88.

Hoo cemetery in East Anglia, and fragments from the Staffordshire Hoard found in the West Midlands. The exact mechanisms that linked England and Scandinavia in this period are hard to define with precision, but artefactual, iconographic, linguistic, literary and mortuary parallels demonstrate a degree of contact and the sharing of cultural concepts. The geographical remit of the papers presented in this volume reflects the fact that ideas about the natural world – especially the ways in which its fauna were represented and imagined – were fluid around what might be described as a 'north sea cultural zone': they certainly did not respect the political boundaries of modern nation states. How and in what ways ideas changed over time and were shared among the inhabitants of this zone will be explored by some of the chapters directly, and will also (we hope) be illuminated by the juxtaposition of studies treating the theme of 'beasts' from a variety of disciplinary and regional perspectives.

Scholarship has been undergoing something of a renaissance in recent years as far as understanding the relationship between humans and non-humans is concerned, whether the latter are mammals, fish, fowl, plants, or even objects which those in the modern developed West would not customarily think of as living.[2] While interest in this aspect of the 'natural' world is nothing new in medieval studies, the important contribution that animals made to the lives and cultures of early medieval people in northern Europe is often addressed within relatively narrow disciplinary contexts. The aim of this book, whose individual chapters engage with a range of disciplines, is to offer new insights into the way that beasts of all kinds were represented among the peoples of early medieval England, Scandinavia, and other related cultures. This volume refers to 'beasts' not only because the word evokes a sense of wild and untamed creatures, but because the non-humans whom the reader will encounter in its pages are primarily those which *cwice hwyrfaþ* ('move around with life'), as the hall-singer puts it in *Beowulf*'s song of creation.[3] This is not, therefore, a book about non-humans that were rooted to the ground in the same

---

[2] One of the principal advocates of object-oriented philosophical approaches has been Graham Harman, who also builds on the work of Bruno Latour; see Graham Harman, *Tool-Being: Heidegger and the Metaphysics of Objects* (Chicago, 2002); Graham Harman, *Towards Speculative Realism* (Winchester, 2010); Graham Harman, *The Quadruple Object* (Winchester, 2011); Graham Harman, *Prince of Networks: Bruno Latour and Metaphysics* (Melbourne, 2009); see also Bruno Latour, *Reassembling the Social: An Introduction to Actor-Network Theory* (Oxford, 2005).

[3] *Klaeber's Beowulf and the Fight at Finnsburg*, ed. R. D. Fulk, Robert E. Bjork and John D. Niles (Toronto, 2008), line 98. This, of course, might be comfortably applied to plants as well as mammals, in so far as new philosophical approaches to plants are revealing behaviours once thought limited to animals with a consciousness apparently closer to our own. Some written works from early medieval England and Scandinavia also suggest the plants had their own agency, and were sometimes thought of in similar terms to humans. See discussion in Matthew Hall, *Plants as Persons: A Philosophical Botany*

way as trees and rocks, but rather those which (arguably) had more direct interaction with humans in both symbolic and practical terms. The discussions cover domesticated animals, like pigs, cows, sheep and poultry, as well as wild animals that were hunted and killed for food and sport, like boars, deer, and wolves; some chapters feature animals that could impart hidden knowledge – both in the waking world, like ravens, and in sleep, where they had the potential to be far more exotic; also considered are animals more obviously mythical to modern readers, like dragons, whose forms appeared in literary works and visual art; and smaller, creeping and crawling creatures whose ubiquity could be both a blessing and a curse. Then there are the humans themselves, whose savagery or religious affiliations were sometimes cast in a bestial light, and, finally, certain objects which, though created by humans, were thought to possess their own vitality. However, no suggestion is made here that this final class of beasts, and what defined it, was any more or less important than other non-humans; much work remains to be done before the full range of relationships between these various categories can be adequately represented.

In many ways this book endeavours to set a precedent for the further exploration of these relationships, by reflecting both on certain topics that are already the focus of long-established study, and on others that have received comparatively little attention. In each case, the studies included here address what the representation of beasts in early medieval England and Scandinavia can tell us about how their inhabitants defined themselves in relation to the non-humans who shared their world – whether real or imagined. Each chapter endeavours to advance the field (or fields) it represents, while simultaneously contributing to a broader understanding of the interaction and interchange between humans and non-humans.

The importance of defining and delineating the characteristics of non-humans, and, indeed, stratifying their role in the life of the earth, was known to European thought long before Carl Linnaeus. Matthew Hall has argued that the Classical philosophical tradition and the Judaic religion, as cornerstones of the Western Christian tradition, bear significant responsibility for subsequent modes of thought which have encouraged humans to think of themselves as in some way distinct from 'animals' and 'nature'.[4] Realisations to the contrary, born out of twentieth-century countercultures, have only recently gained a foothold in mainstream scholarship. However, the questioning of social boundaries and definitions is often symptomatic

---

(New York, 2011), esp. pp. 119–35; see also Michael D. J. Bintley, *Trees in the Religions of Early Medieval England* (Woodbridge, 2015).

[4] Hall, *Plants as Persons*, pp. 17–71.

of the erosion of self or group identity – a phenomenon far more likely to be found among those working at the frontiers of intellectual enquiry. For the majority of early medieval people, living their lives at some remove from the learned and literate world of ecclesiastical scholarship, category questions would not only have been irrelevant but probably incomprehensible. Moreover, as art, poetry, place-names and chronicles suggest, this was an age better acquainted and more comfortable than our own with shape-shifters, monsters, talking animals, and the repeating cycle of the agricultural year: the boundaries observed between humans and animals throughout much of the modern world would have been far less rigid to many in the early Middle Ages.[5] New approaches to the interaction between humans and non-humans within these networks (or entanglements, as Ian Hodder calls them) are beginning to represent the extent to which these relationships, and even dependencies, were recognised.[6] This book aims to contribute to this understanding, by examining some of these relationships within one group of linguistic and cultural relatives during the early medieval period.

This focus derives from growing interest in the degree to which the 'natural' world contributed to daily life in early medieval cultures.[7] The majority of those living in the developed world today exist at a significant distance from raw materials and the means of production, and many of the tools, products and foodstuffs that we encounter are largely divorced from their point of origin. Humans at all levels of early medieval society were far better acquainted with the origins of these things – albeit to different degrees. Additionally, they were also better aware of the way in which the products of animals (and other non-humans) were essential to everyday life on multiple levels. For example, the material products of animal husbandry, hunting, fishing, and fowling were not only a vital source of sustenance, but also offered up other materials, such as leather, bone, horn, fur and feathers. While all of these products are still in use today (albeit often in different capacities), the distance at which the majority of people reading this book will live from their cultivation and harvest is probably great. The early medieval understanding of this 'natural'

---

[5] Jeffrey Jerome Cohen has helmed the most extensive body of criticism on this subject so far; see, for example, *Animal, Vegetable, Mineral: Ethics and Objects*, ed. Jeffrey J. Cohen (Washington, DC, 2012); Jeffrey J. Cohen, *Medieval Identity Machines* (Minneapolis, 2003); Jeffrey J. Cohen, *Hybridity, Identity and Monstrosity in Medieval Britain: Of Difficult Middles* (Basingstoke, 2006); Jeffrey J. Cohen, *Of Giants: Sex, Monsters, and the Middle Ages* (Minneapolis, 1999).

[6] See Ian Hodder, *Entangled: An Archaeology of the Relationships between Humans and Things* (Malden, MA, 2013).

[7] See also discussion by Michael D. J. Bintley and Michael G. Shapland, 'Introduction to Trees and Timber in the Anglo-Saxon World', in *Trees and Timber in the Anglo-Saxon World*, ed. Michael D. J. Bintley and Michael G. Shapland (Oxford, 2013), pp. 1–18.

Introduction

world was complex and multi-faceted, displaying a understanding of the need for nuanced approaches to managing and maintaining certain relationships, while actively seeking to disrupt and destroy others – however wisely or unwisely. It is worth remembering that the very medium upon which knowledge was most permanently recorded and preserved – vellum – was itself an animal product. For the monk hunched over in the scriptorium, the relationship between the technological and the spiritual was mediated through the interplay of human hand and animal skin. How this symbiosis affected the way that a monk understood and thought about his world is not, perhaps, recoverable; nor is it unique to northern European experience. But the fact of the matter is worth bearing in mind as we try to make sense of medieval mentalities from the perspective of an electronic age.

The chapters in this volume make use of a variety of evidence from numerous sources, in the belief that correspondences between different types of material and documentary evidence are indicative of deeper levels of 'cultural structure and practice', as John Hines has put it.[8] Documentary sources include literary, historical, religious, devotional and magical texts, in addition to linguistic and place-name evidence. Onomastic evidence also contributes to those chapters that are more broadly grounded in historical geography and landscape archaeology. In addition, several chapters also engage with the more obviously manufactured products of material culture, whose various levels of artistry reflect interactions between humans and animals in a shared world.

Critical and Theoretical Contexts

Given that the subject of this book is the relationship between humans and aspects of the 'natural' world, it inevitably engages to some degree with ecology and ecocriticism, though the range of approaches within these fields, many of which are still emergent (not to mention conflicting), complicates detailed discussion. The range of eco-philosophies that have already developed distinct identities makes it difficult for this introduction to offer more than a brief overview of how this book engages with existing ecological and ecocritical discourse. Furthermore, its chapters have been written from a range of perspectives, and it would be misleading for the

---

[8] John Hines, 'Literary Sources and Archaeology', in *The Oxford Handbook of Anglo-Saxon Archaeology*, ed. Helena Hamerow, David A. Hinton and Sally Crawford (Oxford, 2011), pp. 968–85 (p. 974).

authors of this introduction to suggest otherwise.⁹ This volume has not been assembled from an ecological or ecocritical perspective, in so far as it does not present an ecological agenda either in its individual parts, or as their sum. This said, it does nevertheless reflect elements of contemporary ecocritical approaches to the relationship between humans and non-humans, in so far as these have contributed to the development of the current academic climate, and have helped to foster approaches in medieval studies (or 'ecomedievalisms') which will better represent how humans have engaged with and attempted to understand non-humans.

The title of this book, *Representing Beasts*, ostensibly draws a sharp line between humans and non-humans. The Old English word *deor*[10] or the Norse *dýr*[11] may seem more appropriate here, given their shared origin and the volume's geographical focus,[12] rather than the Middle English word derived from Latin *bestia* via OFr *beste*.[13] 'Beast' still has the same connotations in Modern English that it had for Latin speakers (denoting non-humans, as opposed to 'animal', which includes humans), whilst *deor* has come to represent only deer.[14] Whatever conception pre-Christian Anglo-Saxons and Scandinavians may have had of their relationship with animals, the conversion of northern Europe drew more definite lines between beasts and humans. Before this, lacking written representations of human relationships with the 'natural' world, we cannot represent these cultures in their own words, even if we can understand them through archaeology. There can be little doubt that, by the end of the period, the rational Christian human was recognised as something quite different from the beasts of the field, the air and the sea. This is before one even considers 'lower' orders of life, such as vegetation, or material, like stone – the latter being the sort of thing we would still not normally think of as possessing life

---

[9] 'Nature' is used in this introduction as a problematic term of convenience that is nevertheless often used by deep ecologists (e.g. Bill Devall and George Sessions, *Deep Ecology: Living as if Nature Mattered* (Layton, UT, 1985)). Broadly speaking, deep ecology rejects the dualist separation of humans from 'nature' that underpins the history of western philosophical thought, humans being nothing if not natural. The Judaeo-Christian tradition, as reflected in the vast majority of medieval writing, *did* draw a marked distinction on certain levels between the human and the non-human (see below). An important work to have challenged deep ecological approaches, proposing an alternative 'dark ecology', in which 'nature' is no longer held at an aesthetic distance, is Timothy Morton, *Ecology without Nature* (Cambridge, MA, 2007); see also Timothy Morton, *The Ecological Thought* (Cambridge, MA, 2010).
[10] *DOE* [accessed 11 December 2013].
[11] Geir T. Zoëga, *A Concise Dictionary of Old Icelandic* (Toronto, 2004), p. 100.
[12] Vladimir Orel, *A Handbook of Germanic Etymology* (Leiden, 2003), p. 71.
[13] *DOE* [accessed 11 December 2013].
[14] *A Latin Dictionary Founded on Andrews' Edition of Freund's Latin Dictionary*, ed. E. A. Andrews, Charlton T. Lewis and Charles Short (Oxford, 1879), p. 234.

Introduction

outside of models such as Lovelock's 'Gaia' hypothesis.[15] This is not to say that everyone thought in this way; these divisions primarily reflect mainstream Christian thought. An anonymous Middle English lyric encapsulates the uncertainty with which those in the later Middle Ages were still consciously considering their own bodies in relation to those of beasts:

> Foweles in the frith,
> The fisses in the flod,
> And I mon waxe wod.
> Mulch sorw I walke with
> For beste of bon and blod.[16]

Like many anonymous Middle English lyrics, there are riddling qualities to these lines which resist definitive interpretation, much like the Old English riddles of the Exeter Book. They do, however, expose uncertainties regarding the bodies of beasts of bone and blood in the world in which the speaker exists, and the fear of their own mortality and the final destination of the soul.

In a general sense, then, it can be said that humans throughout the period understood that they shared with other living things a vitality that could be extinguished. This commonality is perhaps most obviously shared with the majority of the beasts considered in this book, whether they were domestic animals, wild animals, or supernatural creatures – humanoid or otherwise. But it was also true that life could be extinguished in trees and plants and, perhaps, in inanimate objects that could be imbued with a degree of sentience or mortality. Objects like swords and buildings could be named and possess unique and well-defined corporeal forms – even, perhaps, identities independent of their human wielders and fabricators. They might also be destroyed: rapidly, like Heorot by fire, or by a slower process of decay, like the treasure from the dragon's barrow in *Beowulf*. They might even be deliberately destroyed in the context of funerary or votive deposition – one of the clearest indications that objects could be imagined to retain a power independent of human manipulation.[17] It would be a mistake, however, to suggest that people during this

---

[15] James Lovelock proposed his Gaia hypothesis (later Gaia theory) of the earth as a self-regulating organism in *Gaia: A New Look at Life on Earth* (Oxford, 1979). Lovelock revisited this idea in various works, including *The Ages of Gaia: A Biography of our Living Earth*, 2nd edn (Oxford, 2000), and *The Revenge of Gaia: Why the Earth is Fighting Back, and How we Can Still Save Humanity* (London, 2006), by which time he claimed that 'Gaia' had received a degree of general acceptance.

[16] *Middle English Lyrics*, ed. Maxwell S. Luria and Richard L. Hoffman (New York, 1974), p. 7.

[17] Hilda E. Davidson, *The Sword in Anglo-Saxon England: Its Archaeology and Literature* (Oxford, 1962), pp. 10–11.

period were maintaining (at any phase in their religious history) an idyllic balance with the animals and the environment in which they dwelt. It would also be an error to suggest that paganism or Christianity invariably privileged certain relationships between humans and non-humans. Christians and pagans both made use of and manipulated their environment in order to suit their own ends. If the conversion to Christianity introduced dividing lines between humans and non-humans that had not hitherto been so clearly marked, these did not segregate the two so much as draw attention to the mutability of the boundaries between them.

* * *

The chapters in this volume have been arranged in order to bring together topics which naturally lend themselves to proximate discussion, rather than to separate them according to disciplinary boundaries. It begins with four studies, by Adams, Brunning, Symons and Osborn, which address some of the ways in which real and mythological animals appear in early medieval English and Scandinavian culture, offering insight into how cultural creators conceptualised and ordered systems of belief, exchange, and the transmission of goods and ideas.

Noël Adams discusses the unique position of Anglo-Saxon animal art, poised between the 'reality' of the Classical tradition, which provided much of the visual source material for craftsmen, and the 'myths' of the Germanic tradition recorded in literary sources. Although mythological traditions recorded many centuries later are often used to interpret early Anglo-Saxon art, often with questionable results, this chapter argues that it is important not to lose sight of the influence of earlier Roman and contemporary Late Antique and Byzantine imagery. In addition, Classical literary evidence expresses certain fundamental concepts regarding the relationship between humans and animals which remain outside the mythic themes of Germanic literature. Adams argues that this is particularly true in relation to representations of animals of the hunt – a central theme of much early Anglo-Saxon animal imagery.

Sue Brunning then considers connections between snakes and swords in Viking-age Scandinavian culture, focusing on serpentine ornament on swords and other artefacts, in addition to written descriptions of swords as serpents in contemporary literature. Brunning compares literary descriptions of swords and the patterns created by pattern-welding, in a discussion which illuminates the complex relationship between humans, animals and artefacts, and raises important questions about the boundaries between what are commonly thought of as distinct categories of 'beings'. As do many of the chapters in this book, Brunning suggests that these boundaries

Introduction

were mutable, and that there was great potential for overlap, as well as the lending and borrowing of individual characteristics. Brunning shows that a nuanced appreciation of these associations reveals the networks of meaning which connected serpents, swords and humans in the minds of those who crafted and wielded these weapons.

Victoria Symons also confronts serpents and serpentine imagery, focusing her discussion on the relationship between dragons and runes in Old English and Old Norse literature, but also considering the rune stones which bear dragon decorations in Denmark, Norway, and Sweden. While dragons function as a symbol of impending doom in sources like the *Anglo-Saxon Chronicle*, in literary works like *Beowulf* they tend to lie coiled beneath the earth, in barrows piled with hoarded treasure – a tendency which stands in opposition to the circulation of wealth in the world of men, where material exchange is essential to the maintenance and development of social bonds. Runes, by contrast, which are associated with both treasure *and* dragons, can be understood as a means of uncovering hidden knowledge. Thus Symons argues that dragons and runes, as representatives of concealment and revelation, are frequently set in opposition to one another in ways that reveal underlying anxieties concerning wealth and its appropriate distribution in early medieval England and Scandinavia.

Moving away from serpents, but not southern Scandinavia, Marijane Osborn's chapter is centred upon the tiny Viking-age sculpture discovered at Lejre in 2009, which depicts an enthroned figure flanked by a pair of ravens, who have been identified as Óðinn and his corvid companions, Huginn and Muninn. Questioning this admittedly attractive interpretation, Osborn's chapter addresses a number of issues concerning the transmission and reception of artistic motifs, and the way in which these can develop as they encounter new cultural traditions and – in this case – their specific relationship with indigenous avifauna. In this wide-ranging study, Osborn considers representations of enthroned figures with birds in late Antiquity; the reception of this imagery in early medieval northern Europe; the materiality of the sculpture itself; birds in 'Germanic' and 'Celtic' visual art; and relations between humans and ravens in ancient and modern Iceland. Although, as Osborn writes, the various characteristics associated with ravens *can* be taken to identify the enthroned figure with Óðinn's feathered friends, there is no reason that the ravens flanking the Lejre throne need be Huginn and Muninn, nor that the central figure, similarly, need be the one-eyed god himself.

In the following two chapters, Lacey and Chardonnens move away from the discussion of objects and towards written sources, considering how the cultures of early medieval England and Scandinavia were influenced by animals in the pursuit of hidden knowledge, whether this was revealed through divination, prognostication, or even by means of non-human speech. Like Marijane Osborn, Eric Lacey is also interested in ravens; in this case the blithe-hearted bird whose song heralds sunrise over Heorot in *Beowulf* – a curious episode in which the raven's customary morbid associations are at odds with positive events in the narrative. Lacey addresses a number of issues raised by the communication gap between humans and beasts, including the raven's ambiguous symbolism (either of triumph or impending doom), and its role as a bringer of knowledge in Old Norse–Icelandic analogues. The chapter further connects this aspect of the raven with a wider body of evidence for bird-augury among the early Germanic and Anglo-Saxon peoples, arguing that this literary motif in *Beowulf* draws on longstanding cultural traditions in which birds revealed hidden knowledge of future events.

Sandor Chardonnens addresses similar questions in his chapter about the role of exotic beasts in Anglo-Saxon prognostics: in other words, those beasts of which the early English would have had only limited experience, such as lions, camels, and elephants. This was a group that also included fantastical beasts such as phoenixes, which existed at a similar geographical abstraction, unlike the far more familiar domestic dragon. Both indigenous and exotic beasts appeared in prognostics, but here Chardonnens tackles the interesting question of how the early English would have imagined such animals, which they were familiar with through religious texts, but whose physical forms were ultimately alien to their everyday experience. The chapter considers beasts in Anglo-Saxon prognostics in a variety of different capacities: as symbolic animals; as an equivalent to animals used in modern laboratory research; and as means of assisting seasonal forecasts. Chardonnens addresses some of the reasons why certain animals appear in certain capacities, and discusses the prevalence of 'exotic' animals in dream books, in contrast with the rather more limited presence of husbandry animals and their products in year prognoses.

This is followed by two studies in which North and Williams examine the influence of beasts upon the identity of peoples and landscapes, both as untamed denizens of the wilderness, and as animals that symbolised kinship groups within 'Germanic' cultures. Richard North focuses upon the curious depiction of a pet pig in a Latin poem written by Luxorius of Carthage (*c.* 520), arguing that it may represent the tamed Vandals whose kings ruled Carthage from 439–533, and who patronised North African poets like Luxorius himself. North connects Luxorius's pet pig with boar cults in Vandalic and other Germanic cultures through a variety of documentary and material sources. He discusses boar symbolism and boar deities in the ancient heathenism which the Vandals inherited, particularly in

Introduction

the Vanic god variously known as Enguz, Ing and Ingvi-freyr, and compares this with surviving boar motifs in Old English and Old Norse literature of the Christian era. North argues that although the Vandals themselves were Arian Christians in Tunisia at the time of the poem's composition, they could still have maintained the boar symbolism of warfare and fertility seen elsewhere among Germanic cultures. In this light, Luxorius's depiction of a pet pig in a Roman villa is presented as a parodic depiction of his Vandal rulers, as a once ferocious beast domesticated by the comforts of Carthage.

The boar raises his tusked head again as one of a number of creatures that were associated with violence and warfare in the Anglo-Saxon imagination. Williams reviews the evidence for beast symbolism in archaeological and poetic contexts, placing this in relation to a wider cosmology that equated violence with the outpouring of energies that could be conceived of as monstrous or bestial, and thus imagined to occupy a space 'outside' the realm of the normal sphere of human behaviour. In particular, he compares the descriptions, place-names and investigable topography of Anglo-Saxon battlefields with the imagined landscapes of conflict presented in the poetic and hagiographic corpus, revealing how these places spoke to a sense of marginality and 'wilderness' that reveals some of the concepts that underpinned ideologies of violence in early medieval England. Using evidence from related social phenomena such as judicial and administrative processes in the landscape, Williams shows how identities could become blurred and mutable in violent contexts, and how warfare occupied a liminal cognitive space where the symbolic boundaries between man and monster were negotiated in a visceral process of semiotic exchange.

Williams's discussion of beasts as denizens of wild places and perpetrators of bestial deeds is further developed by Bintley, who also considers how landscapes and settlements were attributed particular qualities in Old English poetry according to the virtuous or sinful actions of rational beings within them. Dangerous beasts, both real and imagined, have primarily been represented in Anglo-Saxon studies as occupying marginal spaces on the fringes of human society, whether they are the beasts of battle waiting in the forests, the Grendels in their sub-aquatic lair, or dragons clutching their gold in ancient barrows. Conversely, this chapter considers the depiction of humans as beasts when they act in the manner of beasts, and the way in which this influences the presentation of a variety of landscapes. Bintley's discussion also considers Nebuchadnezzar's bestial madness in the Old English *Daniel*, and the satanic cannibal Mermedonians of *Andreas*, arguing that any landscape can be made monstrous by its inhabitants if they act as beasts – that is, if they reject those virtuous practices that bound together Christian Anglo-Saxon society. Correspondingly, any space – be it rural or urban – might be reclaimed as a place for humankind, if those who inhabited it were seen to behave as virtuous Christians.

The final two chapters of the volume, which focus on place-name evidence from charters and other sources, present some of the most enduring evidence of animal–human interaction in Anglo-Saxon England: that which has left its influence imprinted on the landscapes of today. John Baker presents the first study of the way that place-names reflect the smallest of beasts – the invertebrates that are much neglected in studies of the early medieval societies, either through their lack of prominent cultural symbolism, or because they represent an unpleasant intrusion into our modern separation from the land. These mini-beasts are nevertheless a vital part of our ecosystems, and although they are not culturally represented to quite the same extent as dragons or wolves, Baker shows that they nevertheless made a significant contribution to the way in which early medieval people thought about their world. This chapter raises important questions about how the Anglo-Saxons, at the very least, conceived of their landscape as being underpinned by the actions of mesofauna, in ways which permit valuable insight into other aspects of medieval society and economy, including agricultural and pastoral arrangements and preoccupations.

Della Hooke also examines charter and place-name evidence, questioning what it reveals about the relationship between animals and humans in Anglo-Saxon England, and how people viewed and interacted with their local environment. As Hooke demonstrates, the vast majority of references to beasts in the landscape of early medieval England indicate the practical use of the land, and there are relatively few instances in which fantastical creatures have left their mark. This evidence reveals a great deal about the way in which animal husbandry took place, indicating varieties of livestock, their management, the locations of enclosures, and how this varied on a seasonal basis. Elsewhere, terms for wild beasts and other animals of the hunt show animal exploitation and management in other respects, extending to avifauna and other creatures whose presence in the British Isles has been perhaps irrevocably diminished. This final chapter reveals the depth of the Anglo-Saxons' local knowledge and understanding of the beasts with whom they shared the landscape, presenting a rich and intimate picture of early England as it was understood by the people who lived and toiled in its fields and woods, and of the beasts that were variously incorporated into their lives.

1

Between Myth and Reality

Hunter and Prey in Early Anglo-Saxon Art

Noël Adams

> '… most swift and wise and divine'.
> Arrian (*Cynegetica*, V.6) on his Celtic
> hunting dog named Horme (Impulse)

Isidore of Seville (*c.* AD 560–636), in his *Etymologiae siue Origines*, interpreted the Latin word for animal as deriving from *animans* (living), 'because they are animated (*animare*) by life and moved by spirit'.[1] Isidore derived much of his information directly from the great imperial Roman author Pliny (d. AD 79), whose Books VIII–XI in his *Naturalis Historia* divided the animal world into creatures of land, sea and sky. The Romans not only observed and commented upon creatures of every sort but also depicted them with varying degrees of naturalism in the major and minor arts.[2]

Anglo-Saxon animal art was of a very different nature. Surviving 'art' from the fifth to the seventh centuries consists primarily of ornamental metalwork, worn as personal jewellery or used to embellish arms and armour, horse harness and containers. With few exceptions, animals were not made as sculptures in the round but were cast in low relief in copper alloy; high-status ornaments displayed animals shaped with filigree wire on precious metal or fashioned in gold and garnet cloisonné cellwork. Many of these images were highly stylised and

---

[1] *Latine autem animalia sive animantia dicta, quod animentur vita et moveantur spiritu*: Isidore of Seville, *Etymologiae siue Origines*, XII.i, *De animalibus*. The above translation is in Steven A. Barney, Wendy J. Lewis, Jennifer A. Beach and Oliver Berghof, *The Etymologies of Isidore of Seville* (Cambridge, 2006), p. 247. Isidore's thesaurus of Latin terminology suggested etymologies for a vast number of terms, some accurate, others bastardised, invented or mnemonic, combined with commentaries upon them. His categories ranged from mathematics, medicine and law to all aspects of the Church, humans and animals, stones and metals, buildings and agriculture, war, ships and domestic accessories. Virtually every medieval library is recorded as holding a copy.

[2] For examples in the minor arts, with further bibliography, see Debra Noël Adams, 'Roman Empire', in *When Orpheus Sang*, ed. Debra Noël Adams, Emma C. Bunker, Trudy Kawami, Robert Morkot and Dalia Tawil (Paris, 2004), pp. 182–243.

decorative. Accompanying representations in organic materials such as bone, wood, leather and textile are virtually lost to us.

The creatures that can be identified in Anglo-Saxon period metalwork are principally quadrupeds and birds, complemented by snakes and fish. The quadrupeds included canines, boars and probably horses; birds were generally raptors with curved beaks. In some cases these appear only as disembodied heads or as heads united with interlace to form ambiguous zoomorphs. There are, in addition, a few identifiable mythological composites derived from Classical forms, notably winged griffins, marine creatures with coiled tails, and hybrids derived from these. Both Pliny and Isidore included griffins in their compendia, Pliny judging them to be fabulous (*Naturalis Historia* X.lxx), but Isidore accepting their existence (*Etymologiae* XII.ii.17). Isidore (*Etymologiae* XII.vi.8) also simply accepted the existence of vast sea monsters, distinct from or related to whales. For the purposes of this paper, all these creatures – mammals, birds, reptiles and fantastic hybrids – are broadly referred to as animals.

Before beginning this study it is worth considering the animals from the Graeco-Roman pantheon that are largely or completely missing on Anglo-Saxon period metalwork. The large exotica with which Pliny opened his study of land animals – elephants, lions, tigers, panthers – are absent or not visible to us. The horned herbivores which were essential food animals – cattle, sheep, goats – do not feature, although they appear on Scandinavian bracteates. Deer, the prize wild game animal, are under-represented, but do appear on cremation urns[3] and on high-status objects, often with Celtic/Romano-British influence, such as the stag figurine on the Sutton Hoo Mound 1 sceptre.[4] There are several famous representations of boars, always identifiable by their tusks, but none of pigs, another key domestic food animal. Birds that can be classified are, for the most part, limited to raptors and doves. Cockerels, the consorts of Mercury and symbols of good fortune, are missing, together with other barnyard animals, like geese. Wading birds and the Christian peacocks found on Late Roman belt plates in Britain disappear. Game birds are represented only by the ducks on the purse lid from Sutton Hoo Mound 1 (see Fig. 1.20 below)

---

[3] Catherine Hills, Kenneth Penn and Robert Rickett, *The Anglo-Saxon Cemetery at Spong Hill, North Elmham*, part IV: *Catalogue of Cremations*, EAAR 34 (Norwich, 1987), p. 60, fig. 73, no. 2594; Carola Hicks, *Animals in Early Medieval Art* (Edinburgh, 1993), fig. 1.6, pp. 22–3; Catherine Hills, Sam Lucy et al., *Spong Hill*, part IX: *Chronology and Synthesis* (Cambridge, 2013), p. 391 (phase A/B, *c.* AD 400–80).

[4] Carola Hicks, 'A Note on the Provenance of the Sutton Hoo Stag', in *The Sutton Hoo Ship-Burial*, vol. 2: *Arms, Armour and Regalia*, ed. Rupert L. S. Bruce-Mitford (London, 1978), pp. 378–82; Hicks, *Animals in Early Medieval Art*, pp. 26–9. See also discussion of the bowl found at Lullingstone, Kent, p. 42 below.

and a brooch from Fairford, Gloucestershire.[5] There are no obvious mice or rats (another Roman favourite), and we can detect no lizards or amphibians. On the other hand, marine creatures with coiled tails appear sporadically, fish can be traced throughout the period, and serpents put in a dramatic appearance in the sixth century. With one exception (a butterfly or moth in cloisonné on the triangular buckle from Sutton Hoo Mound 17),[6] there are no winged insects or bees – Isidore's 'tiny flying animals', or *minutis volatibus* (*Etymologiae* XII. viii).

Anglo-Saxon animal representations were therefore confined to a very limited repertoire. We know from Isidore of Seville and other sources that the names and characteristics of different species were not lost to the educated clergy in the West, and they were certainly never forgotten by the common man who dealt with them.[7] Nor were they absent in Church literature, although Christian enquiry into the nature of animals was often tinged by judgements regarding their inherent good or evil in the eyes of God.[8] For the most part, this outlook was also characteristic of animal representations produced in the early medieval period in Scandinavia and the Continent by craftsmen acquainted at some level with Classical art. Contemporary societies living across Britain (termed variously Romano-British, Celtic and Pictish) retained only a slightly wider animal repertoire.[9]

The representation of the full spectrum and variety of animal life, therefore, was simply not 'part of the program' in the early medieval period. At the most basic level, as Salisbury has demonstrated, the defining factor in the relationship between humans and animals was the provision of food.[10] Yet rather than domestic food animals, the animals depicted were those obtained in the noble pursuit of the hunt. Much animal imagery was, of course, decorative and presumably symbolic in ways that remain difficult for us to fully understand. It is clear, however, that the specific range of animals on metalwork was

---

[5] Arthur MacGregor and Ellen Bollick, *A Summary Catalogue of the Anglo-Saxon Collections (Non-ferrous Metals)*, BAR British Series 230 (Oxford, 1993), p. 154, no. 22.1.

[6] Martin O. H. Carver, *Sutton Hoo: A Seventh-Century Princely Burial Ground and its Context*, Society of Antiquaries of London and British Museum Press (London, 2005), p. 244, fig. 103.

[7] The runes spelling out roe deer (*raihan*), engraved on a gaming piece made from a deer's astragal, is perhaps the earliest surviving English word: Alfred Bammesberger, *Old English Runes and their Continental Background* (Heidelberg, 1991), p. 403.

[8] For example St Eucherius, Bishop of Leon (*c.* AD 380–449), *Formularum spiritualis intelligentiae ad Uranium, V, De animantibus* (*PL* 50, 749–54), where animals are divided up into those which are holy (*sanctus*), those which are devilish (*diabolus*), and those whose nature is mixed (such as ravens and dogs).

[9] See Hicks, *Animals in Early Medieval Art*, pp. 39–55, fig. 1.9, for examples of Pictish stones carved with linear representations identifiable as bulls, geese and stags, in addition to the canines, eagles, snakes, fish and horses noted above.

[10] Joyce E. Salisbury, *The Beast Within: Animals in the Middle Ages* (New York, 1994), pp. 32–9.

selected because it was considered appropriate for certain types of object, many of which were worn by people of high or relatively high status. Our task, therefore, is to describe them objectively and attempt to interpret them.

Literature

No insular texts contemporary with the early Anglo-Saxon period survive to illuminate how people at the time regarded the creatures they depicted. The desire to find meaning in animal imagery, however, has given rise to an extensive scholarly literature on the broader subject of Germanic animal art. A survey of the research history on this topic has recently been published by Høilund Nielsen,[11] and I would like to draw attention to only a few trends here.

First, the study of Anglo-Saxon animal imagery has been intertwined with Scandinavian material for over half a century.[12] This is not unjustified, as key art styles such as Style I[13] and Style II[14] were imported from the Continent and Scandinavia to England. The discovery of the some of the finest surviving Style II metalworking in Sutton Hoo Mound 1 further embedded discussion of insular styles into the Scandinavian orbit, particularly as key objects such as the shield and helmet from the grave find their best parallels in Vendel Sweden.[15]

Hand in hand with this orientation is the reliance upon the mythology of Viking and post-Viking period poems and sagas to

---

[11] Karen Høilund Nielsen, 'Germanic Animal Art and Symbolism', in *Altertumskunde – Altertumswissenschaft – Kulturwissenschaft: Erträge und Perspektiven nach 40 Jahren: Reallexikon der Germanischen Altertumskunde*, ed. Heinrich Beck, Dieter Geuenich and Heiko Steuer, Ergänzungsbände zum Reallexikon der Germanischen Altertumskunde 77 (Berlin, 2012), pp. 595–611.

[12] E.g. George Speake, *Anglo-Saxon Animal Art and its Germanic Background* (Oxford, 1980), p. 85; Høilund Nielsen's title 'Germanic Animal Art' embraces Anglo-Saxon England as part of the larger Germanic and particularly Scandinavian world.

[13] See, *inter alia*, E. Bakka, *On the Beginning of Salin's Style I in England*, Universitet i Bergen Årbok Historisk-Antikvarisk Rekke 3 (Bergen, 1958); Sonia Chadwick Hawkes, 'The Jutish Style A', *Archaeologia*, 98 (1962), 29–74. Leeds initially believed Style I to have come from the Continent (E. T. Leeds, *Early Anglo-Saxon Art and Archaeology, being the Rhind Lectures Delivered in Edinburgh, 1935* (Oxford, 1936), pp. 41–78); but post-Sutton Hoo (and the work of Chadwick-Hakwes), inclined more towards southern Scandinavian influence – see E. T. Leeds, 'Notes on Jutish Art in Kent', *MedArch* 1 (1957), 5–26.

[14] On Style II, see the references in nn. 30–1 below.

[15] On the helmet, see Bruce-Mitford, *The Sutton Hoo Ship-Burial*, vol. 2, pp. 205–220; Sonja Marzinzik, *The Sutton Hoo Helmet* (London, 2007), pp. 33–5. The shield boss is a Scandinavian type with no other parallels in Anglo-Saxon England: see *Anglo-Saxon Graves and Grave Goods of the Sixth and Seventh Centuries AD: A Chronological Framework*, ed. John Hines and Alex Bayliss, Society for Medieval Archaeology (Leeds, 2013), p. 161.

interpret animal imagery.[16] At the beginning of the twentieth century, Salin (the Swedish academic who first defined Style I and Style II) and others suggested that animals such as ravens and wolves might be identified with those named as companions of the Norse god Odin.[17] In the second half of the twentieth century Hauck used Old Norse religion as the basis for complex interpretation of the images on Scandinavian gold bracteates as iconographic renderings of mythological passages.[18] In many works he argued for the complete transformation of Classical imagery and myth into those of a Germanic realm dominated by the high god Odin. Bracteates remain a special object type, represented in England by only one class (D-bracteates) whose ornament may have influenced the development of Style II in Kent.[19] To a large extent, however, the range of animals on bracteates is not dissimilar to that found on metalwork of the Anglo-Saxon period.

The Skaldic and Eddic poems were written down under Christian influence in the eleventh to thirteenth centuries, but are generally considered to preserve older oral traditions.[20] Although these myths and heroic tales can never be dismissed as expressions of northern thought, neither can the grave methodological problems presented by these late sources be overcome.[21] A widespread belief in the Germanic high god Woden/Odin, identified in early sources with the Roman god Mercury, and later in the tenth century with Mars, cannot, of course, be doubted,[22] but whether all animal art must be embedded in this mythology remains to be proven. In England Woden (together with Caesar) heads up the genealogical lists of some Anglo-Saxon royal houses, and is mentioned in a few other ninth- to tenth-century sources,[23] but does not appear in *Beowulf*. Furthermore, there was never any corresponding development of the individual tales and

---

[16] *Inter alia*: Speake, *Anglo-Saxon Animal Art*, pp. 77–92; Tania M. Dickinson, 'Symbols of Protection: The Significance of Animal-Ornamented Shields in Early Anglo-Saxon England', *MedArch* 49 (2005), 109–63 (pp. 154–60); Leslie Webster, *Anglo-Saxon Art: A New History* (Ithaca, NY, 2012), p. 17.

[17] Bernhard Salin, *Die altgermanische Tierornamentik* (Stockholm, 1904). Salin was director of the Statens Historiska Museum in Stockholm in the late nineteenth century.

[18] The primary source is Karl Hauck et al., *Die Goldbrakteaten der Völkerwanderungszeit*, 3 vols. (Munich, 1985–9), but he published over sixty further articles and books on the subject.

[19] Speake, *Anglo-Saxon Animal Art*, pp. 66–72.

[20] A good introductory survey in Theodore M. Andersson, 'Old Norse-Icelandic Literature', in *Early Germanic Literature and Culture*, ed. Brian Murdoch and Malcolm Read, Camden House History of German Literature I (Rochester, NY, 2004), pp. 171–204.

[21] See the comments in Dickinson, 'Symbols of Protection', pp. 111–12.

[22] Most recently see Wilhelm Heizmann, 'Die Bilderwelt der Goldbrakteaten', in *Altertumskunde – Altertumswissenschaft – Kulturwissenschaft*, ed. Beck et al., pp. 689–736 (p. 710).

[23] Rudolf Simek, 'Germanic Religion and the Conversion to Christianity', in *Early Germanic Literature and Culture*, ed. Murdoch and Read, pp. 73–101 (pp. 82–3).

mythic structure around these Germanic gods in Christian England comparable to that in pagan Viking and post-Viking societies.

Another modern research strand applies anthropological theory to the interpretation of the execution and the conceptual ideology behind animal art. Kristoffersen, for example, presented an interpretation of Style I based on the principles of Lévi-Strauss.[24] Parallel with other forms of 'primitive', 'native' art, he argued that split representations of animals into masks in Style I ensured a 'transformation of meaning from the ritual to the social sphere'; he envisioned Germanic societies at this time as alienated from the Classical world and its means of expression. Pluskowski, following literary speculation by Glosecki, saw animals as 'mediators between the natural and supernatural worlds' in an animistic and pagan society.[25] Deities like Odin/Woden were shamanistic shape-shifters, therefore, in this world of magic, where 'the conceptual boundaries between human and animals were mutable and certain species facilitated connections with the otherworld.'[26] Wild animals, notably the wolf, boar and raptor (although rarely represented in archaeological finds), represented an inner beast to be channelled or controlled. From this perspective, for example, all canines can be identified as wolves, as the elite themselves identified with wild, fiercely aggressive predators.[27]

Moving from the anthropological to the political, Hedeager proposed that cultic practices such as shamanism were deeply embedded in the political structures in Scandinavia.[28] She rightly questioned whether 'myth' can ever be embedded in objects. As some of the later epic poetry refers to earlier historical periods, however, she supports the idea that 'mythic structures encode history' and thus explain the appearance and disappearance of art styles such as Style I and Style II. From this perspective Style I corresponded to the political structures of the Migration period, while Style II represented the state of affairs following the Langobardic invasion of Italy in AD 565.

---

[24] Siv Kristoffersen, 'Transformation in Migration Period Animal Art', *Norwegian Archaeological Review* 28:1 (1995), 3–17.

[25] Stephen O. Glosecki, *Shamanism and Old English Poetry* (New York, 1989); Stephen O. Glosecki, 'Movable Beasts: The Manifold Implications of Early Germanic Animal Imagery', in *Animals in the Middle Ages*, ed. N. C. Flores (New York, 2000), pp. 3–23; Aleks Pluskowski, 'The Beast Within? Breaching Human-Animal Boundaries in Anglo-Saxon Paganism', *Saxon* 45 (2007), 1–4; Aleks Pluskowski, 'Animal Magic', in *Signals of Belief in Early England: Anglo-Saxon Paganism Revisited*, ed. Martin O. H. Carver, Alexandra Sanmark and Sarah Semple (Oxford, 2010), pp. 103–27.

[26] Pluskowski, 'The Beast Within', p. 1.

[27] Ibid., p. 2 (the common animals within Style II); Aleks Pluskowski *Wolves and the Wilderness in the Middle Ages* (Woodbridge, 2006), pp. 26–7, 134–7, 142–4, 155–8.

[28] Lotte Hedeager, 'Myth and Art: A Passport to Political Authority in Scandinavia during the Migration Period', *ASSAH* 18 (1999), 151–6; Lotte Hedeager, 'Migration Period Europe: The Formation of a Political Mentality', in *Rituals of Power from Late Antiquity to the Early Middle Ages*, ed. Frans Theuws and Janet L. Nelson (Leiden, 2000), pp. 15–57.

Whether this approach can be applied to Anglo-Saxon England is uncertain, as at present there is no clear evidence of shamanistic beliefs in Britain.

Thirdly, the application of science to animal art should be noted. Høilund Nielsen has produced a series of sophisticated correspondence analyses suggesting regional groupings and chronological development of Style II animals.[29] Her approach derives directly from that of Salin, who defined these styles for discussion by isolating key elements of the animals – heads, joints, legs, feet – and separating them into categories. Høilund Nielsen extended her results to hypothesise that Style II originated in south Scandinavia and spread to other regions, including Vendel Sweden and Anglo-Saxon England, as a means of prestigious display and identification among elites who, in some cases, cultivated myths of their Scandinavian origins.[30] In addition, she has also attempted to construct 'family trees' tracing the stylistic evolution of the key species of Style II animals, based upon entire beasts as opposed to their parts.[31]

Finally, two recent studies should be commended. Wamers has recently documented Style II on undisputed Christian objects, putting to rest the assumption that 'where there is an animal style, there is also Germanic paganism'.[32] Adetorp traced the close similarity between images and symbols on Celtic coins with those on bracteates, thereby throwing new light on the models available to metalworkers.[33] He purposefully makes no attempt to read meaning into the imagery, but simply documents the availability and correspondence between certain representations.

One topic that is rarely encountered in current appraisals of animal art is that of the Classical motif of the hunt, a key occupation

---

[29] Karen Høiland Nielsen, 'Animal Style – A Symbol of Might and Myth: Salin's Style II in a European Context', *Acta Archaeologica* 69 (1998), 1–52; Karen Høiland Nielsen, 'Female Grave Goods of Southern and Eastern Scandinavia', in *The Pace of Change: Studies in Early-Medieval Chronology*, ed. John Hines, Karen Høiland Nielsen and Frank Siegmund (Oxford, 1999), pp. 160–94; Karen Høiland Nielsen, 'Style II and the Anglo-Saxon Élite', *ASSAH* 10 (1999), 185–202; and Høiland Nielsen, 'Germanic Animal Art'.

[30] Høiland Nielsen, 'Animal Style'; Høiland Nielsen, 'Style II and the Anglo-Saxon Élite', pp. 185–6. She has observed ('Germanic Animal Art', pp. 592–4) that Style II is found on only a very small percentage of Continental objects from the period (approx. 0.1%), compared to 15–30% of objects in cemeteries on Bornholm; the forms in Scandinavia are also much more varied and diverse.

[31] Høiland Nielsen, 'Germanic Animal Art', pp. 612–18. This was based upon Scandinavian art, where, as she notes, the distinctions between different forms of 'wolves', birds and boars are easier to detect.

[32] Johan Adetorp, *De guldglänsande ryttarna, C-brakteaternasikinografi I ny belysning* (Lund, 2013).

[33] Egon Wamers, 'Behind Animals, Plants and Interlace: Salin's Style II on Christian Objects', in *Anglo-Saxon/Irish Relations before the Vikings*, ed. James Graham-Campbell and Michael Ryan, Proceedings of the British Academy 157 (Oxford, 2009), pp. 151–204 (p. 153).

involving animals. Scholars in the early twentieth century and around the period of World War II explored the theme,[34] but interest had dwindled by the end of the century.[35] Yet animals extracted from hunting scenes were prominent on Late Roman chip-carved metalworking, whose repertoire remains fundamental to the analysis of early medieval animal styles.[36] Hunting motifs are certainly not the only explanation for every creature represented in the Anglo-Saxon period, but, given their prevalence and importance in Roman and Early Byzantine art, evidence for animals associated with hunting deserves careful exploration. The following essay traces this particular theme from the fourth to the seventh centuries. Our image bank remains extremely limited, and many of these representations have been explored before. However, in England the data is changing rapidly thanks to new excavations and finds, many of them made by local metal detectorists, and recorded under the Portable Antiquities Scheme. It seems worthwhile, therefore, to place familiar and new objects together within a wider context that underlines the continuity between Classical and medieval imagery of hunter and prey.

The Hunt

Different forms of hunting were universal across many levels of society. As Oppian of Apamea, the author of a famous early third-century hunting manual, wrote: 'Common is hunting with nets, common are traps, and common is the chase of all the swift footed tribes by men with horses and dogs, or sometimes without dogs pursuing the quarry with horses only.'[37] Oppian noted particularly 'one valiant breed of tracking dogs' bred specifically by the Britons,[38] perhaps the famous

---

[34] Rudolf Henning, *Der Helm von Baldenheim und die verwandten Helme des frühen Mittelalaters* (Strassburg, 1907); Leeds, *Early Anglo-Saxon Art*, pp. 4–6, *passim*; Wilhelm Holmquist, *Kunstprobleme der Merowingerzeit*, Kungl. Vitterhet, Historie och Antikvitets Akademiens Handlingar 47 (Stockholm, 1939); Joachim Werner, *Die beiden Zierscheiben des Thorsberger Moorfundes* (Berlin, 1941); Hans Zeiss, *Das Heilsbild in der germanischen Kunst des frühen Mittelalters*, Sitzungsberichte der Bayerischen Akademie der Wissenschaften, Philosophische-Historische Abteilung II:8 (Munich, 1941), pp. 3–71.

[35] Thomas Köves-Zulauf, 'Die Verehrung von Tieren in der griechische-römischen Antike: Die römische Fuchshetze', in *Zum Problem der Deutung frümittelalterlicher Bildinhalte*, ed. H. Roth (Sigmaringen, 1986), pp. 57–66.

[36] *Inter alia*: Günther Haseloff, 'Zum Ursprung der germanischen Tierornamentik – die spätrömische Wurzel', *Frühmittelalterlicher Studien* 7 (1983), 406–42.

[37] Oppian of Apamea, *Cynegetica*, IV, 43–5, in *Oppian, Colluthus, Tryphiodorus*, trans. Alexander William Mair (London, 1987). This volume combines Oppian of Apamea's treatise, dedicated to the Emperor Caracalla (188–217), with another written by Oppian of Corycus (*fl. c.* 169) on fishing.

[38] *Cynegetica*, I, 468–71; called Agassian dogs, these British dogs are described as possessing a poor appearance rather like a plump lapdog, but remarkable courage. According to Oppian they were 'small indeed but as worthy as large dogs to be the theme of song'.

hunting dogs that Strabo listed along with furs and slaves as Britain's primary exports.[39] The genre of ancient literature known as *Cynegetica* descends from the earliest surviving hunting manual written by Xenophon (*c.* 431–355 BC),[40] whose title evokes the Greek word for dog: κύων (kýon). Treatises and poems on hunting,[41] complemented by manuals on fishing and fowling, were produced throughout the Roman period.[42] The subject was not inimical to Christians, as Synesius of Cyrene (*c.* 373–*c.* 414), bishop of Ptolemais (in modern Libya), wrote a lost book of hunting.[43] Knowledge of hunting and dog and horse breeding therefore constituted a very long tradition that continued unbroken into the Middle Byzantine and Islamic periods. The tenth-century manuscript of Oppian of Apamea's *Cynegetica* preserved in the Bibliotheca Marciana in Venice, for example, copied an illustrated archetype, probably of the Constantinian period (*c.* AD 300–350).[44]

The chase encapsulated man's complex relationship with animals in the natural world. There were three types of hunting – fowling (*aucupium*), hunting (*venatio*) and fishing (*piscatus*) – representing the three elements – air, earth and water – that provided food for man. Hare and birds were always the primary quarry, and could be obtained individually, with traps, or with dogs. Hunting large or dangerous animals required cooperation between men, horses and dogs as well as great courage. Preparing for a stag hunt, for example, then as now, was a major operation. Hunting, therefore, provided not only food and the pleasure of the chase, but also opportunities for

---

Their feet were 'armed with grievous claws', their mouths with 'close-set venomous tusks'. 'With its nose especially the Agassian dog is most excellent and in tracking it is best of all; for it is very clever at finding the track of things that walk the earth but skilful too to mark the airy scent' (*Cynegetica*, I, 474–80).

[39] Strabo, *Geographica*, 199, in *The Geography of Strabo*, trans. Horace Leonard Jones and John Robert Sitlington Sterrett, The Loeb Classical Library, 8 vols. (Cambridge and London, 1917–32).

[40] Xenophon, *Scripta minora*, trans. Edgar Cardew Marchant (London, 1925), ΞΕΝΟΦΩΝΤΟΣ, Kynigetikoz, *Cynegeticus*, pp. 366–457. Xenophon, a wealthy military officer, also wrote a treatise on horsemanship and horse breeding: *Peri Hippikes*.

[41] Grattius (Augustan period), *Cynegetikon*, in *Minor Latin Poets*, vol. 1, trans. John Wight Duff and Arnold Mackay Duff (London, 1935), pp. 141–205; Nemesianus, *Cynegetica*, in ibid, pp. 457–513. Arrian (AD 86–160), *Xenophon and Arrian: On Hunting*, ed. and trans. A. A. Phillips and Malcolm M. Willcock (Warminster, 1999); Phillip A. Stadter, 'Xenophon in Arrian's Cynegeticus', *Greek, Roman, and Byzantine Studies* 17 (1976), 165–7; Denison B. Hull, *Hounds and Hunting in Ancient Greece* (Chicago, 1964).

[42] Oppian of Corycus, *Halieutica*, in *Oppian, Colluthus, Tryphiodorus*, pp. 200–51; Dionysius Periegetes (*c.* 2nd century AD), *Dionysii Ixeuticon; seu, De Aucupio libri tres in epitomen metro solutam redacti*, ed. Antonio Garzya, Bibliotheca Scriptorum Graecorum et Romanorum Teubneriana (Lipsiae, 1963); Nemesianus, *De aucupio*, in *Minor Latin Poets*, vol. 1, pp. 513–15.

[43] In a letter to Hypatia, the mathematician in Alexandria, Synesius complained that 'my *Cynegetics* disappeared from my house, how I know not …' <http://www.livius.org/su-sz/synesius/synesius_letter_154.html> [accessed 30 December 2014].

[44] Ioannis Spatharakis, *The Illustrations of the 'Cynegetica' in Venice, Codex Marcianus Graecus Z 139* (Leiden, 2004), pp. 224–31.

acquiring important skills, particularly those required for proficiency in battle.[45] Hunting wild beasts thus became a metaphor for war.[46] Killing animals in a circus *venatio* was related to the noble hunt but, of course, required primarily raw courage for the slaughter.

A corresponding strand in the following investigation is imagery depicting two animals in the roles of hunter and prey, symbols of triumph parallel to victory in the hunt involving men. In Anglo-Saxon art, these motifs consist primarily of images of raptors and their prey. As we cannot distinguish the species of raptors, these are referred to in the conventional way as 'eagles'. Two of these motifs – the eagle and snake, and eagle and fish – were integrated into the iconography of sixth- and seventh-century military equipment produced by official arms factories in Europe and the Eastern Roman Empire.

In addition to animal hunts observed in nature on land, in the sea and in the sky, combats incorporating mythological hybrids formed part of the hunting repertoire. These were primarily griffins and marine sea monsters. Griffins appear among real animals of the chase on mosaics, tomb paintings and metalwork in the Greek and Roman periods; in some cases they seem to be simply another type of animal,[47] while in others they are clearly predators killing prey.[48] As they are capable of tearing men apart, according to Isidore, and are violently hostile to horses (*Origines* XII. ii.17), griffins are to be feared and are not always on the side of humans. In this regard they function as supernatural hunters, halfway between the air and the earth.

---

[45] Grattius applied a number of military terms to the chase (hunts, traps, spears, etc. are described as *arma*), and the *Cynegeticus* of Nemesianus opens: *Venandi cano mille uias hilaresque labores discursusque citos, securi proelia ruris, pandimus* ('I sing of the thousand roads of the chase, its joyful labours and swift rovings – the safe battles of the country we reveal'). The *Strategikon*, an Early Byzantine military manual attributed to the Emperor Maurice (r. AD 582–602), describes hunting from horseback as a complementary discipline to warfare, keeping men alert, exercising their animals and teaching them tactics; see *Maurice's Strategikon: Handbook of Byzantine Military Strategy*, trans. George T. Dennis (Philadelphia, 1984), D, 165.

[46] For example, Arrian 24.5: 'This is how those hunt who have good dogs and good horses, not tricking the animals with snares, nets, nooses, cunning or traps but challenging them openly. How different the spectacles are! The one resembles piracy or theft, the other a war fought out with all one's strength.'

[47] Spatharakis, *Venice Cynegetica*, p. 19, fig. 188 (Tomb 1, Necropolis of Marissa, Israel, c. 200 BC); p. 49 (Orpheus mosaic, Shahba-Philippopolis, Syria, fourth century AD)

[48] Gerard Brett, Günter Martiny, Robert B. K. Stevenson and W. J. Macaulay, *The Great Palace of the Byzantine Emperors, being a First Report on the Excavations Carried out in Istanbul on Behalf of the Walker Trust (The University of St. Andrews), 1935–1938* (London, 1947), pp. 75–6, pl. 33; Kenneth Painter, *The Mildenhall Treasure: Roman Silver from East Anglia* (London, 1977), p. 63, flanged bowl no. 5 (two griffins attacking a horse); Catherine Johns, *The Hoxne Late Roman Treasure: Gold Jewellery and Silver Plate* (London, 2010), pp. 36–40, figs. 3.25 and 3.26, bracelets 11 and 12.

Late Roman Models

Snapshots from the narrative of the chase, often focused upon the heat of pursuit, were among the most popular of all figural representations in the Late Roman and Byzantine periods. As Anglo-Saxon metalwork also depicts animals of the hunt and abbreviated hunting scenes, it is useful to consider a few extended representations of the hunt found on portable items ranging from domestic vessels to personal jewellery in the fourth and fifth centuries (Figs. 1.1–1.3). The most naturalistic and widely distributed of these were engraved glass vessels with scenes of the chase made in the Rhineland. The example illustrated here, dated to the mid-fourth century, was excavated at Wint Hill, Somerset (Fig. 1.1).[49]

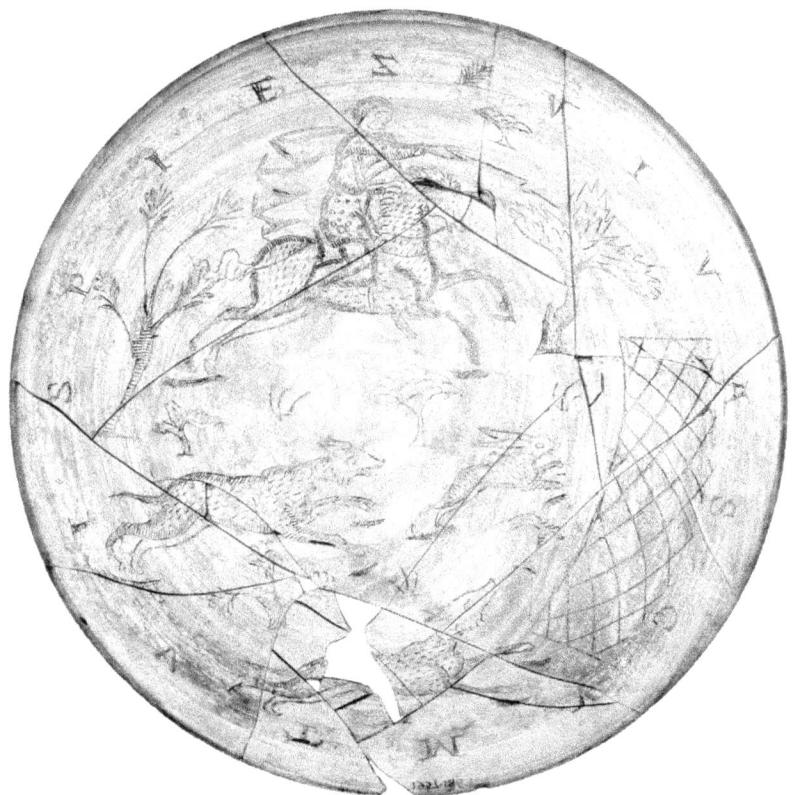

Fig 1.1 Late Roman glass bowl from Wint Hill, Somerset

---

[49] Donald B. Harden, 'The Wint Hill Hunting Bowl and Related Glasses', *Journal of Glass Studies* 2 (1960), 44–81. The hunting scenes consist of hare hunts, boar hunts and stag hunts; the other categories of subjects are Roman gods and goddesses and Christian scenes.

The animals can be divided into the creatures that serve men – horses and hounds – and their prey in the natural world – a hare is shown here, with boar and stags appearing on other bowls. All the creatures have open mouths, breathing in exertion and signalling that they are *animans*, animated with life. While their heads are not particularly well shaped, their ears illustrate their action – long and laid back to show the speed of the racing hounds and their prey, pricked in attention for horses. The dogs wear collars and have large paws marked by parallel lines. Both animal and human bodies have contour outlines filled with vertical hatching, while the fur is shown as short angled strokes. The hare is being driven into a net, without which, as Isidore notes, this sort of hunting is pointless (*Etymologiae* XIX.v.4).

The spectacle and symbolism of a large imperial stag hunt decorates the metal rim mounts of a wooden bucket excavated in grave 41 at Giberville (Calvados), France (Fig. 1.2).[50] The bucket was found in a robbed female grave of the early sixth century but was made in the fourth century, perhaps at the nearby military camp of Bénouville on the Saxon *limes*. The excavators suggest it may have been an official gift on behalf of the emperor. The scene opens at one end with a profile bust copying a coin of Valentinian (and bearing the letters DN VAL), and closes with the frontal head of a Gorgon at the other. The diademed hunter in profile with a spear may be the emperor himself, riding a horse shown at the same scale as a large stag being worried by seven leaping hounds of different breeds. To the right, the emperor bearing a military standard above a small fallen captive (also copying a coin type) unites the hunting theme with military victory. In addition the scene shows the head and shoulders of another animal (behind the horse's hooves), a snake on the ground between the horse and stag, and, at the far right, a composite creature with a fish tail and an animal head at the end above what may be a bird. Pairs of *en face* animals decorate the triangular tabs; the position and shape of their heads and tails support their identification as horses.[51] No metal bucket mounts found in England are comparable to this

---

[50] Christian Pilet, Armelle Alduc-Le Bagousse and Luc Buchet, 'Les Nécropoles de Giberville', *Archéologie Médiévale* 20 (1990), 3–140 (pp. 23–33, figs. 15–21, pls. 10–11); Christian Pilet, Luc Buchet, Jacqueline Pilet-Lemière *et al.*, 'L'Apport de l'archéologie funéraire à l'étude de la présence militaire sur le limes saxon, le long des côtes de l'actuelle Basse-Normandie', in *L'Armée romaine et les barbares du IIIe au VIIe siècle*, ed. Françoise Vallet and Michel Kazanski, AFAM, Musée des Antiquités Nationales (Saint-Germain, 1993), pp. 157–73 (p. 159, pl. 9).

[51] Chris Fern, 'Horses in Mind', in *Signals of Belief in Early England*, ed. Carver, pp. 128–57. The excavators, however, identify these animals as dogs (Pilet, Alduc-Le Bagousse and Buchet, 'Les Nécropoles de Giberville', pp. 31–2, fig. 21).

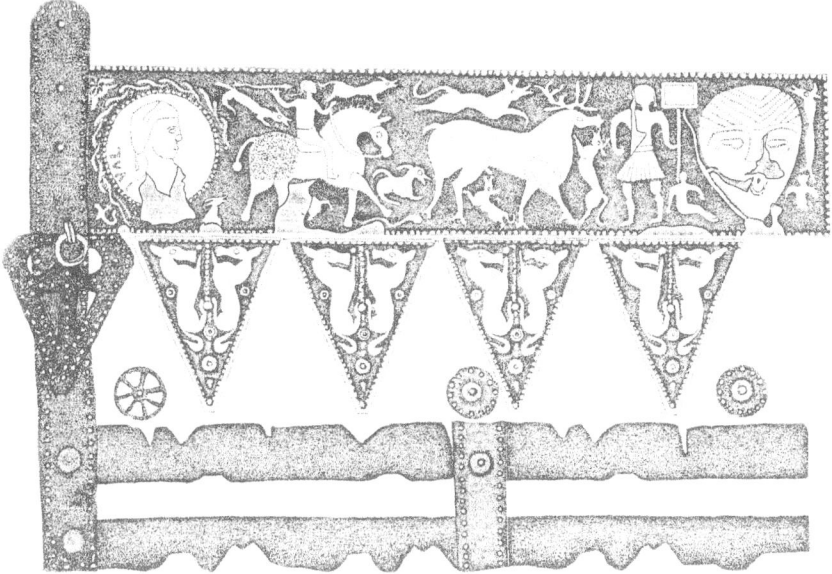

Fig 1.2 Bucket mounts from Giberville, Calvados

special example,[52] but an insular quoit brooch found near Bénouville and Kentish brooches found in other graves are proof of the close connection between Britain and this area in the fifth century.[53]

Finally we should consider hunting scenes in a female context. On the gold bracelets found in the Late Roman hoard at Hoxne, Suffolk,[54] humans appear as small figures in profile holding spears, and as frontal and profile heads, always male. Three of the Hoxne bracelets incorporate a wide range of animals, including panthers, lions and bulls, which could suggest that a circus *venatio* rather than a natural hunt is depicted (Fig. 1.3). One Hoxne bracelet depicts a sea goddess, a nereid, being pulled by a marine leocamp with a curled tail. The Hoxne bracelets show that hunting motifs were never restricted to male equipment. The patron of the hunt, of course, was the goddess Artemis/Diana, and these motifs were symbolic of a full and bounteous life.

---

[52] Jean M. Cook, *Early Anglo-Saxon Buckets: A Corpus of Copper Alloy- and Iron-bound, Stave-Built Vessels* (Oxford, 2004). On these the pairs of decorative animal terminals can only be described as raptors and quadrupeds, together with human heads.

[53] Claude Lorren, 'Des Saxon en Basse-Normandie au Ve siècle?', *Studien zur Sachsenforschung* 2 (1980), 231–59 (p. 233, fig. 2.2); Pilet, Alduc-Le Bagousse and Buchet, 'Les Nécropoles de Giberville', pp. 34–5.

[54] Johns, *The Hoxne Late Roman Treasure*, pp. 36–45, figs. 3.23–33. Identifiable animals include goat/ibex, bull, hounds, panthers, leopards, bear, lion, lioness, hares, ram, stag and wild boar.

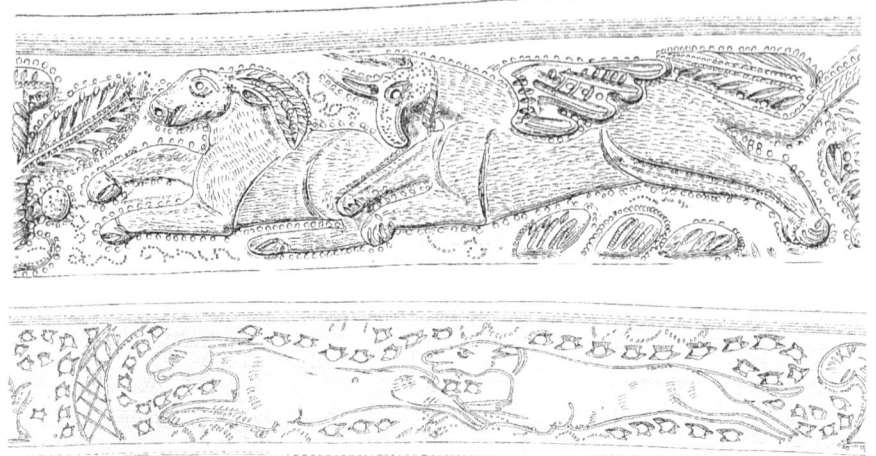

Fig 1.3 Bracelets 11 and 21 from Hoxne, Suffolk

First Germanic Art Styles

In the course of the later fourth and fifth centuries a wide range of increasingly abstract animal imagery developed on relief-cast metalworking made on the Continent and in southern Scandinavia. Reviews of these styles (Military Style, Nydam Style and Sösdala Style)[55] are beyond the scope of this essay, but key points are the appearance of pairs of animals, often with open mouths, springing towards or away from one another, and double animals flanking a human head. Animals included quadrupeds, birds and marine creatures, combined with human masks, but the accurate identification of these becomes increasingly challenging for the modern viewer. Roman and eastern Germanic traditions influenced these styles: for example, the appearance of animal heads springing outwards found on belt buckles and above the footplates of brooches derived from bronzes depicting horse and chariots,[56] while the open-mouthed sea creatures flanking a human head derive from images of Oceanus flanked by dolphins.[57] The appearance of bird heads reflects

---

[55] The classic sources are Horst Wolfgang Böhme, *Germanische Grabfunde des 4. bis5. Jahrhundert zwischen unterer Elbe und Loir* (Munich, 1974); Günther Haseloff, *Die Germanische Tierornamentik der Völkerwanderungszeit, Studien zu Salin's Stil I*, 3 vols. (Berlin, 1981); Günther Haseloff, 'Bild und Motiv im Nydam-Stil und Stil I', in *Zum Problem der Deutung fruhmittelalterlicher Bildinhalte*, ed. Roth, pp. 67–100.

[56] For examples of the former, see Horst W. Böhme, 'Das Ende der Romerherrschaft in Britannien und die Angelsächsische Besiedlung Englands im 5. Jahrhundert', *Jahrbuch des Römisch-Germanischen Zentralmuseums Mainz* 33 (1986), 469–74 (pp. 505–7, fig. 27).

[57] Haseloff, *Die Germanische Tierornamentik*, p. 8.

the spread of military equipment among eastern Germanic peoples in the Migration period, referencing both the imperial eagle of Jupiter and the eagles of the Roman legionary standards.[58]

Certain classes of relief cast (or 'chip-carved') male belt equipment present hunting animals alone and with their prey, as well as naturalistic scenes of humans hunting. These types have been found in England in fifth-century contexts, along with a wide range of Roman buckle loops that featured various animal heads (dolphins, horses and quadrupeds).[59] Production of military belt equipment of Böhme's type A with animals along their edges was clearly closely related to the more elaborate forms of equal-arm brooches, the Sahlenburg, Dösemoor and Nesse types from the Saxon regions between the Elbe and Weser.[60] The lions, leocamps and griffins that appear on the male belt sets and strap ends, such as the example from Furfooz, Namur, shown here (Fig. 1.4), are not as common on female brooches,[61] although distinct animals such as hares, hounds, deer and marine creatures can be distinguished on these.[62] A fragmentary silver gilt *Stützarmfibel* found in England has hares clearly modelled on the arms; the heads of three hunting dogs appear along the headplate below (Fig. 1.5); a related but not identical brooch was found at Riensförde (Stade), north Germany, with a equal-arm brooch of Nesse Type II.[63] A Nesse Type I brooch found recently near Maidenhead in Berkshire depicts a hound taking a hare along the lower arms (Fig. 1.6);[64]

---

[58] Consider Pliny, *Naturalis Historia*, X.v, on nature's response to the adoption of eagles as the military symbol in 104 BC: *Ex eo notatum non fere legionis umquam hiberna esse castra ubi aquilarum non sit iugem*. ('From this it was noted that there was scarcely ever a legion's winter camp where there was not a continued presence of eagles.') Isidore (*Etymologiae*, XVIII.iii.2) was aware of Lucan's comments: 'Standards against standards, eagles matching eagles and javelins threatening javelins'. On the development of the *aquila* standards see Christopher A. Matthew, *On the Wings of Eagles: The Reforms of Gaius Marius and the Creation of Rome's First Professional Soldiers* (Cambridge, 2010), pp. 51–62.

[59] *Inter alia*: Böhme, *Germanische Grabfunde*, pp. 357–62, find-lists and maps 11 and 12; Vera Evison, 'Supporting-Armed and Equal-Armed Brooches in England', *Studien zur Sachsenforschungun* 1 (1977), 127–47; Kevin Leahy, 'Soldiers and Settlers in Britain, Fourth to Fifth Century – Revisited', in *Collectanea Antiqua: Essay in Memory of Sonia Chadwick Hawkes*, ed. Martin Henig and Tyler Jo Smith (Oxford, 2005), pp. 133–43; Barry Ager, 'Appendix: A Note on the Continental Background to Late Romano-British Belt Fittings with Zoomorphic Features', in ibid., pp. 141–2; Peter A. Inker, *The Saxon Relief Style*, BAR British Series 410 (Oxford, 2006).

[60] Böhme, *Germanische Grabfunde*, pp. 18, 346–8, 361–2, lists and maps 5 and 2; Böhme, 'Das Ende der Romerherrschaft in Britannien', pp. 542–5; Dorothee Bruns, *Germanic Equal Arm Brooches of the Migration Period*, BAR International Series 1113 (Oxford, 2003), p. 37; Inker, *The Saxon Relief Style*, pp. 41–2, 78, 180, figs. 5–11, maps 2–4.

[61] Böhme, *Germanische Grabfunde*, vol. 1, pp. 57–8, 289, fig. 18; vol. 2, pl. 88, 4 (Furfooz (Namur) grave 3). The winged creatures are identified here as eagles, but as they have ears, they must be griffins.

[62] Bruns, *Germanic Equal Arm Brooches*, p. 19.

[63] Böhme, *Germanische Grabfunde*, pp. 247–8, pl. 34, 10; the illustrated brooch, a metal-detector find from 1990s, is in a private English collection.

[64] PAS number FASW-948D00, copyright Stuart Laidlaw.

this type has not previously been recorded in England. Nesse Type II brooches, however, are widely distributed across England,[65] and the example in C2376/3 at Spong Hill is considered to belong to Phase B of the cemetery (c. AD 430–80).[66]

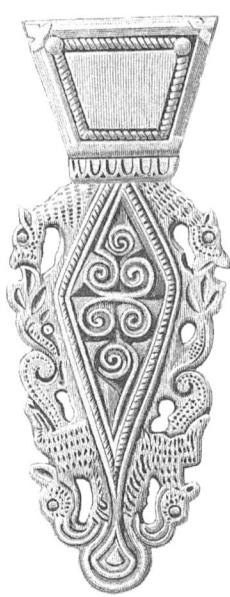

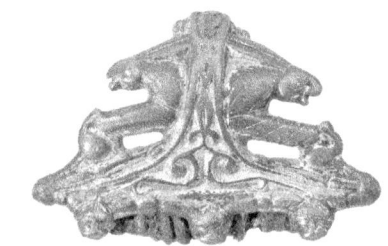

Fig 1.5 *Stutzarmfibel* in private collection, London

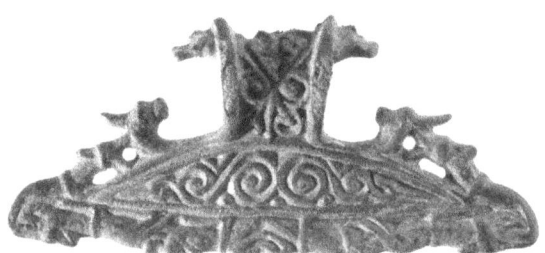

Fig 1.4 Strap end from Furfooz, Namur, grave 3

Fig 1.6 Nesse Type 1 brooch from Maidenhead, Berkshire

---

[65] Examples are known from Abingdon, Berkshire; Collingbourne Ducis, Wiltshire; Hollingbourne, Kent; Westgarth Gardens, Suffolk; and Spong Hill, Norfolk; see Vera Brieske, *Schmuck und Trachtbestandteile des Gräberfelds von Liebenau, Kr. Nienburg/Weser: Vergleichende Studien zur Gesellschaft der frühmittelalterlichen Sachsen im Spannungsfeld zwischen Nord und Süd*, Studien zur Sachenforschung 5, 6 (Oldenburg, Isensee, 2001), fig. 13; Inker, *The Saxon Relief Style*, pp. 42, 180, map 3; Hills and Lucy, *Spong Hill*, p. 39).

[66] Hills and Lucy, *Spong Hill*, pp. 39, 232, 387, fig. 2.5 (C2376/3).

Insular Production in the Fifth Century

The transmission by trade and immigration of Late Roman and Germanic art styles into England cannot be traced in detail here. A closer look at the transformation of these by insular craftsmen in the fifth century, however, provides a second portal into understanding Anglo-Saxon animal art. The final publication of the large cremation cemeteries at Spong Hill, Norfolk, has shown that burials of Germanic incomers in East Anglia had begun in the early fifth century,[67] and in the course of the century populations across eastern Britain were increasingly an admixture of native and Continental peoples.

The most familiar art style of the fifth century incorporating animals, the Quoit Brooch Style (QBS), was named after a native British form of cloak brooch.[68] The style originated in provincial workshops in northern Gaul, but the majority of examples have been found on English soil. The buckle set excavated in a female grave at Mucking (grave 217)[69] carries animal and geometric ornament reflecting the overall trends of Late Roman relief-cast metalwork in terms of imagery and layout. The casting is shallower and the silver inlays with engraved surface decoration are unique to the style. QBS is also found on military equipment.[70] A recent discovery of a fragmentary scabbard mouthpiece at Cheriton, Hampshire, preserves one of a pair of hounds with a spiral marking its front shoulder (Fig. 1.7).[71]

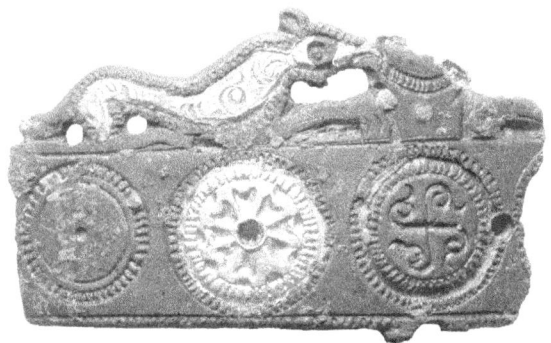

Fig 1.7 Scabbard mount from Cheriton, Hampshire

---

[67] Ibid., pp. 157–232, esp. pp. 229–32 (487 cremation burials in Phase A).
[68] *Inter alia*: Vera I. Evison, 'Quoit-Brooch Style Buckles', *Antiquaries Journal* 48 (1968), 231–46; Barry M. Ager, 'The Smaller Variants of the Anglo-Saxon Quoit Brooch', *ASSAH* 4 (1985), 1–58; Seiichi Suzuki, *The Quoit Brooch Style and Anglo-Saxon Settlement: A Casting and Recasting of Cultural Identiy Symbols* (Woodbridge, 2000).
[69] Sue M. Hirst and Dido Clark, *Excavations at Mucking*, vol. 3: *The Anglo-Saxon Cemeteries: Excavations by Tom and Margaret Jones, part ii*, Museum of London Archaeology (London, 2009), pp. 662–8, figs. 368–72.
[70] MacGregor and Bollick, *A Summary Catalogue of the Anglo-Saxon Collections*, pp. 235–6, no. 45.4 (scabbard from Brighthampton, Oxfordshire).
[71] PAS SUR-029B13; copyright PAS and Surrey County Council.

The most elaborate quoit brooches, cast in silver and gilded, have been found in graves in Kent (Figs. 1.8, 1.9). On the fragmentary brooch from Howletts grave 13 (Fig. 1.8) the hounds, rendered with contour outlines and feathered with short strokes, have flattened ears, large paws that are ribbed to indicate claws, and lean whip tails that curl backwards into plumed tips; their front shoulders are marked by a crescent. On the Sarre brooch (Fig. 1.9) the animals in the outer ring have their front legs held up and their clawed feet bent backwards, while their open mouths show predatory rows of teeth; the inner ring of animals with bobbed tails, looking over their shoulders, may represent prey. The birds cast in the round on the Sarre and Howletts grave 13 brooches[72] resemble doves, used either with a hunting[73] or

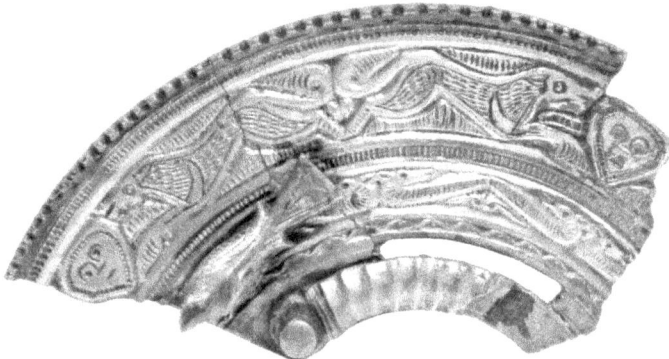

Fig 1.8 Fragmentary quoit brooch from Howletts grave 13

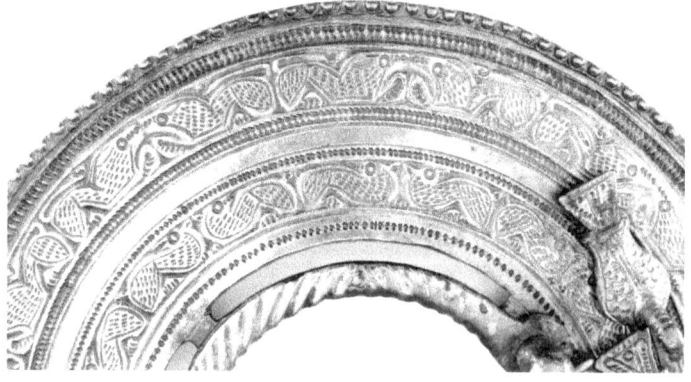

Fig 1.9 Quoit brooch from Sarre grave 1

[72] These derive from a class of Gallo-Roman brooches with free-standing and spinning animal figures: Hicks, *Animals in Early Medieval Art*, p. 19; Noël Adams, *Bright Lights in the Dark Ages: The Thaw Collection of Early Medieval Ornaments*, The Morgan Library and Museum (New York, 2014), pp. 32–3, cat. no. 1.14.

[73] Oppian, *Cynegetica*, I, 73: 'the fowler with his reeds takes doves'. Doves were also traditionally used to lure other birds into nets.

a Christian significance. On other quoit brooches, such as that from Howletts grave 1, the animals in the outer row clearly reference marine creatures with coiled tails, completing the trinity of the beasts of land, sea and sky.

An enamelled disc found in 2013 at St Mary Bourne, Basingstoke and Dean, Hampshire, provides a new example of animal imagery related to QBS (Fig. 1.10).[74] Reserved against the red enamel, three pairs of hounds set back to back with long ears, open mouths and clawed paws turn their heads backwards to snap at their long whip tails. The function of the piece is not entirely clear, although horse harness is certainly a possibility. On balance it is likely to represent insular work in the Celtic enamelling tradition.

Finally, a bow brooch in the Canterbury Museum (unprovenanced, but certainly Kentish) depicts two naturalistic hounds flanking a human head (Fig. 1.11);[75] as shown here these would have been facing upwards rather than downwards when worn. This, like another recent metal-detector find of a similar brooch from Gillingham, Kent, is probably not a Scandinavian import as earlier authors suggested, but a local variant, perhaps made in the second half of the fifth century.[76]

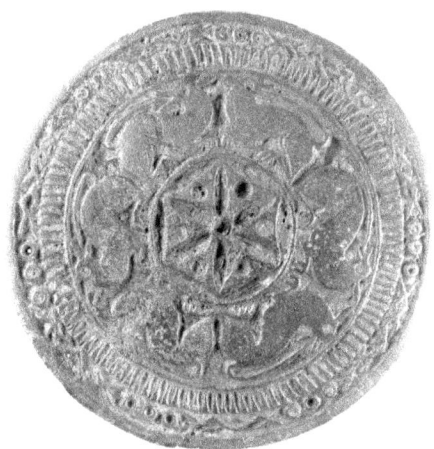
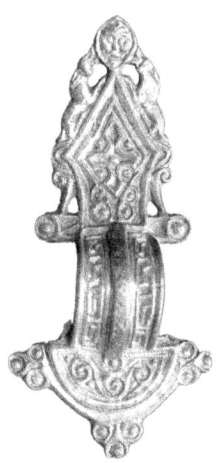

Fig 1.10 Enamelled disc from St Mary Bourne, Basingstoke and Dean, Hampshire

Fig 1.11 Brooch in the Canterbury Museum

[74] PAS HAMP-FFCDF4: copyright Winchester Museums Service.
[75] Bakka, *On the Beginning of Salin's Style I in England*, p. 9, fig. 2; Andrew F. Richardson, *Anglo-Saxon Cemeteries of Kent*, BAR British Series 391, 2 vols. (Oxford, 2005), vol. 2, p. 16, fig. 2a (where it is considered south-east Scandinavian).
[76] See comments by Richardson *et al.* in the PAS entry for the Gillingham brooch, PAS KENT-3A7463.

Style I

By the last decades of the fifth century, insular metalworkers had been exposed to the relief-cast ornament known as Style I that had arisen in Scandinavia and northern Europe.[77] Objects in Insular Style I are quite distinctive, one of their features being a certain degree of naturalism. From the considerable Anglo-Saxon corpus that was produced throughout the first half of the sixth century we will look at only a few examples that can be clearly connected to hunting themes.

Some of the finest Style I in England was used on a range of metalwork designed to be riveted to the leather straps of belts and horse harness. On a small strap end from Sarre, Kent, the hound at the left with triple-clawed paws rests its front paw (detached from its body) atop the hindquarters of a smaller creature with an arched back and flat paw (Fig. 1.12).[78] The position is certainly that of a predator and prey, even if the animals can be distinguished only by viewers with the visual background outlined above. On a hinged harness fitting found at Long Marston (Harrogate, Yorkshire) the Style I clawed creature has a narrow snout and what appears to be a wing springing from its front shoulder (Fig. 1.13).[79] This perhaps was intended to convey its speed (always one of the major features of hounds), or may be an indication that this creature is a mythological composite. On the basis of comparative material from Eriswell, it probably belonged on a brow band.[80]

Relief-cast saucer brooches worn in areas with Saxon populations also incorporate profiled quadrupeds nose to tail in a circle. On a brooch from Long Wittenham grave 46 (Berkshire), the beasts retain the typical ribbed feet and are shown with slightly differing ears and heads, either to suggest different creatures or different types of canines (Fig. 1.14).[81] The interlacing of the sinuous bodies of the canines may be an attempt to convey the speed of the animals. The creatures on the Long Wittenham brooch are exceptionally clear, as

---

[77] Style I horse trappings excavated in Eriswell 104, grave 323 (RAF Lakenheath), have recently been radiocarbon dated to c. AD 490–510; see Hines and Bayliss, *Anglo-Saxon Graves*, pp. 234, 24. There are good drawings of the pieces in Chris Fern, 'The Archaeological Evidence for Equestrianism in Early Anglo-Saxon England, c. 450–700', in *Just Skin and Bones? New Perspectives on Human-Animal Relations in the Historic Past*, ed. Aleks Pluskowski, BAR International Series 1410 (Oxford, 2005), pp. 43–71 (pp. 48, 50, 53, figs. 5.1 and 5.9 – here given the number grave 4116 before the finds were renumbered).

[78] Salin, *Die altgermanische Tierornamentik*, p. 325, fig. 702; Reginald A. Smith, *British Museum Guide to Anglo-Saxon Antiquities 1923* (London, 1923), p. 57, fig. 62 (BM P&E 1893,0601.237).

[79] PAS YORYM-A74BF7, copyright York Museums Trust.

[80] I am grateful to Angela Care Evans for this suggestion.

[81] Nils Åberg, *The Anglo-Saxons in England during the Early Centuries after the Invasion* (Uppsala, 1926), p. 19, fig. 23; Speake, *Anglo-Saxon Animal Art*, p. 63, fig. 10b.

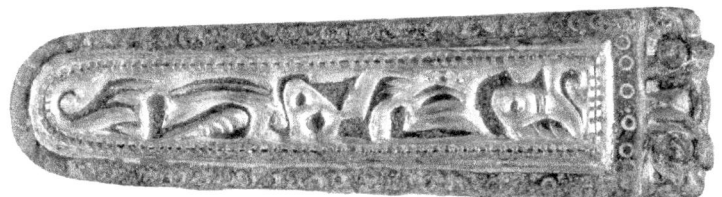

Fig. 1.12 Strap end from Sarre, Kent

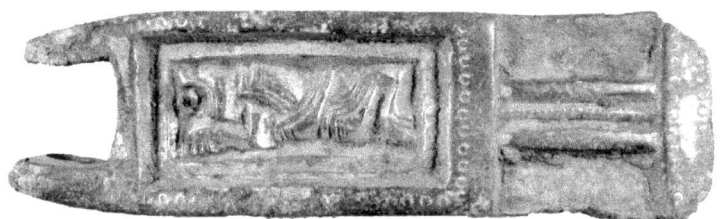

Fig. 1.13 Harness fitting from Long Marston, Harrogate, Yorkshire

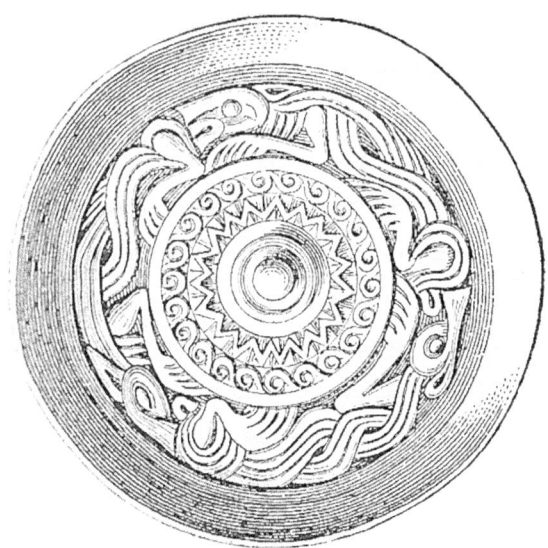

Fig. 1.14 Saucer brooch from Long Wittenham grave 46, Berkshire

are those Dickinson defined as 'Coherent Style' brooches.[82] On many saucer brooches, however, the component parts are increasingly chopped up, randomly mixed and abbreviated until they achieve the degenerate state which Haseloff appropriately termed *Tiersalat*.

The same is true of many Style I creatures on the great square-headed brooches worn by Anglian populations. Many of these reference large and elaborately decorated Scandinavian brooches in gilded silver,[83] but the animal frieze along the top of a brooch from Suffolk is unusual in being rendered in relief in a manner unlike most Style I.[84] It is a high-status production in gilded base silver with garnet inlays. This is one of a group of square-headed brooches (Hines Group IV) that differ from Scandinavian-derived types in representing a complete animal (often referred to as a 'rampant beast') above the footplate.[85] This feature is related to brooches produced in Kent, although it cannot be determined whether they represent a derivative or independent development in England from Continental models.[86] Hines dated Group IV to the first quarter of the sixth century, while the first Kentish brooches with this feature were made in Kentish Phase II (*c.* AD 500–530/40).[87] On a brooch from Ruskington, Lincolnshire, winged bird-headed quadrupeds are shown in openwork around the headplate, and rampant between the bow and footplate (Fig. 1.15).[88] On a Group IV brooch now in the Morgan Library and Museum in New York the animals in the corners of the headplate are also clearly rendered as winged, bird-headed quadrupeds (Fig. 1.16).[89]

---

[82] Tania M. Dickinson, 'Translating Animal Art: Salin's Style I and Anglo-Saxon Cast Saucer Brooches', *Hikuin* 29 (2002), 1–25 (pp. 2–3). Many of these feature a human head flanked by birds.

[83] Thorleif Sjøvold, *The Scandinavian Relief Brooches of the Migration Period*, Norske Oldfunn XV (Oslo, 1993); John Hines, *A New Corpus of Anglo-Saxon Great Square-Headed Brooches* (Woodbridge, 1997). Examples of these have never been found in England.

[84] MacGregor and Bollick, *A Summary Catalogue of the Anglo-Saxon Collections*, p. 114, no. 13.5; Hines, *A New Corpus*, pp. 48–58, 340, pl. 17a.

[85] Hines, *A New Corpus*, pp. 48–58, 223–34, 227–8. At present examples are known from Rothley (Leicestershire), Holywell Row grave 11 (Cambridgeshire), Farforth and Ruskington (Lincolnshire), Suffolk (unprovenanced) and J. Pierpont Morgan Library and Museum, New York (unprovenanced, see Fig. 1.16).

[86] The brooch from Idstedt (Schleswig-Holstein) cited by Hines (cf. Haseloff, *Die Germanische Tierornamentik*, vol. 3, pl. 95–6) as a prototype for the group has rampant creatures with double heads that are not similar to the Group IV brooches; it is related but not necessarily the only model. There is a range of the earlier Kentish variants in Åberg, *The Anglo-Saxons in England*, figs. 121–2, 125–9.

[87] Cf. Sonia E. Chadwick, 'The Anglo-Saxon Cemetery at Finglesham, Kent', *MedArch* 2 (1958), 1–71 (pp. 46–52, fig. 9b (grave D3), 11b (E2); Birte Brugmann, 'The Role of Continental Artefact Types in Sixth-Century English Chronology', in *The Pace of Change*, ed. Hines *et al.*, pp. 37–64 (p. 42, table 3.3).

[88] Hines, *A New Corpus*, figs. 23d, 25e, pl. 16a.

[89] Adams, *Bright Lights*, pp. 202, 220–1.

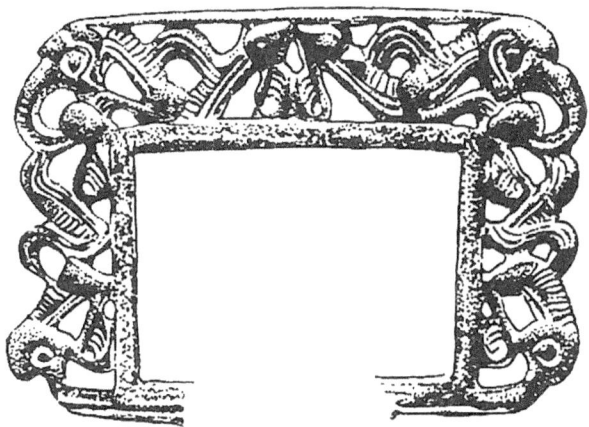

Fig. 1.15 Headplate of great-square-headed brooch from Ruskington, Lincolnshire

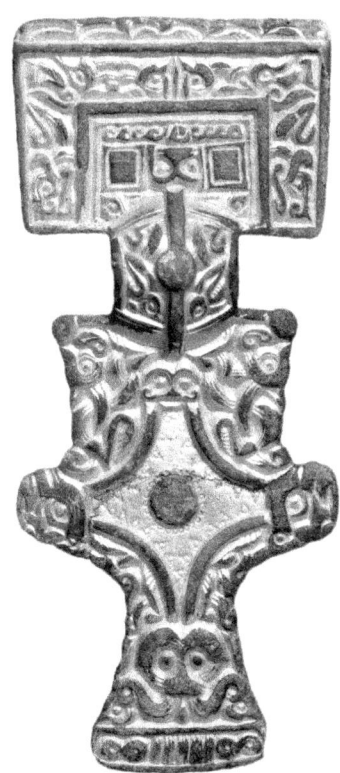

Fig. 1.16 Great square-headed brooch in the Morgan Library and Museum

As we have seen above, griffins were one of the typical animals of hunt friezes, although they came to have specifically Christian associations.[90] Style I shield mounts such as those found in Bergh Apton grave 26 (Norfolk),[91] apparently depicting hippogriffs (griffin heads with horse bodies), seem to fuse the mythological enemies into a single image. Griffin imagery on Merovingian brooches of the first half of the sixth century[92] may suggest that the near Continent was the immediate source of this motif for the Anglo-Saxons.

Transitional Style I to Style II

A further group of Anglian shield mounts, which Dickinson rightly identifies as transitional between Style I and Style II, depict birds of prey combined with snakes. On the shield mount from Bromeswell, Suffolk, the bird's neck, tail and talon are overlaid with silver, as is the oval head of the snake (Fig. 1.17); the shield boss apex depicted two chasing quadrupeds.[93] Other new finds, such as a strap mount from Dean and Shelton, Bedfordshire,[94] show that the eagle and snake motif was used across England and in other contexts as well (Fig. 1.18).[95] The silver sheet overlays and other factors suggest these were being made throughout the first half of the sixth century.

Eagles grasping snakes, together with other scenes of eagles and their prey, have a long Classical history.[96] Pliny notes that snakes ate

---

[90] Griffins, initially associated with Apollo, were seen as guardians of light, hence their popularity on Early Byzantine lamps (cf. Anna Gonosová and Christine Kondoleon, *Art of Late Rome and Byzantium in the Virginia Museum of Fine Arts* (Richmond, VA, 1994), pp. 250–1, no. 85). They also appear on Early Christian funerary monuments.

[91] Dickinson, 'Symbols of Protection', pp. 135–7, fig. 13e.

[92] Cf. *Die Franken – Wegbereiter Europas 5. bis 8. Jahrhundert n. Chr.*, ed. Alfred Wieczorek, Patrick Périn, Karin von Welck and Wilfried Menghin (Mainz, 1996), pp. 987–8, cat. VII.5.40.

[93] Dickinson, 'Symbols of Protection', pp. 127–35, figs. 4d–e, 5a, 9–11 (fish) and 12 (eagles). The Bromeswell finds are identified here as Sutton Hoo 018; full publication of this cemetery is in pre-publication phase.

[94] PAS WMID-E4F0C5; copyright Birmingham Museum and Art Gallery.

[95] Devolved forms are also known: see Tania M. Dickinson, Chris Fern and Andrew Richardson, 'Early Anglo-Saxon Eastry: Archaeological Evidence for the Beginnings of a District Centre in the Kingdom of Kent', *ASSAH* 17 (2001), 1–86 (p. 34, fig. 11).

[96] Ernst Künzl, 'Die Adler und die Kobra – Ein seltenes Motiv im römischen Waffendecor', *Archäologisches Korrespondenzblatt* 38:1 (2008), 87–95 (fig. 2); Leonard Forrer, *Descriptive Catalogue of the Collection of Coins Formed by Sir Hermann Weber, 1823–1918*, vol. 2: *Greek Coins* (London, 1924), pp. 441, 446, 451, pl. 147 no. 4023, pl. 148 nos. 4029 and 4033, and pl. 149 no. 4053 (Olympia, mint of the temple of Zeus, *c.* 454–32, *c.* 432–21 and *c.* 343–23 BC, respectively). The motif reviewed in Rudolf Wittkower, 'Eagle and Serpent: A Study in the Migration of Symbols', *Journal of the Warburg Institute* 2 (1938–9), 239–325. The image appears as a device on Minerva's shield on an Attic vase of the mid-sixth century BC.

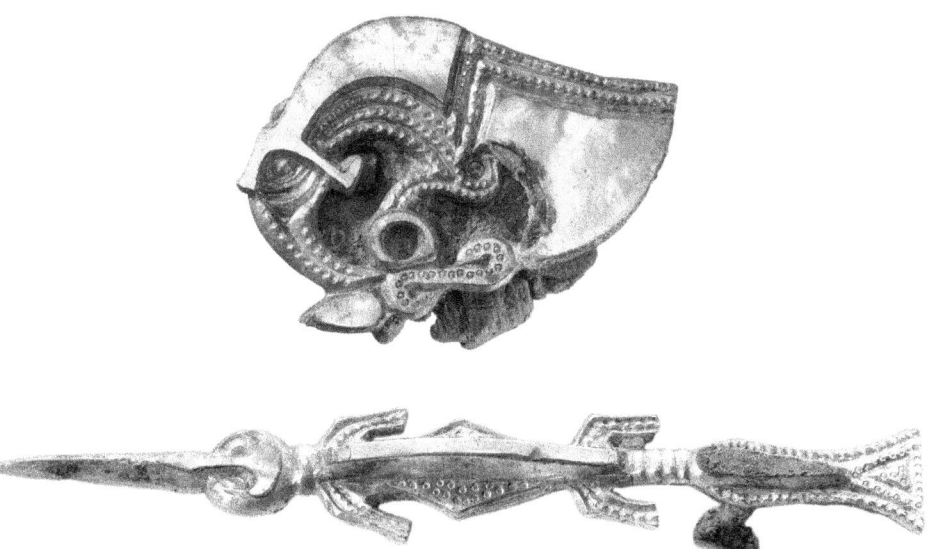

Fig. 1.17 Shield mounts from Bromeswell, Suffolk, depicting an eagle and snake (top), and a fish resembling a pike (bottom)

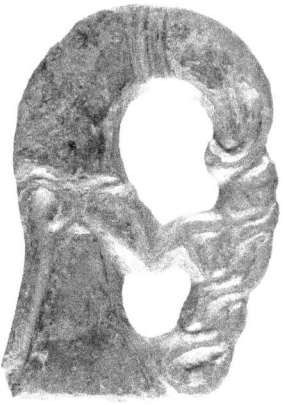

Fig. 1.18 Bird and snake mount from Dean and Shelton, Bedfordshire

eggs and therefore had to be destroyed by birds.[97] The inspiration for this particular image in Anglo-Saxon metalwork is uncertain, as it is more prevalent in England than elsewhere. The snakes and birds of prey that appear among the marching warriors on the helmet plaques from Välsgarde 7 (Uppland), Sweden, are not shown in this naturalistic adversarial pose.[98] The eagle and snake combat is recorded occasionally on Roman[99] and Byzantine military equipment,[100] and its appearance on the floor mosaics at the Great Palace in Constantinople shows it had acquired prominence in the imperial capital by the sixth century.[101] Military equipment may have influenced personal metalwork, but as the recent discovery at Aldgate in London of a large sculpture of an eagle and a snake carved c. AD 100[102] demonstrates, the image adorned public spaces as well, even in Roman Britain. The piece came from a tomb or mausoleum in the eastern cemetery of Londinium, so perhaps was still visible in the sixth century. On the Bromeswell shield noted above, excavated near the royal mounds at Sutton Hoo, the eagle/snake mount was displayed with another mount in the form of a pike-like fish seen from above (see Fig. 1.17). The shield board mount of an eagle and fish from Eriswell 104, grave 232, is complemented by three silver fishes on the cone of the boss.[103] And, of course, on the Sutton Hoo Mound 1 shield the crouching eagle is combined with the most fearsome prey of all, a winged dragon. One cannot help but think of Pliny, who wrote that having defeated a stag by throwing a snake onto its horns, the eagle will immediately seek another enemy:

---

[97] Pliny, *Naturalis Historia*, X. V.17.

[98] Greta Ardwidsson, *Die Gräberfunde von Valsgärde III: Valsgärde 7* (Uppsala, 1977), figs. 115, 120. This helmet remains the closest parallel for the Sutton Hoo Mound 1 helmet. These remarks also apply to the snakes on the cloisonné bird among filigree snakes on the brooch from Skodborg, Denmark; see Haseloff, *Die Germanische Tierornamentik*, vol. 3, pl. 32).

[99] Künzl, 'Die Adler und die Kobra', figs. 1, 4–5. See also Bernard Goldman, 'Pictorial Graffiti of Dura-Europos', *Parthica* 1 (1999), 19–106 (p. 63, E.11; Late Roman graffiti at Dura-Europos, Syria).

[100] A silver eagle statuette with a snake in its talons found in a late seventh- to early eighth-century hoard at Voznesenka (Zaporož'e, Ukraine), with a cruciform monogram and official Byzantine control stamps, was probably the finial of an eastern Roman army standard; see Igor Gavrituhin, 'La Date du 'Trésor' de Pereščepina et la chronologie des antiquités de l'époque de formation du Khaganat Khazar', in *La Crimée entre Byzance et le Khaganat Khazar*, ed. Constantin Zuckerman (Paris, 2006), pp. 13–30, fig. 3.10. See also Adams, *Bright Lights*, pp. 122, no. 3.13 (a Visigothic or Early Byzantine strap end found in Spain).

[101] Brett *et al.*, *The Great Palace of the Byzantine Emperors*, p. 79, pl. 36, with a griffin to the side and a hunter with spear, sword and shield below.

[102] 'Rare Roman eagle sculpture found on hotel building site', BBC News, 30 October 2013, online at <http://www.bbc.co.uk/news/uk-24740273> [accessed 30 December 2014].

[103] Dickinson, 'Symbols of Protection', pp. 126, 135, figs. 10f and 12c.

not content with one foe, it has a fiercer battle with a dragon, of more doubtful result, even if it is in the air. This serpent with wicked greed pursues the eagle's eggs; hence the eagle carries it off whenever seen. It (the serpent) coils itself so closely around the wings that that they both fall to the ground.[104]

A related motif, that of an eagle carrying a fish, has ancient Near Eastern origins.[105] Its continued use in the West probably owes much to its appearance on Greek coinage issued in Sicily in the late fifth century BC,[106] and to the eagle and dolphin coin series still in issue by cities on the Black Sea as late as the first century BC.[107] It occasionally appears on Late Iron Age finds in Europe.[108] An eagle and fish feature on a bracteate now in the British Museum,[109] but I know of no other occurrence in Scandinavian art of the early medieval period.

Of greater interest is the use of the motif and its context on *Spangenhelme* of Baldenheim type made in Italian and Byzantine arms factories.[110] On the *Spangenhelm* from grave 1782, Krefeld Gellep (Nordrhein-Westphalia), each inset panel bears a large eagle and fish set against a punched scale background.[111] The band below features a vine scroll inhabited by birds pecking grapes and, in the centre, a human head flanked by birds and horses. An even more extensive range of iconography was engraved on the six panels of a *Spangenhelm* from Montepagano, Italy.[112] These show the following scenes:

---

[104] Pliny, *Naturalis Historia*, X.v.17: *Nec unus hostis illi satis: est acrior cum dracone pugna multique magis anceps, etiamsi in aere. Ova hic consectatur aquilae aviditate malefica; aquila hoc rapit ubicumque visum. Ille multiplici nexu alas ligat ita se inplicans ut simul decidat ipse.*

[105] Anna Roes, 'Birds and Fishes', *Jaarbericht van het Vooraziatisch-Egyptische Genootschap Ex Oriente Lux* 10 (1945–8), 461–72.

[106] *British Museum Catalogue of Greek Coins, Sicily*, vol. 2, ed. R. V. S. Poole, B. V. Head and P. Gardner (London, 1876), no. 86 (Sicily, Akragas (Agrigentum)).

[107] *British Museum Catalogue of Greek Coins*, vol. 3: *Thrace* (London, 1877), no. 1 (Olbia, third to first century BC), no. 2 (Istros, 400–350 BC); Forrer, *Descriptive Catalogue of the Weber Collection*, p. 162, pl. 100, no. 2603 (eagle to right flying with dolphin) and no. 2606 (eagle to left pecking dolphin) (both Olbia, third to second century BC); p. 169, pl. 101, nos. 2637 and 2638 (eagles to left pecking dolphin) (both Istrus, fourth century BC).

[108] Claus von Carnap-Bornheim, 'Der 'Helmbeschlag' aus Domagnano – Überlegungen zur Herkunft des 'Vogel-Fisch' Motivs', in '... *Trans Albium Fluvium': Forschungen zur vorrömischen, kaiserzeitlichen und mittelalterlichen Archäologie: Festschrift für Achim Leube zum 65. Geburtstag*, ed. Michael Meyer (Rahden, 2001), pp. 223–38 (p. 231, fig. 6d, a fitting from the mid-third-century grave 5 at Langen Jarchow (Mecklenburg), and fig. 7, the early fifth-century Gallehus horns).

[109] Hauck, *Die Goldbrakteaten der Völkerwanderungszeit*, I, 2, pp. 68–9; I, 3, pl. 33 (IK33 in BM).

[110] For a survey of current thinking on this subject, see Jörg Drauschke, '"Byzantine" and "Oriental" Imports in the Merovingian Empire from the Second Half of the Fifth to the Beginning of the Eighth Century', in *Incipient Globalization? Long-Distance Contacts in the Sixth Century*, ed. Anthea Harris, BAR International Series 1644 (Oxford, 2007), pp. 53–73 (pp. 58–9, fig. 5).

[111] Renate Pirling, 'Krefeld-Gellep im Fruhmittelalter', in *Die Franken*, ed. Wieczorek *et al.*, pp. 261–5, fig. 193.

[112] Karl Hauck, 'Von einer spätantiken Randkultur zum karolingischen Europa', *Frühmittelalterliche Studien* 1 (1967), 3–93 (pp. 17–19); Volker Bierbrauer, *Die Ostgotischen*

(1) an eagle, stag and boar; (2) a horse before a cup and two horned animals; (3) a frontal eagle above an eagle standing on a fish; (4) a man spearing a boar attacked by a hound; (5) a standing man holding a fish in his right hand and a vessel in his left, with a lion below; and (6) a man carrying a cross above two eagles with a fish between them (Fig. 1.19). The purposeful combination of imagery that the modern mind separates into 'secular', 'pagan' and 'Christian' encapsulates the framework of ideas and beliefs of the early Byzantine and medieval periods. No *Spangenhelme* have been found in England, but the recent discovery of a Frankish helmet type on the Isle of Wight proves that Continental military equipment did find its way here.[113]

There are a few other examples of naturalistic raptors and fish, such as the two birds and fish on a gilt copper alloy buckle from Faversham,[114] but nothing could have prepared us for the large mount in the form of two eagles and a fish in heavy gold sheet in the Staffordshire Hoard.[115] The purpose of this mount remains unknown, but its high value and fine execution suggest it was a piece of official paraphernalia, whether secular or Christian (or both). The balance perhaps tilts slightly towards the latter in light of the appearance of the bird and fish motif among the appliqués on the hanging bowl found near Lullingstone, Kent.[116] The date of this bowl is debated,[117] but on current evidence it is likely to be from the late sixth to the first half of the seventh century. The association of stags, birds and fish is a construct of the Christian Byzantine world.

It is not surprising that the motif passed seamlessly into the Christian art and iconography of insular manuscript illustration.[118] In the Book of Armagh the eagle gripping a fish symbolised John the Evangelist, while on an early Carolingian manuscript the motif appears alongside an image of a bird and a snake.[119] The meaning assigned to the subject in this context is assumed to be that of Christ the redeemer

---

Grab- und Schatzfunde in Italien, Centro Italiano di Studi sull'alto Medioevo (Spoleto, 1975), pp. 288–92, fig. 28.

[113] Jamie Hood, Barry Ager, Craig Williams, Susan Harrington and Caroline Cartwright, 'Investigating and Interpreting an Early-to-Mid-Sixth-Century Frankish Style Helmet', *British Museum Technical Research Bulletin* 6 (2012), 83–95.

[114] Speake, *Anglo-Saxon Animal Art*, p. 58, fig. 6n, pl. 2a; fig. 4m and n.

[115] Kevin Leahy and Roger Bland, *The Staffordshire Hoard* (London, 2009), pp. 40–1.

[116] Rupert L. S. Bruce-Mitford and Sheila Raven, *The Corpus of Late Celtic Hanging Bowls with an Account of the Bowls Found in Scandinavia* (Oxford, 2005), pp. 72, 175–9, colour pl. 5.

[117] Hicks, *Animals in Early Medieval Art*, pp. 26–9 (fifth to sixth century); Bruce-Mitford and Raven, *The Corpus of Late Celtic Hanging Bowls*, p. 178 (late seventh or early eighth century).

[118] Florentine Mütherich, 'Der Adler mit dem Fisch', in *Zum Problem der Deutung frümittelalterlicher Bildinhalte*, ed. Roth, pp. 317–40 (pp. 317–318, figs. 2–4).

[119] Ibid., pp. 318, 325–6, figs. 3 (Armagh) and 13. The eagle and hare, another of the great predator and prey motifs found on Greek coinage, also appears on a ninth-century Ottonian manuscript (ibid., p. 321, fig. 9).

Hunter and Prey in Early Anglo-Saxon Art

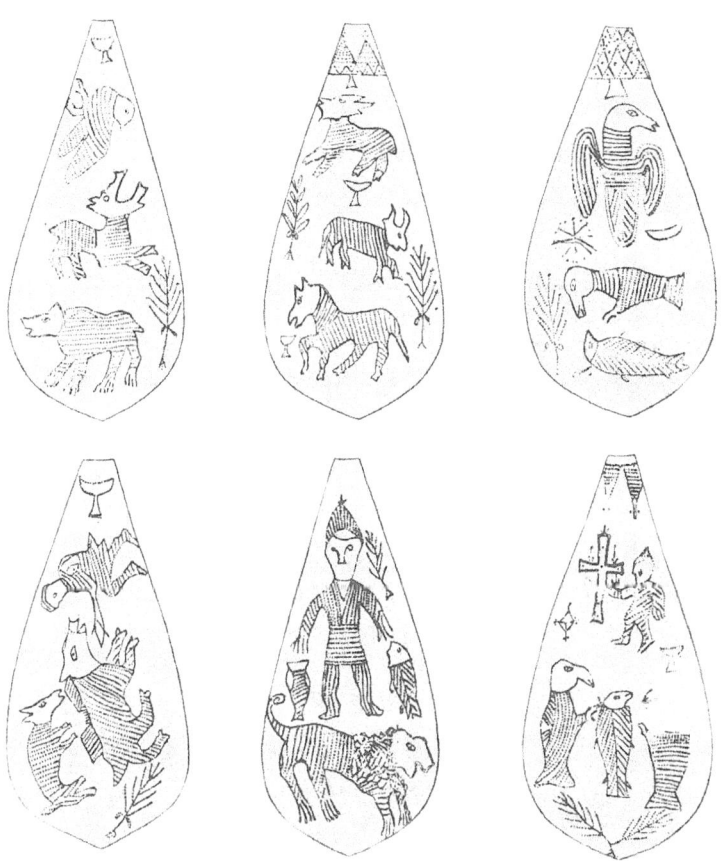

Fig. 1.19 Panels of *Spangenhelm* from Montepagano, Teramo, Italy

bearing the baptised believers whose souls he has saved.[120] It is of some interest that Pliny's observation regarding the eyesight of a bird being keen enough to spot a fish in the water was made with specific reference to the osprey or sea hawk (*haliaëtus*, Naturalis Historia X.iii8), whereas Isidore ascribes this remarkable quality to eagles in general (*Etymologiae* XII.vii.10).[121] The eagle, singled out as a hunter of fish in the Eddic poem *Vǫluspá*,[122] is yet another aspect of the poem which echoes Roman and Christian literature.

Naturalism and Style II

In the second half of the sixth century a new decorative style developed in metalwork. Its vital component was interlace, both regular and asymmetric, to which animal heads and limbs were attached.[123] The elegant Style II found on the objects in Sutton Hoo Mound 1 did not form part of the recent Anglo-Saxon dating project,[124] but the style was probably present in England on metalwork from c. AD 565/80–610/30,[125] and of course longer in manuscripts.[126] Style II in England has its own particular character, distinct from both the Continent and Scandinavia. Correspondence analyses have shown how Kentish and Anglian styles can be distinguished, but the large amount of new material from the Staffordshire Hoard has considerably blurred this

---

[120] Ibid., pp. 319–20; Helmut Roth, 'Kleine cloisonnierte Adlerfibeln', in *Gedenkschrift für Jürgen Driehaus*, ed. Frank M. Andraschko and Wolf-Rüdiger Teegen (Mainz, 1990), pp. 267–76 (pp. 272–3).

[121] The ninth-century Frankish author Rabanus Maurus glossed this passage (e.g. *PL* 111, 243B), but elsewhere wrote metaphorically of the eagle as Christ and the fish as saved human souls: 'For just as the sharp-eyed eagle is elevated on motionless wings above the sea, out of human sight, and from such a height sees the small fish to be plundered swimming in the sea, seizes and draws them to the shore; so our Redeemer, physically raised from corporeal form and exalted above all in heaven, yet in the ocean of this world his divine majesty sees at a glance which of the prey to deliver salvation to, and pulls them by his rope of love onwards to the shores of eternal bliss. Hence He says in the Gospel: "And I, if I be lifted up from the earth, will draw all things to myself (John 12)"' (*Enarrationis super Deuteronomium liber IV*, PL 108, 974C–D).

[122] *The Poetic Edda*, ed. Ursula Dronke, vol. 2: *Mythological Poems* (Oxford, 1997), p. 23 (*Vǫluspá* 56), one of the scenes at the renewal of the world; analysis of the Christian context of the poem at pp. 93–8.

[123] *Inter alia*: Salin, *Die altgermanische Tierornamentik*; Haseloff, *Die Germanische Tierornamentik*; Speake, *Anglo-Saxon Animal Art*; Høiland Nielsen, 'Style II and the Anglo-Saxon Élite'; Karen Høilund Nielsen, 'Animal Style – a Symbol of Might and Myth: Salin's Style II in a European Context', *Acta Archaeologica* 69 (1998), 1–52; Wamers, 'Behind Animals, Plants and Interlace', all with further references.

[124] Hines and Bayliss, *Anglo-Saxon Graves*, p. 252.

[125] Høilund Nielsen, 'Animal Style', pp. 8, 10, 12, fig. 4g–h, Phase D.

[126] A review of some of the dating considerations in Høiland Nielsen, 'Style II and the Anglo-Saxon Élite', pp. 194–5.

picture.[127] Wamers has demonstrated how Style II was fully embraced by Christian art,[128] and, as discussed above, some key motifs preceding this style were part of the wider Christian image bank from the outset.

Høilund Nielsen has attempted to trace the descent of Style II zoomorphs from identifiable 'wolves', horses and dragons.[129] She believes that this is more feasible with Scandinavian than Anglo-Saxon Style II and is careful to use the term wolf in inverted commas. Thus, while it is clear that birds and fish, for example, continued to be found on some Style II ornaments,[130] for the purposes of this paper it is not practical to attempt species identification in interlaced zoomorphic representations. Contemporary with Style II, however, are a range of naturalistic representations whose subject matter is relevant to our theme of the hunt.

The Sutton Hoo Mound 1 Purse Lid

If the battles between eagles and snakes/dragons present a quarry worthy of destruction, and those of the eagle and fish symbolise acuity of vision and Christian conversion, the raptor and duck plaques on the Sutton Hoo Mound 1 purse lid show animals in the service of man obtaining food for his consumption (Fig. 1.20).[131] Hicks rightly compared the plaques to a scene of fowling showing falcons taking ducks on an early Byzantine mosaic at Argos dated *c.* AD 500.[132] Although the Sutton Hoo raptors have been given classic Style II bird heads, here it is perhaps appropriate to refer to them as hawks or falcons rather than eagles. The Argos fowling scene appears on the floor mosaics of the dining room (*triclinium*) of a villa, mosaics which illustrated a complete hunt episode from preparation and departure to the falcon catching a duck, hounds coursing and capturing hares, and ending with the party's return home.[133] This belongs within a tradition

---

[127] See Karen Høilund Nielsen, 'Style II and All That: The Potential of the Hoard for Statistical Study of Chronology and Geographical Distributions', online at <http://beta.finds.org.uk/staffshoardsymposium/papers/karenhoilundnielsen> [accessed 30 December 2014], where some of the Style II animal components from the Staffordshire Hoard now appear at both early and late phases in her correspondence analyses.
[128] Wamers, 'Behind Animals, Plants and Interlace'.
[129] Her earlier theories now reviewed in Høilund Nielsen, 'Germanic Animal Art', pp. 612–18.
[130] E.g. Speake, *Anglo-Saxon Animal Art*, p. 70, fig. 6a and pl. 2h (gold buckle from Faversham, Kent.)
[131] Bruce-Mitford, *The Sutton Hoo Ship-Burial*, vol. 2, pp. 487–522.
[132] Carola Hicks, 'The Birds on the Sutton Hoo Purse', *ASE* 15 (1986), 153–65.
[133] Gunilla Åkerström-Hougen, *The Calendar and Hunting Mosaics of the Villa of the Falconer in Argos: A Study in Early Byzantine Iconography*, Skrifter Utgivna av Svenska Institutet I Athen 4 XXIII (Stockholm, 1974), pp. 28–32, figs. 12–13, 16, pls. 4–6.

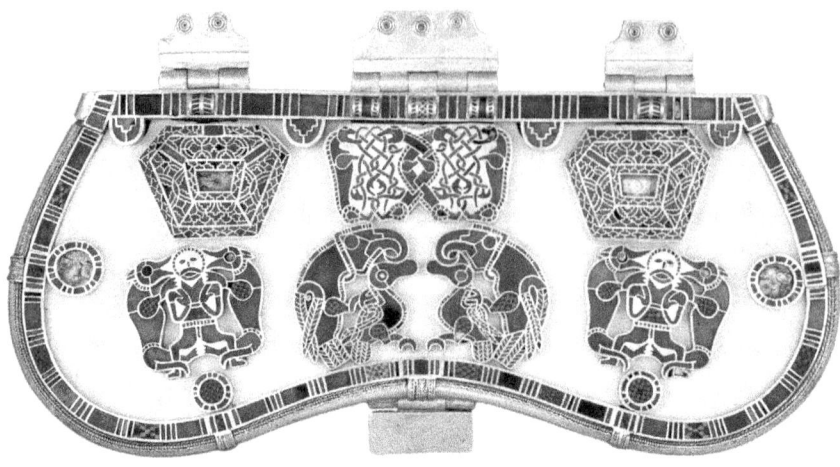
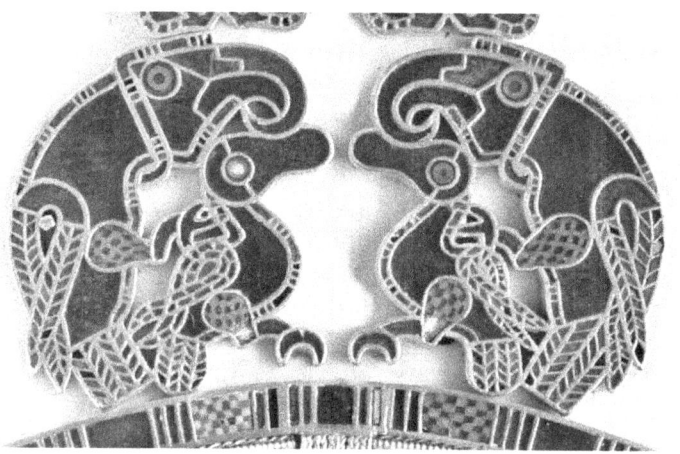
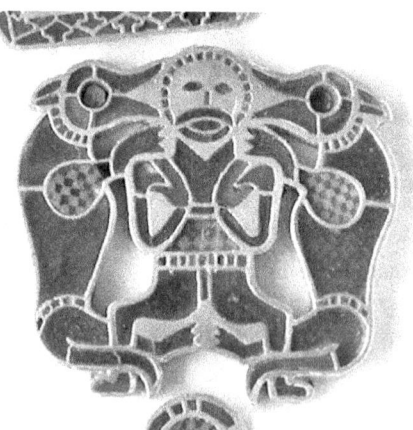

Fig. 1.20 Purse lid from Mound 1, Sutton Hoo, Suffolk, general view (above) and two details (below)

of mosaics made for luxurious villas on great estates, best known from Vandal and early Byzantine mosaics in North Africa.[134] The motif was used on metalwork as well, as shown by a Sasanian bowl featuring a falcon and duck, among other game animals, all within a vine scroll and arranged around a winged horse (Fig. 1.21). The horse faces an inscription that dates the piece to the later sixth or seventh century.[135] I know of no further examples of the raptor and duck motif from the Byzantine world, but it occurs repeatedly in the corpus of Islamic metalworking.[136] It is of some interest in the context of this essay that in medieval Persian art and poetry the duck symbolised purity and

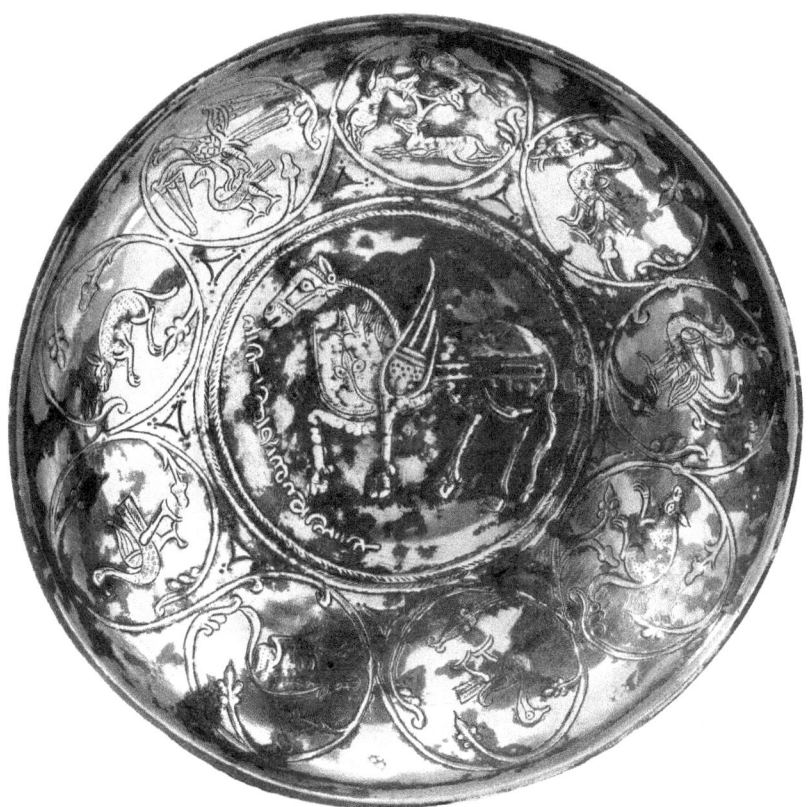

Fig. 1.21 Small Sasanian bowl in private collection, London

[134] Michele Blanchard-Lemée, Mongi Ennaïfer, Heidi Slim and Latifa Slim, *Mosaics of Roman Africa: Floor Mosaics of Tunisia* (London, 1995), figs. 129 (Kelibia), 131 (Bordj-Djedid near Carthage).

[135] The bowl is in a private collection in London and I am grateful to the owner for allowing its publication here. The epigraphy dates the piece to the Late Sasanian period, see below, n. 154.

[136] E.g. Rachel Ward, *Islamic Metalwork* (London, 1993), pp. 33, 117, pls. 22, 93.

enlightenment, as well as sorrow caused by the conflict between its mixed aquatic and terrestrial nature.[137] As with many other grave goods in the kingly burial at Sutton Hoo in eastern England, we have the impression of high-status contacts with the Byzantine empire and wider Mediterranean world.

Falconry, of course, was perhaps the most refined of the hunting methods,[138] practised largely by elites who could afford to keep and train birds. It is significant, therefore, that the large raptor and duck plaques are the central focus of the Sutton Hoo purse lid, flanked by plaques in the form of a man between canines. Although the latter are frequently referred to as wolves,[139] these are not the shaggy-coated, fierce-fanged beasts shown on contemporary depictions of wolf warriors,[140] but smooth-coated hounds with deep chests and long tails. Whatever interpretation is applied to these plaques, it is clear what creature the artist intended. Unlike contemporary Christian and Continental representations based upon Daniel in the lion's den, the hounds are upright and neither fierce, nor subjugated. And in contrast to contemporary representations of the man-between-beasts motif,[141] the man on the purse lid is not killing the canines, but rather resting his hands on his companions' paws, signalling not destruction but harmony. This unadulterated realism lacks the thrill of later Viking period mythology but sits well with the privileged status of the king who wore this purse. The other plaques on the lid are beyond the scope of this discussion, but if Bruce-Mitford's identification of the upper plaques as horses is correct, this is not at odds with an overall narrative of the chase.

---

[137] Abbas Daneshvari, *Animal Symbolism in Warqa wa Gulshāh* (Oxford, 1986), pp. 83–6. A twelfth-century Persian poem praises an *amir* by combining the predator and prey images: 'Your lordship's heart is a royal scale: on one side there is the sadness of the duck and on the other the desires of the falcon' (p. 85).

[138] As Oppian (*Cynegetica*, I, 60) noted regarding fowlers: 'to their hunt the fowlers carry nor sword nor bill nor brazen spear, but the hawk is their attendant when they travel to the woods'.

[139] *Inter alia*: Bruce-Mitford, *The Sutton Hoo Ship-Burial*, vol. 2, p. 512 ('wolf-like'); Glosecki, *Shamanism and Old English Poetry*, pp. 181–210; Pluskowski, *Wolves and the Wilderness*, pp. 143–4; Høilund Nielsen 'Germanic Animal Art', pp. 620–6, fig. 15.

[140] Høilund Nielsen, 'The Wolf-Warrior'– Animal Symbolism on Weaponry of the 6th and 7th centuries', *Archäologisches Zellwerk, Beiträge zur Kulturgeschichte in Europa und Asien, Festschrift für Helmut Roth zum 60. Geburtstag*, ed. Ernst Pohl, Udo Recker and Claudia Theune (Rahden, 2001), pp. 471–81, fig. 6.

[141] Bruce-Mitford, *The Sutton Hoo Ship-Burial*, vol. 2, p. 522, fig. 385 (Torslunda die); Margarete Klein-Pfeuffer, *Merowingerzeitliche Fibeln und Anhänger aus Preßblech*, Marburger Studien zur Vor- und Frühgeschichte 14 (Marburg, 1993): antithetical quadrupeds, pp. 171–3, fig. 53.203, pp. 368–71, no. 128 (Illingen, Baden-Württemberg) and no. 131 (Inzing, Bayern); man between upright beasts, pp. 446–8, no. 293; possible Christ with animals below his arms, p. 202, fig. 64.4. Production began in first decades after 600 and lasted until the middle of the century (p. 17).

An emphasis upon the realm of the hunt is confirmed by the appearance of boars on the shoulder clasps, which I have discussed elsewhere, suggesting that, as the feet of these naturalistic boars do not touch the ground, the creatures on these clasps are not alive but dead.[142] They are trophies of the hunt – indeed, one of the finest trophies of the hunt, available only to the bravest and most highly trained member of the elite: the king with his horses. It is possible that the beasts around the border represent hounds and the central pattern of stepped rhomboids a net, but these thoughts are speculative.

However we read the meaning of the relatively naturalistic depictions of canines, boars and raptors on the Sutton Hoo Mound 1 objects, they partake of the same symbolic world as those which form a trinity on high-status buckles preserved in Merovingian France, Denmark and Hungary.[143] One of the earliest representations of this motif may be that in Style I on the apex of a shield boss from Barton-Seagrave, Northamptonshire;[144] as yet, no examples in Style II have been found in England. Hauck's interpretation of these motifs as the *Drei-Tier-Signum* of Odin is problematic.[145] First, boars in the Germanic world, whatever their kingly associations, were not symbols of Odin, but of Freya. Secondly, as later medieval sources make perfectly clear, the wolf in relation to society was not a cherished animal.[146] While one might argue that wearing a wolf image allows the bearer to acquire wolf-like characteristics or protect against wolf attacks (surely never a common occurrence), the objects bearing supposed wolves show little to none of the animal's fearsome properties. Neither is it feasible to see these beasts as symbols of Christ, as Arrhenius has argued.[147] Høilund Nielsen has shown how the so-called 'wolf' motif spread

---

[142] Noël Adams, 'Rethinking the Shoulder Clasps and Armour in Sutton Hoo Mound 1', in *Intelligible Beauty, Recent Research on Byzantine Jewellery*, ed. Chris Entwistle and Noël Adams, British Museum Press Research Publication 178 (London, 2010), pp. 87–116 (pp. 88–9).

[143] Karen Høilund Nielsen, 'The Wolf-Warrior', pp. 471–81; Attila Kiss, *Das awarenzeitliche Gräberfeld in Kölked-Feketekapu B*, Monumenta Avarorum Archaeologica 6 (Budapest, 2001), pp. 331–2, fig. 149, colour pl. V.4, and pp. 303–4, fig. 131.

[144] Dickinson, 'Symbols of Protection', p. 120, figs. 4a, 7a. Åberg (*The Anglo-Saxons in England*, p. 169) had already spotted the boar in 1926, but not the significance of the combination.

[145] Karl Hauck, 'Zum zweiten Band der Sutton-Hoo-edition', *Frühmittelalterliche Studien* 16 (1982), 317–62 (p. 326). Other critical literature regarding the association of these animals with Odin is cited in Høilund Nielsen, 'The Wolf Warrior', pp. 473–6.

[146] Salisbury, *The Beast Within*, pp. 69–70; Pluskowski, *Wolves and the Wilderness*, pp. 1–17, 28–31, 73–84, 95–7, *passim*. Salisbury notes that wolves were considered useless because the meat was inedible, and were hunted only to remove a threat. Even hounds would not eat wolf meat, and had to be rewarded by placing chopped mutton in the cavity of the slain wolf.

[147] Birgit Arrhenius, 'Einige Christliche Paraphrasen aus dem 6. Jahrhundert', in *Zum Problem der Deutung frümittelalterlicher Bildinhalte*, ed. Roth, pp. 129–51 (pp. 138–45, figs. 11–13).

outwards from Merovingian Europe as one of the emblems of male elites. In a wider context, it is most satisfactory to see these canines as hounds, who, like falcons and boars, were key creatures of the hunt. Continental Germanic law codes, for example, made perfectly clear the value of hunting hounds, whose worth ranged from 2 to 12 *solidi*; Alamannic and Bavarian codes also included fines for hunting hawks which accidently killed domestic barnyard and water birds.[148]

Conclusions

This essay has attempted to open another door onto how the Anglo-Saxons may have seen some of their animal ornament. Images of hunters and prey in the early medieval period are mutations of, and variations upon, standard motifs, with continuity with the Classical past an undiminished theme. We might turn Wamer's statement around and suggest that 'Where there is naturalistic animal art, there is a Roman background', the foundation, the *Grundlagen*, of the Classical world that never went away.

The animal friezes on the brooches and belt sets from northern Europe that first reached England in the first half of the fifth century reflected the Late Roman origins of this type of relief cast metalworking. Predators and prey such as hunting hounds and hares were common motifs among the small border animals on these pieces. Such metalworking was one of the sources for the QBS objects in England and northern Gaul, some of which depict canines in a relatively naturalistic way. We have suggested that even abstract Style I objects in England in some cases retain an awareness of hound and hare coursing. Also in the period of Style I, a fantastical beast of the hunt – the griffin – was added to the repertoire, probably transmitted via the Continent into Anglo-Saxon Kent and East Anglia.

While the Late Roman derived imagery of QBS can still be detected in Style I, the rise of hunter and prey images in the middle decades of the sixth century correspond to a different worldview. In this phase specific combinations of predator and prey motifs appear – the

---

[148] *Laws of the Alamans and Bavarians*, trans. Theodore J. Rivers (Philadelphia, 1977): *Pactus Legis Alamannorum* XXVI.4 (hawk kills goose, 3 *solidi*); *Lex Alamannorum* LXXVIII.1–6; *Lex Baiuvariorum* XX1.7 (stolen or killed hunting dogs, 3–12 *solidi*, depending upon the dog). The latter two codes distinguish between first and second dogs, lead dogs, pig and bear dogs, dogs that guard cattle, trained greyhounds and sheepdogs that kill wolves. These sums are put into perspective by the fact that the price for killing a cow or swine was also 6 *solidi*. To the best of my knowledge dogs do not feature in Anglo-Saxon law codes until the *Laws of Alfred*, cap. 23, and then only in reference to biting men: see *The Laws of the Earliest English Kings*, trans. Frederick L. Attenborough (Cambridge, 1922).

eagle/snake, eagle/fish and eagle/dragon – used in Anglo-Saxon England on high-status male gear such as shields and horse harness. The source of these was most probably arms and armour from the Continent, with the rare eagle/dragon motif on the Sutton Hoo shield demonstrating that these images spread to Scandinavia as well. These hunters and their prey are stylised, but identifiable to a degree that many Style I creatures are not. There is evidence that, although they represent a victorious battle, in some cases they may also have conveyed ideas of Christian conversion. From an historical perspective, the Byzantine reconquest of Italy, worldwide climatic disruption *c.* 536, plague, the consolidation of power by new elites, and the inexorable spread of Christian imagery are among the factors that may have played a role in the transformation of animal imagery.

The most naturalistic animals of the Anglo-Saxon period are those found on the objects from Sutton Hoo Mound 1, representing both the classic animals of the hunt (hounds and boars) as well as a scene of falconry with a hawk and a duck. These should be seen in the same light as the naturalistic boars, raptors and canines popular *c.* AD 600 in continental Europe, whose context, like Style II, lies in the realm of male elites and their hunting fellowships.

Wearing objects whose motifs had religious connotations neither implies nor denies that their users were Christians, but simply demonstrates participation in the wider figurative world. While hunting was not an activity permitted to monks,[149] killing for food was never inimical to the Church,[150] and hunting and seasonal mosaics similar to those made for villas were used to decorate churches in the eastern Mediterranean.[151] This explains why much animal imagery moved seamlessly into the Christian world, not because the Church sought to take over paganism or impress the pagans, but simply because the metalworkers, their patrons and their clients drew upon a common pool of imagery.

---

[149] According to the Benedictine Rule (*PL* 66, 971C–972A), *Et monachus non venetur* ('And monks do not hunt').

[150] St Jerome (*PL* 23, 290), glossing David in Psalm 8:5 asking why man was set over all the beasts of the field, the birds of the heaven and fish of the sea, answers: *Esto, inquit, bos ad arandum, ad sedendum equus, canis ad servandum, caprae ad lac, oves ad lanatae conditae sint. Quis usus porcorum, absque esu carnium? quid caprae, cervuli (cervi), damulae, apri, lepores, et hujusmodi venatio? … Si non comeduntur, haec omnia frustra a Deo create sunt* ('To live, he said, these are the foundation: an ox to plow, a horse to sit upon, a dog to keep watch, she-goats to milk, sheep for wool. What use are swine, without eating meat? Why are there goats, stags, deer, boar, hares and hunting of this kind? … If you do not partake of them, all these things are created by God in vain').

[151] Micjele Piccirillo, 'Il mosaico bizantino di Giordania come fonte storica di un'epoca all luce dell recenti scoperte', in *III Colloquio internazionale sul mosaico antico, Ravenna, 6–10 settembre 1980*, ed. Raffaella Farioli Campanati (Ravenna, 1983), pp. 199–217 (pls. 4–5, 7, 14 (Mount Nebo, Jordan)); Maria Teresa Canivet, 'I mosaici di Hūarte d'Apamene (Siria)', in ibid., pp. 247–52 (figs. 2, 7).

In the above discussion it is clear that the range of animals was restricted by what was considered fitting for the object types themselves. This was obviously true of male military equipment, where familiar themes of the hunt and victory were deemed the appropriate activity to depict. But the outcome of the chase, the food preparation and consumption, were household activities in charge of women, who therefore also had a vested interest in successful hunting. In the end we can never know what societies, much less individuals, thought about all of the animals on their personal ornaments, but we can demonstrate the origins and development of the imagery.

This selective survey reveals the unique character of Britain, whose insular (Celtic, Romano-British and Pictish) and mixed Germanic populations (Angles, Jutes, Saxons, Franks, Frisians, southern Scandinavians and Norwegians) transformed existing and outside influences into an animal art that was in many cases distinctly naturalistic. Many topics await further exploration, such as the importance of dogs in Celtic mythology, the archaeology of dog burials in England, the Continent and Scandinavia,[152] the minimal evidence for wolves and wolf hunting in graves,[153] and, of course, a review of animals in insular manuscript illumination, where some of the 'missing' Roman creatures miraculously reappear.

Later expressions of animal imagery lie beyond the remit of this chapter, but there is one shared aspect of earlier and later representations that is of particular interest here – the pairing of hunting images with specific stock phrases of beneficence. The Wint Hill bowl with which this investigation began was inscribed: VIVAS CVMTVIS ('Life to you and yours'), combined with PIEZ, copying the Greek phrase ΠΙΕ ΖΗΣΑΙΣ, meaning 'Drink and good health to you'. The Pahlavi inscription on the Sasanian bowl with the hawk and duck image discussed above (see Fig. 1.21) reads: 'Be immortal ... and prosperous!'[154] An eleventh-century Saljūq sabre depicts a row of hounds (one of which is winged) and hares outstretched in the chase (Fig. 1.22); the accompanying inscription reads: 'Might, good fortune, good luck, blessing'.[155] Finally, a twelfth- to thirteenth-century

---

[152] Anne Sofie Graslund, 'Dogs in Graves – A Question of Symbolism', in *PECUS: Man and Animal: Proceedings of the Conference of the Swedish Institute in Rome, September 9–12, 2002*, ed. Barbro Santillo (Rome, 2004), pp. 167–76 (p. 169).

[153] Aleks G. Pluskowski, 'Where are the Wolves? Investigating the Scarcity of European Grey Wolf (*Canis lupus lupus*) Remains in Medieval Archaeological Contexts and its Implications', *International Journal of Osteology* 16:4 (2006), 279–95.

[154] The Pahlavi can be transcribed 'anōš ud <špwm> (?) ud ābād bāš!'. I am grateful to P. Oktor Skjaervø for this reading, provided in a personal communication via Nicholas Sims-Williams, 22 April 2014.

[155] The form and decoration reflects weaponry developed by the Kievan Rus', Magyars and Carolingians in the tenth century; see Bashir Mohamed, *The Arts of the Muslim Knight*

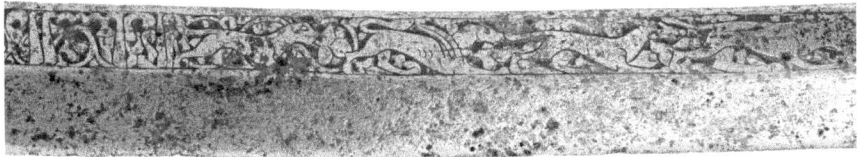

Fig. 1.22 Eleventh-century Saljūq sabre (detail)

Crusader dagger from the Frankish kingdom of Outremer in modern Lebanon and Syria is engraved with a sequence of motifs congruent with many of those discussed here: a hare and hound, a griffin on a stag, a mounted saint riding over a snake with a quadruped head (Fig. 1.23). Its inscription translates as: 'Perpetual glory, increasing prosperity, penetrating authority and ascending good fortune'.[156]

The fruits of the hunt were one of the primary benefits of humans working together with hounds, hawks and horses; the supplementary food they provided was sometimes vital to survival and always worthy of celebration. A man alone traps animals; with the help of a dog a man can drive small animals into a net; two men with hounds or a man on horseback with a javelin can face a boar; a hunting party seeks a stag; and those with falcons enjoy the thrill of birds caught on the wing for their pleasure. The more privileged members of society, who wore and commissioned the best metalwork, had the time to breed and keep hunting animals, exercise them in the chase and practise tactics in preparation for battle. This is, to be sure, a human-centred universe, as many of the images shown above prove, but one whose successful companionship with animals through hunting provides precisely what the Late Roman and Islamic inscriptions promise to their owners – abundance, prosperity and vitality. Success in this realm was triumph in reality, not in myth.[157]

(Milan, 2005), p. 39.
[156] Ibid., pp. 155–7.
[157] This essay stems from an exhibition I curated in 2004 at the National Trust Visitor Centre at Sutton Hoo: 'Between Myth and Reality: Animals in Anglo-Saxon Art'. The display positioned animal images from the Anglo-Saxon period alongside Roman-period bronzes found in Britain, supplemented by passages from Latin, Old English and Norse-Icelandic literary sources.

As always, I am grateful to Angela Care Evans for reading and improving drafts of this paper. Barry Ager has also kindly read and commented on the text. I would also like to thank Tom Williams and Mike Bintley for their patience with the missed deadlines. Remaining errors are my own. The Latin translations are again my own, unless otherwise credited.

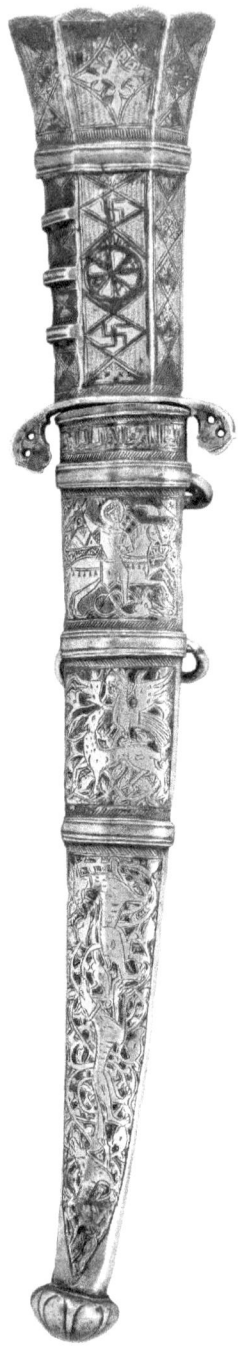

Fig. 1.23 Dagger and scabbard from Outremer

2

'(Swinger of) the Serpent of Wounds'

Swords and Snakes in the Viking Mind

Sue Brunning

The existence of a link between snakes and swords in Viking[1] thought has long been suspected. Poetry dated to the Viking period (roughly 750–1050) likens swords to serpents,[2] while snakes are part of the menagerie of animals used to decorate sword fittings (and other artefacts) at this time. Comparisons have also been drawn between literary descriptions of sword blades and real swords made by pattern-welding, a technique that created blades with sinuous, serpentine designs.[3] These correlations seem neat, but there are hints of greater complexity underneath. In recent years, research into the relationship between humans, animals and artefacts has shown that the boundaries between these categories were once far less defined than they are today. In early medieval thinking, any one of these categories could acquire the qualities of another, and shape-shifting was possible.[4] As a result, it has become helpful to view the members of these categories as co-existent 'beings' which were not taxonomically separate. These themes, which have formed part of the impetus for this volume, offer a useful framework within which to

---

[1] The term 'Viking' is problematic, and carries many different connotations. Despite various scholarly discussions, it remains in general use as a convenient means of denoting 'the peoples and culture of Scandinavia in the "Viking Age" (800–1050)': Gareth Williams, 'Introduction', in *Vikings: Life and Legend*, ed. Gareth Williams, Peter Pentz and Matthias Wemhoff (London, 2014), p. 17. 'Viking' is used here in this broad sense.

[2] In this chapter, 'snake' and 'serpent' are used synonymously to describe the limbless reptile, following popular modern convention. In Old Norse, these terms could also denote large winged dragons, as discussed below. See also the discussion by Symons, Chapter 3 in this volume.

[3] Hilda R. Ellis Davidson, *The Sword in Anglo-Saxon England* (Oxford, 1962), pp. 106–7, 130, 132, 166–7; Brian Gilmour, 'Swords, Seaxes and Saxons: Pattern-Welding and Edged Weapon Technology from Late Roman Britain to Anglo-Saxon England', in *Collectanea Antiqua: Essays in Memory of Sonia Chadwick Hawkes*, ed. Martin Henig and Tyler Jo Smith, BAR International Series 1673 (Oxford, 2007), pp. 91–109 (p. 103).

[4] Lotte Hedeager, *Iron Age Myth and Materiality* (London, 2011), pp. 12–3, 85; Kristina Jennbert, *Animals and Humans: Recurrent Symbiosis in Archaeology and Old Norse Religion* (Lund, 2011).

explore and understand the Vikings' cognitive link between swords and snakes.

This chapter constitutes an interdisciplinary study of the relationship between swords and snakes in Viking thought. The evidence is reviewed and analysed in order to determine the strength and significance of the link, and explanations are proposed. The geographical and temporal focus is Viking Scandinavia, although evidence from other regions where Scandinavians settled or were active is discussed where relevant. Literary and archaeological sources form the core of the enquiry, and the parallels between them are assessed. All evidence is viewed in proper context: this is vital because snakes were not the only animals that were associated with swords in Viking Scandinavia. These relationships must also be considered if the sword-snake link is to be properly understood.

Firstly, it is necessary to negotiate a perennial problem relating to written sources. Before the spread of Christianity from the mid-tenth century, an oral culture prevailed in Scandinavia, and literacy was extremely limited. The only truly contemporary texts of the era are runic inscriptions on monuments and portable artefacts, which, due to their formulaic and/or commemorative nature, contain little information that is useful for this enquiry.[5] A rich body of later texts survives in the form of Icelandic sagas, written down from the twelfth century, with many set in the Viking period.[6] However, their later date and Icelandic genesis, together with uncertainty surrounding the extent of their oral or literary origins, have raised questions about their validity as sources for the Viking Scandinavian mainland.[7] Recent work has argued that while sagas may not be reliable for historical facts, they can (and should) be used in studies of ideologies, customs and attitudes which, being slow to change over time, render their late dating less problematic.[8]

---

[5] Judith Jesch, *Ships and Men in the Late Viking Age: The Vocabulary of Runic Inscriptions and Skaldic Verse* (Woodbridge, 2001), pp. 7, 14; Terje Spurkland, *Norwegian Runes and Runic Inscriptions* (Woodbridge, 2005), pp. 20ff, 86ff.

[6] Lars Lönnroth, 'The Icelandic Sagas', in *The Viking World*, ed. Stefan Brink and Neil Price (London, 2008), pp. 304–10 (p. 304).

[7] Judith Jesch, *Women in the Viking Age* (Woodbridge, 1991), p. 4; Lönnroth, 'The Icelandic Sagas', pp. 305–6; Preben Meulengracht Sørensen, 'Historical Reality and Literary Form', in *Viking Revaluations: Viking Society Centenary Symposium, 14–15 May 1992*, ed. Anthony Faulkes and Richard Perkins (London, 1993), pp. 172–81 (pp. 172–4); Eric Christiansen, *The Norsemen in the Viking Age* (Oxford, 2001), pp. 305, 309.

[8] Hedeager, *Iron Age Myth*, pp. 3, 22; Jesch, *Women in the Viking Age*, pp. 4–5; Lönnroth, 'The Icelandic Sagas', pp. 301–11; Meulengracht Sørensen, 'Historical Reality', with references; Maria Domeij Lundborg, 'Bound Animal Bodies: Ornamentation and Skaldic Poetry in the Process of Christianization', in *Old Norse Religion in Long-Term Perspectives: Origins, Changes and Interactions*, ed. Anders Andrén, Kristina Jennbert and Catharina Raudvere (Lund, 2006), pp. 39–44 (p. 40).

More promisingly, a substantial corpus of Old Norse poetry survives that, although preserved in later medieval manuscripts, is widely believed to have been composed in the Viking period. Many sagas incorporate so-called 'skaldic' poems, named after the skalds (poets) who created them, which have been dated to the late tenth to eleventh centuries.[9] A few may be older still, such as Bragi inn gamli Boddason's *Ragnarsdrápa*, thought by some to belong to the mid ninth century.[10] The complex form and metre of skaldic poetry means that it was likely to have been transmitted through the ages without corruption or interpolation, until it was eventually written down centuries later. Furthermore, many poems are attributed to named skalds whose works were intended for public recitation in honour of a named person's known historical exploits:[11] in other words, skalds might exaggerate in order to flatter, but they were unlikely to create complete fabrications. Another collection of Scandinavian poetry is preserved in the thirteenth-century *Codex Regius* or *Konungsbók*, and commonly referred to as the *Poetic Edda*. Eddic verses have traditionally been approached with more caution than skaldic poems, since their authors are anonymous, their subject matter mythological rather than historical, and their simpler form more open to corruption over time. While this means that Eddic poetry cannot be securely attributed to the early medieval period, some have argued with conviction that these works contain genuinely archaic material.[12]

In view of these literary complexities, this study concentrates primarily on Old Norse skaldic and Eddic poetry that has been widely dated to the Viking period. This is not to deny the significance of Icelandic sagas on the chosen topic: on the contrary, not only do they preserve numerous skaldic verses as mentioned above, but they also contain many well-known allusions to serpentine swords – the weapon called Adder wielded by the anti-hero Egill, and Skǫfnungr, a temperamental sword that was said to have a snake crawl out from

---

[9] Judith Jesch, 'Poetry in the Viking Age', in *The Viking World*, ed. Brink and Price, pp. 291–8 (p. 296).

[10] John Lindow, 'Narrative Worlds, Human Environments, and Poets: The Case of Bragi', *Old Norse Religion*, ed. Andrén et al., pp. 21–5; but see cautionary notes in Judith Jesch, 'Eagles, Ravens and Wolves: Beasts of Battle, Symbols of Victory and Death', in *The Scandinavians from the Vendel Period to the Tenth Century*, ed. Judith Jesch (Woodbridge, 2003), pp. 251–71 (p. 273), and Russell G. Poole, *Viking Poems on War and Peace* (Toronto, 1991), pp. 18–19, on the possibility that some later skalds deliberately composed verses in the style of earlier poetry.

[11] Christopher Abram, *Myths of the Pagan North: The Gods of the Norsemen* (London, 2011), pp. 11–13; Hedeager, *Iron Age Myth*, p. 23; Jesch, 'Eagles, Ravens and Wolves', p. 251; Jesch, 'Poetry in the Viking Age', pp. 295–6.

[12] Abram, *Myths of the Pagan North*, p. 11; Jesch, 'Poetry in the Viking Age', pp. 293–5; Jesch, 'Eagles, Ravens and Wolves', pp. 251, 261, 263–4; Jesch, *Ships and Men*, p. 18; Christiansen, *The Norsemen in the Viking Age*, p. 309.

the hilt if one breathed upon its blade.[13] So many memorable swords, acting as instruments of fate and drivers of plot, feature in Icelandic sagas that the proper forum for discussion is a lengthy, dedicated study rather than a short chapter such as this. Consequently, this study refers to the sagas only where they are particularly relevant. All written sources are quoted in English translation.

Signals of Serpentine Swords

Complex linguistic constructions known as kennings dominate written evidence for a link between snakes and swords in the Viking mind. Somewhat metaphorical in nature (although usually termed 'periphrastic' or 'circumlocutory'), kennings were used as replacements for simple nouns in skaldic poetry. For instance, a basic kenning for 'fire' was 'harm of the forest' because fire was able to destroy, or harm, wood.[14] Hundreds of sword kennings dating to the Viking and later medieval periods are recorded in modern compilations and the *Skaldic Poetry of the Scandinavian Middle Ages Project*'s scholarly online database.[15] The imagery they employ is diverse, ranging from parts of the body to natural forces and, crucially, animals: namely snakes, fish and dogs, with snakes being the most popular.[16] Across these kenning compilations, fourteen sword kennings that refer to snakes have been dated to the Viking period by the *Skaldic Poetry* project. Five describe swords as 'wound snake',[17] four as 'battle snake',[18] two as 'corpse

---

[13] *Egils saga* 53, trans. Bernard Scudder, *Egil's Saga* (London, 1997); *Kormáks saga* 9, trans. William Morris and Eiríkr Magnusson, *The Story of Kormak the Son of Ogmund* (London, 1970).

[14] Bjǫrn krepphendi, *Magnússdrápa* 3, trans. Kari Ellen Gade, *Poetry from the Kings' Sagas 2, Part 1* (Turnhout, 2009), pp. 395–405; Abram, *Myths of the Pagan North*, pp. 13–15.

[15] Rudolf Meissner, *Die Kenningar der Skalden: Ein Beitrag zur skaldischen Poetik* (Bonn, 1921); Hjalmar Falk, *Altnordische Waffenkunde* (Kristiania, 1914); Skaldic Poetry of the Scandinavian Middle Ages Project <http://skaldic.arts.usyd.edu.au/db.php> [accessed 7 December 2013].

[16] Sue Brunning, 'The "Living" Sword in Early Medieval Northern Europe: An Interdisciplinary Study' (unpublished PhD thesis, Institute of Archaeology, University College London, 2013), chart 55.

[17] Bersi Skáld-Torfuson, *Flokkr about Óláfr helgi* 3, trans. Lee M. Hollander, *Heimskringla: History of the Kings of Norway* (Austin, TX, 1995); Einarr skálaglamm Helgason, *Lausavísa* 2a, trans. Hollander, *Heimskringla*; Þormóðr Kolbrúnarskáld, *Þorgeirsdrápa* 4, 6, trans. Martin S. Regal, 'The Saga of the Sworn Brothers', in *The Complete Sagas of Icelanders including 49 Tales*, vol. 2, ed. Viðar Hreinsson (Reykjavík, 1997); Hólmgǫngu-Bersi Véleifsson, *Lausavísa* 13, in *Kormáks saga*, trans. Morris and Magnusson, *The Story of Kormak*.

[18] Óttar svarti, *Hǫfuðlausn* 8, trans. Jonathan Grove, 'Recreating Tradition: Sigvatr Þórðarson's *Víkingarvísur* and Óttarr svarti's *Hǫfuðlausn*', in *Á austrvega. Saga and East Scandinavia. Preprint Papers of the 14th International Saga Conference, Uppsala, 9th–15th August 2009*, vol. 2, ed. Agneta Ney, Henrik Williams and Frederik Charpentier

snake',[19] two as 'shield-snake'[20] and one as 'sword-part snake'[21] (Table 2.1). In a similar vein, the Eddic poem *Helgakviða Hundinsgbana I* refers to a sword as a 'blood snake'.[22]

Apart from the kennings, Old Norse poems depict swords with bodily attributes that can be interpreted as snake-like. A defining physical characteristic of a snake is its fangs, which are capable of nasty and even poisonous bites. Likewise, the biting sword is a common image in Old Norse poetry. In *Hamðismál*, thought by some to be one of the oldest surviving Eddic poems,[23] the formidable Guðrún goads her sons into avenging their sister Svanhildr by saying that 'every man should bring about death for others, / with a sword that bites into wounds.'[24] In another poem Sigrún, a Valkyrie, curses her brother Dagr, who has slain her husband, with the words 'may the sword that you wield never bite for you'.[25] Skaldic poems also refer to biting swords:[26] Eyvindr skáldaspillir Finnsson's *Hákonarmál*, composed for the Norwegian king Hákon the Good (r. 934–61), boasts that the king's sword bites through armour;[27] but in *Vikingarvísur*, Sigvatr Þórðarson's poem celebrating King Óláfr Haraldsson's (r. 1015–28) early exploits, it is the enemy's swords that bite.[28]

Archaeological evidence for snake-like swords rests chiefly upon weapons with serpentine decoration. The pattern-welding technique, popular into the ninth century, created intricately patterned blades

---

Ljungqvist (Gävle, 2009), pp. 327–35; Egill Skallagrímsson, *Lausavísá* 28, in *Egils saga*, trans. Scudder, *Egil's saga*; Hólmgǫngu-Bersi Véleifsson, *Lausavísa* 8, in *Kormáks saga*, trans. Morris and Magnusson, *The Story of Kormak*.

[19] Sigvatr Þórðarson, *Nesjavísur* 14, trans. Hollander, *Heimskringla*; Þórarinn svarti máhlíðingr Þórólfsson, *Máhlíðingavísur* 1, in *Eyrbyggja saga*, trans. Hermann Pálsson and Paul Edwards, *Eyrbyggja Saga* (London, 1989).

[20] Þormóðr Kolbrúnarskáld, *Lausavísa* 15, trans. Regal, 'The Saga of the Sworn Brothers'; Þorleifr jarlsskáld Rauðfeldarson, *Lausavísa* 2, in *Svarfdæla saga*, trans. William Bryant Bachman and Gudmundur Erlingsson, *Svarfdale Saga and Other Tales* (Lanham, MD, 1994).

[21] Einarr þveræingr Eyjólfsson, *V. Lausavísa* 1, in *Víga-Glúms saga*, trans. John McKinnell, *Viga-Glums Saga, with the Tales of Ogmund Bash and Chatterbox* (Edinburgh, 1987).

[22] *Helgakviða Hundinsgbana I* 8, trans. Carolyne Larrington, *The Poetic Edda* (Oxford, 2008).

[23] Larrington, *The Poetic Edda*, p. 238.

[24] *Hamðismál* 8, trans. Larrington, *The Poetic Edda*.

[25] *Helgakviða Hundinsgbana II* 33, trans. Larrington, *The Poetic Edda*.

[26] Arnórr jarlaskáld Þórðarson, *Þorfinnsdrápa* 16, trans. Gade, *Poetry from the Kings' Sagas*; Hallfreðr vandræðaskáld Óttarsson, *Erfidrápa Óláfs Tryggvasonar* 15, 24, trans. Alan Boucher, *The Saga of Hallfred the Troublesome Scald* (Reykjavík, 1981); Magnús inn góði Óláfsson, *Lausavísa* 3, trans. Gade, *Poetry from the Kings' Sagas*; Sigvatr Þórðarson, *Erfidrápa Óláfs helga* 16, trans. as part of the Skaldic Poetry of the Scandinavian Middle Ages Project; Þjóðólfr Arnórsson, *Magnússflokkr* 8, trans. Gade, *Poetry from the Kings' Sagas*.

[27] Eyvindr skáldaspillir Finnsson, *Hákonarmál* 5, trans. Alison Finlay, *Fagrskinna: A Catalogue of the Kings of Norway* (Leiden, 2004).

[28] Sigvatr Þórðarson, *Vikingarvísur* 6, trans. Christine Fell, in *Speculum Norroenum: Norse Studies in Memory of Gabriel Turville-Petre*, ed. Ursula Dronke, Gudrun P. Helgadóttir, Gerd Wolfgang Weber and Hans Bekker-Nielsen (Odense, 1981), pp. 106–22.

Table 2.1 Sword kennings incorporating references to snakes

Poet	Poem	Proposed date	Kenning in ON	Modern translation
Bersi Skáld-Torfuson	Flokkr about Óláfr helgi 3	1000–20	linnr sára	snake of wounds
Egill Skallagrímsson	Lausavísa 28	900–83	rógnaðr	battle snake
Einarr skálaglamm Helgason	Lausavísa 2a	975–1000	sárlinnr	wound snake
Einarr þveræingr Eyjólfsson	Lausavísa 1	1000–1100	þremjalinnr	sword-part snake
Hólmgǫngu-Bersi Véleifsson	Lausavísa 8	950–1000	róglinnr	battle snake
Hólmgǫngu-Bersi Véleifsson	Lausavísa 13	950–1000	benja linnr	wound snake
Óttar svarti	Hǫfuðlausn 8	1000–50	dolglinnr	battle snake
Óttar svarti	Hǫfuðlausn 8	1000–50	linnr éla Yggs	snake of the storms of Yggr [Óðinn]
Sigvatr Þórðarson	Nesjavísur 14	1000–50	hrælinnr	corpse snake
Þorleifr jarlsskáld Rauðfeldarson	Lausavísa 2	950–1000	rítormr	shield snake
Þormóðr Kolbrúnarskáld	Lausavísa 15	before 1030	linnr randar	snake of the shield
Þormóðr Kolbrúnarskáld	Þorgeirsdrápa 4	before 1030	undlinnr	wound snake
Þormóðr Kolbrúnarskáld	Þorgeirsdrápa 6	before 1030	undlinnr	wound snake
Þórarinn svarti máhlíðingr Þórólfsson	Máhlíðingavísur 1	950–1000	valnaðr	corpse snake

Sources: The kennings in this table were collected from Meissner, *Die Kenningar*, and the Skaldic Poetry of the Scandinavian Middle Ages Project. Their date was determined as Viking period from the latter.

Swords and Snakes in the Viking Mind

by hammering together twisted iron rods to form a core which was then ground and polished to bring out sinuous designs.[29] Comments in contemporary writings seem to suggest that early medieval people thought pattern-welded swords resembled serpents. The most famous reference appears in a late sixth century letter of Cassiodorus, secretary to the Ostrogothic king Theoderic the Great, in which he thanks the King of the Warni (a Germanic people) for sending him swords that appeared to be 'grained with tiny snakes'.[30] More abstract are several unusual Old English terms applied to sword blades in the Anglo-Saxon poem *Beowulf*: *wægsweord* (translated by Seamus Heaney as 'wave-sword', line 1489), *hringmæl* ('coiling pattern', line 1521), *wundenmæl* ('twisted pattern', line 1532), and *atertanum fah* ('gleaming with twigs of venom / tiny serpents', line 1460).[31] Analogous Scandinavian references mostly post-date the Viking period and derive from sagas, such as *Þiðreks saga*, in which the blade of the sword Ekkisax is marked with a snake from hilt to tip, and *Kormáks saga*, in which Skǫfnungr has a serpent beneath its hilt.[32] Eddic poems may record earlier expressions of similar ideas. In *Helgakviða Hjǫrvarðssonar* a Valkyrie describes a sword with a 'blood-dyed snake' along its edge,[33] while the weapon that separates Brynhildr and Sigurðr in *Brot af Sigurðarkviðu* is 'patterned with acid marks'.[34]

Certain pattern-welded designs correlate more convincingly with literary descriptions than others. The commonest pattern on surviving swords is a herringbone or chevron effect[35] which, depending on one's view, may call snakes to mind; the markings could equally be interpreted as fish-like, connecting with sword kennings that refer to this creature. Interestingly, however, fish are common reference points in snake kennings.[36] Perhaps sword kennings that referred to fish

---

[29] Gareth Williams, 'Warfare and Military Expansion', in *Vikings: Life and Legend*, ed. Williams *et al.*, pp. 76–121 (p. 108); Lee A. Jones, 'Blade Construction and Pattern-Welding', in Ian Peirce and Ewart Oakeshott, *Swords of the Viking Age* (Woodbridge, 2005), pp. 145–51.

[30] Cassiodorus, *Variae* V.1, trans. Sam J. B. Barnish, *Cassiodorus: Variae* (Liverpool, 1992).

[31] *Beowulf*, trans. Seamus Heaney (London, 2000); Caroline Brady, '"Weapons" in *Beowulf*: An Analysis of the Nominal Compounds and an Evaluation of the Poet's Use of Them', *ASE* 8 (1979), 79–142 (pp. 94, 101); John R. Clark-Hall, *A Concise Anglo-Saxon Dictionary* (Toronto, 1960), s.v. these terms.

[32] *Kormáks saga* 9, trans. Morris and Magnusson, *The Story of Kormak*, interpreted by Ellis Davidson, *The Sword*, pp. 166–7.

[33] *Helgakviða Hjǫrvarðssonar* 9, trans. Larrington, *The Poetic Edda*, pp. 123–31.

[34] *Brot af Sigurðarkviðu* 19, trans. Larrington, *The Poetic Edda*, pp. 174–6; Ellis Davidson, *The Sword*, p. 132.

[35] Gilmour, 'Swords, Seaxes and Saxons', pp. 103–4.

[36] For example: 'the fish of the heather' in Sigvatr Þórðarson, *Erfidrápa Óláfs helga* 3, translated as part of the Skaldic Poetry of the Scandinavian Middle Ages project; and 'the whale of the heath' (a fish-like mammal in this case), in Einarr skálaglamm Helgason, *Vellekla* 30, trans. Daphne L. Davidson, 'Earl Hakon and his Poets' (unpublished PhD thesis, University of Oxford, 1983).

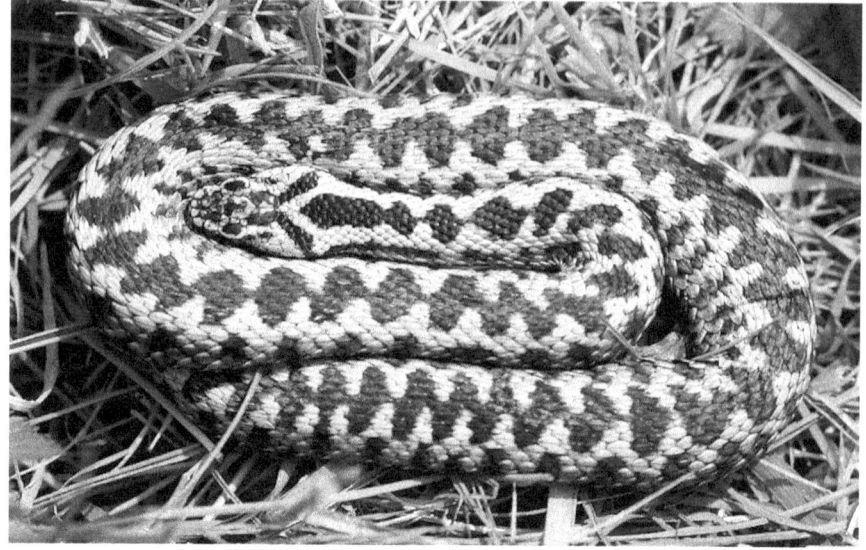

Fig. 2.1 The characteristic diamond-shaped markings of the adder (*Vipera berus*)

could still summon the image of a snake – thereby preserving their link with swords, albeit at one remove.

A more overtly serpentine pattern comprises a single undulating line running along the centre of the blade. It is known only from a handful of surviving north European swords, including an extraordinary weapon from Vehmaa in Lahdinko, Finland, whose pattern transforms from chevron to wavy line along the blade's length.[37]

Clearer representations of snakes form part of interlacing designs on prestige hilts,[38] echoed in the Eddic poem *Helgakviða Hjǫrvarðssonar*, which describes a hilt decorated with a serpent chasing its tail.[39] More abstract visual references to snakes may be found in another type of decoration, if one is prepared to speculate: geometric designs on certain types of hilt appear to resemble scales or the diamond-shaped markings distinctive to the common viper, or adder (*Vipera berus*),

---

[37] Brian Gilmour, 'West Heslerton: A Snake Patterned Sword', English Heritage AML Reports, new series 129 (1991), 1–12 (pp. 1–2 with references); Gilmour, 'Swords, Seaxes and Saxons', pp. 103–4, figs. 10a–c; Jones, 'Blade Construction', pp. 148–9; J. Lepäaho, *Späteisenzeitliche Waffen aus Finland: Schwertinschriften und Waffenverzierungen des. 9.–13. Jahrhunderts* (Helsinki, 1964), p. 66, Taf. 31–2.

[38] Simple ribbon interlace decoration without snake heads may also have been interpreted as representative of serpents, e.g. on the five-lobed pommels categorised as part of Type O in Jan Petersen's typology: Jan Petersen, *De norske vikingsverd: En typologiskkronologisk studie over vikingtidens vaaben* (Kristiania, 1919), pp. 126–34.

[39] *Helgakviða Hjǫrvarðssonar* 8–9, trans. Larrington, *The Poetic Edda*.

native to northern Europe for millennia (Fig. 2.1).[40] Two types in Jan Petersen's seminal typology of Viking swords are particularly relevant.-

Type D (ninth century) is characterised by ornate hilt fittings decorated with cells or panels[41] that, it could be ventured, look like scales or adder markings. One example from Vang in Oppland, Norway, is covered with scale-like decoration in the form of sub-circular lozenges.[42] Another, from Bjørnsholm in Søndersø, Denmark, has defined diamond-shaped motifs arranged in rows which, between them, create scale-like lozenges. The diamond-shaped elements are copper alloy, while the scale-like lozenges are inlaid with silver wire, creating a polychrome effect that resembles the streak of dark-on-light markings along an adder's back.[43] A second (lesser known) sword from Søndersø, and one from Trælnes, Norway, demonstrate similar effects (Fig. 2.2).[44] Other Type D swords are less suggestive. Cells decorating hilts from the Isle of Eigg, Scotland, and Ved Moss, Norway, contain tiny creatures, reducing the scale-like effect and warning against inferring too much from these weapons.[45]

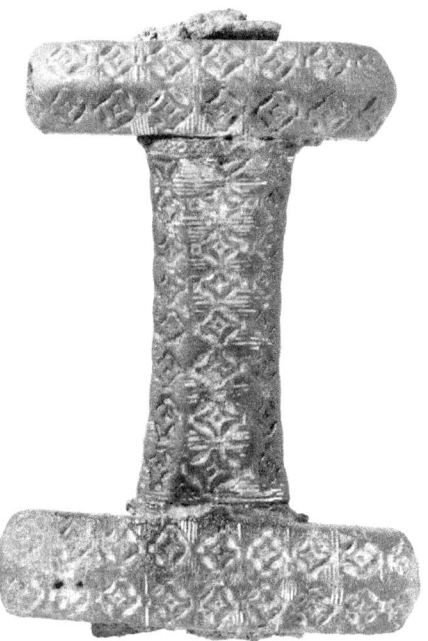

Fig. 2.2 Type D sword hilt from Trælnes, Norway

Swords of Petersen's Type H (ninth to mid-tenth century) have iron hilt fittings decorated with different coloured wires arranged in striped and geometric patterns.[46] Some involve colour-contrasting bands of diamonds that again, in many cases, resemble adder markings. The

---

[40] Martin Carlsson and Håkan Tegelström, 'Phylogeography of Adders (*Vipera Berus*) from Fennoscandia', in *Biology of the Vipers*, ed. Gordon W. Schuett, Mats Hoggren, Michael E. Douglas and Harry W. Greene (Eagle Mountain, UT, 2002), pp. 1–9 (p. 1).

[41] Petersen, *De norske vikingsverd*, p. 70; James Graham-Campbell, *Viking Artefacts* (London, 1980), p. 70.

[42] Kulturhistorisk museum, Oslo, registration number C24887a.

[43] Nationalmuseet, Copenhagen, registration number C1572; Peirce and Oakeshott, *Swords of the Viking Age*, pp. 45–5.

[44] Knud Labohn, 'Gamle pragtsværd fik ny værdighed', news article published at *Nordjyske.dk*, 30 May 2011, online at <http://nordjyske.dk/nyheder/gamle-pragtsvaerd-fik-ny-vaerdighed/1dc9123c-b155-4f2a-b0d9-cecfcb75072f/4/1513> [accessed 10 January 2015]; Trondheim Museum, Norway, registration number T 14309:1.

[45] Haakon Shetelig, *Viking Antiquities in Great Britain and Ireland*, vol. 2 (Oslo, 1940), fig. 37, p. 64; Petersen, *De norske vikingsverd*, fig. 60.

[46] Petersen, *De norske vikingsverd*, pp. 90–1.

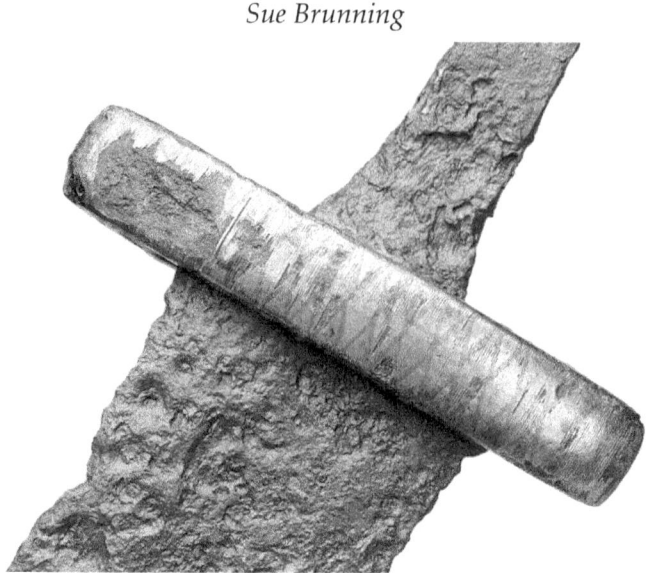

Fig. 2.3 Type H sword hilt of unknown provenance

likeness is especially convincing where a single line of dark diamonds appears against a lighter ground, for instance along the lower guard of a sword of unknown provenance in Historiska Museet, Stockholm (Fig. 2.3),[47] another from Utgården, Norway, and one more from Kjølstad, Norway.[48] Slightly different is the sword from grave 561 at Birka in Uppland, Sweden, whose hilt is decorated with silver stepped motifs arranged so that dark lozenges are created between them.[49] Comparable dark-on-light diamond motifs woven into the Oseberg tapestry from Norway (patterns L and M in particular) may suggest that this was simply a popular geometric design in Viking Scandinavia, rather than something that was perceived as especially snake-like;[50] but while the intention of the craftsmen who made these sword fittings cannot be recovered, the possibility that they may have related to, or could be read as, the markings of snakes can at least be entertained.

---

[47] Registration number 266352.
[48] Kulturhistorisk Museum, Oslo, registration numbers C1648 and C37550a, respectively.
[49] Object number 34000: Bj 561; Holger Arbman, *Birka: Die Gräber 2* [*Tafelband*] (Stockholm, 1940), Taf. 1:2; Holger Arbman, *Birka: Die Gräber 1* [*Text*] (Stockholm, 1943), pp. 180–1.
[50] Sophie Krafft, *Pictorial Weavings from the Viking Age: Drawings and Patterns of Textiles from the Oseberg Finds* (Oslo, 1956), p. 47.

Significance of the Link

Archaeological and written sources both suggest that a link did exist between snakes and swords in the Viking mind. The significance of this link, however, is challenged when the material is viewed in broader context. For instance, much of the evidence for a link between snakes and swords also applies to spears.[51] In his vast kenning compilation, Meissner remarked upon the difficulty of distinguishing sword from spear kennings because the imagery used in both was so similar – including allusions to snakes.[52] Such references apparently became standard. In a thirteenth-century work about poetic conventions, the Icelander Snorri Sturluson states that 'thrusting weapons can appropriately be referred to as snakes or fish'.[53] He clearly excludes swords from this, since they are defined as 'cutting weapons', which are typically denoted as 'the fires of blood or wounds' or 'the fires of Óðinn'. Furthermore, spearheads – like sword blades – were sometimes made by pattern-welding. Impressive examples from the Viking world include one from Uosukkala, Valkjärvi, in Finland, and another from near Twyford in Berkshire, England, upon which the chevron effect of the twisted rods forming the blade's core is exposed.[54] Like sword-hilt fittings, the sockets of prestige spearheads were sometimes inlaid with polychrome lozenge motifs that resemble adder markings, exemplified by tenth- to eleventh-century spearheads from Alsøy, Norway, and Valsgärde, Sweden.[55] Interlacing snakes decorated other fine spearhead sockets.[56] Indeed, serpent motifs were a popular part of the Vikings' zoomorphic repertoire, ornamenting a range of artefacts including jewellery, carved stones, equestrian equipment

---

[51] Spears and arrows are described as 'battle adders' in the Old English poems *Elene* (line 140) and *Judith* (line 222), trans. Sid A. J. Bradley, *Anglo-Saxon Poetry* (London, 1982). This may suggest that the connection between snakes and certain weapons had a broader cultural relevance, but since both poems are preserved in manuscripts that date to the period of Scandinavian settlement in Anglo-Saxon England, a Scandinavian influence cannot be ruled out. This issue lies beyond the scope of the current chapter, but see Roberta Frank, 'Did Anglo-Saxon Audiences Have a Skaldic Tooth?', *Scandinavian Studies* 59 (1987), 338–55; and Roberta Frank, 'North-Sea Soundings in *Andreas*', in *Early Medieval Texts and Interpretations: Studies Presented to Donald G. Scragg*, ed. Stuart Rosser and Elaine Traherne (Tempe, AZ, 2002), pp. 1–11.

[52] Meissner, *Die Kenningar*, pp. 145–6.

[53] Snorri Sturluson, *Skáldskaparmál* 48, trans. Russell G. Poole, 'Poetic References from *Skáldskaparmál*', in *The Prose Edda*, ed. Jesse L. Byock (London, 2005), pp. 108–18.

[54] Graham-Campbell, *Viking Artefacts*, cat. no. 256, p. 72; Williams, 'Warfare and Military Expansion', fig. 51, p. 108.

[55] Kulturhistorisk Museum, Oslo, registration number C5613; Graham-Campbell, *Viking Artefacts*, cat. no. 258, p. 72.

[56] E.g. from Finland: see Lepäaho, *Späteisenzeitliche Waffen*, Taf. 45:2a, pp. 94–5.

and even churches.⁵⁷ The implication is that the snake, rather than the item it adorned, was important.

Ultimately, however, the link between spears and snakes appears to have been weaker than the link with swords. Far fewer serpentine spear kennings have been securely identified, whereas equivalent sword kennings survive in quantity and were used well into the post-Viking period. From an aesthetic point of view, it is reasonable to venture that pattern-welded swords were more likely to have been viewed as snake-like than pattern-welded spearheads, because their long, thin shape was more evocative of the serpent than the shorter leaf- or lozenge-shaped spearheads.

Pattern-welding provides a further challenge to evidence for a link between swords and snakes. Most literary allusions to snake-like swords date to the later Viking period, when pattern-welding was being replaced by techniques that created blades from a single piece of metal (after the ninth century).⁵⁸ Researchers have viewed this phenomenon as a sign that the memory and prestige of pattern-welded swords outlived their period of use, and serpentine descriptions became a stock way of referring to such weapons in poetry and saga.⁵⁹ However, the writers of medieval Scandinavia may have had more than just memories of these swords to go on. Archaeological evidence of repaired, modified and badly worn swords from Viking Scandinavia and beyond demonstrates that they were sometimes kept for generations, for instance as heirlooms or precious gifts.⁶⁰ This practice also appears in skaldic poetry. An eleventh-century verse by Óttar svarti refers to *éarnhringar* – variously translated as 'iron swords', 'old iron swords' or even 'far-famed swords' – being destroyed in a battle.⁶¹ Heirloom swords feature prominently in the sagas themselves, and it is feasible that some pattern-welded swords survived into saga times, if not in functional use then as display or ceremonial pieces. Viewed contextually in this way, the chronological mismatch between pattern-welded swords and the texts that seem to describe them is less problematic.

Another query posed by pattern-welding is that the majority of surviving designs do not appear all that snake-like. As noted above, the most overtly serpentine designs (in the form of wavy lines) are

---

⁵⁷ Domeij Lundborg, 'Bound Animal Bodies', p. 39; Bo Jensen, *Viking Age Amulets in Scandinavia and Western Europe* (Oxford, 2010), p. 37.
⁵⁸ Graham-Campbell, *Viking Artefacts*, p. 67; Jacqueline Simpson, *The Viking World* (London, 1980), p. 114; Williams, 'Warfare and Military Expansion', p. 108.
⁵⁹ Ellis Davidson, *The Sword*, pp. 166–7; Simpson, *The Viking World*, p. 114.
⁶⁰ Brunning, 'The "Living" Sword', ch. 5.
⁶¹ Óttar svarti, *Hǫfuðlausn* 8, interpreted by J. R. Hagland and B. Watson, 'Fact or Folklore: The Viking Attack on London Bridge', *London Archaeologist* 12 (2005), 328–33 (p. 331); Guðrún Nordal, *Tools of Literacy: The Role of Skaldic Verse in Icelandic Textual Culture of the Twelfth and Thirteenth Centuries* (Toronto, 2001), p. 28; Hollander, *Heimskringla*, p. 253.

rare, while the ubiquitous chevron and herringbone patterns do not necessarily resemble snakes or their markings. There are indications, however, that the Vikings did see serpents in these designs. An amulet from Denmark in the form of a coiled snake is incised with chevron markings similar to those on pattern-welded swords, hinting that this design was one way in which snakes were referenced visually.[62] A similar snake amulet from the Hon Hoard in Norway has zigzag markings that create a line of diamonds along its back, leading one scholar to interpret it as a viper or adder.[63] This could support the proposal that diamond-shaped motifs on sword fittings may have been viewed, at least by some, as snake-like.

Explanations

Having established that a significant connection between snakes and swords was likely to have existed in the Viking mind, we can look for possible explanations. It appears that these beings had much in common in Viking Scandinavia, both physically, in their outward aspect, and symbolically, in the way they were perceived.

Physical Analogues

The properties of swords appear to have been a leading inspiration for kennings. While these linguistic puzzles were deliberately complex, they were also designed to be meaningful so that the audience (with the proper knowledge of Norse mythology and skaldic conventions) could decode and enjoy them.[64] Referring to the properties, function or close physical analogues for a given item in a kenning was an obvious way of achieving this. Kennings that describe swords as 'rods' or 'wands' are probably alluding to their long, narrow shape: hence Hallfreðr Óttarsson's 'helmet-rods' and 'rod of mail-coat';[65] Eyvindr Finnsson's 'wound wand';[66] Sigvatr Þórðarson's 'wand of Gjǫll';[67]

---

[62] Miriam Koktvedgaard Zeiten, 'Amulets and Amulet Use in Viking Age Denmark', *Acta Archaeologica* 68 (1997), 1–74 (cat. no. 19, p. 13).
[63] Jensen, *Viking Age Amulets*, pp. 37–9; Neil Price, 'Belief and Ritual', in *Vikings: Life and Legend*, ed. Williams *et al.*, fig. 16, p. 176.
[64] Abram, *Myths of the Pagan North*, p. 15; Margaret Clunies Ross, *A History of Old Norse Poetry and Poetics* (Cambridge, 2005), pp. 107–9.
[65] Hallfreðr vandræðaskáld Óttarsson, *Erfidrápa Óláfs Tryggvasonar* 5, 6, trans. Boucher, *The Saga of Hallfred*.
[66] Eyvindr Finnsson, *Lausavísa* 5, trans. Finlay, *Fagrskinna*.
[67] Sigvatr Þórðarson, *Erfidrápa Óláfs helga* 27, trans. Skaldic Poetry of the Scandinavian Middle Ages Project. Gjǫll was a Valkyrie in Norse mythology.

and Vígfúss Víga-Glúmsson's 'wands of Viðrir'.[68] Einarr Helgason's 'war-lath' should probably be included too.[69] Sword kennings referring to ice conjure the impression of their cold iron blades,[70] while kennings describing swords as light, lightning, sun, beam, gleam or flash bring to mind their silvery brightness.[71] More prosaic, though still effective, are kennings that mention materials, maintenance and accessories associated with swords. In *Vikingavísur*, Sigvatr Þórðarson describes a sword as a 'mouth of metal',[72] while whetstones used to keep blades sharp were also appropriate referents.[73] Other sword kennings allude to scabbards and even rivets that held sword hilts together.[74] Swords shared many physical and behavioural characteristics with snakes, and this may have given rise quite naturally to serpent kennings. Sword blades were long, thin and glossy, like the body of a snake, and they had 'markings' if made by pattern-welding. On a more abstract level, swords may have been thought to behave like snakes, shedding their 'skin' when unsheathed from their scabbard, weaving around quickly when in battle, and giving sharp, fatal 'bites' if provoked.[75]

It is certainly possible that kenning allusions created, helped to create, or popularised cognitive connections between seemingly disparate things until these links became so conventional that they were enshrined by Snorri Sturluson's work *Skaldskaparmál*. In the case of snakes and swords, it is worth querying whether kennings first created the link between them, or if they drew upon an existing

---

[68] Vígfúss Víga-Glúmsson, *Lausavísa* 1, trans. Finlay, *Fagrskinna*. Viðrir was another name for the god Óðinn.

[69] Einarr skálaglamm Helgason, *Vellekla* 12, trans. Davidson, 'Earl Hakon and his Poets'.

[70] 'Ice of sword-belts': Hallvarðr háreksblesi, *Knútsdrápa* 2, trans. Hermann Pálsson and Paul Edwards, *Knytlinga Saga: The History of the Kings of Denmark* (Odense, 1986); *Liðsmannaflokkr* 8, trans. Poole, *Viking Poems*; Guthormr sindri, *Hákonarmál* 5, trans. Hollander, *Heimskringla*; Eyvindr skáldaspillir Finnsson, *Lausavísa* 7, trans. Finlay, *Fagrskinna*; Haraldr harðráði Sigurðarson, *Lausavísa* 14, trans. Gade, *Poetry from the Kings' Sagas*; Vígfúss Víga-Glúmsson, *Poem about Hákon Jarl*, trans. Finlay, *Fagrskinna*.

[71] Bjǫrn krepphendi, *Magnússdrápa* 7, trans. Gade, *Poetry from the Kings' Sagas*; Hallvarðr háreksblesi, *Knútsdrápa* 3, trans. Pálsson and Edwards, *Knytlinga Saga*; Halldórr ókristni, *Eiríksflokkr* 1, 4, trans. Finlay, *Fagrskinna*; Þjóðólfr Arnórsson, *Sexstefja* 3, trans. Gade, *Poetry from the Kings' Sagas*.

[72] Sigvatr Þórðarson, *Vikingavísur* 14, trans. Hollander, *Heimskringla*.

[73] 'Whetstone land': Hallvarðr háreksblesi, *Knútsdrápa* 5, trans. Pálsson and Edwards, *Knytlinga Saga*; 'hollow of whetstones': Glúmr Geirason, *Gráfeldardrápa* 4, trans. Hollander, *Heimskringla*.

[74] 'Nail-riveted one': Bragi inn gamli Boddason, *Ragnarsdrápa* 5, trans. Hollander, *Heimskringla*; 'sharp scabbard-tongues': Glúmr Geirason, *Gráfeldardrápa* 3, trans. Hollander, *Heimskringla*; 'scabbard-covered masts [blades] of rivet [hilt]': Þjóðólfr Arnórsson, *Fragment* 3, trans. Gade, *Poetry from the Kings' Sagas*; 'sword-belt stabber': Arnórr jarlaskáld Þórðarson, *Magnússdrápa* 6, trans. Gade, *Poetry from the Kings' Sagas*; Þjóðólfr Arnórsson, *Lausavísa* 3, trans. Gade, *Poetry from the Kings' Sagas*.

[75] Gro Mandt, 'Myter og materiell kultur: slangesymbolikk i nordisk forhistorie', in *Frøyas hus: Rapport fra faseminaret «Kvinne- og daglig liv i sagatid», som ble holdt på Hamar 28.–29. april 1994*, ed. Oddveig Foldøy et al. (Stavanger, 1997), pp. 101–26 (p. 101); Christopher Abram personal communication.

connection. The latter seems likeliest. Earlier literature, notably Cassiodorus (sixth century) and Anglo-Saxon poems like *Beowulf* (perhaps eighth century, although continually debated)[76] reveals that similar attitudes were circulating in England and elsewhere on the Continent before the Viking period, and may have influenced later poets.

Physical similarities between swords and snakes were unlikely to have been the sole inspiration for sword kennings. The most skilled skalds were creative wizards who, despite the constraints of skaldic poetry's notorious *dróttkvætt* metre, were able to employ whatever imagery they wished in their kennings – meaning that they probably matched snakes with swords for other reasons, too. This seems especially likely given the importance of serpents in Norse cosmology.

Symbolic Analogues

Snakes have held special significance in the beliefs, folklore and mythology of many cultures for millennia. Their peculiar and often startling qualities – slithering movement, shedding of skin, dangerous bite, swallowing of prey whole and uncanny appearance with forked tongue, piercing eyes and smooth scaly bodies – make them both fascinating and frightening, and probably helped elevate them to such an enduring and universally special status.[77] Old Norse poetry illustrates the extent to which snakes permeated Scandinavian thought. In the pre-Christian Norse universe, the great serpent Jǫrmungandr enclosed the world of men (Miðgarðr) in his coil,[78] while other serpents, including the dragon-like Níðhǫggr, lived beneath and bit upon Yggdrasill, the vast ash tree at the heart of the cosmos.[79] In the realm of Hel, below, stood a hall with a roof made from snakes' spines.[80] Snakes were instruments of torture used against the errant god Loki, father of Jǫrmungandr;[81] and tools of execution for the hero

---

[76] Bradley, *Anglo-Saxon Poetry*, p. 407; cf. Roberta Frank, 'Skaldic Verse and the Date of *Beowulf*', in *The Beowulf Reader*, ed. Peter S. Baker (New York, 1981), pp. 155–80 (pp. 169–70).

[77] Mandt, 'Myter og materiell kultur', p. 101; Anne-Sofie Gräslund, 'The Material Culture of Old Norse Religion', *The Viking World*, ed. Brink and Price, pp. 249–56 (p. 254); Anne-Sofie Gräslund, 'Wolves, Serpents and Birds: Their Symbolic Meaning in Old Norse Belief', in *Old Norse Religion*, ed. Andrén *et al.*, pp. 124–9 (p. 126); Hedeager, *Iron Age Myth*, p. 85; Koktvedgaard Zeiten, 'Amulets', p. 13.

[78] *Vǫluspá* 55, trans. Larrington, *The Poetic Edda*; Hedeager, *Iron Age Myth*, p. 86.

[79] *Grímnismál* 34, trans. Larrington, *The Poetic Edda*; Jennbert, *Animals and Humans*, pp. 50–2; Mandt, 'Myter og materiell kultur', pp. 108–9.

[80] *Vǫluspá* 38, trans. Larrington, *The Poetic Edda*.

[81] Aðalheiður Guðmundsdóttir, 'Gunnarr and the Snake Pit in Medieval Art and Legend', *Speculum* 87 (2012), 1015–49 (p. 1029).

Gunnar.[82] Most devastatingly, it was a serpent (Jǫrmungandr again) who sealed the god Thor's fate at Ragnarǫk, the battle at the end of the world.[83] Serpents were also linked to the highest god, Óðinn, who used a snake's form to reach the mead of poetry so that he might become a skilled poet.[84]

Serpents continued to play an important role after Christianity began to spread in Scandinavia. As the creature that tempted Adam and Eve in the Old Testament, snakes embodied evil and the Devil, and probably symbolised heathen beliefs too.[85] They also appear to have had more positive connotations. Serpents adorned Christian stave churches and sacred reliquaries, and were also the vehicle for commemorative inscriptions on rune stones (often in conjunction with crosses), where they may have served a protective function.[86] Apotropaic concerns may also help to explain the popularity of snake motifs on highly personal effects like weapons and jewellery, including the aforementioned snake amulets with their heads raised to strike – presumably – anyone or anything that threatened their wearers.[87] Snakes were such powerful symbols that in the 1020s–1030s King Knútr (Cnut) chose to depict them on his Danish pennies, which, as Gullbekk has pointed out, can be 'considered as the first nationalised coin type in Scandinavia'.[88]

The symbolic resonance that snakes held in the Scandinavian cultural psyche is confirmed by Old Norse kennings. These often associate snakes with instruments of power or status in the Viking world. They appear in kennings for arm-rings,[89] multivalent artefacts that functioned both as a means of portable currency and as symbols of status. Given as rewards for service or as gifts to secure loyalty, rings

---

[82] *Atlamál* 59, trans. Larrington, *The Poetic Edda*; Guðmundsdóttir, 'Gunnarr and the Snake Pit', pp. 1024–9.

[83] Mandt, 'Myter og materiell kultur', pp. 107–9. In the Old English *Nine Herbs Charm* snakes are similarly sinister; their poison must be overcome by Woden, the Anglo-Saxon equivalent of Óðinn. See László Sándor Chardonnens, 'An Arithmetical Crux in the Woden Passage in the Old English *Nine Herbs Charm'*, *Neophilologus* 93 (2009), 691–702.

[84] Snorri Sturluson, *Skáldskaparmál* 1, trans. Poole, 'Poetic References'; Hedeager, *Iron Age Myth*, p. 86; Abram, *Myths of the Pagan North*, p. 113; Jennbert, *Animals and Humans*, pp. 209–10; Catharina Raudvere, 'Popular Religion in the Viking Age', in *The Viking World*, ed. Brink and Price, pp. 235–43 (p. 241); Gräslund, 'The Material Culture of Old Norse Religion', p. 254.

[85] Hedeager, *Iron Age Myth*, p. 86; Jennbert, *Animals and Humans*, pp. 209–10; Jensen, *Viking Age Amulets*, p. 37; Koktvedgaard Zeiten, 'Amulets', p. 13.

[86] Gräslund, 'Wolves, Serpents and Birds', p. 126; Jennbert, *Animals and Humans*, pp. 209–10; Mandt, 'Myter og materiell kultur', p. 107.

[87] Jensen, *Viking Age Amulets*, pp. 37–9; Koktvedgaard Zeiten, 'Amulets', p. 13; Mandt, 'Myter og materiell kultur', pp. 109–10.

[88] Svein Harald Gullbekk, 'Coinage and Monetary Economies', in *The Viking World*, ed. Brink and Price, pp. 159–69 (p. 161, fig. 10.3).

[89] E.g. 'serpent of the fore-arm': Eyvindr skáldaspillir Finnsson, *Háleygjatal* 10, trans. Davidson, 'Earl Hakon and his Poets'.

may also have represented specific social and political allegiances. For these reasons, lords and kings are frequently described as 'ring-givers' in Old Norse poetry.[90] Gold or wealth is described as 'snake land', 'land of the snake' and 'snake's lair',[91] connecting with the idea that snakes lived underground where gold might be hoarded, as well as where it was made and mined. In Norse mythology, for instance, the snake-dragon Fáfnir guarded a spectacular hoard beneath the earth.[92] Snakes are also prominent in kennings for ships – the (literal) driving force of Viking power and expansion, and one of the most potent symbols in their world.[93] This association was arguably based on symbolic rather than physical resonances, for while the best warships were long and slender, their parallels with snakes are few: ships do not shed their skin like snakes; snakes do not live primarily in water like ships; and while some ships may have been decorated with serpent motifs, like the prow and stern of the Oseberg ship from Norway, the evidence is sparse (painted designs, though hinted at in poetry, would probably not survive).[94] The linking of snakes with these culturally significant items implies that swords were seen in this way, too, providing a further explanation for their association in the Viking mind.

The ambivalence with which snakes were viewed may also have made them appropriate symbolic analogues for swords.[95] In a stimulating survey of snake symbolism in Scandinavia, Mandt has shown how serpents stood for both death and destruction (Níðhǫggr chewing at Yggdrasill; Jǫrmungandr rampant at Ragnarǫk) and order and protection (Fáfnir guarding the hoard; Jǫrmungandr as the physical 'belt' holding the world together, exemplified by his kennings).[96] Positive and negative views of snakes certainly colour Old Norse poetry: in *Rígsþula* the highest-born child of the god Heimdallr (symbolically called 'Lord') is said to have 'piercing' eyes

---

[90] Thor Ewing, *Viking Clothing* (Stroud, 2007), p. 68; Gareth Williams, 'Kingship, Christianity and Coinage: Monetary and Political Perspectives on Silver Economy in the Viking Age', in *Silver Economy in the Viking Age*, ed. James Graham-Campbell and Gareth Williams (Walnut Creek, CA, 2007), pp. 177–214 (p. 178 with references).

[91] Sigvatr Þórðarson, *Poem about Erlingr Skjálgsson* 1, trans. Diana Whaley, *Poetry from the Kings' Sagas 1: From Mythical Times to c. 1035* (Turnhout, 2012); Þjóðólfr Arnórsson, *Lausavísa* 3, trans. Gade, *Poetry from the Kings' Sagas* 2; Steinn Herdísarson, *Nizarvísur* 6, trans. Gade, *Poetry from the Kings' Sagas* 2.

[92] E.g. *Gripisspá* 11, 13, trans. Larrington, *The Poetic Edda*; the tale is told more fully in the later *Vǫlsunga saga*. Jensen, *Viking Age Amulets*, p. 37; Mandt, 'Myter og materiell kultur', p. 15. For the ambiguity between dragons and snakes, see below, pp. 71–2.

[93] Peter Pentz, 'Ships and the Vikings', in *Vikings: Life and Legend*, ed. Williams *et al.*, pp. 202–37; Jesch, *Ships and Men*, p. 127.

[94] Mandt, 'Myter og materiell kultur', p. 110; Jesch, *Ships and Men*, p. 144.

[95] Hedeager, *Iron Age Myth*, p. 86.

[96] Mandt, 'Myter og materiell kultur', p. 109. An example of such a kenning for Jǫrmungandr is 'girdle of the world': Snorri Sturluson, *Skáldskaparmál* 43, trans. Poole, 'Poetic References'.

'like a young snake's',[97] but in *Skírnismál* the 'shining serpent' is 'hateful to men'.[98] Furthermore, snakes appear to have been loosely defined beings in Viking thought, so synonymous with worms and dragons that a creature like Níðhǫggr appears both as a serpent and as a dragon soaring over the battlefield at Ragnarǫk, carrying the slain in his wings.[99] Such depictions are a reminder that the Viking worldview did not parcel beings into strict categories. Indeed, this taxonomic mutability probably applied to snakes above all creatures, since they changed their bodies annually by shedding their skin and swallowed their prey alive, becoming what Lotte Hedeager vividly describes as 'double beings'.[100] This tension of complex and opposing feelings towards snakes, together with their apotropaic power, probably fuelled their continuing popularity in Christian Scandinavia despite their having been so interwoven with pre-Christian cosmology.[101] They were special creatures, to be respected but also feared – and here the connection with swords emerges. In Viking Scandinavia, swords were also ambiguous entities: instruments of both order (protecting one's self, comrades, territory, kingdom) and chaos (destroying those of an enemy); rulers gave swords as rewards and guarantees for loyal service, thus promoting social cohesion, but also expected that they be used on command to win wealth or destroy foes. The esteem in which swords were held is clear from the lavish decoration of some weapons, together with glorifying descriptions in poetry and later sagas; but a particularly vivid example of the dual perceptions applied to swords appears in *Helgakviða Hjǫrvarðssonar*, concerning the snake-ornamented weapon mentioned earlier in this chapter. A Valkyrie claims she knows of forty-six swords on Sigarsholmr, one of which is 'better than all the rest' – but it is also 'the evil one among battle-needles'.[102] These two lines of poetry appear to encapsulate why swords and snakes were such perfect symbolic analogues: two beings that were at once alluring and deadly.

---

[97] *Rígsþula* 34, trans. Larrington, *The Poetic Edda*.
[98] *Skírnismál* 27, trans. Larrington, *The Poetic Edda*.
[99] Snorri Sturluson, *Skaldskaparmál* 57, trans. Poole, 'Poetic References'; *Vǫluspá* 66, trans. Larrington, *The Poetic Edda*; Gräslund, 'Wolves, Serpents and Birds', p. 126; Mandt, 'Myter og materiell kultur', p. 101; Jensen, *Viking Age Amulets*, pp. 37, 172.
[100] Hedeager, *Iron Age Myth*, p. 85.
[101] Mandt, 'Myter og materiell kultur', p. 111; Koktvedgaard Zeiten, 'Amulets', p. 13.
[102] *Helgakviða Hjǫrvarðssonar* 8–9, trans. Larrington, *The Poetic Edda*.

Swingers of the Serpent of Wounds

This investigation has shown that swords were cognitively linked to snakes in Viking Scandinavia, and has proposed some reasons why this was the case. Given the permeable boundary between categories of being, and the shape-shifting ambiguity of snakes in Viking minds, one final question arises: were swords viewed as simply *like* snakes – or *as* snakes, in a literal, living sense? In battle, were swords thought able to transform into serpents, as the more dramatic kennings hint?

Interestingly, kennings that describe swords as snakes typically show them under the direction of a warrior: for instance, Þormóðr Kolbrúnarskáld's sword kenning 'wound snake' is actually part of the warrior kenning 'reddener of the wound snake'.[103] Given the honorific function of skaldic poetry, it may have been inappropriate for a poet to depict his subject's weapons as sharing, or even responsible for, his victories.[104] However, Eddic poetry – which did not have the same glorifying function – paints a matching picture. 'Biting' swords in both *Hamðismál* and *Helgakviða Hundingsbana II* are wielded by warriors,[105] while *Skirnismál* records that the god Freyr's sword 'will fight by itself', but only 'if he who wields it is wise'.[106] These references do not negate the possibility that some people may have thought swords were capable of 'becoming' snakes, but do suggest that swords could not act without a wielder. This image of synergy between weapon and warrior invites us to read these sword kennings in another way: the sword is a snake, which is part of the warrior – all three are one being, with no clear boundary between them. This interpretation correlates well with ideas of blurred taxonomies described in the introduction to this chapter.

It is hard to find shape-shifting swords outside the world of literature. Some researchers have hypothesised that animal motifs on artefacts (including swords) were believed to magically transform into those beasts under certain circumstances;[107] but in general, archaeological evidence requires a good deal more speculative

---

[103] Þormóðr Kolbrúnarskáld, *Þorgeirsdrápa* 4, trans. Regal, 'The Saga of the Sworn Brothers'.
[104] Brunning, 'The "Living" Sword', p. 203.
[105] '... every man should bring about death for others, / with a sword that bites into wounds': *Hamðismál* 8, trans. Larrington, *The Poetic Edda*; '... may the sword that you wield never bite for you': *Helgakviða Hundingsbana II* 33, trans. Larrington, *The Poetic Edda*.
[106] *Skirnismál* 8–9, trans. Larrington, *The Poetic Edda*.
[107] Stephen O. Glosecki, 'Movable Beasts: The Manifold Implications of Early Germanic Animal Imagery', in *Animals in the Middle Ages*, ed. Nora C. Flores (New York, 1989), pp. 3–23 (pp. 4, 7, 9); Fedir Androshchuk, 'The Gift to Men and the Gift to the Gods: Weapon Sacrifices and the Circulation of Swords in Viking Age Society', in *Zwischen Fjorden und Steppe: Festschrift für Johan Callmer zum 65. Geburtstag*, ed. Claudia Theune, Felix Biermann, Ruth Struwe and Gerson H. Jeute (Rahden, 2010), pp. 263–76.

consideration if new interpretations are to be reached. There is, however, no reason to avoid such an exercise. The average inhabitant of Viking Scandinavia was fairly likely to have been familiar with the characteristics and behaviour of snakes. Most were not travellers or town dwellers, but rural people living on the land, with a detailed knowledge of the flora and fauna of their environment. Encounters with snakes were probably a part of their lives. As such, it is possible that some individuals who saw swords with pattern-welded blades, diamond-marked fittings and scale-like hilts related these features to snakes, even if the weapons' makers had not intended this result. Those who were part of the milieu of combat, who heard praise poetry describing swords as serpents, and who went into the teeth of battle wielding a long, silvery weapon might have been most susceptible to making the connection, empowered by the thought that the sword they wielded was like, or even was, a terrible snake.

   It is difficult to know how strong or widespread such ideas may have been. Much would have depended on an individual's social conditioning, a hugely influential factor in shaping peoples' perceptions. Even if the archaeological evidence cannot prove a belief in snake-like swords, Old Norse poetry leaves no doubt that the connection existed. The physical and behavioural parallels, together with powerful symbolic correspondences between snakes and swords, might just make these weapons the epitome of taxonomic fluidity in the Viking mind.

3

Wreoþenhilt ond wyrmfah

Confronting Serpents in *Beowulf* and Beyond

Victoria Symons

Serpents or dragons make several appearances in the Old English poem *Beowulf*.[1] Famously, the narrative concludes with a dragon-slaying, in which both the beast and the eponymous hero are mortally wounded. Earlier in the poem, after his first encounter with Grendel, a young Beowulf is approvingly compared to the dragon-slayer Sigemund. There is, in addition, a subtle evocation of dragons in the description of a hilt recovered from Grendel's mere after Beowulf's second encounter with the monstrous hall-scourge. This hilt, an ancient record of the world's first strife, is said to be both inscribed with *runstafas* ('rune letters', line 1695) and adorned with *wyrmfah* ('serpent-patterned', line 1698).[2]

Runes and dragons have only been tangentially connected in medieval scholarship as lingering remnants of ancient Germanic mythology adapted for Christian audiences. This chapter argues that the reference to both dragons and runes in the description of *Beowulf*'s ancient hilt is more than a momentary nod to the distant past.[3] The same two elements, dragons and runes, are united in a number of other Anglo-Saxon and Old Norse sources, often in relation to treasure and worldly riches. Such instances, I would suggest, are not merely

---

[1] The Old English word *draca* 'dragon' (ON *dreki*) is derived ultimately from Greek δράκων; such creatures are also referred to using the Germanic word *wyrm*, meaning 'dragon', or 'serpent' (ON *ormr*). The terms are often used interchangeably, as in *Beowulf* (e.g. lines 2211b and 2287a). In the contexts covered in this paper, the words *draca* and *wyrm*, and their Old Norse cognates, are understood to refer to the same serpentine, mythological creature. See Jonathan Evans, '"As rare as they are dire": Old Norse Dragons, *Beowulf*, and the *Deutsche Mythologie*', in *The Shadow-Walkers: Grimm's Mythology of the Monstrous*, ed. Tom Shippey (Tempe, AZ, 2005), pp. 207–69 (p. 217). Biblical and hagiographic dragons were also incorporated into Anglo-Saxon concepts of the creature, for which see Christine Rauer, *Beowulf and the Dragon* (Cambridge, 2000), pp. 52–61.

[2] For further discussion of swords, see Brunning, Chapter 2 in this volume.

[3] Seth Lerer, *Literacy and Power in Anglo-Saxon Literature* (Lincoln, NE, 1991), p. 167. For the suggestion that runes were included in poems to give the text a 'distressed' appearance, see John D. Niles, 'The Trick of the Runes in The Husband's Message', *ASE* 32 (2003), 189–223 (p. 196).

coincidental. Instead, we find dragons and runes, and the cultural concepts they represent, repeatedly set in opposition to one another, with the concealment associated with dragons being countered by the revealing nature of runic letters. An awareness of this opposition serves to emphasise the thematic and structural significance of the hilt in *Beowulf*. As Hrothgar gazes at the serpent-patterned heirloom he muses on the dangers of hoarded gold. In doing so he both speaks to social anxieties surrounding the appropriate distribution of wealth, and incidentally sets the stage for the poem's closing lines, in which Beowulf confronts his own treasure-hoarding dragon and the greed it represents.

The Serpent-Patterned Hilt

After successfully overcoming the Grendels in their own habitat, Beowulf returns to Hrothgar's hall in triumph. He arrives bearing both the head of the monster Grendel and the hilt of the sword that decapitated the monster's mother: tangible tokens of the hero's double victory and the Danes' long-awaited salvation.[4] Beowulf announces his entrance to Heorot with a triumphant *Hwæt* (line 1652), and presents Hrothgar with the plunder. While the king gazes at the hilt in his lap, the narrator describes its account of the origins of worldly strife. The description concludes:

> Swa wæs on ðæm scennum   sciran goldes
> þurh runstafas   rihte gemearcod
> geseted ond gesæd   hwæm þæt sweord geworht
> irena cyst   ærest wære,
> wreoþenhilt ond wyrmfah.[5]

Likewise on the plate of shining gold it was clearly written through rune-letters, set and recorded, for whom that sword was first made, the best of iron, with woven hilt and serpent-patterns.

(*Beowulf*, lines 1694–8)

Having taken in this opulent sight, Hrothgar addresses Beowulf. He does not, however, express the relief or gratitude that we might expect of a king newly delivered from a threat that has plagued his people for more than a decade. Instead, Hrothgar uses the opportunity to deliver a sermon on the dangers of greed.[6] He uses the example of Heremod,

---

[4] See also the discussion by Bintley, Chapter 9 in this volume.
[5] Text from *Beowulf: An Edition*, ed. Bruce Mitchell and Fred C. Robinson (Oxford, 1998). Unless otherwise indicated, all translations are my own.
[6] For analysis of the content and structure of this 'sermon', see Elaine Tuttle Hansen, *The Solomon Complex* (Toronto, 1988), pp. 55–67.

a king who grew arrogant in his power and *nallas beagas geaf / Denum æfter dome* ('gave no rings for the glory of the Danes', lines 1719–20). Heremod's meanness is contrasted with the generosity of God. It is He, Hrothgar tells Beowulf, who provides wisdom, land, power, and an easy life (lines 1724–39). However, the king who benefits from God's generosity must himself be generous in turn. If not, the results can be disastrous:

> 'þinceð him to lytel   þæt he lange heold,
> gytsað gromhydig,   nallas on gylp seleð
> fætte beagas   ond he þa forðsceaft
> forgyteð ond forgymeð   þæs þe him ær god sealde,
> wuldres waldend,   weorðmynda dæl.
> Hit on endestæf   eft gelimpeð
> þæt se lichoma   læne gedreoseð,
> fæge gefealleð;   fehð oþer to
> se þe unmurnlice   madmas dæleþ
> eorles ærgestreon,   egesan ne gymeð'.

'It seems to him too little, that which he long held. Angry minded he covets, never proudly distributes plated rings, and he forgets and neglects that future destiny, because previously God, the ruler of glory, gave to him a measure of prosperity. Afterwards it happens at the end that the transitory body declines; it falls, fated to die; another one, he who ungrudgingly shares out treasures, takes up the nobleman's ancient wealth, and does not heed fear.'

(*Beowulf*, lines 1748–57)

Although in keeping with the general ethos of the poem, the timing of this speech and its position in the narrative is jarring. It contrasts with Hrothgar's joyous reaction to the news of Grendel's earlier flight from Heorot (lines 928–56), and has little direct relevance to the preceding action, since neither Beowulf, nor Grendel (nor indeed the Danes themselves) has been particularly greedy prior to this point in terms of the hoarding of material goods.[7] Crucial to understanding the significance of this speech, and the factors that motivate it, is an appreciation of the connotations of the *wyrmfah* appearance of the hilt.

---

[7] Johann Köberl, 'The Magic Sword in *Beowulf*', *Neophilologus* 71.1 (1987), 120–8 (pp. 121–2); Margaret E. Goldsmith, *The Mode and Meaning of Beowulf* (London, 1970), p. 183.

Dragons: Hiding and Hoarding

The *wyrm*, or serpent-like dragon, was a figure firmly rooted in the medieval Germanic imagination.[8] The existence of such creatures is taken as fact by the author of the *Anglo-Saxon Chronicle* entry for 793, recording the raid on Lindisfarne:

> Her wæron reðe forebecna cumene ofer Norþanhymbra land ond þæt folc earmlic bregdon: þæt wæron ormete þodenas ond ligrescas, ond geseowene fyrene dracan wæron on þam lyfte fleogende. Þam tacnum sona fyligde mycel hunger, ond litel æfter þam þæs ilcan geares on .vi. idus Ianuarii earmlice heðenra manna hergung adiligode Godes cyrican in Lindisfarenaee þurh reaflac ond mansleht.[9]

> In this year dire forewarnings came over the lands of Northumbria, and terrified those people miserably. These were violent winds and lightning without measure, and fiery dragons were seen flying in the sky. These tokens were soon followed by a great hunger, and a little afterwards in the same year, on the 8th of January, the harrowing of the heathen men wretchedly destroyed God's church in Lindisfarne through theft and slaughter.

Although the dragons in the *Chronicle* are a visible symbol of impending misfortune, dragons encountered elsewhere in Old English writing are more often hidden from sight. *Maxims II* states that *draca sceal on hlæwe, / frod, frætwum wlanc* ('the dragon will be in the barrow, old, proud in adornments', lines 26–7).[10] This subterranean dragon, concealed in its mound, is the same kind of dragon found in *Beowulf*, where it is referred to as a hoard-guardian on four occasions (lines 2293, 2302, 2554, 2593). This dragon, the narrator tells us, inhabits a *hord on hrusan þær he hæðen gold / warað wintrum frod; ne byð him wihte ðy sel* ('a hoard in the earth where, old in winters, he guards heathen gold. It does him not a bit the better', lines 2276–7).

Like the *draca* in *Maxims*, the *Beowulf* dragon is old, and lives hidden in a mound guarding its pile of even more ancient treasure. Anglo-Saxon dragons, then, are associated with subterranean concealment. They live far from the spheres of the human world, hidden beneath

---

[8] See Jonathan D. Evans, 'Semiotics and Traditional Lore: The Medieval Dragon Tradition', *Journal for Folklore Research* 2.2.3 (1985), 85–112. See also Hooke, Chapter 11 in this volume.
[9] *The Anglo-Saxon Chronicle: A Collaborative Edition*, vol. 7: MS E, ed. Susan Irvine (Cambridge, 2004), p. 42.
[10] *The Anglo-Saxon Minor Poems*, ed. Elliott van Kirk Dobbie, ASPR 6 (New York, 1942), pp. 55–7. See also Chardonnens, Chapter 6 in this volume.

the earth in ancient barrows.[11] Such creatures, and the mounds they inhabit, are also closely associated with treasure. The *Maxims II* dragon is 'proud in adornments'. The dragon's hoard in *Beowulf*, meanwhile, is an ancient remnant of a forgotten people, having been buried in the earth by the last survivor of a fallen civilisation (lines 2231–46). Just as dragons are associated with concealment, so too is their treasure.[12] How the dragon in either poem came across its hoard is not recorded, but a clue to how this situation may have come about is to be found in the story of Sigurd and Fáfnir.

The legend of Sigurd the dragon-slayer appears to have been well-known in Anglo-Saxon England.[13] Sigurd's father Sigemund is identified as a dragon-slayer in *Beowulf* to parallel the poem's hero:

> Sigemunde gesprong
> æfter deaðdæge   dom unlytel
> syþðan wiges heard   wyrm acwealde
> hordes hyrde;   he under harne stan
> æþelinges bearn   ana geneðde
> frecne dæde   ne wæs him Fitela mid;
> hwæþre him gesælde   ðæt þæt swurd þurhwod
> wrætlicne wyrm   þæt hit on wealle ætstod
> dryhtlic iren;   draca morðre swealt.
> Hæfde aglæca   elne gegongen
> þæt he beahhordes   brucan moste
> selfes dome;   sæbat gehleod,
> bær on bearm scipes   beorhte frætwa
> Wælses eafera;   wyrm hat gemealt.

For Sigemund there arose, after his death-day, no little glory, since the fierce warrior killed the dragon, guardian of the hoard. Beneath the grey stone he, the prince's son, went alone to the daring deed; Fitela was not with him. However it was granted to him that the sword pierced the wondrous serpent, so that it stuck in the wall, the noble iron. The dragon died in the attack. The fearsome one ensured through courage that he may himself choose to enjoy the ring-hoard. He loaded the sea-boat, Wæl's son carried into the bosom of the ship bright adornments; the hot dragon melted.

(*Beowulf*, lines 884b–897)

---

[11] On barrows in Anglo-Saxon culture, and their association with dragons, see Sarah Semple, 'A Fear of the Past: The Place of the Prehistoric Burial Mound in the Ideology of Middle and Later Anglo-Saxon England', *World Archaeology* 30.1 (1998), 109–26 (esp. pp. 109–15).

[12] Rauer, *Beowulf and the Dragon*, p. 34; Hilda Ellis Davidson, 'The Hill of the Dragon', *Folklore* 61.4 (1950), 169–85 (p. 178); Evans, 'Semiotics and Traditional Lore', p. 95.

[13] Evans, 'As rare as they are dire', p. 216; Sue Margeson, 'The Vǫlsung Legend in Medieval Art', in *Medieval Iconography and Narrative: A Symposium*, ed. Flemming G. Anderson, Esther Nyholm, Marianne Powell and Flemming Talbo Stubkjær (Odense, 1980), pp. 183–211.

Elsewhere in England, scenes from the narrative survive carved on stone sculptures.[14] In Old Norse literature, Sigurd's dragon-slaying episode is represented in four sources: the *Poetic Edda*, the *Prose Edda*, *Þiðreks saga*, and *Vǫlsunga saga*.[15] Here, the reader learns that Sigurd was asked to fight the dragon by his adoptive father, Regin. It transpires that Regin and Fáfnir were brothers who, in common with their father, all received a share of treasure from the gods as compensation for the murder of their third brother. Driven by greed for the gold, however, Fáfnir kills his father and steals from his brother in order to keep all the treasure for himself. The effects of this behaviour are impressive and transformative. Fáfnir, Sigurd is told, *varð síðan at inum versta ormi, ok liggr nú á fé* ('became the most evil serpent, and lies now upon the treasure', *Vǫlsunga saga*, ch. 14).

The Fáfnir episode highlights an important aspect of the relationship between dragons and treasure. Treasure plays a significant role in medieval Germanic society and literature. It is used to seal the social bonds of the heroic world that forms that backdrop to *Beowulf*, *Vǫlsunga saga* and other such narratives. At the start of *Beowulf*, Heorot is built specifically as a place in which Hrothgar *beagas dælde / sinc æt symle* ('shared out rings, treasures at the feast', lines 80–1). Gift-giving in reward for heroic feats and the distribution of the spoils of war continually strengthen and define the relationship between a lord and his retainers.[16] After Beowulf rids Heorot of the scourge of the Grendels, he is rewarded by Hrothgar with lavish gifts of treasure, weapons, and horses. Upon his return to Geatland, Beowulf presents these riches to his king, Ecgtheow. In turn, Ecgtheow gives a portion of the booty straight back to Beowulf.[17] Such a society can be said to operate 'not so much in economic transactions as in reciprocal gifts'.[18] In the course of this elaborate process of gift-giving and gift-receiving, the significance of treasure as the delineator of social bonds can be fully appreciated.

---

[14] Richard N. Bailey, 'Scandinavian Myth on Viking-Period Stone Sculpture in England', *Old Norse Myths, Literature and Society: Proceedings of the 11th International Saga Conference*, ed. Geraldine Barnes and Margaret Clunies Ross (Sydney, 2000), pp. 15–23 (pp. 16–17); Margeson, 'The Vǫlsung Legend', pp. 185–91; see also Klaus Düwel, 'On the Sigurd Representations in Great Britain and Scandinavia', in *Languages and Cultures: Studies in Honor of Edgar C. Polomé*, ed. Mohammad Ali Jazayery and Werner Winter (Berlin, 1988), pp. 133–56.

[15] Rauer, *Beowulf and the Dragon*, pp. 41–2; Evans, 'As rare as they are dire', pp. 231–6.

[16] John M. Hill, *The Anglo-Saxon Warrior Ethic: Reconstructing Lordship in Early English Literature* (Gainesville, FL, 2000), pp. 19–46; Robert E. Bjork, 'Speech as Gift in *Beowulf*', *Speculum* 69.4 (1994), 993–1022 (pp. 993–5); Michael J. Enright, 'Lady with a Mead-Cup: Ritual, Group Cohesion and Hierarchy in the Germanic World', *Fruhmittelalterliche Studien* 22 (1988), 170–203 (esp. pp. 188–9).

[17] Bjork, 'Speech as Gift', pp. 1003–4.

[18] Claude Lévi-Strauss, *The Elementary Structures of Kinship*, trans. James H. Bell, John Richard von Sturmer and Rodney Needham (Boston, MA, 1969), p. 52.

However, in order to achieve this, treasure must necessarily be in constant movement from individual to individual. When treasure becomes stationary, as it must be in a dragon's hoard, it ceases to fulfil the positive functions of gift-giving and instead becomes a threat to the stability of the heroic world.[19] It is greed for gold that leads Fáfnir into the dual crimes of theft and murder, and the subsequent hoarding of this tainted gold that turns Fáfnir himself into a hateful dragon.[20] In *Beowulf*, it transpires that the dragon's hoard is cursed to such a degree that it can be of no benefit to mankind (lines 3069–75); it simply exists, buried in the ground, of use to no one.[21] Dragon treasure, then, is treasure that is hidden and secret, at best redundant to human society and at worst a source of significant menace.

The association between dragons and treasure, specifically harmful treasure, is one aspect of Hrothgar's sermon. The focus of this speech is the importance of gift-giving. Through the story of Heremod, Hrothgar offers the parable of a greedy king who, rather than distributing his treasure among his retainers, instead keeps it all to himself. In so doing, he loses both the respect and the loyalty of his younger warriors, one of whom eventually assumes his position and possessions. This new king acknowledges what his predecessor ignored: treasure is only useful when it is in circulation. As a generous ruler, this new king proves popular and has no fear. Thus Hrothgar presents an important lesson to the young hero Beowulf.

In Hrothgar's description of the king's greed and the malicious effects of hoarded treasure, there are hints of Fáfnir's narrative. In both cases, the same lust for gold is presented in strongly negative terms. In *Vǫlsunga saga*, its effects are so strong that they physically transform the human Fáfnir into a bestial dragon. The transformation in Hrothgar's sermon is spiritual and moral, rather than physical, but it is no less complete. Moreover, Hrothgar's sermon is directly motivated by the sight of the hilt, ancient and *wyrmfah*, recovered from Grendel's mere. The association between dragons and hidden treasure found elsewhere in Germanic literature, including at the end of *Beowulf*, is here subtly evoked as a precursor to Hrothgar's meditation on greed and generosity. It is the sight of the ancient hilt, long removed from the sphere of human interactions, and the traces of serpents upon it, that leads Hrothgar to warn Beowulf of the perils

---

[19] Evans, 'Semiotics and Traditional Lore', p. 100; see also Kathryn Hume, 'The Concept of the Hall in Old English Poetry', *ASE* 42 (1974), 63–74 (p. 68).
[20] Further examples in Old Norse literature of gold-hoarding men transforming into dragons include Válr and his sons, and subsequently Thorir, in *Gull-þoris saga*; see Evans, 'Semiotics and Traditional Lore', pp. 103–7.
[21] Hill, *The Anglo-Saxon Warrior Ethic*, p. 32; Alvin A. Lee, *Gold-Hall and Earth-Dragon: Beowulf as Metaphor* (Toronto, 1998), p. 234.

of human greed and the dangers of hoarding wealth.[22] Although this warning may appear incongruous in the context of Beowulf's recent triumph over the Grendels, it is nevertheless apt, as Beowulf will himself encounter the perils of hidden treasure and greedy dragons before the poem's conclusion. The description of the hilt is therefore far from incidental to the nature of the speech that follows. The *wyrmfah* pattern on the heirloom prefigures Hrothgar's meditation on greed by evoking the close association between dragons and concealed treasure. If the appearance of the hilt is so central to this scene, then, what is to be made of the other aspect of the hilt's decoration, its runic letters? The letters that relate this narrative are described not – as we might expect – as *stafas* or *bocstafas*, but rather more specifically as *runstafas*. Unlike the first two terms, which refer to letters in general, this word is used in Old English to refer only to specifically runic script.[23] This detail is especially significant as references to runic letters are uncommon in Old English literature. Seven lines later, at the start of Hrothgar's sermon, the scribe uses a similarly rare runic abbreviation. By writing ᛟ, 'oe', to stand for the word *eþel*, 'homeland' (line 1702a), the scribe reinforces on the manuscript page the importance of runic letters to the meaning of this passage.[24]

Runes and Dragons

Runes, like dragons, are on occasion associated with treasure.[25] In the Old English *Solomon and Saturn I*, dated to the early tenth century, the letters of the Pater Noster are described in terms of their visual appearance and material value (lines 63–7), and their ability to physically harm the devil in often surprisingly visceral ways (lines 111–45).[26] Immediately before listing the individual letters of the prayer, the narrator describes the letters themselves as either *wyrma wlenco* ('pride of dragons', CCCC 41) or *wyrma welm* ('surge of dragons', CCCC 442).[27] In the latter version, the letters of the Pater

---

[22] Lerer, *Literacy and Power*, p. 166.
[23] *ASD*, p. 805; R. I. Page, *An Introduction to English Runes*, 2nd edn (Woodbridge, 1999), p. 107.
[24] See Andy Orchard, *A Critical Companion to Beowulf* (Cambridge, 2001), p. 40 n. 113; for the use of runes to abbreviate *eþel*, see René Derolez, *Runica Manuscripta: The English Tradition* (Brugge, 1954), pp. 399–40; on the rarity of runic abbreviations see p. 385.
[25] On the association between runic letters and material or aesthetic value, see Victoria Symons, 'Runes and Roman Letters in the Writing of Old English Manuscripts' (unpublished doctoral thesis, University College London, 2013), pp. 178–84.
[26] On the dating of the poem, see *The Old English Dialogues of Solomon and Saturn*, ed. Daniel Anlezark (Cambridge, 2009), p. 56.
[27] Text from *Solomon and Saturn*; on the phrase *wyrma wlenco* in this passage, see Victoria Thompson, *Dying and Death in Later Anglo-Saxon England* (Woodbridge, 2004), p. 135; on further instances of *wyrm* and *draca* in *Solomon and Saturn I*, see below.

Noster are then supplied in both runes and Roman script, whereas the former uses runic letters to partially abbreviate the name Solomon.[28] The poem unites the spiritual value of letters, in one case specifically runic letters, with the material and aesthetic value of earthly treasure. In both versions it also associates these letters with *wyrms*. The motif of treasure, physical as a well as spiritual, is therefore associated in these lines with both runic letters and with dragons – the same combination of elements that is encountered in *Beowulf* through the description of the hilt and the speech it inspires.

This combination of treasure, dragons and runes is also found in the Old Norse rendering of the Sigurd episode in *Vǫlsunga saga*. I have already described the greed of Fáfnir that leads to his hoarding of treasure and subsequent transformation into a dragon. However, the woes brought to Fáfnir by this hoard of gold do not end with his transformation. It is for this gold that Sigurd kills Fáfnir, at the request of the dragon's surviving brother, Regin. Before asking Sigurd to kill the dragon, Regin fulfils his role as foster-father by teaching Sigurd *tafl ok rúnar ok tungur margar at mæla* ('checkers and runes and to speak many tongues', ch. 13).[29]

Immediately after his encounter with Fáfnir, Sigurd travels to a castle in which he finds the Valkyrie Brynhild. She, too, offers to teach him about *rúnum eða ǫðrum hlutum er liggja til hvers hlutar* ('runes or other things concerning everything', ch. 21).[30] Brynhild then presents Sigurd with a series of verses concerning, among other things, *sigrúnar* ('victory runes'), *brimrúnar* ('sea runes'), *málrúnar* ('speech runes'), and *ǫlrúnar* ('ale runes').[31] In this way, the episode recounting Sigurd's fight with the dragon Fáfnir is book-ended by references to runic letters and the learning of runes. The fight with Fáfnir is specifically motivated by greed for treasure; Regin sends Sigurd to kill Fáfnir in order to retrieve the gold that turned his brother into a dragon in the first place. Once again, the dual elements of dragons and runes are united through the third element of earthly treasure.

That this association is more than coincidental is perhaps most clearly demonstrated by the opening verse of the Icelandic *Rune Poem*. In most modern editions, the first verse reads:

> **F** (fé) er frænda róg
> ok flæð ar viti
> ok grafseiðs gata.[32]

---

[28] On the addition of runic letters to *Solomon and Saturn I*, see Derolez, *Runica Manuscripta*, p. 420.
[29] *Vǫlsunga saga*, p. 23.
[30] Ibid., p. 35.
[31] Ibid., pp. 35–9.
[32] Maureen Halsall, *The Old English Rune Poem: A Critical Edition* (Toronto, 1981), pp. 183–6.

Treasure is discord among family, and fire of the sea, and the grave-serpent's path.

(Icelandic *Rune Poem*, lines 1–3)

This text is from the appendix to Maureen Halsall's edition of the Old English *Rune Poem*, which is based on previously published editions by L. F. Wimmer and Bruce Dickens.[33] As Page pointed out, however, such editions can give the mistaken impression that the Old Icelandic *Rune Poem* exists as a single, unified text. This is far from the case. The text commonly referred to as the 'Icelandic *Rune Poem*' in fact survives in several different versions from a number of different manuscripts dating between *c.* 1500 and *c.* 1750.[34] These variations, as Page demonstrated, make it problematic to talk about a single 'Icelandic *Rune Poem*', and the text he provided in his own edition of the poem represents an amalgam of several different versions.[35] Page concluded that, rather than a single poem, Icelanders instead had a 'fund of phrases' from which to draw when referring to runic letters, and from which the different versions of the *Rune Poem* were composed.[36]

When considering runes and serpents, these differences are revealing. The verse quoted above unites the same three elements of runes, serpents and treasure that are found in *Beowulf*. ᚠ, 'f', the first rune, is said to stand for *grafseiðs gata* ('the path of the grave-serpent'). Other versions of the *Rune Poem* replace this kenning with phrases including *grafþvengs gata*, *Fáfnisbani* and *Fáfnisbeðr*.[37] The *grafseið* and the semantic equivalent *grafþveng* ('grave-serpent') are both kennings for fish. The phrase *Fáfnisbani*, on the other hand, refers to the dragon Fáfnir, whose *bani* ('bane') is the treasure for which Sigurd kills him. These variant lines clearly carry very different connotations. What is interesting, however, is that they all introduce a reference to serpents or dragons, and that one or other is found in every surviving version of the Old Icelandic *Rune Poem*.[38] Despite their variations, then, it would seem that some reference to these creatures was considered appropriate when beginning a poem about runic letters.

The danger of dragons and the menace posed by their hoarded gold is reinforced by a comparison between the Icelandic and Old English *Rune Poems*. As outlined above, all extant versions of the Icelandic poem include a reference to dragons, and describe treasure

---

[33] Ibid., p. 183.
[34] R. I. Page, *The Icelandic Rune-Poem* (London, 1999), p. 1.
[35] Ibid., pp. 27–30, with corresponding translation, pp. 35–7; see also Halsall, *The Old English Rune Poem*, pp. 183–6.
[36] Page, *The Icelandic Rune-Poem*, p. 18; see also Margaret Clunies Ross, 'The Anglo-Saxon and Norse *Rune-Poems*: A Comparative Study', *ASE* 19 (1990), 23–39 (pp. 25–6).
[37] Page, *The Icelandic Rune-Poem*, p. 27.
[38] Ibid.

in negative terms, as *frænda róg* ('discord amongst family'). The Old English *Rune Poem*, on the other hand, takes a more positive view of treasure:

> ᚠ (feoh) byþ frofur fira gehwylcum.
> Sceal ðeah manna gehwylc miclun hyt dælan
> gif he wile for drihtne domes hleotan.[39]

> F (wealth) is a comfort to everyone. However, each man must share it greatly if he wishes to gain the lord's good opinion.
>
> (Old English *Rune Poem*, lines 1–3)

In the Old English *Rune Poem*, the concept of *feoh* ('wealth') is presented as a benefit to mankind, but with the stipulation that men must *miclun hyt dælan* ('share it widely'). In the differences between these two verses we can see the transition of wealth from *frofur* ('comfort') to *róg* ('discord'), when dragons make an appearance.

Concealing Dragons and Revealing Runes

The concealment that characterises dragons, through their hiding and hoarding of treasure, could perhaps offer an explanation for the runic letters that appear in tandem with them. Initially, this explanation seems attractive. It has often been suggested that specifically runic letters held connotations of secrecy and concealment for the medieval writers who used them. Elizabeth Okasha, assessing a number of epigraphic runic inscriptions, asserts that 'it is difficult to avoid the conclusion that runes were probably considered "secret" and "difficult to read" in a way that Roman script was not.'[40] Others have suggested that runes, being used to carve highly visible inscriptions that the majority of the population, at any point in the Anglo-Saxon period, would have been unable to read, carried from their earliest use dual connotations of concealment and revelation.[41] The fact that Old English *run* means 'secrecy, concealment' has been offered in support of these theories. Although the word *run* alone is never used to refer to runes, and is etymologically distinct from the modern word

---

[39] Text from Dobbie, *Anglo-Saxon Minor Poems*, pp. 28–30.
[40] Elisabeth Okasha, 'Script-Mixing in Anglo-Saxon Inscriptions', in *Writing and Texts in Anglo-Saxon England*, ed. Alexander R. Rumble (Cambridge, 2006), pp. 62–70 (p. 67); see also Niles, 'The Trick of the Runes', p. 197.
[41] Michelle Igarashi, 'Riddles', in *The Companion to Old and Middle English Literature*, ed. Laura Cooner Lambdin and Robert Thomas Lambdin (London, 2002), pp. 336–51 (p. 342); also see Ralph W. V. Elliott, *Runes: An Introduction* (New York, 1989), p. 57, discussing the simultaneous concealing and revealing by runes in Cynewulf's signatures.

'rune', nevertheless Anglo-Saxons did use the word *runstaf* to refer to specifically runic letters.[42]

A more contemporary explanation for the word *runstaf* is provided in a short medieval treatise on five alphabets, previously known as the *De inventione linguarum* ('On the invention of languages'), but now more commonly, and accurately, referred to as the *De inventione litterare* ('On the invention of writing').[43] The treatise was probably written towards the end of the eighth or beginning of the ninth century, at the monastery of Fulda, in what is now Germany, and its composition therefore coincides with the beginnings of a scholarly interest in runic alphabets on the Continent.[44]

Runes appear as the last alphabet in the treatise, following the Hebrew, Greek and Latin scripts, and the invented alphabet of Æthicus Ister.[45] Each alphabet is written out in full, and preceded by an introductory paragraph outlining its features, usage and history.[46] In its original form the final introductory paragraph for runes states:

> Litteras quippe quibus utuntur Marcomanni, quos nos Nordmannos vocamus, infra scriptas habemus (a quibasus originem qui Theodiscam loquuntur linguam trahunt); cum quibus sua incantationesque ac divinationes significare procurant, qui adhuc pagano ritu involvuntur.
>
> The letters which are used by the Marcomanni, whom we call Northmen, we have written below (from them [i.e. the Northmen] those people descend who speak German); with these [letters] they signify their incantations and divinations, because they are still given to pagan practices.[47]

Derolez doubted that the writer of this passage had first-hand knowledge of contemporary runic writing, arguing that 'the magic use has been stressed as an afterthought', and does not reflect any real knowledge of runes.[48] Nevertheless, the treatise was copied repeatedly over the following decades.[49] At some stage during its

---

[42] For example, *Riddle* 46, line 6a, *Riddle* 58, line 15a; see above n. 20.
[43] *De inventione linguarum*, PL 112, cols. 1579–82; the altered title is proposed by Derolez, *Runica Manuscripta*, p. 285.
[44] René Derolez, 'Scandinavian Runes in Continental Manuscripts', in *Medieval and Linguistic Studies in Honor of Francis P. Magoun Jr*, ed. Jess B. Bessinger and Robert P. Creed (New York, 1965), pp. 30–9 (p. 31).
[45] This alphabet is taken from the eighth-century *Cosmographia*, which narrates the travels and encounters of its probably fictional protagonist, Aethicus Ister. See *The Cosmography of Aethicus Ister: Edition, Translation and Commentary*, ed. M. Herren (Turnhout, 2011).
[46] The most recent edition of the treatise is Migne's *Patrologia Latina* publication. Derolez provided a copy of each of the alphabets (*Runica Manuscripta*, pp. 349–54) but stressed that it was not intended as a critical edition.
[47] Text and translation from Derolez, *Runica Manuscripta*, pp. 354–5.
[48] Ibid., p. 357.
[49] Ibid., pp. 348–9.

transmission, the passage discussing runes underwent a major revision; the resulting 'B' version reads:

> Hae quoque literarum figurae in gente Northmannorum feruntur inventae; quibus ob carminum eorum memoriam et incantationum itu adhuc dicuntur; quibus et runstabas nomen imposuerunt, ob id, ut reor, quod his res absconditas vicissim scriptitando aperiebant.
>
> These forms of letters are said to have been invented among the people of the Northmen; it is said that they still use them to commit their songs and incantations to memory. They gave the name runstabas to these letters, I believe because by writing them they used to bring to light secret things.[50]

There is convincing evidence to suggest that the revisions in the 'B' text were carried out by an Anglo-Saxon scholar, and one who, moreover, was familiar with runic writing and was attempting to correct the misconceptions propagated in the 'A' text. In support of this theory, Derolez cited the treatment of the word *runstabas*, which is cognate with OE *runstafas*, arguing that the revision 'can only be due to somebody who really understood the word'.[51] He also pointed out that the author of the 'B' version tones down the relation of runes to pagan practices found in 'A', and cuts the reference to *divinationes* entirely.[52] Runes were in current, although declining, use in ninth-century England, and it may be that the author of 'B' was familiar with the script as a prosaic writing tool.

Like modern scholars, the author of this paragraph notes the semantic association between the word *run* ('secrecy'), and the first element of the term *runstaf* ('runic letter'). Unlike many modern scholars, however, he suggests that the runic script is named in this way not because it had any connotations of concealment or secrecy, but because of its association with revelation and openness, and the bringing to light of hidden or unknown information. The *De inventione* passage is the most explicit surviving source for contemporary Anglo-Saxon thought on runes, and the author of the treatise specifically highlights the revealing, rather than concealing, connotations of the letters.

Christine Fell's detailed examination of the semantic range of the terms *run* and *geryne* in Old English literature agrees with the definition of *runstabas* provided by the treatise author. Fell concludes that 'most uses of *run* and *geryne* refer to sharing of thoughts and

---

[50] Text and trans. ibid., p. 355.
[51] Ibid., p. 358.
[52] Ibid.

dissemination of knowledge'.⁵³ The term *run* is associated with concealment, she argues, simply because of its relationship with private thoughts: 'that thoughts are private, if not secret, till they are spoken is obvious. That knowledge is a mystery until it is explained is obvious'.⁵⁴ In the same way, the author of the treatise suggests that runic letters are connected with *run* ('secrecy'), not because they themselves had connotations of concealment, but because they were able to facilitate the dissemination of private thoughts, by bringing 'to light secret things'.

Runic letters, then, are very much unlike the concealed dragons that inhabit subterranean barrows in medieval literature. Whereas dragons, and the treasure in which they take such pride, occupy places that are hidden and sealed off from the spheres of the human world, runic letters are a human construct carrying connotations of revelation and openness, used to 'bring to light secret things' as they convey private information to the wider world. I would suggest that the runes that accompany the serpents of *Beowulf*, *Solomon and Saturn I*, *Vǫlsunga saga* and the Icelandic *Rune Poem* do not complement the beasts' connotations of secrecy and concealment, but rather oppose them. In *Solomon and Saturn I*, the letters of the Pater Noster are said to be both the object of serpents' desire (line 82) and particularly effective against devils, the *draca* (line 26), that go about *in wyrmes lic* ('in serpent's form', line 152). That at least one scribe of the poem, when encountering this imagery, thought it appropriate to associate such letters with runes demonstrates the resonance of this opposition between serpents and runic letters. What *wyrms* seek to hide, runes reveal.

Dragons and Runes in Opposition

The opposition between *wyrms* and runes is evoked in the Old English *Nine Herbs Charm*, recorded in the tenth-century Lacnunga medical handbook (Bodleian MS Harley 585).⁵⁵ The charm begins by addressing various herbs and describing their efficacy against ailments. It then continues:

---

⁵³ Christine E. Fell, 'Runes and Semantics', in *Old English Runes and their Continental Background*, ed. Alfred Bammesberger (Heidelberg, 1991), pp. 195–229 (pp. 215–6).

⁵⁴ Derolez, *Runica Manuscripta*, p. 216.

⁵⁵ J. H. G. Grattan and Charles Singer, *Anglo-Saxon Magic and Medicine: Illustrated Specially from the Semi-Pagan Text 'Lacnunga'* (London, 1952), pp. 151–5; M. L. Cameron, *Anglo-Saxon Medicine* (Cambridge, 1993), pp. 144–7; Edward Pettit, *Anglo-Saxon Remedies, Charms, and Prayers from British Library MS Harley 585: The Lacnunga* (New York, 2001). On the *Lacnunga* manuscript, see Godfrid Storms, *Anglo-Saxon Magic* (The Hague, 1948), pp. 16–24; Oswald Cockayne, *Leechdoms, Wortcunning, and Starcraft of Early England*, vol. 2, Rolls Series 35 (London, 1864), pp. vii–xxxviii.

> Þas VIIII magon   wið nygon attrum.
> Wyrm com snican,   toslat he man;
> ða genam Woden   VIIII wuldortanas,
> sloh ða þa næddran,   þæt heo on VIIII tofleah.[56]

These nine [herbs] have strength against nine venoms. A worm came sneaking, he slashed a man; then Woden took hold of nine glory-twigs, he slew the adder, which flew into nine parts.

(Nine Herbs Charm, lines 30–3)

The nine glory-twigs that Woden seizes in this charm are elaborated upon in the Norse poem *Hávamál*, in which Óðinn takes hold of runic letters and then passes them to mankind.[57]

> Veit ek, at ek hekk
> vindga meiði á
> nætr allar níu,
> geiri undaðrok gefinn Óðni,
> sjálfr sjalfum mér,
> á þeim meiði
> er manngi veit
> hvers hann as rótum renn.
>
> Við hleifi mik sælduné við hornigi,
> nýsta ek niðr,
> nam ek upp rúnar,
> œpandi nam,
> fell ek aptr þaðan.[58]

I know that I hung on a windy tree all of nine nights, wounded with a spear and given to Óðinn, self to myself, on that tree of which no man knows from where its roots run.

No bread did they give me, nor a drink from a horn. I looked down, I took up runes, took hold of them screaming, then I fell back from there.

(Hávamál, v. 138–9)

The reference to Woden in the *Nine Herbs Charm* is one of only two such examples which survive in Old English poetry.[59] In addition, the number nine, 'familiar' in Germanic numerology, is associated

---

[56] Text from Dobbie, *Anglo-Saxon Minor Poems*, pp. 119–21.
[57] Lerer, *Literacy and Power*, p. 36; Mindy MacLeod and Bernard Mees, *Runic Amulets and Magic Objects* (Woodbridge, 2006), p. 127; Richard North, *Heathen Gods in Old English Literature*, CSASE 22 (Cambridge, 1997), pp. 87–8.
[58] *Hávamál*, ed. David A. H. Evans (London, 1986), pp. 68–9.
[59] The second occurrence is *Maxims I* C, line 63a. Woden is euhemerised as a historical figure in Old English sources, including royal genealogies and Bede's *Historia Ecclesiastica* (I:15); see North, *Heathen Gods*, pp. 111–32; on the worship of Woden in England, see pp. 78–84.

with Woden or Óðinn.[60] The affinity between these two passages would suggest that the nine glory-twigs taken up by Woden in the Old English charm, then, are one and the same with the runes seized by Óðinn in *Hávamál*.[61] In that case, their efficacy against the *wyrm* would seem to be built upon a perceived opposition between runes and serpents. The same opposition, I would argue, underlies the association of runes and dragons in the literary sources outlined above. When runes are introduced to narratives about serpents in *Vǫlsunga saga* and *Beowulf*, or serpents are evoked in descriptions of runes in *Solomon and Saturn I* and the Icelandic *Rune Poem*, the appearance of the letters is in direct opposition to that of the treasure-hoarding beasts. Serpents and dragons, by their very nature according to *Maxims II*, hide both themselves and their treasure in subterranean concealments. Runes, on the other hand, are intended for the opposite purpose: to bring to light things that are secret, or hidden, or concealed. Dragons and runes, then, are representations of conceptually opposing forces.

The extent of this opposition can be seen most clearly on Scandinavian memorial stones, in which dragons and runic letters occupy the very same space on the carved stone surface. Memorial stones are among the most common type of medieval runic inscription surviving in Scandinavia. They are found in Denmark, Norway, and Sweden, and date from as early as the fourth century.[62] The majority, however, are found in Eastern Sweden and date from the tenth and eleventh centuries.[63] From the late Viking Age onwards, these Swedish memorial inscriptions are often accompanied by images of intertwining serpents or dragons, with the runic inscription following the lines of the creature's body.[64] Among the most famous examples of this type of carving is the Ramsund stone from Södermanland (Sö 101).[65] The carving dates from around 1030 and is unusual in that it is inscribed on a flat rock face rather than a free-standing stone.[66] The border is made up of two, or possibly three, intertwining serpents, with scenes from the legendary story of Sigurd in the centre. That these serpents should be seen as dragons is demonstrated by the inclusion, in the lower right-hand corner, of Sigurd stabbing the

---

[60] S. O. Glosecki, '"Blow these vipers from me": Mythic Magic in *The Nine Herbs Charm*', in *Essays in Old, Middle, Modern English and Old Icelandic: In Honor of Raymond P. Tripp Jr*, ed. Loren C. Gruber (Lampeter, 2000), pp. 91–123 (pp. 98–9).

[61] North, *Heathen Gods*, pp. 86–7; David Wilson, *Anglo-Saxon Paganism* (London, 1992); Ralph W. V. Elliott, 'Runes, Yews and Magic', *Speculum* 32.2 (1957), 250–61 (p. 257).

[62] Birgit Sawyer, *Viking Age Rune Stones* (Oxford, 2000), p. 7.

[63] Ibid., p. 7.

[64] For a detailed overview and classifications of the different styles of decoration and rune creatures found on Swedish memorial stones, see Claiborne W. Thompson, *Studies in Upplandic Runography* (Austin, TX, 1975), pp. 22–32.

[65] Sven Jansson, *Runes in Sweden*, trans. Peter Foote (Stockholm, 1987), pp. 145–6.

[66] Düwel, 'On the Sigurd Representations', p. 133.

underbelly of one of the creatures, which identifies it as Fáfnir.[67] The central image shows Sigurd again, this time sucking the finger he burnt while roasting the dragon's heart. This gives him the ability to understand the speech of birds, seen on Sigurd's right, who warn him that Regin will betray him. Finally, on the left of the scene we see the result of this warning: Regin beheaded in his smithy. The inscription itself reads: 'Sigrid, mother of Alrik, daughter of Orm, made this bridge for Holmger's soul, her husband and Sigröd's father'.[68]

The Ramsund stone is notable for its use of images to portray a narrative. It is also interesting that the serpent on which the runic inscription is written can be identified as a character central to that narrative – the dragon Fáfnir. It is thus clearly significant to the stone's design, rather than merely an interesting and decorative way of forming a border. Ramsund is one of the best-known depictions of Sigurd in the context of memorial stones, but it is not unique. Sven Jansson points out that 'to judge from the pictures on Swedish rune stones, by far the most popular hero of legend was Sigurd, the slayer of Favner the dragon.'[69] The image of Sigurd stabbing a rune-inscribed serpent is also found on the Gök stone (Sö 327), which may be an imitation of Ramsund and is located close by,[70] the Drävle stone (U1163), and the Årsunda stone (Gs9).[71] There are other identifiable narratives on Swedish rune stones which incorporate serpents or dragons. These include Gunnar in the snake pit (also from *Vǫlsunga saga*), which is depicted on an inscribed and decorated stone from Västerljung, Södermanland (Sö 40), and Thor fishing for the Midgard serpent on a stone from Altuna church, Uppland (U1161).[72] Both of these differ slightly from the Sigurd stones in that the 'narrative' serpents are separate from the runic ones, carved as completely discrete scenes on separate faces from those bearing the runic inscriptions and conventional serpent borders.

Most of the serpents on Scandinavian memorial stones do not have a narrative function such as those outlined above; they serve simply to form a band upon which the runes are inscribed. They are numerous and were clearly popular. They also suggest that the

---

[67] On the identification of the pictoral elements of Ramsund, see ibid., pp. 133–8.
[68] Sawyer, *Viking-Age Rune-Stones*, p. 126 n. 7; Düwel, 'On the Sigurd Representations', pp. 146–7.
[69] Jansson, *Runes in Sweden*, p. 144.
[70] Düwel, 'On the Sigurd Representations', p. 147 n. 1; Thompson, *Studies in Upplandic Runography*, p. 8, suggests 'there is evidence that fashion played a large role in the proliferation of the monuments, so that to a certain extent one may say that "one rune stone breeds another." Thus, one often finds two inscriptions that have been executed only a few yards apart, one of them clearly an imitation of, or at least inspired by, the other'.
[71] Düwel, 'On the Sigurd Representations', p. 169; Jansson, *Runes in Sweden*, p. 147.
[72] Jansson, *Runes in Sweden*, pp. 145–9.

connection between runes and serpents hinted at in the *Beowulf* passage above may be more pervasive than is immediately obvious. Although memorial stones from eleventh-century Sweden are somewhat geographically and temporally removed from earlier Anglo-Saxon poetry, it is nevertheless reasonable to posit a conceptual overlap between these examples.[73] Clearly, the word *wyrmfah* would not be misplaced if used to describe the memorial stones, especially when one considers that a primary meaning of *fah* is 'to write', and that the verb's Scandinavian equivalent is very often associated with the act of writing, or painting, specifically runic letters.[74] The reason for incorporating serpents into the design of Swedish memorial stones does not, at first, seem to be related to the connection between dragons and treasure. Usually the use of intertwining creatures is explained as a purely aesthetic device, bringing to the design of the monument 'a lively play of line'.[75] Others have seen in the serpents a reference to death, in keeping with the primary function of the stones as memorials for the dead.[76]

I would like to suggest a different motivation for the incorporation of the serpent-like dragon motif on these stones. Birgit Sawyer points out that 'the prominence given to sponsors [on memorial stones] shows that Viking-Age rune-stones are monuments to the *living* as much as to the *dead*', and that 'in commemorating their deceased relatives *all* sponsors, male and female, were at the same time stating their claims to what had been owned and controlled by the dead.'[77] Runic memorial stones, then, are markers of inheritance and the transfer of wealth from one person or generation to another. In this capacity they stand in direct opposition to the association between serpents and treasure outlined above. The creatures in *Beowulf*, *Vǫlsunga saga* and the Icelandic *Rune Poem* all symbolise, or are responsible for, the hoarding and concealing of treasure. It is the failure to correctly distribute wealth that leads to *frænda róg* ('strife amongst kin', Icelandic *Rune Poem*, line 1). If the Scandinavian memorial stones signify the transfer of wealth between relations, then the depiction of dragons on many of the Swedish stones becomes something of a playful irony or visual pun. The image carries connotations of concealed and hoarded treasure, with all the negative results that implies, while the runic inscription, carved onto the body

---

[73] For further linguistic similarities between the hilt in *Beowulf* and inscriptions on Scandinavian rune stones, see Lerer, *Literacy and Power*, pp. 167–9.
[74] Jansson, *Runes in Sweden*, p. 156; Lerer, *Literacy and Power*, p. 170 and p. 230 n. 33.
[75] Thompson, *Studies in Upplandic Runography*, p. 30.
[76] Terje Spurkland, *Norwegian Runes and Runic Inscriptions*, trans. Betsy van der Hoek (Woodbridge, 2005), p. 91; see also Hilda Ellis Davidson, *Gods and Myths of Northern Europe* (London, 1990), p. 161; and Thompson, *Dying and Death*, pp. 132–69.
[77] Sawyer, *Viking-Age Runes-Stones*, p. 2.

of the dragon and therefore following its exact shape and movement, confirms inheritance rights and informs viewers that in this case the deceased's wealth has been properly distributed. The dragon and the runes, occupying exactly the same space on the monument, act in direct opposition to one another.

On most of the Swedish runestones, this dichotomy is only very subtly implied. However, on stones such as Ramsund and Gök, the implications of the serpent are more overt. By incorporating elements of the Sigurd story, the carvers of these monuments ensure that the runic serpent is explicitly identifiable as the dragon Fáfnir. It is Fáfnir's denial of his brother's inheritance that leads to his death at the hands of Sigurd, which is the moment depicted on these stones. On monuments erected specifically for the purpose of recording and communicating inheritance claims, the incorporation of the Fáfnir narrative brings an extra nuance of meaning to the overall design. The reason for incorporating serpents into the iconography of memorial stones, then, is not their associations with death, or just their aesthetic value, but the underlying connection between dragons and the distribution or hoarding of treasure and wealth. Even the very design of these serpents implies the sealing or binding up of treasure. Snakes are frequently associated with binding in Scandinavian literature,[78] and most of the serpents on the memorial stones are depicted intertwined with their own bodies, biting their tails, or fixed to themselves or other serpents with a fastening.[79] The runic letters, meanwhile, stand in direct opposition to this serpentine binding and concealing. By revealing the inheritance claims that underlie the stones' commissions, these runes confirm the distribution of wealth that dragons would otherwise so greedily guard. The design of these stones provides a visual analogue to the opposition of dragons and runes in the literary sources outlined above.

Returning to *Beowulf*, an appreciation of this conceptual opposition between dragons and runes brings additional significance to Hrothgar's sermon. The king's meditation on the tension between greed and generosity is encapsulated by the inscribed hilt's own appearance, with the revelation and openness of its runic letters set against the concealment and avarice of hoarding dragons. It is not simply the sight of the hilt, nor its description as *wyrmfah*, that instigates Hrothgar's seemingly incongruous speech. Instead, it is specifically the interplay between the revealing runic letters and the concealing serpents patterning the hilt's surface that Hrothgar muses upon as he addresses the young hero. This address assumes

---

[78] As, for example, Gunnar in the snake pit, as described in *Vǫlsunga saga* and depicted on the Västerljung stone (above).

[79] Thompson, *Studies in Upplandic Runography*, pp. 22–32.

central importance at the end of the poem, when Beowulf, now an aged king himself, finally comes face-to-face with a dragon of his own. Although Beowulf must unquestionably fight the dragon, his decision to do so alone, and the ambiguous morality that underlies that choice, has been debated widely.[80] Some see Beowulf's decision as the final act of a good king protecting his people even at the cost of his own life.[81] Others take a dimmer view, however, and suggest that Beowulf's refusal to allow his retainers to help him is the folly of a man blinded by greed or overcome by pride.[82] Taken in the context of Hrothgar's earlier speech, it would seem that this second interpretation is closer to the mark. As outlined at the start of this chapter, in his youth Beowulf eagerly shares his hard-won fame and fortune with Ecgtheow, his king. In age, however, he acts more in line with the ancient, hoarding dragon he has come to challenge. In choosing to fight his final adversary alone, Beowulf overlooks both the substance of Hrothgar's words and their inspiration. Aiming to lay sole claim to both the fame and the rewards of this encounter, he fails to gain either.

Conclusion

Anglo-Saxon dragons and serpents are closely associated with concealment and the hoarding of treasure. Such associations are evoked repeatedly in *Beowulf*, and are found diversely in the literature and art of medieval Germanic culture. Runes, on the other hand, are connected with revelation and openness, as demonstrated by the anonymous author of the *De inventione* treatise. It should be no surprise, then, to find the two brought together as representations of opposing forces in such disparate texts as *Solomon and Saturn I*, the *Nine Herbs Charm*, *Vǫlsunga saga*, the various Icelandic *Rune Poems*, and a veritable multitude of Scandinavian rune stones. In many instances, the opposition of runes and dragons is evoked in relation to treasure and its distribution. The resulting conflict, whether narrative in the case of *Vǫlsunga Saga*, gnomic in the Icelandic *Rune Poem*, or visual

---

[80] See R. D. Fulk and Christopher M. Cain, *A History of Old English Literature* (Oxford, 2003), pp. 210–11.

[81] Peter Baker, *Honour, Exchange and Violence in Beowulf* (Woodbridge, 2013), pp. 209–21; Lee, *Gold-Hall and Earth-Dragon*, pp. 249–50; Stanley Greenfield, 'Gifstol and Goldhoard in Beowulf', in *Old English Studies in Honour of John C. Pope*, ed. Robert B. Burlin and Edward B. Irving Jr. (Toronto, 1974), pp. 107–17 (p. 109).

[82] Scott Gwara, *Heroic Identity in the World of Beowulf* (Leiden, 2008), pp. 239–309; Fred C. Robinson, *Beowulf and the Appositive Style* (Knoxville, TN, 1985), pp. 80–2; John Leyerle, 'Beowulf the Hero and King', *Medium Ævum* 34.2 (1965), 89–102 (p. 89); Goldsmith, *The Mode and Meaning of Beowulf*, pp. 226–30; J. R. R. Tolkien, 'The Homecoming of Beorhtnoth Beorhthelm's Son', *Essays and Studies* (1953), 3–24 (p. 20).

in the case of rune stones, reflects wider social concerns surrounding the fair and proper distribution of worldly wealth. The extent of these anxieties is demonstrated by the different treatments of the concept of treasure in the Old English and Old Icelandic *Rune Poems*. In the former, wealth is a benefit to all, but only when it is shared fairly. Conversely, the latter evokes dragons and their connotations of greed, to describe treasure as a menace to mankind. What dragons attempt to hide, however, runes are able to reveal. Thus, Scandinavian rune stones bring the two concepts together such that they literally occupy the same physical space. The hoarding nature of the intertwining serpents is challenged, and overcome, by the runic letters written on their bodies. By recognising the dichotomy of dragons and runes, it is possible to more fully appreciate Hrothgar's sermon. His speech both looks outward, at the bonds that hold society together and the tensions that threaten to overcome them, and looks forward to the poem's own conclusion. As a meditation on the interplay between greed and generosity, Hrothgar's words are directly inspired by the relationship between revealing *runstafas* and concealing *wyrmfah* that decorate the hilt's surface. This same interplay is evoked by the runic serpents on Scandinavian stones, and reflects wider social anxieties surrounding the proper distribution of wealth. At the same time, a speech about greed elicited by the sight of dragon-patterns looks forward to the end of the poem and Beowulf's own conduct in his final encounter with the last of the poem's monsters.

4

The Ravens on the Lejre Throne

Avian Identifiers, Odin at Home, Farm Ravens

Marijane Osborn

'God rewards those who favour the raven'
(modern Icelandic proverb).[1]

On 2 September 2009, an amateur archaeologist digging at Lejre in Denmark discovered a tiny silver and niello sculpture, only 17.5 mm high, of a person seated on a decorated throne and flanked by two ravens. It has been dated to the tenth century (the Viking Age).[2] The drawing in Fig. 4.1 shows the sculpture from the side, with the back of a raven clearly visible. While not common, miniature metal chairs or thrones are not unknown in this period in Scandinavia; they are usually unoccupied and found in women's graves. Suggesting that such chairs are probably amulets, Fuglesang added (in 1989) that 'so far, 13 examples are known from Sweden (including Gotland) and Denmark (including Bornholm). They date from the mid-Viking period (875/900–950/975) and have been connected by some archaeologists to the cult of Odin.'[3] The fact that someone sits on the Lejre throne is an unusual feature in the context of these miniatures. Moreover, while the collared beasts on the back of the throne are clearly ornamental, with their long necks continuing down into interlocked ribbons,[4] the

---

[1] Hjalmar R. Bardarson, *Birds of Iceland* (Reykjavík, 1986), p. 233.
[2] See description at the Roskilde Museum online: <http://www.roskildemuseum.dk/Default.aspx?ID=442> [accessed 31 December 2014].
[3] Signe Horn Fuglesang, 'Viking and Medieval Amulets in Scandinavia', *Fornvännen* 84 (1989), 15–27 (p. 16), referring to Birgit Arrhenius, 'Vikingetidens miniatyrer', *Tor* 7 (1961), 139–64, and Hans Drescher and Karl Hauck, 'Götterthrone des heidnischen Nordens', *Frühmittelalterliche Studien* 16 (1982), 237–301. Christie Ward expresses some scepticism about the use of these 'Odin cult' amulet chairs: 'It could be that they have nothing more than ornamental significance, but many scholars assume a symbolic function in representing thrones or high seats within the pagan context, relating these to the High Seat of Óðinn, or to Hrothgar's *gifstol* in *Beowulf*'; <http://www.vikinganswerlady.com/Birka.shtml> [accessed 31 December 2014]. I am grateful to Christie Ward for furnishing me with the reference to Fuglesang's essay and other useful sources. See also discussion by Lacey, Chapter 5 in this volume.
[4] Carl Anderson examines the possibility that these animals represent Odin's companion wolves in 'The Backrest Beasts of Óðinn from Lejre', *Society for Medieval Archaeology*

The Ravens on the Lejre Throne

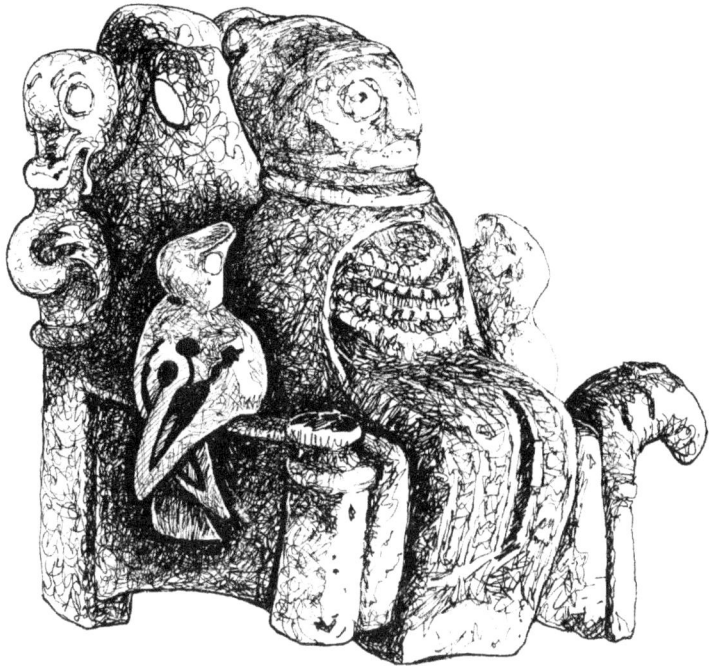

Fig. 4.1 The Lejre Raven Throne

two birds flanking the seated figure are neither decorations nor part of the chair. Their size compared to that of the seated figure, their slightly bent but not hooked beaks, the detail of their wings with primaries crossed when at rest,[5] and their intent attitude looking up at the human figure, are all realistic enough to allow one to identify them as corvids. In fact, some might find the realism of these birds, each only about a quarter of inch high, the most surprising detail of the sculpture.

Newsletter 44 (October 2010), 7–8. Similar throne ornamentation is found, however, in contexts having nothing to do with Odin, such as the finials on the throne of King David in the Durham Cassiodorus illustration (Durham Cathedral Library MS B.II.30, fol. 81v), in scenes on the Bayeux Tapestry, and even on the throne of Octavian Augustus on fol. 45 of the Paris manuscript of Lambert of Saint-Omer's *Liber floridus* (held by the Bibliothèque nationale de France). Kris Kershaw explores the association with wolves of Odin and related heroes or deities in ch. 8, 'Canis and the *koryos', of *The One-Eyed God: Odin and the Indo-Germanic Männerbunde*, Journal of Indo-European Studies Monograph 36 (Washington, DC, 2000), pp. 133–79. He focuses on earlier material, deities and rituals behind Odin, and mentions ravens only in passing (pp. 1 and 267 n. 22).

[5] For a modern sculpture showing a raven with crossed primaries (wingtips), see Tony Angell, *Puget Sound through an Artist's Eye* (Seattle, 2009), p. 119. The two 'nature artists' living a millennium and continents apart, one in Denmark *c.* 950 and the other in Washington State in 1990 (the date of Angell's sculpture), give remarkable attention to this small realistic detail. Their artwork shows that both artists have actually looked closely at ravens, not merely imagined or thought about them (though the blunt fan-shape of the Lejre birds' tails is more like that of a crow than a raven).

These two birds, which are large relative to the person between them, perch on the armrests of the throne and gaze upward at the seated figure. Even had there not been a previous association of the miniature chairs with a cult of Odin, those who first saw the Lejre object would have been inclined to assume the person occupying the chair to be that god, because the sculpture appears to echo the Icelander Snorri Sturluson's famous description in his *Prose Edda* (*c*. AD 1200) of Odin's hall, his throne and his ravens:

> There is also the great place called Valaskialf; it belongs to Odin. The gods built it and roofed it with pure silver. Inside this hall is Hlidskialf, as this throne is called. When All-Father sits in this seat, he sees over all the world ...
>
> Two ravens sit on Odin's shoulders, and into his ears they tell all the news they see or hear. Their names are Hugin [Thought] and Munin [Mind, Memory]. At sunrise he sends them off to fly throughout the whole world, and they return in time for the first meal. Thus he gathers knowledge about many things that are happening, and so people call him the raven god.[6]

Following this information, Snorri quotes stanza 20 of the poem *Grímnismál*: 'Hugin and Munin/ fly each day/ over the wide world./ I fear for Hugin/ that he may not return,/ though I worry more for Munin'.[7] This earlier poem does not mention either Odin's hall or the situation of the birds on his shoulders, nor are these two sites mentioned when Snorri refers to Odin's ravens one other time, in chapter 7 of his *Ynglingasaga*: 'He had two ravens on whom he had bestowed the gift of speech. They flew far and wide over the lands and told him many tidings. By these means he became very wise in his lore.'[8] Even though the ravens are associated only once with a seated god, as the only named pair in any ancient narrative of which I am aware, Hugin and Munin would seem natural choices for the identity of the ravens on the Lejre throne, thereby identifying the person seated between them as Odin.

There are two problems with this 'natural' assumption. The major one is the date. Although a figure of a man's head with a quadruped and a bird that may represent Odin with his horse and raven is frequently found in early Scandinavian bracteates,[9] *Grímnismál* is

---

[6] *The Prose Edda*, trans. Jesse L. Byock (London, 2005), pp. 28 and 47 (chs. 17 and 38).

[7] Quoted by Snorri Sturluson, trans. Byock, pp. 47–8.

[8] *Snorri Sturluson: Heimskringla: History of the Kings of Norway*, trans. Lee M. Hollander (Austin, TX, 1964), p. 11. Of the date Hollander says, 'we have no certain indications when *Heimskringla*, a work of so much larger scope than these earlier works, was composed. Most likely it was the occupation of a lifetime', pp. xvi–xvii.

[9] See, for example, the so-called 'Odin' series of Migration Period bracteates, one of which John Lindow uses to illustrate his brief discussion of bracteates in *Norse Mythology: A Guide to the Gods, Heroes, Rituals, and Beliefs* (Oxford, 2001), p. 85.

the earliest source we have for the notion that Odin had a pair of ravens, and that poem may not be any older than the tenth-century Lejre artefact; indeed, it may even be more recent. Lindow argues that 'The core of [*Grímnismál*] represents a catalogue of mythological knowledge. [...] The poem is impossible to date, but it is not difficult to imagine something like it being performed during the pagan period'.[10] Moreover, the specific image of Odin on his throne being told the news by two birds sitting on his shoulders may have been invented in the thirteenth century by Snorri himself, possibly deriving the idea from Christian imagery (discussed below) or Irish lore.[11] The possibility of Snorri's personal experience of tame ravens should not be ruled out, either.[12] The other problem with identifying the sculpture as Odin with his ravens is the apparently feminine garb of the enthroned person, similar to that on representations clearly of women on other Viking Age objects. This feature has led to heated discussion about the identity of the figure.[13] Whether it represents Odin himself, a cross-dressed shaman, or a prophetess, the way the two ravens are focused intently upon that person between them, as if communicating, would seem to place them in the sphere of Snorri's Odin and his 'magic'. Thus they are probably best regarded as shamanic birds conveying messages about far-away events or things to come – news that can be either good or bad. This prophetic function is familiar enough to require little discussion; it is the lore most frequently associated with ravens the world over, though seldom as picturesquely as here.

The discussion that follows addresses two different issues concerning the ravens on the Lejre throne: their symbolism and their

---

[10] Ibid., p. 151.

[11] At the Irish hero Cuchullain's death the Morrigan comes to rest on his shoulder in her raven form. This image has remained popular in Ireland into modern times and has been adapted to a political purpose by both sides of the North–South conflict. In the south, for example, the dying Cuchullain with a raven on his shoulder appears on the reverse of the elegant ten-shilling coin issued in 1966 to commemorate the fiftieth anniversary of the 1916 Easter Rising; see <http://www.irishcoinage.com/K00003.HTM> [accessed 31 December 2014].

[12] The Icelandic author Kristín Arngrímsdóttir tells me that her most recent children's book, *Arngrímur Apascott og Hrafinn* (Reykjavík, 2010), in which an annoying raven becomes a friend, was partly inspired by the fearless ravens, 'most often in pairs', that teased her and her dog when she was a child growing up on the farm Oddi in the south, from 1953 to 1964 (personal e-mail communication of 12–9–2011). Snorri Sturluson spent part of his childhood on the very same farm 700 years previously, where it is certainly possible that he knew someone who had tamed a raven. For an unrelated connection of paired ravens with Oddi, see ch. 79 of the anonymous *Njal's Saga*, when Hǫgni and Skarpheðinn set out for that farm and 'two ravens flew with them all the way'; *Njal's Saga*, trans. Magnus Magnusson and Hermann Pálsson (London, 1960), p. 174. A discussion of 'farm ravens' follows below.

[13] See Óluva Ellingsgaard, 'Var Odin en Kvinde?', *Videnskab.dk*, 27 January 2010, available online at <http://videnskab.dk/kultur-samfund/var-odin-en-kvinde> [accessed 31 December 2014]. Tom Christensen's rejoinder is discussed below.

realism. First I will discuss avian emblems of deity and power in Late Antiquity and early Christendom, and speculate how artefacts might have carried the association between bird and deity north. Moving then to the realistic aspect of the ravens on the little throne, I will show how the two distinct lifestyles of ravens in the wild – with young ravens roaming in flocks and the mature birds settling in pairs – are reflected in northern literature. I will conclude by observing how the contexts of birds as emblems of deity and the real-life behaviour of ravens are two complementary components of the Lejre throne's significance, and how together they further complicate the issue of its occupant's identity.

Emblems for Deity and Empire: A Numismatic Silver Bridge to the Lejre Throne?

The series of small unoccupied metal chairs mentioned above, possibly amulets, were named 'Odin thrones' mainly because Snorri's description of Odin has the god famously seated on the named throne Hliðskjálf. To the first modern viewers of the tiny Lejre throne, the birds seemed an even better reason for an association with Odin. Just as gods in many cultures are represented as accompanied by an identifying bird or animal, Odin's companion ravens are perceived to mark his identity.[14] Traditional avian motifs in Classical culture include Zeus with his eagle, Athena with her owl, Juno with her peacock, and Apollo with his all-too-talkative raven, and these images of divinity travelled far on portable media, including coins and medals (Fig. 4.2).[15] By the Viking Age, Christianity had appropriated the imagery portraying divinity and majesty, redeploying the theme mainly in two ways: in images of secular rulers wishing to emulate Rome,[16] and in the *maiestas domini* figure showing Christ as ruler of the world. When Christ or a symbol of him is accompanied by a bird, however, it is not the imperial eagle but a dove signifying the Holy Spirit. On a famous coin series of this period, best seen in the AD 1009 Agnus Dei coin of the Anglo-Saxon king Æthelred II, Christ is represented on one side of

---

[14] The identification of Odin by companion ravens is not universally convincing, as will be discussed below. In post-medieval times, however, a pair of ravens consistently sits on Odin's shoulders, as in a well-known eighteenth-century illustration from Snorri's *Edda*. Together with his single eye and his eight-legged horse, the god is most often identified by the raven pair in modern illustrations of him.

[15] This coin image derives ultimately from the sculptor Phidias's 40-foot high statue of Zeus with his eagle at Olympia, formerly one of the Seven Wonders of the Ancient World (destroyed in the fifth century AD). See also the 'coin of Elis' and the imitative sculpture in the Hermitage Museum in St Petersburg, Russia.

[16] Robert G. Calkins provides a useful brief discussion, with illustrations, of the Carolingian use of Roman imperial imagery in *Monuments of Medieval Art* (Ithaca, NY, 1979), pp. 70–6.

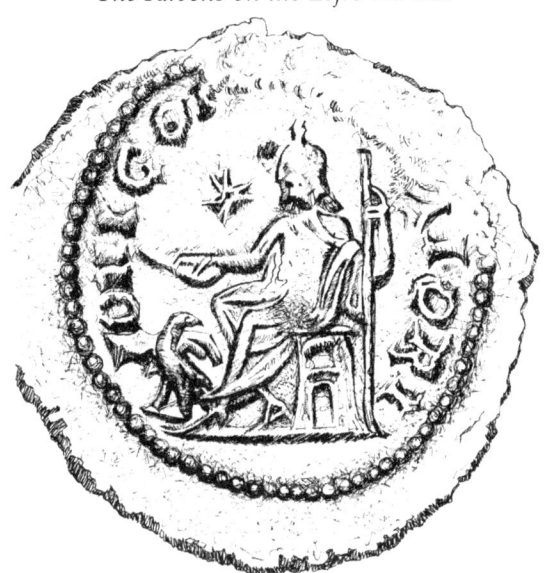

Fig. 4.2 Enthroned Zeus with his eagle

the coin as a lamb with a cross (called in Latin the *Agnus Dei*), while on the other side is an ascending dove.[17] Both Christ and king enthroned become more common about a century later, but these coins derive their iconography from earlier Roman and Byzantine models. Some of those models and their derivants depict women enthroned, including Victory and titular spirits of cities such as 'Roma'. Among the eighteen silver denarii found in Nydam Bog in the 1990s, fifteen have human figures on the reverse, with four being seated on thrones.[18]

Comparing the Lejre object to art forms representing imperial figures, the archaeologist Tom Christensen says that 'we readily recognize the overall symbolism: the ruler on his throne.'[19] Christensen's argument, directed mainly against the identification of the figure as female on the basis of clothing, rests primarily on the depiction of Christ as the '*maiestas domini*, "the lord in majesty", seated on a throne', and related images in which 'enthroned rulers are wearing long robes'.[20] Christensen provides a range of images from

---

[17] N 776, Jeffrey J. North, *English Hammered Coinage*, vol. 1: *Early Anglo-Saxon to Henry III, c. 600–1272*, 3rd edn (London 1994), p. 160. About half a century later, a silver penny of Edward the Confessor (N 827) shows on the obverse the king enthroned, and on the reverse a cross and four birds: ibid., p. 180.

[18] Found during the 1990s, these Roman coins of the period AD 69–217 add to the considerable findings from Nydam Bog. Photographs appear in Helle W. Horsnæs, 'The Coins in the Bogs', in *The Spoils of Victory: The North in the Shadow of the Roman Empire*, ed. Lars Jorgensen, Birger Storgaard and Lone Gebauer (Copenhagen, 2003), p. 331.

[19] Tom Christensen, 'Odin fra Lejre', *ROMU* (2009), 7–25 (p. 21).

[20] Ibid., p. 21.

paintings, relief sculpture and embroidery, but he does not mention that most portable of mediums, coins. In a discussion of the derivation of the form of the *maiestas domini* image in the late seventh-century Codex Amiatinus, Lawrence Nees remarks that 'the influence of coins upon manuscript illumination has been far too little studied.'[21] Better recognised is the influence upon coins of art in other media, as when the mosaic image of Christ enthroned in the Church of Hagia Sophia reappears on Byzantine coins after AD 900.[22] That reuse of imagery is within a single religious culture, but just as Christ Enthroned owes much to the pagan Zeus Enthroned, standard Christian forms could also be 'repaganised' or appropriated in some other way, as, for example, when Sven Estridesen (*c.* 1019–74) appropriated the imagery of Æthelred II's Agnus Dei coin, mentioned above. Sven, or his moneyer, converted the soaring Holy Dove of Æthelred's coin into a fiercely militant imperial eagle on extended wings, thereby marking himself, though Christian, as 'Nordic'.[23] Tom Christensen, in his article on the Lejre throne, concludes the section exploring 'Odin as *Maiestas Domini*' with a suggestion of similar borrowing-back: 'with all the character's harmonious balanced symmetry and the clearly fabricated ruler symbolism, you get the impression that we face a pagan god made in a Classical/Christian tradition.'[24] Could the artist of the pagan, or at least secular, Lejre throne, whose silver medium most likely came from melted-down coins, have found inspiration in a rare *maiestas domini* image upon one of them?

The very material of the silver and niello Lejre throne suggests a coinage source. The Vikings obtained their silver and gold through raiding, trade and tribute, and they were especially interested in payment in silver coins that could be melted down to create objects in native form, to trade in terms of weight, or simply to stockpile for later use. As James Graham-Campbell says:

> The Viking Age was *the* silver age of the northern world – well over a thousand hoards of gold and silver have been found from this period in

---

[21] Lawrence Nees, 'Problems of Form and Function in Early Medieval Illustrated Bibles from Northwest Europe', in *Imaging the Early Bible*, ed. John Williams (University Park, PA, 1999), pp. 121–77 (p. 172 n. 158).

[22] David Elliott, 'The Other Coin: The Changing Image of Christ as Influenced by Byzantine Coins': <http://www.renocoinclub.org/ChristByzcoins.html> [accessed 31 December 2014]. The image of Christ Enthroned was introduced by Basil I and is 'one of the few images on Byzantine coins that can probably be traced to a work of art in another medium, the mosaic over the imperial doorway of the Church of Hagia Sophia in Constantinople': Eric N. Jurgens, online at <http://www.lawrence.edu/dept/art/buerger/catalogue/143.html> [accessed 31 December 2014].

[23] This coin may be seen as the third item at <http://mycoinpage.com/Coin_Samples/Denmark/DenmarkPage1.htm> [accessed 31 December 2014] for comparison to the Æthelred coin (n. 17 above). The description there is also of interest.

[24] Christensen, 'Odin fra Lejre', p. 22.

Scandinavia alone, and their distribution is far wider, from Iceland in the west to the Urals in the east. Despite the enormous wealth of silver that can be seen to have passed through Viking hands into Scandinavian soil, it must be emphasized that there are *no* known native sources of silver that were being worked in Scandinavia during the Viking Age.[25]

The silver flooding north came first from the Islamic world, but later, as Islamic mines began failing in the tenth century, it came mainly from Anglo-Saxon England and Germany, or was funnelled through those countries. Payments of tribute mentioned in Frankish sources alone, Graham-Campbell says, 'amount to 685 pounds of gold and 43,042 pounds of silver, and if some sums were exaggerated, then there were no doubt others that went unrecorded'.[26] When drafting this article in early 2012, I suggested that, with all this flow of coins, it seemed likely that if a good example of the representation of an enthroned person (such as the influential 'Roma') came to hand it would be noticed, and close upon that thought followed confirmation. In August 2012, three amateur archaeologists found a 3.5-kilogram treasure of fifth-century silver and silver-gilt objects buried in a cauldron, near Lejre. Called the 'Mannerupskat' (treasure from Mannerup), the hoard contains, among other items, two 'Roma'-type coins pierced for wearing, possibly as amulets.[27]

Ravens and Birdmen on Other Portable Artefacts

Initially derived from Imperial Roman coins, bracteates are Migration Age pendants found mainly in or adjacent to Scandinavia and bearing designs only on one side. The design on a gold bracteate from Várpalóta in Hungary, possibly Lombardic, bears some resemblance to the Lejre throne in terms of theme (Fig. 4.3).[28] The design shows a man

---

[25] James Graham-Campbell, 'Viking Silver Hoards: An Introduction', in *The Vikings*, ed. R. T. Farrell (London, 1982), p. 34.

[26] Ibid., p. 35. See also *Silver Economy in the Viking Age*, ed. James Graham-Campbell and Gareth Williams (Walnut Creek, CA, 2007). Silver hoards, many dating from the period of the Lejre throne, continue to be found, such as the Viking hoards found in northern England in 2009 and 2011.

[27] These coins may be among the photographs of the treasure on the Roskilde Museum website at <http://www.roskildemuseum.dk/Default.aspx?ID=651> [accessed 31 December 2014]. Although by no means furnishing proof, the fact of the Roma coins turning up so locally, and their being distinguished from the rest of the hoard by piercing, makes more feasible my tentative suggestion that the seated image on coins like these could have inspired the 'Raven Throne' carver.

[28] Gyula László, *The Art of the Migration Period*, trans. Barna Balogh, rev. Paul Aston (Coral Gables, 1974), black and white plate 43, after p. 159 (unnumbered pages). László describes this bracteate with others found in the same Lombard cemetery as 'northern imitations of Late Roman imperial images' ('Appendix C: List of Black and White Plates', p. 151). It is number IK 206 in Karl Hauck, Herbert Lange and Lutz von Padberg, *Die*

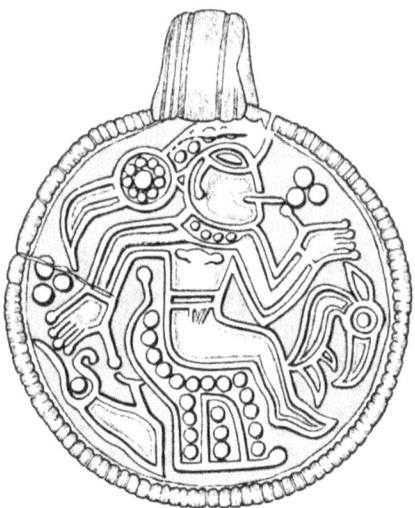

Fig. 4.3 Gold bracteate from Várpalóta, Hungary

in profile sitting on a chair between the heads of birds with raven-like bills. The third beady-eyed bird above him is probably a headdress.[29] With his arms outflung, apparently to grab the birds on either side, perhaps for sacrifice, this lively enthroned man of Várpalóta is very different in mood from the tranquil occupant of the Lejre throne.[30]

Pictures of enthroned rulers flanked by anonymous guards are abundant in this period on various forms of portable media, offering another image of majesty. This initially Roman theme was eagerly adopted for Christian use, showing Christ both enthroned and crucified. Even when crucified, Christ is represented with a strong sense of rulership, in a far-ranging variation upon the theme, with the attending Roman guards with spears now identified as Stephanaton offering Christ a drink on a sponge and Longinus piercing his

---

Goldbrakteaten der Völkerwanderungszeit, 1.3: *Ikonographischer Katalog* (Munich, 1985), p. 273.

[29] A similar headdress is more clearly represented on the Danish Skrydstrup bracteates. Dickinson suggests that this headdress is a reinterpretation of the flowing hair on imperial busts (as on coins), in Tania M. Dickinson, 'Symbols of Protection: The Significance of Animal-Ornamented Shields in Early Anglo-Saxon England', *MedArch* 49 (2005), 109–63 (p. 152). The Skrydstrup bracteate is illustrated by Stephen Pollington, Lindsay Kerr and Brett Hammond in *Wayland's Work: Anglo-Saxon Art, 4th to 7th Century* (Ely, 2010), p. 425. There the authors point out similarities to the Várpalóta bracteate. Whereas I and some others see the Várpalóta creatures as ravens, others more cautiously call them raptors, and the Pollington team sees them as serpents, which demonstrates once again how tenuous these interpretations are. Similarly, Peter Vang Petersen remarks how the popularity of the raven motif around AD 200 is evident from various items, including 'the contemporary "raven head rings" of gold which were earlier called "snakes head rings," but whose heads have nothing to do with snakes'. See Peter Vang Petersen, 'Warrior Art, Religion and Symbolism', in *The Spoils of Victory: The North in the Shadow of the Roman Empire* (Copenhagen, 2003), pp. 286–93 (p. 290).

[30] Enthusiasts identify the man depicted on the Várpalóta bracteate as Odin. Pollington *et al.* conclude more cautiously that he 'may be Godan, the Lombardic name for Woden/ Oðinn'; see Pollington *et al.*, *Wayland's Work*, p. 425. Against Morton Axboe's and Karl Hauck's identification of the figure commonly shown on Type C Migration Period bracteates as Odin, see – among other sceptics – Nancy L. Wicker, 'Context Analysis and Bracteate Inscriptions in Light of Alternative Iconographic Interpretations', giving sources for the interpretations by Hauck and others. Her useful article is a pre-print available online and is cited here with Professor Wicker's permission: <http://www.khm.uio.no/english/research/publications/7th-symposium-preprints/wicker.pdf> [accessed 31 December 2014].

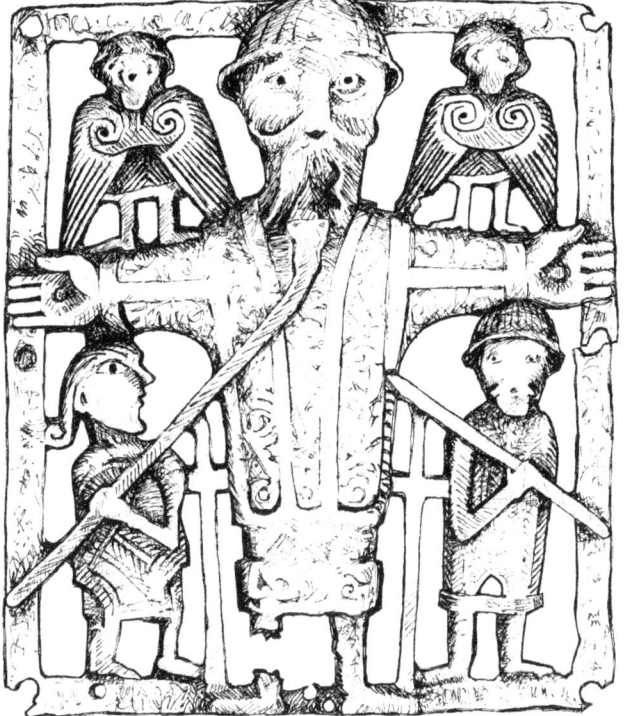

Fig. 4.4 The Clonmacnoise Plaque

side. On the *maiestas domini* page in the early eighth-century Codex Amiatinus the guards with spears have become winged angels,[31] and in the West the image sometimes gains a quadruplex form combining both soldiers and angels. One series of nine Irish crucifixion plaques shows Christ, still alive and clothed, flanked by the Roman guards with small winged angels hovering above.[32] On the famous plaque found at Clonmacnoise in Ireland, the little bird-men perch directly on Christ's shoulders very much as Odin's ravens perch on his shoulders according to Snorri (Fig. 4.4).[33] Several of the Irish high

---

[31] The crucifixion scene in the Syriac Rabbula Gospels of AD 586 has Christ between guards with spears, with the figure on the right offering him a sponge on a spear. Unlike the page in the Codex Amiatinus, on the *maiestas domini* page of the *Gospel Book of Gundohinus* (*c.* AD 754), the angels flanking Christ are unarmed, but still they are 'a heritage from Roman imperial iconography, the angels of the Majesty substituting for the original soldiers'; see Lawrence Nees, 'Carolingian Art and Politics', in *The Gentle Voices of Teachers: Aspects of Learning in the Carolingian Age*, ed. Richard E. Sullivan (Columbus, OH, 1995), pp. 186–226 (p. 193). All these depictions may be seen by searching the manuscript by name online.

[32] Ruth Johnson, 'Irish Crucifixion Plaques – Viking Age or Romanesque?', *Journal of the Royal Society of Antiquaries of Ireland* 128 (1998), 95–106.

[33] The quincunx design is traditional, and this Clonmacnoise plaque is often published; see Johnson, 'Irish Crucifixion Plaques', p. 96. Suggestive in this context of an Irish

crosses share variations on this theme. On the east face of the Doorty Cross at Kilfenora in County Clare, bird-angels rest on the shoulders of a bishop, and the two 'spearmen' are clerics using their croziers to pierce a large bird below their feet; on the worn west face actual birds (ravens or doves?) appear to whisper into the ears of Christ.[34]

The figure of a man between birds is more adaptable than those tending to see Odin might like to think – even with ravens on his shoulders. A figure with what could be ravens whispering in his ears stands on an Anglo-Saxon cross-shaft in Kirklevington, North Yorkshire. It has 'naturally' been taken to represent Odin (or, in England, Woden), but Richard Bailey has shown that 'the iconography can be readily matched on a fifth-century Christian tomb at Tabarka in Tunisia and on an eighth century Augustine manuscript in the Vatican.'[35] In *Animals in Celtic Life and Myth* the archaeologist Miranda Green shows a stone relief in Burgundy of a Romano-Celtic god with a raven on each shoulder.[36] Returning to the Scandinavian context, two birds accompany a rider depicted on a Vendel Mound One helmet plate (Fig. 4.5). John Lindow cautiously suggests that the plate shows 'what might be Odin accompanied by Hugin and Munin'.[37] The difference in the birds' beaks reveals them to be of distinct species, however. An eagle with its significantly curved beak (imitated on the helmet) leads the way, and a raven with barely curved beak follows behind.[38] The birds on this helmet plate are not, therefore, Hugin and Munin, nor is the rider necessarily Odin. He may simply be a warrior associated with birds of prey, or birds like the raven on the famous banner carried into battle by Viking armies.[39] Referring either to such

---

holy object is Snorri's account in *Heimskringla* (Olaf Tryggvason's Saga, ch. 33) of the four *landvættir* (land-spirits) that guard the four quarters of Iceland: dragon, bird, bull and giant. The terms in which Snorri describes them are clearly reminiscent of the Four Evangelical Beasts on Irish high crosses and in the Book of Kells, the tetramorph of Man, Lion, Calf and Eagle representing the gospel writers Matthew, Mark, Luke and John; see Andy Orchard, *Dictionary of Norse Myth and Legend* (London, 1997), p. 103. The idea of *landvættir* predated Snorri; he merely arranged them as the four creatures, or tetramorph, quartering Iceland.

[34] The Doorty Cross may be seen with commentary here: <http://www.clarelibrary.ie/eolas/coclare/archaeology/kilfenora_stone_crosses/doorty_cross.htm> [accessed 31 December 2014].

[35] Richard N. Bailey, *England's Earliest Sculptures* (Toronto, 1996), p. 91. Bailey does not mention the similar depiction of Christ on the Irish Doorty Cross, mentioned above.

[36] Miranda Green, *Animals in Celtic Life and Myth* (London, 1998), p. 179.

[37] Lindow, *Norse Mythology*, p. 187.

[38] This picture recalls the final stanza of Hjalmar's Death Song in the *Saga of Hervorar and King Heidrek the Wise*: 'The raven swoops from the high tree, follows after the eagle in flight'. See Peter Tunstall's translation of this part of *Hervorar Saga* at: <www4.ujaen.es/~lugarcia/litingre/Hjalmar's%20death_texto.doc> [accessed 31 December 2014].

[39] The Vikings' raven banner (*hrafnsmerki*), associated with specific chieftains, is mentioned in various Old Norse sources and also in Old English. For example, the *Anglo-Saxon Chronicle* entry for the year 878 says that when the Vikings came against King Alfred in Devon, the Anglo-Saxons captured the war-flag which they (the Vikings) called 'Raven'.

The Ravens on the Lejre Throne

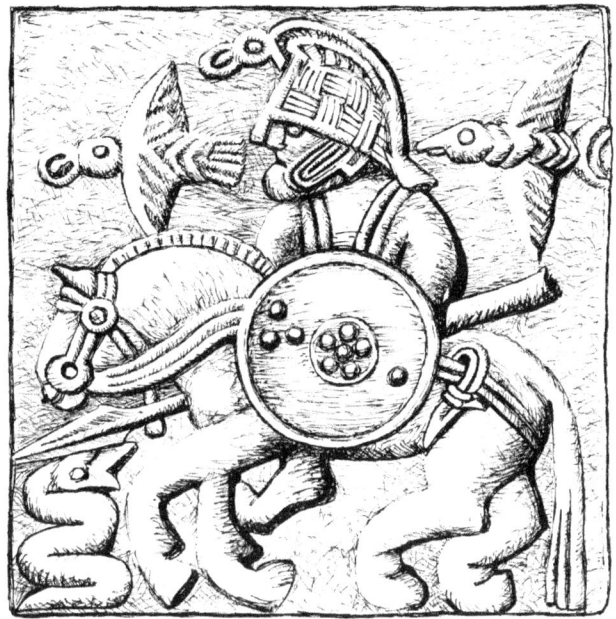

Fig. 4.5 Seventh-century Vendel helmet plate

a banner or to an actual bird, stanza 20 of the Eddic poem *Reginsmál* is respectful toward ravens, but ambiguous: 'A trusty omen for the warrior, I believe,/ is the company of the dark raven'.[40] These two lines may mean that being accompanied by a raven (as above) is lucky for a warrior, or simply that the prophetic message that a raven brings about a battle's outcome is considered to be dependable.

In the Company of Ravens: Life-Stages and Territoriality

While the 'dark raven' preys with its companion beasts on battlefield corpses in poetry and saga, and lone flyers lead hosts into battle or circle above where that violence will occur, mature ravens in story and legend are linked to a 'home' location, and are semi-domesticated. Ravens are not migratory birds. This territorial aspect of raven lore is derived from the observed activity of mature corvids and presents them in an aspect quite unlike the dark scavengers that tear corpses, or the bird of ill omen imagined by Edgar Allen Poe. As mentioned above and here elaborated, ravens in general have two main life-stages. When the fledgling leaves the nest, it typically joins a flock that may travel widely; 'these juveniles constitute a "floater" population

---

[40] *The Poetic Edda*, trans. Carolyne Larrington (Oxford, 1999), p. 155.

without a fixed home.'[41] If the raven survives to reach maturity, with luck it will leave the flock, mate, claim a territory, and nest. Knowledge of this typical (though not universal) life cycle of the raven, as it moves from being a restless and highly social adolescent to a solidly mated bird that will drive 'floater' ravens from its territory, is helpful for an understanding of ravens in early Germanic art and poetry. Additionally significant for this study is the recent observation by ornithologists that ravens in different locations and in different relationships to humans appear to have developed distinctive local 'cultures', to use Marzluff's word.[42] Ravens in California have a local culture different from those in Iceland.

Ravens everywhere are 'opportunistic omnivores', feeding on what is abundant and easily available. In subarctic Iceland, therefore, where life in the wild in winter can be difficult to sustain, easier availability of food leads many ravens, usually in pairs, to claim farms as their territory. If they are fed scraps rather than persecuted for scavenging, they may become an integral – even useful – part of farm life. This openness to integration with humans in a mutually enhanced environment seems to be a local 'culture' specific to Icelandic ravens. The human side of it, the modern concept of farm ravens as a recognised cultural phenomenon, also seems exclusively Icelandic. The closest any ornithologist currently writing in English comes to mentioning farm ravens is when Bernd Heinrich remarks in passing that 'in Iceland, where there is still ancient Nordic respect for ravens, the bird is quite tame.'[43] In *Birds of Iceland* (*Islands Fuglar*) the native author Hjalmar R. Bardarson treats the association of ravens with farms as a commonplace:

> farm-ravens are said to be creatures of habit, always leaving the farm at twilight for their nocturnal roosting place, and returning at dawn the following day to check if anything edible has been thrown out overnight. It is thus considered very unnatural to see or hear a raven at night, and usually means that the bird is possessed by an evil spirit. Such ravens are called night-ravens, as indeed is the name in Icelandic for guests who arrive or leave very late![44]

---

[41] Bernd Heinrich, *Mind of the Raven: Investigations and Adventures with Wolf-birds* (New York, 2006), p. 74.

[42] For justification of this usage, see John M. Marzluff and Tony Angell, 'Chapter One: Cultural Connections', in *In the Company of Crows and Ravens* (New Haven, CT, 2005), pp. 1–35 (and *passim*, e.g. p. 297).

[43] Bernd Heinrich, *Ravens in Winter* (New York, 1989), p. 26. Among my US acquaintances committed to bird-watching, Robin Welch, who has been active for many years, assures me that she has never heard of farm ravens of the Icelandic type.

[44] In contrast to this term is the proper name Dæghrefn, at *Beowulf* line 2501, to which the editors of *Klaeber's Beowulf* compare the raven of line 1801; the latter raven is discussed below. See *Klaeber's Beowulf and the Fight at Finnsburg*, ed. R. D. Fulk, Robert E. Bjork and John D. Niles, 4th edn (Toronto, 2008), p. 217.

Although in general an 'opportunistic omnivore', during fall and winter in Iceland 'the raven appears to be more of a scavenger',[45] and on many farmsteads food is specifically left out for the home ravens.[46]

According to current Icelandic raven lore both oral and written, farm ravens in pairs are a frequent phenomenon. In fact, the frequently observed gathering of many ravens in a circle, called a *hrefnaðing* (raven-parliament), is for the express purpose, I have been told by Icelanders, of assigning the neighbourhood farms to specific pairs.[47] The peculiar activity of ravens in groups on the ground has not been adequately explained, but the human interpretation suggests an awareness of the ravens' territoriality once they are paired and nesting.[48] The only farm raven that I have encountered personally, on a farm at Vik in southern Iceland, was a subsidised predator clearly there for the morning handout, perhaps with the absent mate on the nest or defending it. When these mature birds pair and, in order to breed, become territorial (attached to one location), they keep a firm eye out for intruders of any species, while remaining open to interspecies relationships with handy food-providing humans attached to their territory.

Following are three examples of ravens in Old English and Norse literature and legend that I take to be 'home ravens'. At lines 1801–2 of *Beowulf* the poet gives Heorot, the great hall of the Scyldings, a home raven; however, rather than understanding the raven whose morning call wakes Beowulf as an actual bird, scholars have tended to allegorise it in some way, usually viewing its appearance through

---

[45] Kristinn H. Skarphhédinsson, Ólafur K. Nielsen, Skarphédinn Thórisson, Sverrir Thorstensen and Stanley A. Temple, 'Breeding Biology, Movements, and Persecution of Ravens in Iceland', *Acta Naturalia Islandica* 33 (1990), 1–45 (p. 3).

[46] Hjalmar R. Bárðarson, *Birds of Iceland* (Reykjavik, 1986), p. 235. For a raven coming to seek food in wintertime Sweden, see this YouTube video: <http://www.youtube.com/watch?v=ND6j8l-TVHw> [accessed 31 December 2014]; alternatively, search YouTube for 'Hrafninn sem heimsækir Uppsali'. Marzluff begins *In the Company of Crows and Ravens* with a personal anecdote in which a crow stands in for corvids in general; his story bears on the arguments of this essay: 'It's midmorning, and a single crow has arrived unseen to parade about the lawn outside our open window. Failing to arouse us with visual cues, the crow leaps to the outside railing and calls: two loud, sharp caws in succession. Alerted, we look up from our work, and one of us walks obediently to the kitchen to retrieve a previously saved crust of bread. This morning ritual of bread-fetching for our saucy friend has been going on long enough to become habit', p. xi. Such anecdotes about corvids are ubiquitous.

[47] One of my Icelandic informants even claimed to have witnessed such a gathering. See Marijane Osborn, 'Domesticating the Dayraven in *Beowulf* 1801 (With Some Reference to Alison's *Ston*)', in *Heroic Poetry in the Anglo-Saxon Period: Studies in Honor of Jess B. Bessinger, Jr.*, ed. Helen Damico and John Leyerle (Kalamazoo, MI, 1993), pp. 313–30 (p. 321).

[48] Heinrich writes that 'ravens are almost unique among corvids, and more like raptors in their generally wide nest dispersal and strong territoriality'; see Heinrich, *Mind of the Raven*, p. 90. Once established, the pair will repel others from their territory.

the dark lens of Poe. Sylvia Horowitz is adamant, for example, that the raven is 'a symbol of death, or of the ever present death in life',[49] and Eric Lacey lists other scholars echoing this opinion. He considers the connotations of the bird as 'morbid', and finds the 'blithe-hearted' raven a jarring incongruity.[50] The two-stage life cycle of the raven described above may resolve this apparent incongruity between the evil or portentous battle raven, or bird of death, and the raven comfortable with humans at home. One of these 'opportunistic omnivores' circling above a battlefield or a field about to host a battle, as in lines 34–5 of the 'Finnsburg Fragment',[51] would indeed portend human carnage, and in realistic terms would probably be a young explorer raven. Typically the explorer would return to the flock and guide it back to the potential feasting site, often from a considerable distance.[52] Such opportunistic 'beast of battle' birds are not operating within their own territory, and from the human point of view they are definitely ominous, auguring the Game of Odin (i.e. mayhem in battle).[53] But the 'blithe-hearted' raven in *Beowulf* that unambiguously 'bodes heaven's joy' is at home in the royal hall Heorot. It can be interpreted as a mature bird settled in its own nesting territory, flying to the hall from a night-time roost high in cliff or treetop[54] to announce dawn (and breakfast time); at a more spiritual level it may be seen as a sign that the demonic antagonists of Heorot have now been quelled, and that life on this bright new day can go back to normal. When R. M. Liuzza speaks of 'the irony of the image of the black raven, not

---

[49] Sylvia Horowitz, 'The Ravens in *Beowulf*', *JEGP* 80 (1981), 502–11 (p. 502).

[50] See Lacey, this volume, pp. 113–30.

[51] *Finnsburh Fragment and Episode*, ed. Donald K. Fry (London, 1974), pp. 34–5. Eagle, wolf and raven are the three traditional 'beasts of battle', first analysed as formulaic by Francis P. Magoun Jr. in 'The Theme of the Beasts of Battle', *NM* 56 (1955), 81–90 (p. 83). See also the 'Viking Answer Lady's' well-illustrated discussion at <http://www.vikinganswerlady.com/beasts.shtml> [accessed 31 December 2014]; and Joseph Harris, 'Beasts of Battle, South and North', in *Source of Wisdom: Old English and Early Medieval Latin Studies in Honour of Thomas D. Hill*, ed. Charles D. Wright, Frederick M. Biggs and Thomas N. Hall (Toronto, 2007), pp. 3–25. In his 'Battlescapes' blog, Tom Williams (editor of this volume) offers a photograph of carrion birds flying above the putative field of the Battle of Ringmere, with this accompanying text: 'As I wandered about the site, a great cloud of rooks billowed up into an ominous sky to swirl madly in the gathering dusk. Their hoarse cries were a timeless echo in that bleak landscape – it was hard not to imagine the wide expanse of heathland strewn with the corpses of Saxons and Danes as the birds of battle wheeled in anticipation of their coming feast': available to members at <http://battlescapes.wordpress.com/2012/09/21/ringmere/> [accessed 10 January 2014].

[52] In nature, single 'explorer' ravens, normally vagrant juveniles, will discover and circle a food supply and then return to the flock of other young birds and lead them to it; see, among other sources, observations in Heinrich, *Mind of the Raven*, pp. 13–30.

[53] *Gauts bragða* (i.e. battle), *Landnámabók*, ch. 33, in *Íslendinga sögur* 1, ed. Guðni Jónsson (Reykjavík, 1946), p. 120.

[54] Ravens prefer to roost up high – on cliffs, or in tall trees – somewhere with a broad view across the landscape.

otherwise known as a harbinger of joy, announcing the surprising good news of a dawn without slaughter',[55] his surprise reflects the standard Western view of the raven as ominous. Contrary to Liuzza's idea that the raven is 'not otherwise known' to announce joy, however, Kathryn Hume documents a number of literary examples of the raven as a joyful herald of dawn.[56] An Icelandic farmer might find the entire discussion otiose, recognising the *hræfn* of *Beowulf* as a half-tame bird demanding its morning handout. In any case, this ordinary domestic activity may be read as a marker that the violent and uncanny 'Grendel' part of the poem is finally over.[57]

The ravens associated with the Tower of London have a similar function of representing the fate of a place. As long as they remain there, it is said, Britain is safe. Boria Sax has shown that this supposedly ancient legend is in fact quite recent, although it contains strands of older legendary material, such as the story of Bran recorded in the Welsh *Mabinogion*. In that work the Celtic god-hero, whose name Bran means 'raven' and whose non-human form is that bird, is beheaded and his head buried, at his request, looking toward France on the site where the Tower now stands. The Welsh story contains the admonition that if the head (of Bran the Raven) is ever removed Britain will fall.[58] While it is obvious how the ancient story has influenced the modern legend, another powerful influence on this cautionary tale may well be the real-life activity of ravens haunting farms for forage and staying away when circumstances become adverse, since the natural inclination of that intelligent and opportunistic bird is to forage elsewhere if the farm becomes dangerous or food becomes unavailable. The raven's territorial nature is very strong, however, so it may return to its chosen site. Ravens often occupy their territory in long-living pairs, and they become very interested in humans, particularly when humans are rare in that place, as in bleak Iceland or a desert wasteland,[59] or when they offer the possibility of easy

---

[55] Roy M. Liuzza, *Beowulf: A New Verse Translation* (Peterborough, ON, 2000), p. 108.
[56] Kathryn Hume, 'The Function of the *Hrefn Blaca*: *Beowulf* 1801', *Modern Philology* 67 (1969–70), 60–3.
[57] Osborn, 'Domesticating the Dayraven', p. 324. Both Hume and Puhvel arrive at this same conclusion; see Martin Puhvel, 'The Blithe-Hearted Morning Raven in *Beowulf*', *English Language Notes* 10 (1973), 243–7 (p. 247).
[58] Boria Sax, *City of Ravens: The Extraordinary History of London, the Tower and its Famous Ravens* (London, 2011).
[59] Many stories of 'Beasts and Saints', such as those told by Helen Waddell in her book of that title, are clearly fictions designed to make some kind of moral point, but even when morally framed some are based on actual animal nature. The raven pair that makes friends with Cuthbert on Farne Island reminds me very much of the raven pair I encountered on the Icelandic island Drangey, flying circles above me and watching my every move when the boat left me 'stranded' there, a single human unusually alone on their island. See Gillian R. Overing and Marijane Osborn, *Landscape of Desire: Partial Stories of the Medieval Scandinavian World* (Minneapolis, 1994), p. 115.

forage, as on snowy winter mornings. Perhaps those well-fed Tower of London ravens do not need their wings clipped after all.

Snorri Sturluson himself frames Odin's ravens as allegorical when he calls them Hugin (Thought)[60] and Munin (Memory), yet, as these two raven-familiars accompany Odin in his hall Hliðskjálf, high above all others, they behave like farm ravens when they leave him at dawn to fly out over the world and then return to him and their high roosting place, as Snorri significantly says, 'in time for the first meal'. As observed at the beginning of this essay, a highly unusual aspect of the Lejre throne as a Nordic art object is the realism with which the ravens, clearly interacting with the seated person, are portrayed.[61] The most likely aim of the Lejre throne sculptor is to portray the ravens as real creatures conveying information, not as in augury or in terms of common raven behaviour,[62] but intentionally as speaking from 'person to person', like human messengers. This locates them in an interesting marginal space between species and possibly between mental states,[63] making them suitable companions for a seated god associated less with war and the *männerbund* (male-bonded warrior band) than with visions and supernatural knowledge – a god like Snorri's wise Odin.

---

[60] Alver discusses the Norwegian *hug* (as in Icelandic *hugin*) and other ideas about the soul being separable from the body in Bente G. Alver, 'Concepts of the Soul in Norwegian Tradition', in *Nordic Folklore: Recent Studies*, ed. Reimund Kvideland and Henning K. Sehmsdorf (Bloomington, IN, 1989), pp. 110–27. 'Normally, every person had a *hug*. The *hug* could free itself for long or short periods of time and live its own life outside the body', p. 111.

[61] In opposition to this realism, consider the highly stylised warrior eagle on brooches and coins.

[62] Ravens are highly intelligent birds, and are often mischievous as they interact with humans. These characteristics, together with their interest in us, invite interpretation. For example, long after raven and dove appeared in the story of Noah in Genesis, Church Fathers such as Jerome interpreted the raven's abandoning of the Ark as proof of the bird's evil nature (Letter LXIX, 'To Oceanus'), but such negative symbolism is imposed upon, and misses the point of, a long-standing custom in which the raven's act of 'abandonment' is useful and sought. Before the invention of the compass, ravens hungry for land-based food were used for navigation in various cultures; when the bird flew up to see what lay beyond the seafarers' horizon, if it spotted land it flew in that direction, and the sailors could follow as indicated. The Mesopotamian hero Gilgamesh was said to have released a raven to find his way to land, as did, more historically, Flóki Vilgerðarson, the first Norwegian to travel to Iceland with the intention of settling there, whose story is told in the second chapter of *Landnámabók*. The account of Hrafna-Flóki ('Raven-Floki'), as he came to be called, is the only context in which Iceland normally features in books about ravens; see Heinrich, *Mind of the Raven*, pp. 23–4, for example.

[63] Referring to the ravens' names, John Lindow remarks that 'the ability to send one's "thought" and "mind" may be related to the trance-state journey of shamans. The worry about their return, expressed in the stanza from *Grímnismál*, would be consistent with the danger the shaman faces on the trance-state journey'; see Lindow, *Norse Mythology*, p. 188. Leslie Lockett briefly discusses Anglo-Saxon references to mind and memory travelling birdlike beyond the body, in *Anglo-Saxon Psychologies in the Vernacular and Latin Traditions* (Toronto, 2011), pp. 38–9.

While *Grímnismál*, the poem that Snorri quotes, gives Odin paired ravens and names them, perhaps for the first time, in the ninth or tenth century,[64] only Snorri himself in his description of *c*. 1200, over two centuries after the probable date of the throne sculpture, places them flanking the god and settling on his shoulders. This may also be the first time Odin's ravens are imagined as tame birds comfortable with humans, or at least with one quasi-human situated in a particular place. Although less persuaded than the Roskilde Museum writer who named the sculpture 'Odin fra Lejre', I too like to think (as opposed to firmly believing) that the figure on the Lejre throne is Odin communicating with his ravens – or rather, that the two birds at his side are his ravens intent on communicating with him. In any case, the person who invented this attribute of Odin in the first place, perhaps at the same time settling this god of the Wild Hunt into a fixed and named location, may have had paired farm ravens in mind. That would explain why medieval Icelandic sources give Odin two birds instead of the single bird that commonly identifies a Classical deity.

Once the idea that the ravens on the Lejre throne may be farm ravens is considered, however, the identity and gender of the figure on the throne is open once again to speculation, for tempting as the raven pair is as identifier, one can nevertheless oppose an array of factors against the figure on the Lejre throne's representing Odin – or even a man. Here are three: tiny thrones are associated with women's graves and the practice of *seiðr* (prophecy and magic); the person on the throne is clad in what looks like women's clothing (though Tom Christensen disputes that); and the woman of a farm, in control of after-breakfast scraps of bread, is more likely than a man to make friends with a local raven pair.

So what has this essay achieved, if it cannot come to a firm conclusion about the identity of the throne's occupant, or even his or her gender? The answer is that the calmly seated person is not the primary subject of this exploration; the ravens are, and about them three points have been made with varying degrees of assurance, as follows. The ravens, traditionally associated with prophecy, are in some kind of esoteric communication with the person seated between them on the throne; they *may* partake in the imagery of avian companions identifying deity (and thus may support the Odin hypothesis, though this raises another problem, about date); and their paired status identifies them

---

[64] Although the mythographer Rudolf Simek finds Odin associated with ravens from very early times, he doubts that the god's companion ravens were given names before the ninth or tenth century AD. See his *Dictionary of Northern Mythology*, trans. Angela Hall (Cambridge, 1993), p. 164.

as farm ravens or home ravens associated with fixed place, as opposed to the unfixed wandering of juveniles.

This final point has implications beyond speculations about the tiny Lejre throne and its quiet occupant. It appears that to Odin's earlier aspect as wolf-god leader of the wandering *männerbund*, mounted on his eight-legged horse, associated primarily with death and battle, and often accompanied by ravens (functioning as 'choosers of the slain' upon the battlefield, like Valkyries),[65] a second aspect was added, making Odin also a sedentary raven god seeking wisdom in his high hall. Flanked by a pair of mature ravens, Odin has thus been changed from an icon of aggressive ('adolescent'?) migratory peoples into one better representing a settled, if sometimes violent, population, such as that of Iceland, where already in the time of Snorri Sturluson farmsteads had been inhabited by the same stable family groups for several hundred years.[66]

---

[65] The Old Norse word *valkyrie* is a compound noun meaning 'chooser of the slain' and referring to Odin's winged female assistants who convey dead warriors to Valhalla. (Old English has a cognate form, *wælcyrige*, usually referring to witches.)

[66] It would not have been possible to write this essay without the assistance of the Interlibrary Loan Department at UC Davis and the patient personal help of Librarian Jason Newborn, whom I especially thank with this material that I believe he will enjoy. I am also profoundly indebted for guidance in the realm of bird studies to the ornithologist Cathy Toft, whose loss to cancer I deeply mourn, and to whose dear memory I dedicate my essay.

5

Beowulf's Blithe-Hearted Raven

Eric Lacey

In a curious scene in the middle of *Beowulf*, a raven appears joyfully heralding the arrival of a new day. The scene is entirely unparalleled in the extant Old English literature, where cheerful ravens ordinarily form part of the well-known 'beasts of battle' topos; in this guise they appear either relishing the proliferation of fresh carcasses after battle or eagerly anticipating the forthcoming feast before the fighting commences.[1] In the *Beowulf* passage, there is no such apparent slaughter. After Beowulf hunts down Grendel and his mother in their lair, he presents Hroðgar with the sword found therein (lines 1677–86), prompting Hroðgar to deliver a lengthy sermon on the follies of pride and fame (lines 1700–84) before the entire company feasts and sleeps (lines 1785–98). We are then told that:

> Reste hine þa rumheort;   reced hliuade
> geap ond goldfah;   gæst inne swæf,
> oþ þæt hrefn blaca   heofones wynne
> bliðheort bodode.   Ða com beorht [leoma]
> [ofer sceadwa] scacan;   scaþan onetton,
> wæron æþelingas   eft to leodum
> fuse to farenne;   wolde feor þanon
> cuma collenferhð,   ceoles neosan.[2]

---

[1] There is an extensive bibliography for the 'beasts of battle' topos in Old English. Some key studies are: F. P. Magoun, 'The Theme of the Beasts of Battle in Anglo-Saxon Poetry', *NM* 56 (1955), 81–90; M. S. Griffith, 'Convention and Originality in the Old English "Beasts of Battle" Typescene', *ASE* 22 (1993), 179–99; Adrien Bonjour, 'Beowulf and the Beasts of Battle', *Proceedings of the Modern Language Association* 72.4 (1957), 563–73; Thomas Honegger, 'Form and Function: The Beasts of Battle Revisited', *ES* 79.4 (1998), 289–98; Judith Jesch, 'Eagles, Ravens and Wolves: Beasts of Battle, Symbols of Victory and Death', in *The Scandinavians from the Vendel Period to the Tenth Century: An Ethnographic Perspective*, ed. Judith Jesch (Woodbridge, 2002), pp. 251–80; Joseph Harris, 'Beasts of Battle, South and North', in *Source of Wisdom: Old English and Early Medieval Latin Studies in Honour of Thomas D. Hill*, ed. Charles D. Wright, Fred M. Biggs and Thomas N. Hall (Toronto, 2007), pp. 3–25; Mark C. Amodio, *Writing the Oral Tradition: Oral Poetics and Literate Culture in Medieval England* (Notre Dame, IN, 2004), pp. 51–3.

[2] All references to *Beowulf* are to *Klaeber's Beowulf*, ed. R. D. Fulk, Robert E. Bjork and John D. Niles, 4th edn (Toronto, 2008). Translations throughout, unless otherwise noted, are my own. See also discussion of the raven in Osborn, Chapter 4 in this volume.

The munificent one (lit. 'roomy-hearted one', i.e. Beowulf) rested; the hall towered, spacious and gold-adorned. The guest slept inside until the bright/dark raven happily declared heaven's joy. Then came bright light, hurrying over the shadows; the warriors moved quickly, the princes were eager to journey back to their people; the visitor, bold of spirit, desired to seek out their ship, to voyage far away from there.

(*Beowulf*, lines 1799–806)

Many commentators have been taken aback by the perceived incongruity of the raven, a bird bearing 'sinister associations with death and carnage',[3] appearing as a 'joyous harbinger of the bright, radiant morning' that follows the first night of peaceful slumber after the elimination of Grendel and his mother.[4] The difficulties in interpreting this passage can be usefully categorised as stemming from two details. On the one hand, there is a lexical ambiguity in the adjective *blaca*, which may either be a weak nominative singular form of *blāc* ('bright', 'shining')[5] or a weak nominative singular form of *blæc* ('black').[6] This ambiguity is important because in Old English, as today, 'black' colour terms hold associations with evil and wickedness,[7] whereas 'bright' colour terms do not.[8] On the other hand, there is the puzzlingly positive description of the raven's joy and its resonance with the successful deliverance of Heorot from its monstrous attackers. As mentioned above, the raven's glee is not unusual in itself: glad ravens abound in Old English (and the closely related Old Norse) literature as part of the 'beasts of battle' topos. In *Beowulf* the joy of the *hrefn blaca* is unusual because there is nothing in the preceding or following lines to indicate that something like the 'beasts of battle' topos is at work. Furthermore, the raven's joy appears to be linked to the positive image of the rising sun and the associations of restoration that accompany it.

The discomfort experienced by commentators on this passage has led to some bizarre interpretations. The most unusual must be John Earle's suggestion that the *hrefn blaca* is no raven at all, but a

---

[3] Michael Lapidge, '*Beowulf* and Perception', *Proceedings of the British Academy* 111 (2001), 61–97 (p. 67).

[4] Martin Puhvel, 'The Blithe-Hearted Morning Raven in *Beowulf*', *English Language Notes* 10.4 (1973), 243–7 (p. 243).

[5] *DOE*, s.v. 'blāc'.

[6] *DOE*, s.v. 'blæc'.

[7] Carole P. Biggam, 'The Development of the Basic Colour Terms of English', in *Interfaces between Language and Culture in Medieval England: A Festschrift for Matti Kilpiö*, ed. Alaric Hall, Olga Timofeeva, Ágnes Kiricsi and Bethany Fox (Leiden, 2010), pp. 231–66 (pp. 258–9).

[8] This is not to say, however, that 'bright' colour terms were necessarily positive: OE *blāc* ('bright'), often used of fire and luminous celestial bodies (*DOE*, s.v. 'blāc', 1.a.), had a secondary meaning of 'pale', which could also describe the colour of pallid corpses, *DOE*, s.v. 'blāc', 2.b.

'black-cock', better known today as the Black Grouse (*Tetrao tetrix*).[9] As far-fetched as this suggestion may appear, it ultimately stems from a line of reasoning that is all too common: that the raven, so frequently associated with death, cannot be a good omen. The appeal of such an approach is clear given the prominence of the 'beasts of battle' topos in Old English, and given that all the subsequent raven references in *Beowulf* are associated with destruction.[10] We must be cautious, however, of how we use these later raven references to read into the *hrefn blaca*. As the first raven to be mentioned in *Beowulf*, it is the natural point of comparison for all subsequent ravens in the poem – and the number of these alone suggests their significance. Ravens later in the poem may force us to reconsider the *hrefn blaca* in hindsight, but it is fallacious simply to use the later raven scenes to illuminate the blithe-hearted raven. If anything, the *hrefn blaca* must inform the subsequent ravens.[11] Margaret Goldsmith gives us an example of exactly how we should not approach the matter when she remarks, during an analysis of the slaughter at Hrefnes Holt ('wood of the raven') later in the poem (lines 2922–98) that 'like the raven at Heorot, the ravens of *Hrefnesholt* herald a day of death'.[12] Her reasoning is not clearly articulated, but one cannot help but feel that it is flawed: on the one hand it is circular, and on the other hand, even though all the later raven references – even those contained within proper nouns like Hrefnes Holt, Dæghrefn (line 2501b) and Hrefna Wudu ('wood of the ravens', line 2925b) – are clearly linked with death and destruction, the raven at Heorot is not. The most satisfactory solution to the problems of interpreting this raven, then, must be one which evaluates the *hrefn blaca* on its own terms, and must situate the *hrefn blaca* among the subsequent raven references in the poem. I shall attempt to offer such a solution here.

---

[9] *The Deeds of Beowulf*, trans. J. A. Earle (Oxford, 1892), p. 170.
[10] The subsequent raven references in *Beowulf* are as follows: ravens are mentioned to express the grief felt by Hreðel at the death of his son (and Hygelac's brother) Herebeald (lines 2446b–2449); ravens appear alongside wolves and eagles heralding the destruction of the Geats at the hands of the Swedes (lines 3024b–3027); Hygelac's slayer is named Dæghrefn ('Day-raven', line 2501b); and in the place-names Hrefnes Holt (line 2935a), where the Swedish king Ongenþeow is slaughtered, and Hrefna Wudu (line 2925b), where Hygelac's brother Hæðcyn is killed. The possible mention of ravens in line 2941a is based on a conjecture. See *Klaeber's Beowulf*, ed. Fulk, Bjork and Niles, p. 260 nn. 2939–41.
[11] Sylvia H. Horowitz, 'The Ravens in *Beowulf*', *JEGP* 80.4 (1981), 502–11 (p. 502), echoes this sentiment when she notes that 'the repetition of a given word in various contexts in a poem deepens and modifies its meaning'.
[12] Margaret E. Goldsmith, *The Mode and Meaning of Beowulf* (London, 1970), p. 252. The 'day of death' she refers to here is a speculation buried in a footnote 180 pages earlier in her book (p. 72 n. 2): the intimated future tensions between Hroðgar and Hroðulf on lines 1014b–1017a and 1163b–1165a. It is little wonder that previous studies which cite Goldsmith's view here (such as Horowitz, 'The Ravens in *Beowulf*', p. 505 n. 13) do not explain what 'day of death' the raven at Heorot heralds.

Eric Lacey

Previous Interpretations

Many have attempted to make sense of the blithe-hearted raven, but no single interpretation has held favour for long, let alone reached a position that might be considered generally accepted. They can roughly be categorised into two camps: those who see the *hrefn blaca* as a positive image, and those who view it as bearing negative connotations. Those espousing the latter opinion have, without exception, focused on the raven's general association with death. We have already seen Goldsmith's casual classification of the *hrefn blaca* as a herald of death, a view similarly held by Richard North.[13] Both assume that the raven's widespread association with slaughter must be evoked in this curious scene, and search for reasons why death would be proclaimed at Heorot. Goldsmith's reading is purely circumstantial and not substantiated by the blithe-hearted raven's description at all: she links it with the 'hints of hidden hostility' between Hroðgar and Hroðulf (lines 1014b–1017a, and 1163b–1165a), who both live in Heorot at the time.[14] North's reading is grounded in the circumstances surrounding the *hrefn blaca*: he links the raven at Heorot with Beowulf's subsequent offer of military assistance to Hroðgar in the future (lines 1830–5), and the poem's prior disclosure of Ingeld's destructive raid upon the hall (lines 81–5).[15] However, North's suggestion (like Goldsmith's), does not address the curious link between the raven and the rising sun, which is central to the bird's presentation. Whitney Bolton takes this detail into account in his argument for the raven being 'ominous', viewing the 'alternation of day and night' as a 'token of mortality'.[16] The most sophisticated argument for the *hrefn blaca* being an evil omen – and the one with the most considered methodology – is that of Sylvia Horowitz. She examines this raven among the other raven references in the poem, makes comparative use of the Old Norse evidence, and also ties in references to the Flood before the raven's appearance at Heorot, arguing that it draws on Noah's raven: just as Noah's raven symbolises the postdiluvian survival of evil, so the *hrefn blaca* symbolises the continued presence of evil after the vanquishing of Grendel and his mother.[17] The reading is actually very similar to that of Allan Metcalf, who does not note any biblical nuances, but for whom the bird nevertheless signifies the 'eventual triumph of death

---

[13] Richard North, *The Origins of Beowulf: From Vergil to Wiglaf* (Oxford, 2006), p. 108.
[14] Goldsmith, *The Mode and Meaning of Beowulf*, p. 72 n. 2.
[15] North, *The Origins of Beowulf*, p. 108.
[16] W. F. Bolton, *Alcuin and Beowulf: An Eighth-Century View* (London, 1979), p. 92.
[17] Horowitz, 'The Ravens in *Beowulf*', *passim*; she also argues for ravens in the poem providing a commentary on Beowulf's inevitable death, pp. 506–7.

and sorrowful fate, however bright life seems in a glorious morning'.[18] There are problems with Horowitz's approach, however. Perhaps the single biggest issue is her spurious identification of Óðinn as 'the god of the sun' – and her consequent linking of the blithe-hearted raven's affinity with the sun to its role as this sun-god's messenger.[19]

Around the beginning of the twenty-first century, the so-called 'joke theory' propounded by Michael Lapidge and Andy Orchard became popular.[20] This theory is founded on the assumption that the raven necessarily forebodes slaughter, and proposes that various elements in the passage leading up to the raven's appearance suggest the possibility of another monster attack.[21] It ultimately has its roots in Howard Chickering's reading of the blithe-hearted raven, but seeks to rationalise why there is so much ambiguity in the passage.[22] The idea is interesting, and imaginatively engages with certain troubling phrases, but as with so many interpretations of the blithe-hearted raven, the 'joke theory' does not adequately account for the raven being linked with the sun. Lapidge says that the raven's declaration of the day dispels the tension – but the artful chiastic alliteration between the *blaca* of *hrefn blaca* and the subsequent a-line *bliðeheort bodode* ('proclaimed with joyful heart') suggests that there is a link between this adjective and the reason for the bird's blithe-hearted cry.[23] This will be revisited below, alongside considerations of the details that Lapidge identifies as 'teasing the audience (as it were) with the anticipation of another slaughter-attack'.[24]

In recent years there have been few endorsements of the idea that the blithe-hearted raven might be a good omen, though it was popular enough in the past for Horowitz to have described it as 'the consensus so far'.[25] Herbert Wright was tempted 'to regard it as another example of the employment of the symbol for the triumph of light over darkness and death',[26] and Kathryn Hume argued that the

---

[18] Allan Metcalf, 'Ten Natural Animals in *Beowulf*', NM 64 (1963), 378–89 (p. 381).
[19] Horowitz, 'The Ravens in *Beowulf*', pp. 503–4. Upon making this statement she references Hilda R. Ellis Davidson, *Gods and Myths of Northern Europe* (Harmondsworth, 1975), p. 50, who says nothing of the sort.
[20] Lapidge, '*Beowulf* and Perception'; Andy Orchard, *A Critical Companion to Beowulf* (Cambridge, 2001), pp. 77–8.
[21] Lapidge, '*Beowulf* and Perception', pp. 66–8; Orchard, *A Critical Companion to Beowulf*, pp. 77–8.
[22] *Beowulf: A Dual Language Edition*, ed. and trans. Howell D. Chickering Jr. (New York, 1977), pp. 344–7.
[23] Lapidge, '*Beowulf* and Perception', p. 67. See also Orchard, *A Critical Companion to Beowulf*, p. 77, who notes that this description (and its alliteration) 'is striking ... and surely hints at artifice'.
[24] Lapidge, '*Beowulf* and Perception', p. 67.
[25] Horowitz, 'The Ravens in *Beowulf*', p. 502.
[26] Herbert G. Wright, 'Good and Evil; Light and Darkness; Joy and Sorrow in *Beowulf*', *Review of English Studies* 8 (1957), 1–11, repr. in *Anthology of Beowulf Criticism*, ed. Lewis E. Nicholson (Notre Dame, IN, 1963), pp. 257–67 (p. 260).

raven was a good omen that signified the cleansing of Heorot and the fulfilment of Beowulf's vow that Hroðgar's retinue would be able to sleep peacefully in the hall once more (lines 1671b–1672),[27] though for her the detail of the raven heralding the day was 'an ornithological fact' rather than an item of literary significance.[28] Similarly, Gale Owen-Crocker suggests that the blithe-hearted raven is an expression of joy at the cleansing of Heorot.[29] Martin Puhvel took a structuralist approach to the issue and sought parallels for the raven as a good omen in Indo-European mythical traditions,[30] and such parallels also informed the commentaries on this passage in the editions of *Beowulf* by Michael Swanton and George Jack.[31] Partial endorsement of this idea is given by Horowitz and Chickering, who are both sensitive to the pervasive ambiguities in the passage. For Horowitz the raven initially suggests the triumph of the cleansing of Heorot, but as *Beowulf* progresses comes to symbolise death and the follies of heroic pride;[32] for Chickering the raven's ambiguous status as omen of victory, and its verbal echoes to the earlier attacks on the hall, 'impl[y] that the pattern of the warrior's life is an unending cycle of hall-joy followed by battle-sorrow'.[33]

It is worth briefly noting the varying claims of naturalism (or lack thereof) that have been offered by scholars in relation to the blithe-hearted raven. Metcalf's study of the 'natural animals' in *Beowulf* does not fall into this category, defining 'natural animals' in opposition to 'mythical' or 'supernatural beings',[34] but Hume's morning raven does, as does Marijane Osborn's suggestion that the *hrefn blaca* reflects something like the tame ravens found on Icelandic farms.[35] Lapidge questions any naturalistic presentation of the bird, saying that

---

[27] Kathryn Hume, 'The Function of the *Hrefn Blaca*: Beowulf 1801', *Modern Philology*, 67.1 (1969), 60–3 (p. 63).

[28] Ibid., p. 60.

[29] Gale Owen-Crocker, *The Four Funerals in Beowulf and the Structure of the Poem* (Manchester, 2000), p. 165.

[30] Puhvel, 'The Blithe-Hearted Morning Raven in *Beowulf*', passim.

[31] *Beowulf*, ed. and trans. Michael Swanton (Manchester, 1978), p. 125; *Beowulf*, trans. Burton Raffel (New York, 1963), p. 199: 'there is good evidence in both Norse and Latin literature that the raven was considered a prophetic bird which might augur either good or evil; and that the Anglo-Saxons shared in this tradition is indicated by early penitentials. Ravens characteristically herald daybreak, and the fifth-century Gallo-Roman poet Sidonius Apollinaris found the sound pleasing.' See also *Beowulf: A Student Edition*, ed. George Jack, 2nd edn (Oxford, 1997), p. 133: 'in both Norse and Latin tradition the raven is a bird of augury, which may presage good, and this must underlie its use in *Beowulf* to mark the joyful sunrise that follows the final conquest of Grendel's race'.

[32] Horowitz, 'The Ravens in *Beowulf*', pp. 502, 505–7.

[33] Chickering, *Beowulf*, p. 345.

[34] Metcalf, 'Ten Natural Animals in *Beowulf*', p. 378.

[35] Hume, 'The Function of the *Hrefn Blaca*', pp. 60–1; Marijane Osborn, 'Domesticating the Dayraven in *Beowulf* 1801 (With Some Reference to Alison's *Ston*)', in *Heroic Poetry in the Anglo-Saxon Period: Studies in Honor of Jess B. Bessinger, Jr.*, ed. Helen Damico and John Leyerle (Kalamazoo, MI, 1993), pp. 313–30. See also Osborn, Chapter 4 in this volume.

'ravens have at best a very dubious "dawn song"',[36] and is right in so far as there is little justification for ravens possessing vocalisations specifically for dawn. However, ravens are 'very loquacious',[37] and their vocalisations are heard frequently throughout the day and year.[38] Indeed, the advertising display of calling male ravens involves bowing motions that could easily elicit the notion that the bird is heralding something in the sky.[39] Allowing for naturalistic details does not undermine the bird's potential for literary significance, but can in fact contribute to it. The case in point here is the adjective used of the raven – *blaca* – which is as ambiguous as the passage itself, and warrants some discussion before these lines are analysed in detail.

Ambiguity and the Adjective blaca

Discussions of this passage in *Beowulf* have generally not adequately acknowledged the ambiguity of the adjective *blaca*. To many, it must have seemed like an open-shut case: *blaca* is a form of *blæc* ('black') and ravens are, indeed, black.[40] However, the importance of properly understanding this adjective cannot be overstated. Firstly, as noted above, it is imperative that we correctly identify the colour description used of the raven because the colour may – or may not – carry connotations crucial to our interpretation of the bird and this scene. Thus, when Lapidge asks 'why did the poet choose the *black*

---

[36] Lapidge, '*Beowulf* and Perception', p. 67.
[37] Derek Goodwin, *Crows of the World*, 2nd edn (London, 1986), p. 127.
[38] *Handbook of the Birds of Europe, the Middle East and North Africa: The Birds of the Western Palearctic*, ed. S. Cramp *et al.*, 9 vols. (Oxford, 1977–94), vol. 8, p. 216. This is the authoritative work on the basic zoology of birds in Europe and should be used in preference to the now very much outdated *The Handbook of British Birds*, ed. H. F. Witherby, 5 vols. (London, 1938–41). See also the anecdotal evidence for morning vocal activity in Derek Ratcliffe, *The Raven* (London, 1997), p. 106, and Bernd Heinrich, *Ravens in Winter* (London, 1991), *passim*.
[39] See the commentary and illustrations in Cramp *et al.*, *The Birds of the Western Palearctic*, vol. 8, p. 214.
[40] See, for example, the unqualified translation of *hrefn blaca* as 'the/a black raven' in *Beowulf*, trans. Seamus Heaney (London, 1999), p. 58; *Beowulf*, trans. Dick Ringer (Indianapolis, 2007), p. 95; Swanton, *Beowulf*, p. 125; Raffel, *Beowulf*, p. 79; *Beowulf*, trans. Kevin Crossley-Holland (Cambridge, 1968), p. 84; Chickering, *Beowulf*, p. 153. *Beowulf and the Finnesburg Fragment*, trans. J. R. Clark Hall, rev. C. L. Wrenn (London, 1950), p. 111, calls it a 'swarthy raven', which at least is less loaded than 'black', but which still assumes that *blaca* is a form of *blæc*. See also the glosses and glossaries in Fulk, Bjork and Niles, *Klaeber's Beowulf* (who follow Klaeber's third edition); Jack, *Beowulf*, p. 133; and *Beowulf: An Edition with Relevant Shorter Texts*, ed. B. Mitchell and F. Robinson (Oxford, 1998; repr. 2000), which all pointedly refer the reader, on consulting *blæc*, to line 1801. Without wishing to labour the point, this trend extends to critical studies on *Beowulf*, too: *hrefn blaca* is translated 'black raven' in Harris, 'Beasts of Battle', p. 12; and Lapidge, '*Beowulf* and Perception', p. 67. Orchard, *A Critical Companion to Beowulf*, p. 77, translates it as the 'dark raven', which has the same semantics and menacing connotations as 'black'.

raven to announce the joy of the coming day?' (emphasis mine),[41] his subsequent interpretation is a forgone conclusion: he has already decided that it is black and therefore bears evil connotations. Secondly, the chiastic alliteration between *blaca* and *bliðeheort bodode* on the subsequent line links the concepts and allows for the adjective to colour it: if the bird is black and evil then we should expect its joy to be linked with slaughter; if it is 'bright', then its joy may be linked to something much more pleasant.

It is helpful to provide an explanatory note for the weak form of the adjective *blaca*. Ordinarily weak adjective forms are used in definite constructions, i.e. when a determiner or pronoun modifies the same noun as the adjective.[42] This generalisation does not hold true for poetry, however, where weak adjectives are used more freely, and goes some way towards explaining the usage of *blaca* in the indefinite construction of *Beowulf* line 1801.[43] We must wonder, however, why the weak adjectival forms were used here when the strong forms would have dispelled any ambiguity (e.g. nom. sg. masc. *blæc*, 'black', and nom. sg. masc. *blāc*, 'bright').

There are reasons to be sceptical of the seemingly straightforward reading of *hrefn blaca* as 'black raven'. My major contention is that *blæc* ('black') does not occur anywhere else in *Beowulf*. The semantic field 'black'/'dark' is instead denoted by such terms as *won(n)*, which occurs five times (lines 651a *wann under wolcnum*, 702b *wanre niht*, 1374a *won to wolcnum*, 3024b *wonna hrefn*, and 3115 *wonna leg*); *deorc*, used four times (lines 160a *deorc deaþscua*, 275b *deorcum nihtum*, 1790a *deorc ofer dryhtgumum*, 2211 *deorcum nihtum*); *sweart*, used twice (lines 167b *sweartum nihtum*, 3145a *sweart ofer swioðole*), *myrce*, used once (line 1405a *myrcan mor*); and the verb *sweorcan*, used twice (lines 1737a *sefan sweorceð*, 1789b *nihthelm geswearc*). However, *blac* ('bright') does occur elsewhere in *Beowulf*. As a simplex it only occurs in *blacne leoman* ('bright light', line 1517a), as part of the description of the light radiating from the underwater hall that Beowulf espies as he swims to confront Grendel's mother. It occurs once elsewhere as part of what should presumably be a kenning for a sword (line 2848a), though

---

[41] Lapidge, '*Beowulf* and Perception', p. 67.
[42] Alistair Campbell, *Old English Grammar* (Oxford, 1959), §638; for a more detailed examination of the occurrence of weak adjectives, see Bruce Mitchell, *Old English Syntax*, vol. 1 (Oxford, 1985), §102ff.
[43] Campbell, *Old English Grammar*, 638; Mitchell, *Old English Syntax*, vol. 1, §114. Mitchell supports Campbell's observation that later poetry conforms more regularly to principle of using weak adjectives in definite constructions, though Mitchell is also careful to highlight the unreliability of the so-called 'Lichtenheld's test', a comparative dating technique based on the frequency of weak adjectives in definite and indefinite constructions. See also Ashley Crandell Amos, *Linguistic Means of Determining the Dates of Old English Literary Texts* (Cambridge, MA, 1980), pp. 122–4 (esp. p. 124).

the line is metrically deficient and an element beginning with /h/ is usually supplied.[44]

The argument that *blaca* may actually reflect a weak nominative singular masculine form of *blāc* ('bright', 'shining') has been put forward before. As far as I can tell, this was first advanced by Hume in the conclusion of her study on the *hrefn blaca*.[45] Some years later, Horowitz, despite drawing on Hume elsewhere, does not acknowledge the latter when she suggests that the 'primary meaning' of *blaca* may be 'shining',[46] but develops the idea by suggesting that 'the sound of the word suggests "black"'.[47] It is surprising that Owen-Crocker does not entertain this reading given her arguments for the *Beowulf*-poet playing on *blæc/blāc* elsewhere in the poem and her use of Horowitz's article.[48] North, despite not articulating his reasons for doing so, acknowledges the ambiguity of the adjective when he translates *hrefn blaca* as 'shining black raven'.[49] It has also been argued that *blaca* should mean 'white' here: John Damon argues for it reflecting the white raven in Classical tradition,[50] and Earl Anderson translates the *blaca* of *hrefn blaca* as 'white' with no further comment when arguing for reflexes of Indo-European cosmology in Old English.[51] In light of the other uses of *blāc* in *Beowulf*, as well as on self-evident ornithological grounds, it seems unlikely that 'white' is meant here.

While describing a raven as 'bright' might seem counter-intuitive, there are very plausible reasons for doing so. Ravens and other members of the genus *Corvidae* have iridescent feathers, which would justify the application of *blaca* (< *blāc*, 'bright'). Under the light, dark *Corvidae* feathers exhibit an almost metallic sheen,[52] and this naturalistic detail could be conjured by the description of the raven heralding *heofones wynne* ('heaven's joy', i.e. the sun) being bathed in sunlight at the dawn of a new day. There are similar observations in related literatures. One frequently noted parallel is the simile used by

---

[44] See Fulk, Bjork and Niles, *Klaeber's Beowulf*, p. 85, and the textual notes therein.
[45] Hume, 'The Function of the *Hrefn Blaca*', p. 63.
[46] Horowitz, 'The Ravens in *Beowulf*', p. 506.
[47] Ibid.
[48] Owen-Crocker, *The Four Funerals in Beowulf*, pp. 165–6. Moreover, her phrasing on p. 166, during her discussion of the *blacne leoman* ('radiant light', line 1517a) shining in Grendel's mother's underwater hall suggests that she does not recognise the potential for *blaca* to be a nominative singular masculine weak form of *blāc*: 'The poet plays on the near-homonyms *blāc*, meaning "pale" (related to Modern English "bleach" and "bleak") and *blæc* or *blaca*, meaning "dark", "black".'
[49] North, *The Origins of Beowulf*, p. 108.
[50] John E. Damon, 'The Raven in *Beowulf* 1801: Bird of a Different Color', *Work in Progress: Working Papers by Graduate Students of the English Department at the University of Arizona* 1 (1990), 60–70.
[51] Earl R. Anderson, *Folk Taxonomies in Early English* (London, 2003), p. 438.
[52] Goodwin, *Crows of the World*, pp. 124–5; Ratcliffe, *The Raven*, p. 269.

the Valkyrie Sigrún in the Eddic poem *Helgaqviða Hundingsbana ǫnnur*, at stanza 43.[53] Even though her lover, Helgi, was killed in battle, he is spotted riding into his burial mound; Sigrún rushes over to the mound, sees him, and says:

> Nú em ec svá fegin   fundi ocrom
> sem átfrekir   Óðins haucar,
> er val vito,   varmar bráðir,
> eða dǫgglitir   dags brún siá.[54]

Now I am as glad, at our meeting, as Óðinn's food-hungry hawks [= ravens] when they know of slaughter, the warmth of flesh, or dew-bright, they see the break of day.

The adjective *dǫgglitir* ('dew-bright') is a *hapax legomenon* but its constituent elements (the feminine noun *dǫgg*, 'dew', and the adjective *litr*, 'coloured', 'hued', and in some cases 'light') render its meaning rather clear.[55] Klaus von See *et al.* suggest this is an instance of a motif of 'dew-covered carrion birds' ('taubenetzte Aasvögel'), drawing attention to a semantically similar set of formulaic adjectives found in Old English: *deawigfeðera* ('dewy-feathered'), used of ravens (presumably) in *Genesis* line 1984b and *Exodus* line 164a, and *urigfeðera* ('wet-feathered'), used of the eagle in *The Seafarer* line 25a, *Judith* line 211b, and *Elene* lines 29a and 111a.[56] While the liquids mentioned on the birds' feathers is clearly meant to evoke blood in these Old English parallels (cf. the *deawig sceaftum*, 'dewy spears', in *Exodus* line 344a), there is probably an ornithological reality underlying these descriptions: white-tailed eagles frequently do have wet feathers, as they are fishing eagles,[57] and the gleaming iridescence of a raven's

---

[53] E.g. Harris, 'Beasts of Battle', p. 12; Puhvel, 'The Blithe-Hearted Morning Raven in *Beowulf*', p. 247; Fulk, Bjork and Niles, *Klaeber's Beowulf*, p. 217.

[54] *Edda: Die Lieder des Codex Regius*, ed. G. Neckel and H. Kuhn, 4th edn (Heidelberg, 1962), p. 159. All references to the poetic *Edda* are to this edition.

[55] It is worth noting that *litr* is frequently used of the light at daybreak, justifying the translation 'dew-bright' as much as 'dew-coloured'; the collocation of *dags brun* ('the break of day') makes the meaning 'dew-bright' all the more likely. See Johan Fritzner, *Ordbog over Det gamle norske Sprog*, bd. 4: *Rettelser og tillegg ved F. Hødnebø* (Bergen, 1972), s.v. 'litr'; Sveinbjörn Egilsson and Finnur Jónsson, *Lexicon Poeticum* (Copenhagen, 1931), s.v. 'litr'; Richard Cleasby and Gudbrand Vigfusson, *An Icelandic–English Dictionary* (Oxford, 1874), s.v. 'litr'. See also *The Elder Edda: A Book of Viking Lore*, trans. Andy Orchard (London, 2011), p. 143, who likewise translates *dǫgglitir* as 'dew-bright'.

[56] Klaus von See *et al.*, *Kommentar zu den Liedern der Edda*, bd. IV: *Heldenlieder* (Heidelberg, 2004), p. 784.

[57] The white-tailed eagle (*Haliaeetus albicilla*) was an apex predator and was historically much more common than it is today – indeed, it was the most widespread and common eagle in Anglo-Saxon England. See Derek W. Yalden and Umberto Albarella, *The History of British Birds* (Oxford, 2009), pp. 124–5; and Derek W. Yalden, 'The Older History of the White-Tailed Eagle in Britain', *British Birds* 100.8 (2007), 471–80. For their diets and behaviour, see Cramp *et al.*, *The Birds of the Western Palearctic*, vol. 2, pp. 48–58 (esp. pp. 52–3).

feathers, not dissimilar to the reflection of light from water droplets on a surface, could well have suggested the image of the bird being covered in dew.

A similar observation is made in the Middle Welsh *Angar kyfyndawt*. This poem is preserved in the so-called Book of Taliesin, which is dated on palaeographical grounds to the first half of the fourteenth century. Although the manuscript seems to reflect an older anthology, it is impossible to say how much older.[58] At one point in this rather lengthy poem, the poem's speaker, the supreme poet Taliesin, catalogues the occult and cryptic knowledge he possesses, which includes *pan yw gwyrliw brein* ('why the raven is green/iridescent', line 164).[59] The adjective *gwyrliw* is usually emended to, or translated as, *gwyrddliw* (nominally 'green', though this word is also used to describe the sea);[60] however Marged Haycock has recently proposed that *gwyrliw* may contain the first element *gwŷr* ('bent', 'distorted', 'unjust'),[61] and suggests that 'refracting' or 'reflecting' is a possible semantic extension in *gwyrliw*.[62] Whether *gwyrliw* means 'refracted' or 'green', in one way or another it describes some aspect of the raven's iridescent feathers.[63]

Comparative evidence for the observation of the raven's iridescence, alongside the use of *blac* ('bright') within *Beowulf*, raises the serious possibility that the adjective *blaca* is a form of *blac* rather than *blæc* ('black'). At the very least the adjective is ambiguous, and this ambiguity resonates with the uncertainty that pervades the scene more generally. Mornings are revelatory moments in *Beowulf*, which have the potential to reveal favourable as well as unfavourable tidings. It is at dawn, for example, that the people of Heorot see the extent of Grendel's destruction (lines 126–9, 484), and that news spreads about the subsequent attack by his mother (lines 1311bff.). However, it is also at dawn that the people of Heorot behold Grendel's disembodied hand (lines 837ff., 916bff.), and that Hygelac saves the Geats trapped in Hrefnes Holt by Ongenþeow (lines 2941bff.). It is unclear what sort

---

[58] *Legendary Poems from the Book of Taliesin*, ed. and trans. M. Haycock (Aberystwyth, 2007), pp. 1, 6–9.

[59] Ibid., p. 118. Haycock's edition is authoritative, but can be difficult to acquire; a somewhat more accessible edition (and translation), though lacking Haycock's extensive notes, is found in Sarah L. Higley, *Between Languages: The Uncooperative Text in Early Welsh and Old English Nature Poetry* (University Park, PA, 1993), pp. 284–92. The older edition, with an accompanying translation, available in *Poems from the Book of Taliesin*, ed. and trans. John Gwenogvryn Evans (Llanbedrog, 1915), pp. 10–26, is often unreliable.

[60] R. J. Thomas *et al.*, *Geiriadur Prifysgol Cymru: A Dictionary of the Welsh Language* (Cardiff, 1956–), s.v. 'gwyrddliw'. See also Higley, *Between Languages*, p. 289, and Evans, *Poems from the Book of Taliesin*, pp. 20–1.

[61] *Geiriadur Prifysgol Cymru*, s.v 'gwŷr¹'.

[62] Haycock, *Legendary Poems*, p. 153 n. 164.

[63] See, for example, the comments in Ratcliffe, *The Raven*, p. 269, and Cramp *et al.*, *The Birds of the Western Palearctic*, vol. 8, p. 220.

of morning the blithe-hearted raven heralds. One would expect it to be a joyful occasion, given Beowulf's dispatch of the monsters, but Lapidge, following Chickering, notes that there are verbal collocations which are reminiscent of the previous monster attacks. There is the 'characteristic use of *oþ þæt*, anticipating a reversal', the repetition of *þa wæs eft swa ær* ('then it was as it was previously', lines 642a, 1787a), and the descriptions of the coming of night.[64] Chickering, moveover, draws attention to the unusually hurried pace of the scene, with its possible implication that the warriors are running away from something, as well as to oddly positive nuances, such as the night being described protectively (e.g. as *nihthelm*, 'night-helmet', line 1789b).[65] Horowitz draws attention to further lexical ambiguities in the passage, e.g. *rumheort* ('munificent', but lit. 'roomy-hearted', line 1799a), which could apply to both Beowulf and Heorot; *gæst* (line 1800b), which could mean either 'guest'/'visitor', or 'ghost'/'spirit'; and *scaþan* (lit. 'scathing ones', line 1803b), which is normally used of evil-doers but here applies to Beowulf's party. Horowitz also suggests that the description of the hall (*reced hliuade/ geap and goldfah*, 'the hall towered, spacious and gold-adorned', lines 1799b–1800a) recalls the golden banner on Scyld's burial ship (*segen gyldenne/ heah ofer heafod*, 'the golden banner, high over head', lines 47b–48a), though I find this last connection tenuous.[66]

The implication of all this is that the ambiguity which has troubled commentators so much is intentional, and that the scene is supposed to be disorienting and troubling. In spite of this, it soon becomes apparent that that particular morning brought good tidings: in addition to repaying Ecgþeow's old debt to Hroðgar, Beowulf has fulfilled two boasts he makes on separate occasions. One, previously noted by Hume, is that made by the hero after he presents to Hroðgar the hilt of the sword used to slay Grendel's mother:

> Ic hit þe þonne gehate   þæt þu on Heorote most
> sorhleas swefan   mid þinra secga gedryht
> ond þegna gehwylc   þinra leoda,
> duguðe ond iogðue,   þæt þu him ondrædan ne þearft,
> þeoden Scyldinga,   on þa healfe,
> aldorbealu eorlum,   swa þu ær dydest.

I promise it to you that you will be able to sleep free from cares in Heorot with your retinue of men, and each of your thanes of your country too, old retainers and young retainers, so that you do not need

---

[64] Lapidge, '*Beowulf* and Perception', pp. 66–7 (whence the quotation); Chickering, *Beowulf*, pp. 344–5.
[65] Chickering, *Beowulf*, p. 345.
[66] Horowitz, 'The Ravens in *Beowulf*', p. 506.

to fear any danger, any life-threats to your men on that account, Lord of the Scyldings, as you previously did.

(*Beowulf*, lines 1671–6)

The other boast is made by Beowulf before his initial confrontation with Grendel, during his conversation with Unferð:

> Ac ic him Geata sceal
> eafoð ond ellen   ungeara nu,
> guþe gebeodan.   Gæþ eft se þe mot
> to medo modig,   siþþan morgenleoht
> ofer ylda bearn   oþres dogores,
> sunne sweglwered   suþan scineð.

But now I shall soon demonstrate for him (Grendel) the strength and valour of the Geats in battle. Once again, the one who is able to do so will go mead-drinking in high spirits, after the morning light of another day, the sun clothed in radiance, shines from the south over the children of men'.

(*Beowulf*, lines 601b–606)

The blithe-hearted raven scene thus ultimately becomes – after the ambiguity of the unusual details – an illustration of the accomplishment of Beowulf's goals: Beowulf has killed the monsters, Hroðgar and his retinue have been able to sleep without sorrow, and they are able to rejoice in their ordinary patterns of life in the shining sun. This realisation causes a re-evaluation of the ambiguous details into plausibly innocent flourishes, e.g. that the *gæst* which rested within the hall was Beowulf, not yet another monster, and that the temporal referent of *þa wæs eft swa ær* ('then it was as it was previously') was the time before Grendel's attack, not during it. Yet in order for this to work conceptually, there must also have been some way for the *hrefn blaca* itself to be cast in a more positive light than is normally seen in its role as a beast of battle. Internal evidence, in the pairing of *bliðeheort* (used of the raven's call, line 1802a) and *rumheort* (line 1799a), suggests this too.

The 'Good' Blithe-Hearted Raven

There are no ravens comparable to the seemingly positively depicted *hrefn blaca* in Old English literature, though some can be found in Old Norse texts. In the past commentators have provided the previously quoted stanza 43 from *Helgaqviða Hundingsbana ǫnnur* as a reasonably close parallel to the scene in *Beowulf*.[67] There, as in *Beowulf*, the joy of

---

[67] Puhvel, 'The Blithe-hearted Morning Raven in *Beowulf*', p. 247; Fulk, Bjork and Niles, *Klaeber's Beowulf*, p. 217; Harris, 'Beasts of Battle', p. 12.

the ravens is closely linked with the sun, and despite the arguments of Klaus von See *et al.*, this joy does not seem to be associated with carrion: the coordinator *eða* ('or') suggests that their happiness seeing daybreak is for some other reason.[68] Puhvel and Harris both argue that there was a 'genuine poetic tradition' involving ravens at daybreak, though Harris's scope is more modest, situating this tradition among other Old Norse parallels and not speculating beyond the existence of such a topos.[69] A possible reason for the raven's joy at daybreak may be inferred from *Grímnismál*, which famously describes Óðinn's ravens thus:

> Huginn oc Muninn fliúga hverian dag
>   iǫrmungrund yfir;
> óomc ec of Huginn, at hann aptr né komið,
> þó siámc meirr um Munin.

Huginn and Muninn fly out every day over the enormous earth; I fear that Huginn will not come back to me, yet I fear it even more about Muninn.

(*Grímnismál*, stanza 20)

Snorri Sturluson, who was drawing on *Grímnismál*, elaborates on why Óðinn wants his ravens to return in *Gylfaginning*: the ravens sit upon Óðinn's shoulders and tell him *ǫll tíðindi þau er þeir sjá eða heyra* ('all the tidings which they see or hear').[70] Their joy at daybreak, then, may be linked to the visibility that accompanies the dawn, and the opportunity to clearly perceive, collect and relate events in the world. Ravens similarly act as news-bringers in the eddic poems *Helgaqviða Hundingsbana in fyrri* 5, *Guðrúnarqviða ǫnnur* 8, and *Brot af Sigurðarqviða* 5 and 13, and can also be seen in this role in stanzas of verse attributed to an Icelandic farmer named Hrómundr *halta* ('the limp'), preserved in *Hrómundar þáttr halta* and the *Sturlubók* version of *Landnámabók*.[71] We should note, too, that the raven's two roles as news-bringer and herald of death are not mutually exclusive. For example, in the skaldic poem known variously as *Haraldskvæði* and *Hrafnsmál*, attributed to the ninth-century poet Þórbjorn hornklofi, a Valkyrie converses with ravens who have been following King Haraldr Hárfagri's martial exploits. The ravens tell her the news of his campaigns as well as of

---

[68] Von See *et al.*, *Kommentar zu den Liedern der Edda*, bd. IV: *Heldenlieder*, pp. 782–6 (esp. pp. 783–4).
[69] Puhvel, 'The Blithe-Hearted Morning Raven in *Beowulf*', *passim*; Harris, 'Beasts of Battle', pp. 12 and 23 n. 50.
[70] *Edda: Prologue and Gylfaginning*, ed. Anthony Faulkes (London, 2005), ch. 38.
[71] *Hrómundr þáttr halta* can be found in *Vatnsdæla Saga*, ed. Einar Ól. Sveinsson, Íslenzk Fornrit 8 (Reykjavík, 1939), pp. 303–15; this episode in the *Sturlubók* version of *Landnámabók* can be found in *Íslendingabók: Landnámabók*, ed. Jakob Benediktsson, Íslenzk Fornrit 1 (Reykjavík, 1986), p. 202.

the abundance of carrion they have been able to feast on.[72] Indeed, ravens are depicted similarly in *Beowulf* lines 3024b–2027, as they discuss their plundering of the corpses after the impending conflicts between the Swedes and Geats:

> ... ac se wonna hrefn
> fus ofer fægum   fela reordian,
> earne secgan   hu him æt æte speow,
> þenden he wið wulf   wæl reafode.

> ... but the dark raven, eager for the fated [to die], tells many speeches to the eagle, how he succeeded at the feast when he plundered the corpses against the wolf.
> (*Beowulf*, lines 3024b–3027)

Closer geographically than the Norse material, however, and not previously compared with the *hrefn blaca*, is a curious incident in the Anglo-Latin *Vita Gregorii Magni*.[73] This eighth-century Northumbrian text is notable for its 'unrestrained deployment of folklore motifs' drawn from local tradition.[74] At one point it relates that during the conversion of King Edwin of Northumbria, he and a large group of *genilitati* ('pagans') had been in the royal hall, where they had been *utrumque emendandum hortati* ('exhorted to put ... matters right'), i.e. to undergo baptism.[75] Upon leaving the hall they heard:

> ... stridula cornix ad plagam voce peiorem cantavit. Tunc omnis multitudo regia quę adhuc erat in platea populi, audiens avem, stupore ad eam conversa subsistit, quasi illud canticum novum carmen Deo nostro non esset vero futurum in ecclesia, sed falso ad nihil utile.[76]

> ... a crow set up a hoarse croaking from an unpropitious quarter of the sky. Thereupon the whole of the company, who were still in the public square, heard the bird and turned towards it, halting in amazement as if they believed that the 'new song' in the church was not to be 'praise onto our God' but something false and useless.

According to the narrator, the call of the crow was from an 'unpropitious corner of the sky', though clearly it was not considered unfavourable by those who stopped to listen to it, and moreover, were tempted by its message. The identification of the bird as a *cornix*,

---

[72] *Den norsk-islandske skjaldedigtning*, ed. Finnur Jónsson, 4 vols. (Copenhagen, 1912–15), B1, pp. 22–5.
[73] All references to this text are to *The Earliest Life of Gregory the Great*, ed. and trans. Bertram Colgrave (Cambridge, 1968). This translation is Colgrave's.
[74] Walter Goffart, *The Narrators of Barbarian History (A.D. 550–800): Jordanes, Gregory of Tours, Bede and Paul the Deacon* (Notre Dame, IN, 2005), p. 265.
[75] Colgrave, *Earliest Life of Gregory the Great*, pp. 96–7 (ch. 15).
[76] Ibid., p. 96.

usually translated 'crow', may appear to be a barrier to linking it with the *Beowulf* passage, however it is important to note that *cornix* could refer to the raven as well.[77] In the *Vita Gregorii Magni*, then, we have possible evidence for a tradition in which ravens could impart information outside the realm of carnage and slaughter. If we use the Old Norse evidence to inform both the unusual use of the *cornix* in the *Vita Gregorii Magni* and the *hrefn blaca* – and this seems to be justified somewhat by *Beowulf* lines 3024b–3027 – then we are left with the possibility of the blithe-hearted raven being a good omen, whether in the more general declaration of the purging of the monstrous threat from Heorot or, more specifically, in relation to the deaths of Grendel and his mother themselves. The blithe-hearted raven's joy at the sun's appearance fits both this celebratory context and the inference from *Grímnismál* 20, in which daylight brings the clear revelation of the hall's safety.

The 'Bad' Blithe-Hearted Raven

If the raven initially appears to be a good omen, then this is later revealed to be illusory. In addition to the negative connotations of some of the phrasing at the appearance of the *hrefn blaca*, we must also reckon with the 'meaningful pattern of raven imagery' observed by Horowitz in the poem (though I argue for a far simpler pattern).[78] Each subsequent raven reference in *Beowulf* is closely associated with death. Ravens form part of a comparison for Hreðel's expression of grief and powerlessness at the accidental slaying of Herebeald by Hæðcyn (lines 2446b–2449) and feature in the 'beasts of battle' topos during the unnamed warrior's prophecy following Beowulf's death (lines 3024b–3027). They reappear in the personal name of Hygelac's slayer, Dæghrefn (line 2501b), and the place-names Hrefna Wudu ('wood of the ravens', line 2925b) and Hrefnes Holt ('wood of the raven', line 2935a), referring to a forest in Sweden where Ongenþeow massacres some Geats, the remnants of whom are saved by Hygelac in a daring raid.[79] Moreover, there are two other constants running through these

---

[77] J. André, *Les Noms d'oiseaux en Latin* (Paris, 1967), p. 61. Furthermore, the absence of *hroc* (nominally 'rook') and *crawe* (nominally 'crow') in Old English poetry suggests a poetic register in which all of these members of the crow family were subsumed under *hrefn*. For more on this, see Eric Lacey, 'When is a *hroc* not a *hroc*? When it is a *crawe* or *hrefn*!', in *The Art, Literature and Material Culture of the Middle Ages: Transition, Transformation and Taxonomy*, ed. Megan Boulton, Jane Hawkes and Melissa Herman (forthcoming).

[78] Horowitz, 'The Ravens in *Beowulf*', p. 502.

[79] Hrefnes Holt and Hrefna Wudu, despite the slight difference in meaning, are generally thought to refer to the same place, and to allude to the bird rather than – as is possible for Hrefnes Holt (with its genitive singular) – a man named Hrefn (i.e. 'wood of Hrefn'). See Margaret Gelling, *Signposts to the Past*, 2nd edn (Chichester, 1988), p. 165.

subsequent raven references which have not previously been noted. One is the consistency of allusions to dawn. Hreðel's inability to avenge Herebeald's death is compared with the inconsolable man whose son hangs for the raven's pleasure (*hrefn to hroðre*), and who is reminded of his loss *morna gehwylce* ('each morning', line 2450b). Hygelac rescues the Geats at Hrefna Wudu/Hrefnes Holt in the morning (lines 2941b–2945), and similarly, the raven that eagerly anticipates the Swedish–Geatish conflict at the end of the poem wakes warriors who have *morgenceald* ('morning-cold') spears (line 3021a). The link between the name of Hygelac's slayer, Dæghrefn, and the blithe-hearted raven's unusual ushering in of a new day has been noted before, though without any attempt to explain the significance of the parallel.[80] In each of these cases the combination of raven allusion and dawn/day imagery invites a comparison with the blithe-hearted raven – but how different these scenes are! Especially when viewed in light of the second strand that runs through all raven references after the blithe-hearted raven: a connection with the destruction of the Geats. This is seen in the ravens used to describe Hreðel's grief, but is perhaps clearest in connection with the name of Hygelac's slayer, Dæghrefn. Moreover, despite the celebratory potential for Hygelac's dawn-raid at Hrefnes Holt/Hrefna Wudu, this very event is later identified as the reason for the impending Swedish invasions following Beowulf's death (lines 2999–3007). Indeed, the final raven in the poem (line 3024) portends the complete destruction of the Geatish kingdom with this invasion, and, furthermore, this final raven in the poem harks back to the blithe-hearted raven by being the only other raven described as speaking and described by colour: the *hrefn blaca* is given the verb *bodian* (*bodode*, 'declared', line 1802a), while the final bird is described as sharing many words (*fela reordian*, line 3025b); the blithe-hearted raven's ambiguous description *blaca* ('bright'/'black') becomes coloured by the final raven's unequivocal colouration as *wonna* ('dark').

The effect of this is cumulative. While the blithe-hearted raven initially appears positive because of the context of Beowulf's purging the monstrous threat from Heorot, the presentation of subsequent ravens in the poem resonates with the more sinister connotations of lines 1799–1806, and the repetition of allusions to dawn recall one of the most unusual – and potentially positive – aspects of the *hrefn blaca* scene. Each subsequent raven, therefore, undermines the seemingly auspicious depiction of the blithe-hearted raven, and increasingly links the bird with death until the final raven of the poem, embedded

---

[80] Fulk, Bjork and Niles, *Klaeber's Beowulf*, p. 207 n. 1801, repeats the identification previously made by Klaeber himself in *Beowulf*, ed. F. Klaeber (Lexington, MA, 1950), p. 192 n. 1801.

in the unnamed messenger's prophecy of future ruin, ominously heralds the forthcoming invasion of the Swedes.

The Blithe-Hearted Raven: A New Reading

This chapter argues for an intricate reading of *Beowulf*'s blithe-hearted raven that takes into account the raven's immediate context, the collective use of ravens in *Beowulf*, and the wider cultural contexts. I have stressed the ambiguity of the scene, which has troubled so many commentators on the poem, and suggested that the ambiguity is intentional based on the menacing implications in an otherwise triumphant context, as well as the ambiguous form (and potential meanings) of the adjective *blaca*. Moreover, I have argued for the *Beowulf*-poet's drawing on a tradition in which ravens could bring information which was not necessarily slaughter-related, and that the blithe-hearted raven scene, for all its troubling ambivalence, initially appears to be positive: the raven stands as a harbinger of the success of Beowulf's campaign against Grendel and his mother, and the fulfilment of his previous boasts about the restoration of the hall. However, the scene's sinister nuances, and the striking image of the raven heralding the rising sun, are alluded to and recalled by the subsequent raven references in the poem, inviting comparisons with the first raven while simultaneously recasting it in a more negative light. This culminates in the poem's final raven, which parallels the blithe-hearted raven in colour and vocality, but is unequivocally a portent of future destruction. In retrospect, the bithe-hearted raven can either be seen as presaging Beowulf's death specifically (as other ravens link with specific members of the Geatish royal line, Herebeald and Hygelac), or as a precursor to the *wonna hrefn* that portends the destruction of the Geats. The blithe-hearted raven, then, is a multivalent and unstable image, whose meaning changes over the course of the poem.

6

Do Anglo-Saxons Dream of Exotic Sheep?

László Sándor Chardonnens

In discussing the archaeological record, art, place-names, historiography and literature, the essays in this volume highlight the coexistence of people and animals in early medieval England. The Germanic tribes and few stray Celts who inhabited it lived in close proximity to a range of domestic and wild animals, the former category including cats and dogs, chickens and geese, horses and asses, cattle and pigs, sheep and goats, while the latter included fish, sea mammals, snakes, birds, deer, otters, badgers, rabbits, hares and all kinds of animal pests; particularly notable among the wild species were wolves, ravens and eagles – the three iconic beasts of battle commemorated in heroic poetry. Yet whereas most Anglo-Saxons would have been familiar with these *nytenu* and *deora*, including dragons (as the *Anglo-Saxon Chronicle* reminds us), it would be a stretch to assume that this familiarity extended to exotic animal species, such as camels, elephants, lions, phoenixes and scorpions.[1] The Bible, the *Physiologus*, the *Medicina de quadrupedibus* and other non-Germanic sources testified to the existence of these animals in far-away corners of the world, and readers of the *Wonders of the East* would have encountered descriptions and depictions of fabulous beasts with eight legs, two heads and Valkyries' eyes, of *lertices* with asses' ears, sheep's wool and birds' feet, and many other *ungefregelicu deor* ('extraordinary beasts').[2] However, these written sources represented a world that was utterly different from Anglo-Saxon England, and they targeted highly educated audiences that were presumed to have been able to put these strange beasts into context.

Even though early medieval ideas about the natural world are far more integrative than modern attempts to categorise that world into discrete taxonomic ranks, there would seem to be a divide between the animal world that Anglo-Saxons could readily observe and the beasts that they knew only through religious and learned sources from the Mediterranean and the Near East. While indigenous creatures

---

[1] On dragons in the *Anglo-Saxon Chronicle*, see Symons, Chapter 3 in this volume.
[2] Andy Orchard, *Pride and Prodigies: Studies in the Monsters of the Beowulf-Manuscript* (Cambridge, 1995), p. 186.

were domesticated, processed, hunted, avoided, feared or venerated, exotic animals were read about and marvelled at, and their absence from the Anglo-Saxon natural world led to their becoming the subject of metaphor and allegory. Animals, therefore, could be understood either as the output of God's creation, or as the input for symbolic thought.

A similar distinction can be discerned in early medieval techniques for foretelling the future. Taking dreams, natural phenomena, and significant moments in time as signs of future events, prognostication places that which has yet to happen on the same level of certainty as the present and the past. Whereas prognostication today is largely limited to weather forecasts, the Anglo-Saxons had a wide range of prognostic techniques at their disposal. These were inherited from the same Mediterranean and Near Eastern cultures that provided the basis for religion and learning; they first reached Continental monasteries in the late eighth century, and moved into Anglo-Saxon foundations in the ninth.[3] Prognostication offered tools with which to interpret the future in all areas of life, from human concerns such as war and peace, life and death, health and illness, wealth and poverty, happiness and adversity, to noteworthy events in the natural world, including meteorology, agriculture and animal husbandry. This chapter examines the kinds of beasts that feature in prognostications from Anglo-Saxon England. Depending on the technique employed, prognostications may reveal the fate of animals as part of the output of a prediction, or their symbolic value as part of the input. The former tend to be closer to the Anglo-Saxon natural world than the latter, though some Anglo-Saxon scribes interfered with the homely animal

---

[3] For general studies of prognostication in Anglo-Saxon England, see Rolf. H. Bremmer and László S. Chardonnens, 'Old English Prognostics: Between the Moon and the Monstrous', in *Monsters and the Monstrous in Medieval Northwest Europe*, ed. Karin E. Olsen and Luuk A. J. R. Houwen (Leuven, 2001), pp. 153–66; László S. Chardonnens, *Anglo-Saxon Prognostics, 900–1100: Study and Texts* (Leiden, 2007); László S. Chardonnens, 'Context, Language, Date and Origin of Anglo-Saxon Prognostics', in *Foundations of Learning: The Transfer of Encyclopaedic Knowledge in the Early Middle Ages*, ed. Rolf H. Bremmer and Kees Dekker (Leuven, 2007), pp. 317–40; László S. Chardonnens, 'Appropriating Prognostics in Late Anglo-Saxon England: A Preliminary Source Study', in *Practice in Learning: The Transfer of Encyclopaedic Knowledge in the Early Middle Ages*, ed. Rolf H. Bremmer and Kees Dekker (Leuven, 2010), pp. 203–55; László S. Chardonnens, 'Norm and Practice of Divination and Prognostication in Late Anglo-Saxon England', in *Mantik, Schicksal und Freiheit im Mittelalter*, ed. Loris Sturlese and Katrin Bauer (Cologne, 2011), pp. 51–64; Max Förster, 'Die Kleinliteratur des Aberglaubens im Altenglischen', *Archiv für das Studium der neueren Sprachen und Literaturen* 110 (1903), 346–58; Max Förster, 'Beitrage zur mittelalterlichen Volkskunde I–IX', *Archiv für das Studium der neueren Sprachen und Literaturen* 120 (1908), 43–52, 296–305; 121 (1908), 30–46; 125 (1910), 39–70; 127 (1911), 31–84; 128 (1912), 55–71, 285–308; 129 (1912), 16–49; 134 (1916), 264–93; Roy M. Liuzza, 'Anglo-Saxon Prognostics in Context: A Survey and Handlist of Manuscripts', *ASE* 30 (2001), 181–230; Roy M. Liuzza, *Anglo-Saxon Prognostics: An Edition and Translation of Texts from London, British Library, MS Cotton Tiberius A. iii* (Cambridge, 2011). Studies of specific prognostic techniques are referred to in the notes below.

world displayed in prognostications in order to make the predictions seem more exotic.

That the fate of animals was sometimes not to be envied is poignantly demonstrated by the opening lines of the Old English *De diebus malis*:

> Þa ealdan læcas gesettan on ledenbocun þæt on ælcum monðe beoð æfre twegen dagas þe syndan swyðe derigendlice ænigne drenc on to ðicgenne, oððe blod on to lætenne, forðan þe an tid is on ælcum þæra daga gif man ænige æddran geopenað on þære tide, þæt hit bið his lifleast, oððe langsum sar. Þæs cunnode sum læce, let his horse blod on þære tide, and hit læg sona dead.[4]

> The doctors of old wrote in Latin books that there are always two days in each month on which it is very harmful to drink any [medicinal] potion or to let blood, because there is an hour in each of these days during which a vein that is opened will cause death or protracted pain. A certain physician tried this – bled his horse on such an hour – and it lay dead immediately.

This excerpt reports how a physician experimented (OE *cunnode*) on an animal, with lethal consequences, on one of the so-called Egyptian Days. These were the most feared of evil days in Late Antiquity and the Middle Ages, because it was thought that those who let blood or took medication on one of these days would almost certainly die.[5] Various lists of Egyptian Days existed, recording three, twelve or twenty-four *plihtlice dagas* ('dangerous days').[6] In the type under discussion, two days were arbitrarily assigned to each month (e.g. 1 and 25 January, 4 and 26 February), which together make up the twenty-four Egyptian Days that survive in thousands of medieval manuscripts, particularly in liturgical calendars. As the *De diebus malis* demonstrates, animals

---

[4] London, British Library, MS Harley 3271, fols. 90v–91r; László S. Chardonnens, 'Ælfric and the Authorship of the Old English *De diebus malis*', in *Limits to Learning: The Transfer of Encyclopaedic Knowledge in the Early Middle Ages*, ed. Concetta Giliberto and Loredana Teresi (Leuven, 2013), pp. 123–53 (p. 127). All translations are mine unless noted otherwise.

[5] On Egyptian Days, see Chardonnens, *Anglo-Saxon Prognostics*, pp. 330–92; Chardonnens, 'Norm and Practice of Divination'; Chardonnens, 'Ælfric and the *De diebus malis*'; Max Förster, 'Die altenglischen Verzeichnisse von Glücks- und Unglückstagen', in *Studies in English Philology: A Miscellany in Honor of Frederick Klaeber*, ed. Kemp Malone and Martin B. Ruud (Minneapolis, 1929), pp. 258–77; Heinrich Henel, 'Altenglischer Mönchsaberglaube', *Englische Studien* 69 (1934–5), 329–49; Gundolf Keil, 'Die verworfenen Tage', *Sudhoffs Archiv für Geschichte der Medizin und der Naturwissenschaften* 41 (1957), 27–58; Jules Loiseleur, 'Les Jours égyptiens: Leurs variations dans les calendriers du moyen-âge', *Mémoires de la Société nationale des antiquaires de France* 33 (1872), 198–253; Robert Steele, 'Dies Aegyptiaci', *Proceedings of the Royal Society of Medicine* 12, Section of the History of Medicine, Supplement (1919), 108–21; Lynn Thorndike, *A History of Magic and Experimental Science during the First Thirteen Centuries of our Era*, 8 vols. (New York, 1923–58), vol. 1, pp. 685–8.

[6] London, British Library, MS Cotton Vitellius C. viii, fol. 22r–v (Chardonnens, *Anglo-Saxon Prognostics*, p. 342).

suffered the same fate as humans if they were bled on an Egyptian Day. Though it might be considered cruel and unethical to subject an animal to an experiment whose deadly outcome is fixed in advance, the point to be considered here is that the physician decided to use a horse instead of (for instance) a camel. In fact, this reference to veterinary medicine ensured that this hapless horse was the only animal out of approximately 175 Anglo-Saxon prognostications to make it into Frederick Smith's *Early History of Veterinary Literature and its British Development*.[7] What Smith did not know, however, is that the prognostications which appear in Anglo-Saxon manuscripts do not represent a native Germanic tradition, but reflect older, non-Germanic mantic practices. The reference to a horse, then, is pure chance; it might as well have been a camel, were it not for the fact that the medical experiment in the *De diebus malis* was an *ad hoc* addition by an Anglo-Saxon scribe. The Latin source on which the scribe based his translation reads: *autenticorum in his medicorum cohibentur diuersorum potionum dictione, seu flebotomatum usus adibendi* ('on these [days], they are deterred from [using] various potions or applying bloodletting, on the basis of the assertion of genuine doctors'), which is much more concise than the Old English, and leaves out the medical experiment altogether.[8] Fortunately for Smith, in other words, the horse of the *De diebus malis* had an English pedigree to begin with, because it was introduced into the text by an early eleventh-century Anglo-Saxon scribe.

The same cannot be said for the majority of animals in Anglo-Saxon prognostications. Since most prognostications hail from Mesopotamia, Syria, Egypt, Greece and the Mediterranean, the animals mentioned tend to represent species indigenous to these areas. Some of these species, of course, were also native to Britain, or had become native by the time the Anglo-Saxons arrived, as a result of prior introduction by Celtic or Roman settlers. In such cases, references to these exotic animals could conveniently be retained because they had indigenous counterparts in Anglo-Saxon England. Early Continental texts on the twenty-four Egyptian Days, for instance, sometimes warned that cattle should not be broken on these days – an injunction that was retained in Anglo-Saxon manuscripts.[9] Likewise, early Continental texts warn

---

[7] Frederick Smith, *The Early History of Veterinary Literature and its British Development*, 4 vols. (London, 1919–33), vol. 1, p. 70.
[8] MS Harley 3271, fol. 122r–v (Chardonnens, 'Ælfric and the *De diebus malis*', p. 151).
[9] For early Continental versions, see Bern, Burgerbibliothek, MS 318 (facsimile via e-codices <http://www.e-codices.unifr.ch> [accessed 1 January 2015]); Karlsruhe, Badische Landesbibliothek, MS Aug. perg. 120, fols. 211v–212r (Wilhelm Schmitz, *Beiträge zur lateinischen Sprach- und Literaturkunde* (Leipzig, 1877), pp. 314–15; facsimile via Digitale Sammlungen <http://digital.blb-karlsruhe.de> [accessed 1 January 2015]); MS Aug. perg. 167, fol. 49r (Schmitz, *Beiträge zur lateinischen Sprach- und Literaturkunde*, pp. 313–14; facsimile via Digitale Sammlungen). For Anglo-Saxon examples, see London,

that cattle should not be bled on the Egyptian Days, a stipulation adopted without any change by the Anglo-Saxons; compare the Latin, which notes that *qui in istis tribus diebus hominem inciderit aut pecus, aut statim aut in die quarto morietur* ('he who is bled on these three days, be it man or cattle, he will die immediately or on the fourth day'), with the Old English, which indicates similarly, *se þe on þysum þrim dagum his blod gewanige, sy hit man sy hit nyten, þæs þe we secgan gehyrdan þæt sona on þam forman dæge oþþe þam feorþan dæge his lif geændað* ('he who is bled on these three days, be it man or cattle, of him we have heard say that he will die immediately on the first day, or on the fourth day').[10] The animals that are affected by prognostications are mostly of the kind described here; that is, they had indigenous counterparts in Britain, ensuring a smooth transition from non-Germanic to Anglo-Saxon mantic practices.

The animals of the *Revelatio Esdrae* are a case in point. Ascribed to the prophet Esdras (Ezra), the *Revelatio Esdrae* is an annual prognostication that predicts meteorological conditions, yields in agricultural produce and animal husbandry, and human affairs, based on the weekday of either 1 January or Christmas Day. For instance:[11]

Gif middeswintres messedeg bið on sunnandeg, þonne bið god winter, and lengten windi, and drige sumer and wingeardas gode; and sceap beoð weaxende, and hunii beoð genihtsum and eal sib bið genyhtsummo.[12]

British Library, MS Cotton Caligula A. xv, fols. 129v–130r, and MS Cotton Tiberius C. vi, fol. 114r (both in Chardonnens, *Anglo-Saxon Prognostics*, p. 373).

[10] Paris, Bibliothèque nationale de France, MS lat. 12048, fol. 260v (facsimile via Gallica bibliothèque númerique <http://gallica.bnf.fr> [accessed 1 January 2015]), and London, British Library, MS Harley 585, fol. 190r–v (Chardonnens, *Anglo-Saxon Prognostics*, p. 342), respectively. For early Continental versions, see Karlsruhe MS Aug. perg. 167, fol. 49r; Paris, Bibliothèque nationale de France, MS lat. 2825, fols. 128v–129r (Ernest Wickersheimer, *Les Manuscrits latins de médecine du haut moyen âge dans les bibliothèques de France* (Paris, 1966), p. 59); MS nouv. acq. lat. 1616, fol. 12r (Wickersheimer, *Les Manuscrits latins*, p. 141); Reims, Bibliothèque Carnegie, MS 304, fol. 2r–v (facsimile via Gallica bibliothèque númerique).

[11] On the *Revelatio Esdrae*, see Marilina Cesario, 'Weather Prognostics in Anglo-Saxon England', *ES* 93 (2012), 391–426; Chardonnens, *Anglo-Saxon Prognostics*, pp. 491–500; Hardin Craig, *The Works of John Metham*, EETS os 132 (Oxford, 1916), pp. xxxii–xxxvii; Lorenzo DiTommaso, 'Pseudepigrapha Notes III: Old Testament Pseudepigrapha in the Yale University Manuscript Collection', *Journal for the Study of the Pseudepigrapha* 20 (2010), 3–80 (pp. 16–33); David A. Fiensy, 'Revelation of Ezra (prior to Ninth Century A.D.): A New Translation and Introduction', in *The Old Testament Pseudepigrapha I: Apocalyptic Literature and Testament*, ed. James H. Charlesworth (Garden City, NY, 1983), pp. 601–4; Ria Jansen-Sieben, 'Middelnederlandse Jaarprognosen', *Verslagen en mededelingen van de Koninklijke Academie voor Nederlandse Taal- en Letterkunde* (1971), 210–66; Liuzza, *Anglo-Saxon Prognostics*, pp. 43–50; Edith A. Matter, 'The "Revelatio Esdrae" in Latin and English Traditions', *Revue Bénédictine* 92 (1982), 376–92.

[12] Oxford, Bodleian Library, MS Hatton 115, fol. 149r–v (Chardonnens, *Anglo-Saxon Prognostics*, p. 496). On OE *wingeard* (Latin *uindemia*) as the fourth season, see Cesario, 'Weather Prognostics', p. 395.

If Christmas Day is on a Sunday, winter will be good, spring windy, summer dry and the harvest season good; sheep will grow and there will be honey in abundance, and there will be peace and abundance on earth.

From their first appearance on the Continent in early ninth-century learned manuscripts, the prototypical news and weather reports in the *Revelatio Esdrae* proved hugely popular in monastic circles, and it did not take long for Anglo-Saxons to become acquainted with them. Though the predictions pertained to issues that were relevant to life on the Continent, the fact that the Anglo-Saxons had similar seasons, crops, animals and worries meant that they had plenty of common ground. One version of a *Revelatio Esdrae* from an Anglo-Saxon manuscript, for instance, makes the following predictions:

> Si fuerit kł ianuarius die dominico, hiems bona erit et suauis ac calida, uer uentuosus et sicca estas, uindemia bona; oues crescent, mel habundabit, senes morientur et pax fiet.
>
> Si fuerit kł ianuarius die lunę, hiems mixta, uer bonus, estas uentuosa et tempestuosa, uindemia bona; ualitudo hominum, apes morientur.
>
> Si fuerit kł ianuarius die martis, hiems nobilissima, uer uentuosus et pluuialis, estas bona; mulieres morientur, naues periclitantur in pelago; uindemia laboriosa.
>
> Si fuerit kł ianuarius die mercurii, hiems dura et aspera, uer malus et estas bona, uindemia bona; frumentum bonum, iuuenes moriuntur, mel non erit, mercatores laborabunt.
>
> Si fuerit kł ianuarius die iouis, hiems bona erit, uer uentuosus, estas bona; et habundantia erit, reges et principes peribunt, pax fiet.
>
> Si fuerit kł ianuarius die ueneris, hiems stabilis et nix erit, uer bonus et estas dolor oculorum, uindemia bona; oues et apes peribunt, annona cara fiet.
>
> Si fuerit kł ianuarius die saturni, hiems caliginosa, nix erit; annona cara erit, fructus habundabit, homines egrotabunt et ueterani moriuntur; uindemia bona.[13]

> If 1 January is on a Sunday, winter will be good, mild but warm, spring windy and summer dry, the harvest season good; sheep will grow, honey will abound, old men will die and there will be peace.
>
> If 1 January is on a Monday, winter will be mixed, spring good, summer windy and stormy, the harvest season good; there will be health among the people, bees will die.
>
> If 1 January is on a Tuesday, winter will be most noble, spring windy and rainy, summer good; women will die, ships will be in danger on the sea; the harvest season will be toilsome.

---

[13] London, British Library, MS Cotton Tiberius A. iii, fol. 36r–v (Chardonnens, *Anglo-Saxon Prognostics*, pp. 496–7).

If 1 January is on a Wednesday, winter will be hard and difficult, spring evil, and summer good, the harvest season good; grain will be good, young people will die, there will be no honey, merchants will toil.

If 1 January is on a Thursday, winter will be good, spring windy, summer good; and there will be plenty, kings and princes will perish, there will be peace.

If 1 January is on a Friday, winter will be stable and there will be snow, spring will be good and summer too; there will be pain in the eyes, a good harvest season, sheep and bees will perish; resources will be dear.

If 1 January is on a Saturday, winter will be gloomy, there will be snow; resources will be dear, fruits will abound, people will fall ill and old people will die; the harvest season will be good.

The issues addressed in this text are not so outlandish that Anglo-Saxons would have had trouble relating to them, which is probably why the Anglo-Saxon text does not diverge significantly from the Continental version. A closely related Anglo-Saxon version predicts that sheep will multiply and honey will abound (Sunday); there will be no honey (Wednesday); sheep will die (Thursday and Saturday); and sheep's eyes will be weak (Friday).[14]

These two witnesses of the *Revelatio Esdrae* deal with sheep and bees exclusively, which Marilina Cesario explains by the fact that 'both were of great importance to Anglo-Saxon monastic and lay communities: sheep for the production of parchment, milk, cheese, and textiles, and bees for honey and wax'.[15] But while Cesario is right to point out that sheep and bees fulfilled important roles in Anglo-Saxon animal husbandry, which may account for the *Revelatio Esdrae*'s being one of the most widespread prognostications in Anglo-Saxon England, the absence of other common farm animals (particularly cattle and pigs) is striking nonetheless. Indeed, the earliest Continental texts seem generally to limit themselves to sheep and bees, with cattle and pigs appearing only very infrequently.[16] This might be due to

---

[14] MS Cotton Tiberius A. iii, fols. 41v–42r (Chardonnens, *Anglo-Saxon Prognostics*, pp. 494–5).

[15] Cesario, 'Weather Prognostics', p. 414.

[16] For early *Revelatio Esdrae* with sheep and bees, see, for instance, Leiden, Universiteitsbibliotheek, MS Voss. Lat. Q. 69, fol. 37v (Rolf H. Bremmer, 'Leiden, Vossianus Lat. Q. 69 (Part 2): Schoolbook or Proto-Encyclopaedic Miscellany?', in *Practice in Learning: The Transfer of Encyclopaedic Knowledge in the Early Middle Ages*, ed. Rolf H. Bremmer and Kees Dekker (Leuven, 2010), pp. 19–53 (p. 38)); Munich, Bayerische Staatsbibliothek, MS Clm 14456, fol. 75v (facsimile via Münchener Digitalisierungszentrum <http://www.digitale-sammlungen.de> [accessed 1 January 2015]); MS Clm 22053, fol. 21r–v (facsimile via Münchener Digitalisierungszentrum). For an early *Revelatio Esdrae* with pigs, cattle and bees, see Vatican City, Biblioteca Apostolica Vaticana, MS pal. lat. 1449, fols. 119v–120r (Giovanni Mercati, *Note di letteratura Biblica e cristiana antica* (Rome, 1901), pp. 77–9; facsimile via Manoscritti digitalizzati <http://

farming practices in the region of origin of this version of the *Revelatio Esdrae*. Though Continental scribes sometimes adapted the *Revelatio Esdrae* to local conditions, the Anglo-Saxons saw no need, apparently, to tailor the prognostication to their own specific needs once they were introduced to the sheep and bees variant.[17]

A possible exception is a *Revelatio Esdrae* uniquely attested in an English manuscript from the early post-Conquest period. 'An anomalous text which differs substantially' from other versions, this *Revelatio Esdrae* scales up the usual predictions by reporting more extreme weather conditions, bigger natural disasters, and greater suffering for humans and the natural world.[18] As far as animals are concerned, the text predicts that: *apes proficient, oues morientur* ('bees will multiply, sheep will die', Sunday); *quadrupedia plurima morientur* ('most quadrupeds will die', Monday); *piscatio multa* ('much fishing', Wednesday); *clades quadrupedum* ('the destruction of quadrupeds', Thursday); *monstruosa animalia nascentur, ... piscatio plurima* ('monstrous animals will be born, ... fishing in plenty', Friday); and *oues et porci morientur, mel multum, ... in mari belue et pisces morientur plurimi* ('sheep and pigs will die, much honey, ... in the sea most beasts and fish will die', Saturday).[19] Uniquely, this particular *Revelatio Esdrae* covers a much bigger slice of the animal world than any other version. It includes pigs alongside sheep and bees, and it subsumes large numbers of animal species under general labels, such as quadrupeds, fish and sea animals. The most interesting feature, however, is the unparalleled attention given to aquatic creatures, which suggests that this version was adapted to the needs of a maritime culture. Britain is an island, to borrow Bede's observation, so a *Revelatio Esdrae* reoriented along these lines must have proved helpful. Yet if this is indeed the case, it is a mystery why such a useful prognostication appears only in a single scientific manuscript from the inland abbey of Thorney – a location which can hardly have been conducive to its application in practice.

The example of the *Revelatio Esdrae* demonstrates that it was possible to tailor prognostications to local conditions, but that Anglo-Saxons did not often engage in noteworthy modifications. The sheep and bees from Continental sources were familiar sights in Britain, and Anglo-Saxons would therefore have known which creatures were

---

www.vatlib.it/home.php?pag=mss_digitalizzati> [accessed 1 January 2015]); for cattle and bees, see London, British Library, MS Harley 3017, fols. 63r–64v (Chardonnens, 'Appropriating Prognostics', pp. 253–4; facsimile via Digitised Manuscripts).

[17] See Cesario, 'Weather Prognostics', pp. 396–8.
[18] Ibid., p. 413.
[19] Oxford, St John's College, MS 17, fol. 149rb (Chardonnens, *Anglo-Saxon Prognostics*, pp. 499–500; facsimile via Faith Wallis, 'The Calendar and the Cloister', online at <http://digital.library.mcgill.ca/ms-17> [accessed 1 January 2015]).

meant. Other kinds of prognostications, such as brontologies, probably underwent little modification for the same reason, though Anglo-Saxon brontologies do hold some intriguing surprises. 'Practised in the ancient world and continued into Christian culture as part of a larger interest in forecasting events by means of signs and portents', brontologies predict a range of human and natural affairs by means of the occurrence of thunder at various times or from various directions.[20] Thunder was perceived as a destructive force, and most predictions have a negative outcome, particularly with regard to agriculture and animal husbandry. *Se norð þunor* ('northern thunder'), for instance, *becnað scepa deað, and cealfra and geogoðe* ('signifies the death of sheep, calves and youth').[21] Similarly, *gif on frigedæg geþunrað, þonne getacnað þæt nytena cwealm* ('if it thunders on a Friday, it signifies the death of cattle').[22] Around the time of the Norman Conquest, this prediction from a weekday brontology was redacted to specify that *gif hit on frigedæig þunrige, þæt tacnað sædeora cwealm* ('if it thunders on a Friday, it signifies the death of sea animals'), again testifying to a late eleventh-century interest in maritime life, though early Continental texts indicate that OE *nytena* probably represents the original reading (e.g. *peccora multa moritura esse* ('cattle are to die')).[23] The emphasis on farm animals is also evidenced in hour brontologies. If it thunders in the eighth hour, for instance, it signifies *cwyld on heordum and fyþerfetum* ('destruction among herds and quadrupeds').[24] Month brontologies, on the other hand, address a wider array of animals, as the following text demonstrates:

> Si tonitruum fuerit in mense ianuario multe conuentiones sunt: una de ouibus, alia de hominibus, .iii. de peccoribus, .iiii. de lignis, .v. de equis. Timendum est hoc tonitruum.
>
> Si tonitruum fuerit in mense februario ad aurem pertinet uel ad alia, que referuntur in aliam, areas et semen pertenet.
>
> Si tonitruum fuerit in mense martio timendum est, quia ab eo exspectatur mortalitas uel iudicium.
>
> Si tonitruum erit in mense aprili semina periclitantur uel nabes.

---

[20] Roy M. Liuzza, 'What the Thunder Said: Anglo-Saxon Brontologies and the Problem of Sources', *Review of English Studies* ns 55.218 (2004), 1–23 (p. 7). On brontologies, see also Chardonnens, *Anglo-Saxon Prognostics*, pp. 247–69; Liuzza, *Anglo-Saxon Prognostics*, pp. 51–7.

[21] Cambridge, Corpus Christi College, MS 391, p. 714 (Chardonnens, *Anglo-Saxon Prognostics*, p. 269).

[22] MS CCCC 391, pp. 713–14 (Chardonnens, *Anglo-Saxon Prognostics*, pp. 260–1).

[23] Cologne, Erzbischöfliche Diözesan- und Dombibliothek, MS 102, fol. 52r–v (facsimile via Codices electroni ecclesiae Coloniensis <http://www.ceec.uni-koeln.de> [accessed 1 January 2015]); and MS Cotton Tiberius A. iii, fol. 40r–v (Chardonnens, *Anglo-Saxon Prognostics*, p. 261), respectively.

[24] MS Cotton Tiberius A. iii, fol. 37r–v (Chardonnens, *Anglo-Saxon Prognostics*, pp. 254–5).

Si tonitruum fuerit in mense maio pluuie magne erunt, uel erba uel semina pululabunt.

Si tonitruum fuerit in mense iunio homines perecletantur uel ligna.

Si tonitruum fuerit in mense iulio pisces pericletantur.

Si tonitruum erit in mense agusto bilue uel reptilia perecletantur.

Si tonitruum erit in mense septembri uituli moriuntur.

Si tonitruum erit in mense octobri motantur aure.

Si tonitruum erit in mensis nouembri obes crescunt.[25]

If there is thunder in the month of January, there are many conventions: one of sheep, another of men, a third of cattle, a fourth of trees, a fifth of horses. This thunder is to be feared.

If there is thunder in the month of February, it pertains to the ears, or to something else, as is reported elsewhere; it pertains to threshing floors(?) and seeds.

If there is thunder in the month of March, it is to be feared, because mortality or judgement is to be expected from it.

If there is thunder in the month of April, seeds or ships are in danger.

If there is thunder in the month of May, there will be great showers, and weeds or seeds will sprout.

If there is thunder in the month of June, men or trees are in danger.

If there is thunder in the month of July, fish are in danger.

If there is thunder in the month of August, beasts (monsters?) or reptiles are in danger.

If there is thunder in the month of September, calves will die.

If there is thunder in the month of October, winds will blow.

If there is thunder in the month of November, sheep will grow.

This is the only Latin month brontology from Anglo-Saxon England – a late tenth-century addition to the glossed Regius Psalter. The text reports on a number of natural, agricultural and human concerns, but it is nowhere more outspoken than in its predictions for the animal world. The sheep (January, November), cattle (January) and calves (September) already encountered in other brontologies are here joined by horses (January), fish (July) and beasts and reptiles (August). This mix of farm animals, fish and wild beasts is unique to this text – as we have already seen, other prognostications generally limit themselves to one of these groups of animals. Yet, as early Continental analogues corroborate (such as the pseudo-Bedan *De tonitruis libellus ad Herefridum*), an eclectic assortment of animals is a feature of month

---

[25] London, British Library, MS Royal 2. B. v., fol. 190r–v (Chardonnens, *Anglo-Saxon Prognostics*, p. 265).

brontologies in general.[26] The Latin month brontology from England is no exception, but the reference to reptiles is unattested elsewhere, and may be the fabrication of an Anglo-Saxon scribe who got carried away by the inauspicious topic of thunder. The same may be said of the readings in the only month brontology in Old English, which ignores animals altogether except for during the months of June and July:

> On iunius monðe, hit bodeð mycele windes, and wulfene wodnysse and leona. On iulius monðe, hit bodeð wæstme wel gewænde and oref forfærð.[27]
>
> In the month of June, it [thunder] signifies great storms, and madness among wolves and lions. In the month of July, it signifies crops doing well, and livestock will die.

The reference to *oref* ('livestock') in the prediction for July is not unusual, and wild beasts would not have been out of place either, as the Latin text shows. However, this vernacular text specifically singles out wolves and lions. By mentioning these beasts in one breath, the Old English month brontology bridges the gap between the natural world of Anglo-Saxon England and the exotic world of the Bible and the *Wonders of the East*. The scribe of this text, in other words, seems deliberately to have veered away from what might actually happen on English soil, towards symbolic ways of creating meaning by bringing in creatures from distant, exotic locations.

Similar motivations must have informed the work of the person who translated the sunshine prognostication into Old English. Sunshine prognostications are annual predictions that deliver mostly positive reports on human affairs, produce, and the finding of metals, depending upon which of the twelve days of Christmas is sunny.[28] The English texts feature predictions that can be taken at face value, yet into which a prediction has been inserted that requires some learning before its meaning is understood:

---

[26] For the *De tonitruis libellus ad Herefridum*, see Cologne MS 102, fols. 49r–52v. See also *PL* 90, 609–14, and its appraisal in Charles W. Jones, *Bedae Pseudepigrapha: Scientific Writings Falsely Attributed to Bede* (Ithaca, NY, 1939), pp. 45–7. More manuscript copies of the *De tonitruis* have come to light since Jones's identification of Cologne MS 102; see Hilbert Chiu and David Juste, 'The *De tonitruis* Attributed to Bede: An Early Medieval Treatise on Divination by Thunder Translated from Irish', *Traditio* 68 (2013), 97–124.

[27] London, British Library, Cotton Vespasian D.xiv, fol. 103v (Chardonnens, *Anglo-Saxon Prognostics*, pp. 264–5).

[28] On sunshine prognostications, see Marilina Cesario, 'The Shining of the Sun in the Twelve Nights of Christmas', in *Saints and Scholars: New Perspectives on Anglo-Saxon Literature and Culture in Honour of Hugh Magennis*, ed. Stuart McWilliams (Cambridge, 2012), pp. 195–212; Chardonnens, *Anglo-Saxon Prognostics*, pp. 483–5.

Þy forma dæg drihtnes gebyrde gyf sunne scyneð, mycel gefea byoð mid mannum and genihtsum.

Gyf þy æfteran dæg sunne scyneþ, þonne byð on ængelcynne gold eaðbegeate.

Gyf þy þryddan dæg sunne scyneð, betweoh earmum mannum mycel gefeoht

byoð, and betweoh cynigum and rycum mannum micel sib.

Gyf þy .iiii. dæge sunne scyneð, þonne þa olfenda mycel gold oðberað þan ætmettum þa þone goldhord healden scolden.

Gyf þy .v. dege sunne scyneð, mycel blostman and bleoda beoð þy gere.

Gyf .vi dæge sunne scyneð, driht sendeð mycele meolc.

Gyf .vii. dæge sunne scineð, mycele westmas on treowum beoð.

Gyf þy .viii. dæge sunne scyneð, ðonne byð cwicseolfor eaðgeate.

Gyf þi .ix. dæge sunne scyneð, þonne god sendeð micelne fulluht on geare.

Gyf þi .x. dæge sunne scyneð, þonne byð se and ealle æa mid fixum ontined.

Gyf þi .xi dæge sunne scyneð, micel costung byð deaðes mid mannum.

Gyf þi .xii. dæge sunne scyneð, men beoð wace and byð micel sib on eorðan.[29]

If the sun shines on the first day of the Lord's birth, there will be much joy and abundance among the people.

If the sun shines on the second day, then gold will be easy to get among the English.

If the sun shines on the third day, there will be great strife among poor people, and great peace between kings and powerful men.

If the sun shines on the fourth day, then camels will carry away much gold from the ants that must guard the gold hoard.

If the sun shines on the fifth day, there will be many flowers and fruits in this year.

If the sun shines on the sixth day, the Lord will send much milk.

If the sun shines on the seventh day, there will be much produce on the trees.

If the sun shines on the eighth day, then quicksilver will be easy to get.

If the sun shines on the ninth day, then the Lord will send a great baptism in this year.

If the sun shines on the tenth day, then the sea and all rivers will be full of fish.

If the sun shines on the eleventh day, there will be great suffering of death among the people.

If the sun shines on the twelfth day, men will be weak and there will be great peace on earth.

---

[29] MS Hatton 115, fols. 149v–150r (Chardonnens, *Anglo-Saxon Prognostics*, p. 485).

Most of these predictions can be readily understood, and those pertaining to animals mainly feature creatures already encountered in the *Revelatio Esdrae* and brontologies, that is, cattle (indirectly for day 6) and fish (day 10). But in relation to the discovery of metals, which is a central concern in sunshine prognostications, the prediction for day 4 mentions that 'camels will carry away much gold from the ants that must guard the gold hoard'. Chances were slim, however, that one could simply steal gold from gold-hoarding ants with the help of camels on English soil, because neither animal belonged to the Anglo-Saxon natural world. Rather, the reference is to a passage in the *Wonders of the East* that describes a curious custom:

> Capi hatte seo ea in ðære ylcan stowe þe is haten Gorgoneus, þæt is Wælcyrginc. Þær beoð akende æmættan swa micle swa hundas. Hi habbað fet swylce græshoppan, hi syndon reades hiwes and blaces. Þa æmettan delfað gold up of eorðan fram foran nihte oð ða fiftan tid dæges. Ða menn ðe to ðam dyrstige beoð þæt hi þæt gold nimen, þonne lædað hi mid him olfenda myran mid hyra folan and stedan. Þa folan hi getigað ær hi ofer þa ea faran. Þæt gold hi gefætað on ða myran and hi sylfe onsittað and þa stedan þær forlætað. Ðonne ða æmettan hi onfindað, and þa hwile ðe þa æmettan ymbe ða stedan abiscode beoð, þonne ða men mid þam myran and þam golde ofer ða ea farað. Hi beoð to þam swifte þæt ða men wenað þæt hi fleogende syn.[30]

> The river is named Capi in the same place, which is called Gorgoneus, that is 'valkyrie-like'. Ants are born there as big as dogs, which have feet like grasshoppers, and they are red and black in colour. The ants dig up gold from the ground before night until the fifth hour of the day. People who are bold enough to take the gold bring with them male camels, and females with their young. They tie up the young before they cross the river. They load the gold onto the females, and mount them themselves, and leave the males there. Then the ants detect the males, and while the ants are occupied with the males, the men cross over the river with the females and the gold. They are so swift that one would think that they were flying.

This excerpt from the *Wonders of the East* introduces an ingenious method for stealing gold without having to delve for it: one simply diverts gold-hoarding ants with a free meal of male camels. Since the region described here is far removed from England, it seems unlikely that the prediction in the Old English sunshine prognostication could be taken literally. Sunshine prognostications from the Continent do not contain similar statements, which makes it plausible that the reference to the *Wonders of the East* was devised by an Anglo-Saxon scribe who perhaps wanted to recontextualise a prediction concerning

---

[30] Orchard, *Pride and Prodigies*, pp. 190–1.

gold.³¹ Why the adaptor felt the need to do so is unclear, because less learned users of the sunshine prognostication are unlikely to have known what to make of this prediction. However, Cesario argues that, since 'wisdom literature appealed greatly to the Anglo-Saxons', the obscurity of the reference 'might have been part of the point, as the lack of explanation challenges the reader to determine the intended meaning'.³² Cesario convincingly adduces a range of learned sources on camel-lore and myrmecology that were available to educated Anglo-Saxons, including a riddle by Aldhelm, Isidore of Seville's *Etymologiae*, Gregory the Great's *Moralia in Iob*, the *Physiologus*, and the Bible. In other words, the adaptor may have aimed to showcase the extent of his learning by adding a symbolic layer to the prediction – the part of a prognostication that usually stayed within the bounds of the literal. At the level of output, after all, prognostications had to be as literal as possible, and if the point was to come up with predictions that were concrete enough to give a measure of certainty about the immediate future, then the prediction about the gold-hoarding ants did little to further that agenda, even if it did add an exotic touch.

Symbolism and associative logic were important strategies for creating meaningful patterns at the level of prognostic input. Thunder, for instance, was considered a destructive force, so its occurrence generally did not bode well; sunshine, by contrast, was a constructive force, so its occurrence was a good sign. This is why brontologies tend to predict misfortune whereas sunshine prognostications are auspicious. Thunder and sunshine as symbols of destruction and generation, therefore, condition the outcome of prognostications. A similar mechanism would seem to underlie the *Revelatio Esdrae*, where the day associated with the sun generally offers a positive prediction:

> Si die .i. feria fuerint kł ianuarii, hiemps bona, et uer uentosum erit, aestas sicca et uindemia bona erit; boues crescent et mel abundanter erit, senes morientur et abundantia et pax erit.³³

> If 1 January is on a Sunday, winter will be good, spring windy, summer dry and the harvest season good; sheep will grow and there will be honey in abundance; old people will die and there will be abundance and peace.

Whereas the day associated with Saturn is viewed with greater ambivalence:

---

[31] See, for instance, Liège, Bibliothèque de l'Université, MS 77, fol. 70r (Cesario, 'The Shining of the Sun', pp. 209–12).
[32] Marilina Cesario, 'Ant-Lore in Anglo-Saxon England', *ASE* 40 (2011), 273–91 (p. 283).
[33] London, British Library, MS Cotton Titus D. xxvi, fols. 10v–11v (Chardonnens, *Anglo-Saxon Prognostics*, pp. 497–8).

Si .vii. feria fuerint kł ianuarii, hiemps turbolenta, uer uentosum; et fructus laboriosus erit, oues peribunt et senes morientur.

If 1 January is on a Saturday, winter will be stormy, spring windy; and harvest will be toilsome, sheep will perish and old people will die.

As far as animals are concerned, those at the output level of prognostications generally represent creatures known in the Anglo-Saxon natural world, such as farm animals and fish. Notable exceptions are the lions of the month brontology, and the camels and gold-hoarding ants of the sunshine prognostication, though it is likely that references to these creatures were included by learned scribes with a taste for the exotic. However, animals also feature at the input level of prognostication, where they seem to form an eclectic mix even by Anglo-Saxon standards.

Dream books (collections of dream topics, and their interpretations) are a safe haven for all imaginable concepts, things and creatures, no matter how trivial, controversial or exotic. It mattered little whether the subject of the dream was part of daily life, because the only limiting factor on what takes place in dreams is the human imagination. It was possible, for instance, to dream of having one's teeth fall out (indicating anxiety), of being made emperor (indicating honour), of sleeping with one's sister (harm), or of seeing a fierce elephant (accusation), though none of these events was likely to be included in prognostications. Instead, they were taken as signs of what the future held, which is borne out by the wording of dream book predictions; for instance, *dracones uidere, dignitatem significat* ('to see dragons signifies honour').[34] The dream books known in Anglo-Saxon England were structured on the alphabetical model attributed to the Old Testament prophet Daniel, which went back to Byzantine sources that in turn relied on pre-Byzantine Greek and Near Eastern oneiromantic traditions.[35] As

---

[34] MS Cotton Tiberius A. iii, fols. 27v–32v (Chardonnens, *Anglo-Saxon Prognostics*, pp. 305–23).

[35] Alphabetical dream books have been the subject of considerable study; for relevant sources in the present context, see Chardonnens, *Anglo-Saxon Prognostics*, pp. 290–329; László. S. Chardonnens, 'Dream Divination in Manuscripts and Early Printed Books: Patterns of Transmission, with a Comprehensive Hand List of Sources', in *Aspects of Knowledge: Preserving and Reinventing Traditions of Learning in the Middle Ages*, ed. Marilina Cesario and Hugh Magennis (Manchester, forthcoming); Lorenzo DiTommaso, *The Book of Daniel and the Apocryphal Daniel Literature* (Leiden, 2005), pp. 231–59, 378–402; Andreas Epe, *Wissensliteratur im angelsächsischen England: Das Fachschrifttum der vergessenen artes mechanicae und artes magicae. Mit besonderer Berücksichtigung des Somniale Danielis* (Münster, 1995); Steven R. Fischer, *The Complete Medieval Dreambook: A Multilingual, Alphabetical Somnia Danielis Collation* (Frankfurt am Main, 1982); Jutta Grub, *Das lateinische Traumbuch im Codex Upsaliensis C 664 (9. Jh.): Eine frühmittelalterliche Fassung der lateinischen Somniale Danielis-Tradition* (Frankfurt am Main, 1984); Liuzza, *Anglo-Saxon Prognostics*, pp. 38–43; Lawrence T. Martin, *Somniale Danielis: An Edition of a Medieval Latin Dream Interpretation Handbook* (Frankfurt am Main, 1981); Steven M. Oberhelman, *Dreambooks in Byzantium: Six Oneirocritica in Translation, with Commentary*

Vilmos Voigt once posited, 'dreams reflect place and location', and in the case of the alphabetical dream books that reached Britain in the eleventh century, these texts were strongly coloured by their cultures of origin: one Anglo-Saxon dream book, for instance, includes dreams of eunuchs, emperors and Hercules.[36] This exotic heritage is also apparent from the kinds of animals featured in Anglo-Saxon dream books, which include creatures known in the Anglo-Saxon natural world, such as farm animals, dogs and dragons, but also animals that never lived in England, yet that were nevertheless part of Anglo-Saxon intellectual and religious culture. The following provides an inventory of animals, animal products, and events involving animals from six Anglo-Saxon dream books:

ANIMALS

Ants: to see ~ of any kind: great strife

Asses: to see ~: toil; to eat/to sit on (L (s)*edere*) ~: toil; ~ braying or running free: strife with an enemy

Asses or kids: to see ~: wrongs in business

Bear: to be attacked by a ~: treachery of an enemy

Beasts: to be attacked by ~: to be overcome by enemies; to tame ~: esteem of enemies; ~ running: disturbance; ~ talking: serious trouble

Bees: to be attacked or injured by ~: one's life will be disturbed by men; to be stung by ~: one's mind will be troubled by foreign men; ~ flying into one's house: abandonment/burning down of house; ~ bearing honey: one will get money from prosperous people

Birds: to fight with ~: strife; to catch ~: profit; ~ taking something: harm; ~ in a nest: struggle in business; ~ fighting among themselves: powerful people will fight among themselves; many ~: envy, contention and strife

Buck or goats: to see ~: advancement

Bull: to have a ~: neither good not evil

Camels: to be attacked by ~: harm

Chicken: ~ laying an egg: profit with worry; ~ with chicks: increase in business; many ~: good

Dogs: ~ barking or attacking: enemies seek to overpower one; ~ greeting: guard against one's enemies; ~ playing: thanks; ~ running: much good; many ~: beware of enemies

Doves: to see ~: sadness

Dragons: to see ~: honour/good; ~ flying overhead: treasure

---

and Introduction (Aldershot, 2008); Alf Önnerfors, 'Zur Überlieferungsgeschichte des sogenannten Somniale Danielis', *Eranos* 58 (1960), 142–58.

[36] Vilmos Voigt, 'How Dreams Reflect Place and Location? Georg von Gaal: *Polylogikai Mulatság az Álomról és Alvásról* (1821), *Über den Schlaf* (1823)', *KOHT ja PAIK / PLACE and LOCATION: Studies in Environmental Aesthetics and Semiotics* 5 (2006), 49–59 (p. 49). MS Cotton Tiberius A. iii, fols. 27v–32v.

Eagle: ~ attacking: death/great joy; ~ flying: death of one's wife; ~ overhead: honour; many ~: evil hostility and treachery among the people

Elephant: to see a fierce ~: accusation

Fish: to see ~: rain; ~ in the sea: great anxiety

Foal: to sit on a ~: deception in business

Frogs: to see ~: anxiety

Geese: many ~: good

Goat: to see a ~: hostile enemy close by; many ~: vanity

Horse: to sit on a white ~: good outcome/honour/good news; to sit on a black ~: anxiety/distress in the mind; to sit on a fallow ~: damage/good; to sit on a bay ~: advancement; to sit on a chestnut ~: bad business/loss of one's goods; ~ running free or being attacked by ~: harm

Lion: ~ running: success in business; ~ sleeping: bad business; to be attacked by a ~: rebellion among enemies

Mouse and lion: to see a ~: security

Ox: white or big ~: honour; hornless ~: one will overcome one's enemies; ~ grazing: struggle in business; ~ sleeping: evil in business; to sit on a white ~: honour

Pigs: to see ~: illness; many ~: misery

Quadrupeds: to see ~: anxiety; ~ talking: enmity of a king

Serpent: to see a ~: enemies/malice of an evil woman; to be attacked by a ~: sight of an enemy; ~ coming towards you: guard against evil women

Sheep: shorn ~: harm/not good; white ~: good

Stallions: many ~: destruction of one's goods

ANIMAL PRODUCTS

Butter: to eat ~: good news

Eggs: to have or eat ~: no effect

Honey: to eat ~: distress; to receive ~: be careful not to be deceived

Lard: to handle ~: a parent will die

Ivory: to handle ~: hindrance; to buy or sell ~: great sadness

Silk or fine cloth: to have ~: sometimes good and sometimes evil

EVENTS INVOLVING ANIMALS

Claws: to see ~: anguish

Fish pond: to wash in a ~: joy; to fall into a ~: happiness

Hunt: to ~: wealth/profit/guard against enemies

Plough: to ~: wealth[37]

---

[37] London, British Library, MS Sloane 475, fols. 217v–218r; MS Cotton Tiberius A. iii, fols. 27v–32v, 38r–39v, 42r–v; MS Cotton Titus D. xxvi, fols. 11v–16r; and MS Hatton 115, fols.

The dream topics and their interpretations provide insight into how alphabetical dream books create meaning through associative logic. Animals with negative connotations, for instance, are associated with misfortune, such as the association between serpents and evil women, which is probably based on Scripture. Animals with positive connotations, such as lions, are good signs, except when they turn against the dreamer. Some types of animals (beasts, for instance) stand for human attributes or fellow human beings, and the nature of their interaction with the dreamer dictates the meaning of the dream. Some dreams, on the other hand, create meaning through opposing values, as in the dream of a dove boding sadness. Since most animals and events involving animals would have been familiar to the Anglo-Saxons from daily life or religion and learning, their meaning would have made sense to the audience. That said, the animals portrayed in alphabetical dream books are not native species, strictly speaking, although some might, of course, have existed in Anglo-Saxon England nonetheless. The exceptions (camels, elephants and lions) are a reminder that the roots of alphabetical dream books did not lie in northwest Europe. The Anglo-Saxons would have known these animals, though, since they made an appearance in religious and learned sources, such as the *Wonders of the East* (where camels are even depicted in the section on the gold-hoarding ants), while the dream of the mouse and the lion was probably inspired by Aesop's fable. As far as exotic animal products are concerned, Anglo-Saxons were familiar with ivory, albeit not always from elephants' tusks, and silk would have been a precious import product. Anglo-Saxons would have had no problems, then, in adopting a non-Germanic form of dream divination, because there was sufficient overlap between their own natural world and that of the Mediterranean and Near East.

    Rather than speculate on how far the knowledge of exotic animals extended in Anglo-Saxon England, it is perhaps more interesting to note that the dream books are heavily oriented towards the Mediterranean and the Near East. Asses, for instance, are a stock feature of alphabetical dream books, probably due to their intensive use in the region of origin. Their role in Anglo-Saxon England, however, was minor. Pigs, on the other hand, were important in Anglo-Saxon England, but have strongly negative associations in dream books which probably stem from the earliest Mediterranean oneirocritic sources. Some animals, moreover, are wholly absent from Anglo-Saxon dream books, even though it would have been relatively easy to expand the store of dream images. The Anglo-Saxons would

150v–152v (Chardonnens, *Anglo-Saxon Prognostics*, pp. 297–329).

have understood the simple rules of associative logic underlying the way that meaning is created in dream books, but they did not act on this knowledge. So there are dogs but no cats, and some animals of cultural significance to Anglo-Saxons are completely absent, such as badgers, deer, ravens and wolves. As we have already seen from other prognostic techniques known from Anglo-Saxon sources, it would appear that the Anglo-Saxon scribes who copied alphabetical dream books were content to make do with the predictions handed down through the ages – and they were not alone in this. Badgers and deer, for instance, never made it into alphabetical dream books in the medieval period, while cats and ravens first appeared in early printed dream books from Italy and Germany in the 1470s.[38] Wolves, finally, surface in a thirteenth-century French dream book, but occupy a marginal position.[39]

In conclusion, the natural world that Anglo-Saxons encountered in prognostications resembled the one in which they lived, even if the world in which these prognostications had originated could not be mapped fully onto Anglo-Saxon England. The animals whose fate was predicted in prognostications tend to represent species also known in Britain, such as cattle and bees. This made it easy for Anglo-Saxons to adopt these prognostications without having to undertake major revisions. The animals that formed the input of predictions, however, tend to be more exotic, such as the camels, elephants and lions of alphabetical dream books. Since the Anglo-Saxons were familiar with religious and learned sources that featured these same animals, it was possible for them to grasp their symbolic significance. What is puzzling, though, is that the opportunity to add an indigenous touch to alphabetical dream books was not embraced, though other Anglo-Saxon scribes deliberately complicated prognostications by revising predictions or including references to exotic animals like lions, camels and gold-hoarding ants. It is possible that by diminishing the prophetic potential of predictions in brontologies and sunshine prognostications, scribes removed these techniques from the sphere of divination and drew them into a tradition of learning. Certainly, there are few signs that such prognostications ever fully realised their mantic potential, since the manuscripts in which they were transmitted were firmly situated within a monastic culture of learning. By contrast, other types of prognostications, such as alphabetical dream books, displayed an animal world that was manifestly more exotic, and that would actually

---

[38] For a dream about cats, see *Ego sum Daniel propheta* [...] ([Trent: Albrecht Kunne, c. 1475]; GW 7905); for dreams about ravens, see *Interpretationes seu somnia Danielis prophete* ([Rome: Johannes Bulle, c. 1478/9], GW 7920).

[39] See Paris, Bibliothèque nationale de France, MS fr. 1553, fols. 285v–286v (Walther Suchier, 'Altfranzösische Traumbücher', *Zeitschrift für französische Sprache und Literatur* 67 (1957), 129–67 (pp. 141–6); facsimile via Gallica bibliothèque numérique).

have benefited from some domestication and the inclusion of species more familiar from the English landscape. Needless to say, this never happened, which suggests that if Anglo-Saxons ever dreamt of sheep, it would have been of exotic sheep.

7

You Sexy Beast

The Pig in a Villa in Vandalic North Africa, and Boar-Cults in Old Germanic Heathendom

Richard North

In the early 520s, little more than a decade before the Vandals of North Africa vanished in the wake of Count Belisarius' invasion from Byzantium, the poet Luxorius of Carthage wrote a short *jeu d'esprit* which, in its sole surviving context, the *Latin Anthology*, is entitled *Archilochium de apro mitissimo in triclinio nutrito* ('epigram on a most tame boar fed in the dining room').[1] The pig is described eating quietly among gilded colonnades. Unlike other swine, he refrains from muddying the furniture, and is called a beast no longer of Mars but of Venus. Luxorius' subject belongs to a long Latin literary tradition in which wild animals such as lions and boars are hailed as tamed.[2] This type of poetry is popular in the *Latin Anthology*, in which many aberrant or untypical humans are also described. Luxorius, a *grammaticus* ('teacher of Latin'), was also styled *vir clarissimus et spectabilis* ('most notable and respectable citizen'), possibly in recognition of a teaching award.[3] Yet for all his learning, most poems in Luxorius' *Liber epigrammaton* ('book of epigrams') dwell on the buzz of Carthage, on the people of parks and villas, and on parties, pantomimes and chariot-racing in the circus. His bestial novelties are part of this. Although the vogue for this type of writing began with Martial's epigrams in the reign of Domitian (AD 81–96), Luxorius' poems show that nobody had tired of it in Carthage, second city of the western empire, four centuries later. In the poem before the one on

---

[1] *Anthologia Latina, sive Poesis Latinae Supplementum*, I: *Libri Salmasiani Aliorumque Carmina*, ed. Alexander Riese (Leipzig, 1894), p. 211 (no. 292). Based on Codex Salmasianus (Paris, Bibliothèque nationale de France, Codex Parisinus Latinus 10318), which is copied from a now-lost archetype of 534. Text here taken and translation based upon *Luxorius: A Latin Poet among the Vandals*, ed. and trans. Morris Rosenblum (New York, 1961), pp. 114–15.
[2] Rosenblum, *Luxorius*, p. 181 (n. 6.7). Gregory Hays, '"*Romuleis Libicisque Litteris*": Fulgentius and the "Vandal Renaissance"', in *Vandals, Romans, and Berbers: New Perspectives on Late Antique North Africa*, ed. Andrew H. Merrills (Aldershot, 2004), pp. 101–32 (esp. pp. 112–14).
[3] Rosenblum, *Luxorius*, pp. 39–42 (esp. p. 40).

the boar, Luxorius writes of a fish which fearlessly inhabits the *lacunas regias* 'royal ponds' (no. 5, line 1). Elsewhere he pictures birds who prefer the garden of a Vandal patron, Fridamal, to their old home by the sea (no. 16), as well as a monkey taught to sit on the back of a dog that it fears:

> Quanto magna parant felici tempora regno,
> Discant ut legem pacis habere ferae!
>
> What great things the times hold in store for the happy kingdom,
> That animals may learn to keep the laws of peace!
>
> (no. 44, lines 3–4)

Here the beasts in question might prompt an uneasy comparison, perhaps one between half-Roman Hilderic of Carthage and his Vandal relatives. Luxorius also celebrates a she-bear nursing cubs (no. 47), his own pet puppy (no. 73), leopards trained to hunt with dogs (no. 74), an articulate magpie (no. 84), and a cat that died eating a mouse (no. 89). Finally, there is a wild boar in a painting in a villa, to which Luxorius gives the honour of being speared by his patron Fridamal:

> Hic spumantis apri iaculo post terga retorto
> Frontem et cum geminis naribus ora feris.
> Ante ictum subita prostrate est bellua morte,
> Cui prius extingui quam cecidisse fuit.
> Iussit fata manus telo, nec vulnera sensit
> Exerrans anima iam pereunte cruor.
>
> Here, with spear drawn back behind your shoulder, you strike
> The foaming boar's forehead and face with twin nostrils.
> Before impact the beast was laid low by sudden death,
> Whose lot was to be extinguished before actually falling.
> The hand with lance decreed its fate, nor did its outflowing
> Life-blood feel the wounds with the soul now passing on.
>
> (no. 18, lines 17–22)

Where the live pig in the villa is concerned, however, there appear to be grounds to look beyond Roman trivia, to a Vandal connection with the time-honoured conceit of ferocity tamed.

The Vandals: History, Territory and Culture

The Vandal patrons of Luxorius and his fellow poets were descended from a nomadic military whose kings ruled Africa Proconsularis out of Carthage between 439, when Geiseric forced General Bonifatius to surrender, to 534, when Belisarius took the city for the Byzantine

Empire from Gelimer, last of the Vandal kings.[4] Although by that stage the Hasding Vandals had ruled Carthage for nearly a century, their Mediterranean adventures went back a generation earlier. At first they moved in next to the Suevi, or Sueves, around Galicia in 411 after a two-year pillage of northern Spain.[5] In 418 they found their ranks swelled with Alans when, in a battle further south, the Alans of Lusitania and Siling Vandals of Baetica suffered a crushing defeat to King Wallia of the Goths, who was acting for Rome. With an eye to the main chance, the new Hasding leader, Geiseric, led a conglomerate force southwards. He defeated the Romans in 422 but reasoned that Spain would destroy him in the longer run.[6] In 429 his troops, probably in the tens of thousands, crossed the straits of Gibraltar, advancing slowly eastwards towards Numidia. Encircling Hippo, west of Tunisia, in 435, the Vandals made a treaty with the empire in which they federated to the Roman army. Four years later they took Carthage and confiscated the best lands of the province. In 442 Geiseric had himself recognised by Roman treaty as the independent king of North Africa. He sent his son Huneric to Ravenna to marry Princess Eudoxia, daughter of Emperor Valentinian III (r. 425–55). By now the Vandals were using the Carthaginian merchant fleet to take tribute from the Balearic Islands, western Sicily, Sardinia and Corsica. On the death of Valentinian, King Geiseric sacked Rome and brought Huneric and Eudoxia back to Carthage. His kingdom expanded but remained at war with Rome until his death in 477. To keep it intact he established a new Hasding rule of agnatic succession by the oldest surviving male.[7] Since Geiseric had killed all his son's rivals anyway, Huneric inherited and strengthened his hold by liquidating younger cousins in 481. As he was an Arian Christian (on which more below), he went on to purge Catholics also, in 482–4. When at last he died in 484, having failed to restore primogeniture in favour of his own son, he was succeeded by a cousin, Gunthamund (son of Genton, Geiseric's younger brother). The king after Gunthamund's death in 496 was Thrasamund, another son of Genton and a patron of arts and letters. His was apparently a more tolerant reign in which the Arian persecution subsided, although he treated with the Ostrogoths of Italy.[8]

In 523 Thrasamund died and the crown passed back to Geiseric's side of the family, to Hilderic, son of Huneric and Eudoxia, who had been waiting nearly forty years. This half-Roman Vandal issued an

---

[4] Andrew H. Merrills and Richard Miles, *The Vandals* (Chichester, 2010), pp. 54–5, 228–33.
[5] Ibid., pp. 42–4.
[6] Ibid., pp. 50–1.
[7] Ibid., pp. 74–7.
[8] Ibid., pp. 196–9.

edict of toleration towards Catholic, or Nicene, Christianity in the same year, tilting his diplomacy away from the Arian prefect Theoderic of Italy, and towards Emperor Justinian in Byzantium. In emulation of his imperial ancestors, Hilderic then restored primogeniture, excluding from the succession his second-cousin Gelimer, who was next in line.[9] The reaction came in 531 when Gelimer (otherwise spelt Geilamer), son of Geilarith (Genton's third son and Thrasamund's younger brother), took back the kingdom for a more Vandal style of rule. Gelimer locked up Hilderic and his nephews Hoamer and Hoageis. He blinded Hoamer and two years later, as the Byzantines invaded, sent his brother Ammata to put both Hilderic and Hoageis to death. Hoageis, once a general in Libya, had been a patron of Luxorius, who mourns the passing of Damira, Hoageis' daughter, in a short but effective epitaph.[10] The Vandal collapse which followed in 534 is taken as the *terminus ad quem* for all poems in the *Latin Anthology*, including those of Luxorius, whose epigram on the boar in the dining room (no. 6) is most plausibly dated, at the latest, to the early 520s.[11]

For most of this period of Vandal rule the Catholics, that is to say Nicene or Trinitarian Christians, had endured fierce persecution from their Arian masters – followers of the peculiar but politically dominant version of Christianity in which Jesus is revered as a man created without godhead. When Geiseric was not raiding Spain or the Pelopponese and Zakynthos in Greece, he made sure to torment the North African Catholics with fines, church closures and sporadic violence.[12] Not without reason did ecclesiastical commentators revile the Vandals as fanatics. In one of these persecutions the Vandals are said to have publicly scalped any people in their costume who entered Catholic churches,[13] and in this barbarity they exceeded even their fellow Arians the Visigoths and Ostrogoths (in Iberia and Italy, respectively).

Although when Luxorius eulogised the pig, probably in the quieter reign of Hilderic, it seems that some sense prevailed, things had been different a generation earlier, when King Gunthamund (r. 484–96) imprisoned the lawyer and skilled poet Blossius Aemilius Dracontius for praising the wrong ruler, probably his predecessor, Huneric.[14] In response Dracontius composed a eulogy for Gunthamund entitled *Satisfactio* ('appeasement'). Still imprisoned a few years later, and perhaps feeling guilty for having appeased the king at the cost

---

[9] Ibid., p. 222.
[10] Rosenblum, *Luxorius*, pp. 146–7 (no. 59).
[11] Ibid., p. 43.
[12] Merrills and Miles, *The Vandals*, pp. 111–20, 180–2.
[13] Ibid., pp. 102–3.
[14] Andrew H. Merrills, 'The Perils of Panegyric: The Lost Poem of Dracontius and its Consequences', in *Vandals, Romans, and Berbers*, ed. Merrills, pp. 145–62 (esp. pp. 152–9).

of religious decency, Dracontius may have worsened his lot by composing *De laudibus Dei* ('in praise of God') on the Holy Trinity.[15] Gunthamund, though a survivor of Huneric's familial purges, was no less Arian than his murderous cousin, and Dracontius remained in jail. Released by Thrasamund on his accession (r. 496–523), the old poet emerged to find that both he and his works were *passé*.[16] A generation later it is perhaps unsurprising to find that the poems of Luxorius lack reference to Christianity of any kind. Not even in his epitaph on Damira, the deceased little daughter of Hoageis, does Luxorius refer to God in any way which might permit his religion to be identified:

> Huius puram animam stellantis regia caeli
> Possidet et iustis inter videt esse catervis.[17]
>
> The kingdom of starry heaven possesses her pure soul
> Which it sees living among the throngs of the just.
>
> (no. 59, lines 13–14)

The poet here echoes Horace and Virgil rather than the Bible.[18] The rest of the *Anthology* is similarly pagan. It has poems on biblical or Christian themes, but these may have come from outside North Africa, and there are many more on Mars, Venus, Hylas and Hercules, Leda, Marsyas, Ganymede, Medea and other figures from Classical mythology.[19] It seems likely that the poets of the *Latin Anthology* are imitative and inward-looking[20] in this way partly as an insurance against Arian attack. Some pagan rites continued in Carthage and other cities as a civic formality even into the sixth century,[21] and in poetry the old mythology may have continued for a similar reason, to stay clear of Arian–Catholic tension. Even Dracontius, in his *De laudibus Dei*, remodels Ovid's nude Corinna to make up a line on Eve.[22] Whereas Hilderic's accession enabled more secularisation in 523, few poems in the *Anthology* may be placed after Gelimer's reactionary coup eight years later, when the old persecutions looked set to restart. Despite the fact that Romanisation continued to weaken the North African Vandals in their last few decades of power, it seems from the early *epyllia* of Dracontius and others in the 470s, and from the stock

---

[15] David F. Bright, *The Miniature Epic in Vandal North Africa* (Norman, OK, 1987), p. 17; Merrills, 'The Perils of Panegyric', pp. 149–50.
[16] Merrills and Miles, *The Vandals*, p. 225.
[17] Rosenblum, *Luxorius*, pp. 45–8 (esp. p. 47 – 'the Vandals might have been more unlikely to persecute pagans than Catholics', and pp. 146–7 (text)).
[18] Virgil, *Aeneid* VII; Horace, *Odes*, II.19. Judith W. George, 'Vandal Poets in their Context', in *Vandals, Romans, and Berbers*, ed. Merrills, pp. 133–44 (esp. p. 141).
[19] Hays, 'Fulgentius and the "Vandal Renaissance"', pp. 127–8.
[20] George, 'Vandal Poets in their Context', p. 139.
[21] Anna Leone, *The End of the Pagan City: Religion, Economy, and Urbanism in Late Antique North Africa* (Oxford, 2013), pp. 8–14, 87–101 (esp. pp. 93–6).
[22] Hays, 'Fulgentius and the "Vandal Renaissance"', pp. 128–9.

allusions of other poets between then and the presumed compilation of the *Anthology* in 534, that the language of pastoral gave Catholics safety in the Arian state.[23]

In this way Luxorius' late use of paganism may give the pig a licence to be more Vandal than he first appears:

> Martis aper genitus iugis inesse montium
> Frangere et horrisonum nemus ferocius solens,
> Pabula porticibus capit libenter aureis
> Et posito famulans furore temperat minas.
> Nec Parios lapides revellit ore spumeo
> Atria nec rabidis decora foedat ungulis,
> Sed domini placidam manum quietus appetens
> Fit magis ut Veneris dicatus ille sit sacris.[24]

> A boar of Mars, born to inhabit mountain ridges
> And more fiercely apt to trample the cracking grove,
> Freely takes his fodder among gilded colonnades
> And like a servant, fury abated, checks his threats.
> He neither tears down Parian stone with foaming mouth
> Nor muddies well-furnished rooms with raging trotters,
> But the quiet one seeking his lord's calm hand
> Acts more as if assigned to Venus' rites.

Martial's poetry, too, celebrated wild animals which had become tame, as with a Nemean lion in his *Liber spectaculorum* ('book of shows').[25] Martin Rosenblum, mindful of this heritage, flattens out the phrase *Martis aper* in Luxorius' poem with the words 'a warlike boar', noting that there is 'no mythological allusion to the boar as the favorite animal of Mars'. Venus, he claims, is cited in line 8 apparently in order to complete the 'typical Luxorian contrast', in which the boar is 'now like the gentle doves of Venus'.[26] But Venus' sole connection with a boar, the beast that kills her lover Adonis in Ovid's *Metamorphoses* (Book X, lines 708–89), is not a happy one. There is another contrast between Mars and Venus as divine patrons in Claudian's *De apro et leone* ('on the boar and the lion'), written in Italy in the later fourth century, in which Claudian says of a fight between the animals that *hunc Mars, hunc laudat Cybele* ('Mars praises this one [the boar], Cybele that one [the lion]', line 3).[27] Yet neither Mars nor Venus favours boars in the pastoral of poets of the late Republican and early Imperial

---

[23] Merrills and Miles, *The Vandals*, pp. 225–6.
[24] Rosenblum, *Luxorius*, pp. 114–15.
[25] *M. Valerii Martiali Liber Spectaculorum*, ed. Kathleen M. Coleman (Oxford, 2006), pp. 78–81 (esp. p. 78).
[26] Rosenblum, *Luxorius*, p. 181 (n. 6.8).
[27] *Claudian*, ed. and trans. Maurice Platnauer, Loeb Classical Library 35, 2 vols. (Cambridge, MA, 1976), vol. 2, p. 271 (*Carmina minora* XLII (LIII)).

reigns. Despite its status as a Roman novelty, Luxorius' sixth-century pig presents a mythological puzzle, which we may solve with the help of his patrons.

Luxorius' kings called themselves *Hasdingi*.[28] By this name they appear to have traced themselves back to the Vandal warlords of Pannonia three centuries earlier, whom the Greek historian Cassius Dio, in his *History of Rome* (*c*. AD 171), calls Ἄστιγγοι ('Astingoi', LXXI.12).[29] Whether or not a genuine connection underlay this identity in names, Geiseric's Vandals were a hybrid people. They mixed with other groups, such as the Iranian Alans, East Germanic Goths, West Germanic Sueves, and probably some Romano-Iberians too, if not when they crossed the Rhine (probably near Mainz) in 406, then certainly later, during their Spanish stop-over in 409–29.[30] Procopius, in his *Wars of Justinian* (*c*. 551), comments on the surprising increase of Vandal numbers in North Africa after the invasion of Carthage in the century before him, adding: τὰ δὲ τῶν Ἀλανῶν καὶ τῶν ἄλλων βαρβάρων ὀνόματα, πλὴν Μαυρουσίων, ἐς τὸ τῶν Βανδίλων ἅπαντα ἀπεκρίθη ('but the names of the Alans and other barbarians except the Moors all stood for that of the Vandals', III. 5. 21).[31] In Tunisia some names and titles in funerary inscriptions, as well as in other contemporary textual references, show that people calling themselves Alans and Sueves lived as honorary Vandals among the Vandal aristocracy from the treaty of 442 to the Byzantine invasion of 534. To give a prominent example, an epitaph discovered in the Grand Basilica in Hippo, erected there in 474 in memory of a woman named Ermengon, shows that her husband, Ingomar, named her *Suava* 'a Sueve'; some inscriptions have also been found which contain Alanic names.[32]

Despite the likely racial mix among *Vandali*, the etymology of their name reaches back to Scandinavia. Although neither history nor archaeology confirms it,[33] the *Vandal*-stem points to an early origin or point of provenance either in *Vend*syssel in Jutland or *Vendel* in Swedish Uppland. This is corroborated by the use of the *Wendel*- name in West Germanic vernaculars: not only in OE *Wendelsæ* ('Vandal Sea') for the Mediterranean in Alfredian West Saxon prose, and *Wentilsęo* likewise in the originally Old High German *Hildebrandslied*, line 43 (? *c*. 800);[34] but also in the door-keeper in Danish Heorot, who is

---

[28] Walter Pohl, 'The Vandals: Fragments of a Narrative', in *Vandals, Romans, and Berbers*, ed. Merrills, pp. 31–47 (esp. p. 42).
[29] *Dio's Roman History*, ed. and trans. Earnest Cary and Herbert B. Foster, vol. 9, Loeb Classical Library 177 (London, 1927), 14 (LXXI.12).
[30] Merrills and Miles, *The Vandals*, pp. 84–8, 106–8.
[31] *Procopii Caesariensis Opera Omnia: De Bellis I–IV*, ed. Jacob Haury (Leipzig, 1905), p. 334.
[32] Merrills and Miles, *The Vandals*, pp. 95–7.
[33] Ibid., p. 25. More upbeat, Pohl, 'The Vandals: Fragments of a Narrative', pp. 33–4.
[34] *The Old English Orosius*, ed. Janet Bately, EETS ss 6 (Oxford, 1980), 9.6, 9.9, 10.16 (etc); *The Anglo-Saxon Chronicle: A Collaborative Edition*, vol. 3: *MS A: A Semi-Diplomatic*

known as Wulfgar the *Wendla leod* ('prince of Wendels', *Beowulf*, line 348). There are two equally clear but superficial parallels by which the Goths, on one hand, may be traced to Gotland, and the Burgundians, on the other, to *Borgundahólmr*, or Bornholm, in the southern Baltic.[35] Like the other names of migrating peoples, that of the Vandals was promulgated relatively late. It still seems likely, as was once supposed, that *Andalusia* (Arabic *al-Andalus* (الأندلس), Berber *Wandalus*), the region covering the southern third of the Iberian peninsula, was named for the doomed Vandals of the Siling faction, who had tried to found a new kingdom there in 411–18. The brevity of their stay has been cited as an objection, but other etymologies are more complicated, and it seems best to treat a legend of 'Vandalia' as the most obvious origin, even if only because the Vandals dominated this region from then until 534.[36] *Vandalirice* 'king of the Vandals', a title from Vandalic in the *Latin Anthology* (no. 215) which is reserved for King Hilderic, confirms the use of Latin regal titles: *Vandal-* was the name which defined this kingdom as a new entity.[37]

With the Scandinavian name came a specific language, which has since been defined as East Germanic. Some personal names and even some surviving words attributed to the North African Vandals show that this hybrid aristocracy continued to speak a language related to Gothic, and, through Gothic, to the old language of Scandinavia. *Gunthamund*'s name is identical with Norse *Guðmundr*, while a certain *Becca*, whom Luxorius accuses of buying gay sexual favours with his great-great-grandfathers' inheritance (no. 35), has a name which matches that of an evil Gothic counsellor: *Bikki*, who lurks in Attila's court in the Old Norse *Atlakviða* ('lay of Attila', stanza 14), probably

---

Edition with Introduction and Indices, ed. Janet Bately (Cambridge, 1986), s.a. 885; Leslie Webster, 'Archaeology and *Beowulf*', in *Beowulf: An Edition with Relevant Shorter Texts*, ed. Bruce Mitchell and Fred C. Robinson (Oxford, 1998), pp. 183–94 (p. 60) – references to *Beowulf* from this edition; *Longman Anthology of Old English, Old Icelandic and Anglo-Norman Literatures*, ed. Richard North and Joe Allard, with Patricia Gillies (Harlow, 2011), pp. 122–7 (esp. p. 126 – *Hildebrandslied*).

[35] Herwig Wolfram, *History of the Goths*, trans. Thomas J. Dunlap, 2nd edn (Berkeley, CA, 1979), pp. 19–23.

[36] Ockham's razor would seem to counter the ingenious idea of **landa-hlauts* > **landa-los* > (a)l-andalos 'land-lot [i.e. allocation of lands]', in Heinz Halm, 'Al-Andalus und Gothica Sors', *Der Islam* 66 (1989), 252–63. Other examples of *anda* and *luz* place-name elements in Spain are claimed as the principals, though their meaning is less obvious, by Georg Bossong, in 'Der Name al-Andalus: Neue Überlegungen zu einem alten Problem', in *Sounds and Systems: Studies in Structure and Change: A Festschrift for Theo Vennemann*, ed. David Restle and Dietmar Zaefferer, Trends in Linguistics/Studies and Monographs 141 (Berlin, 2002), pp. 149–64.

[37] Riese, *Anthologia Latina*, p. 154. Nicoletta Francovich Onesti, 'Tracing the Language of the Vandals: A Synthesis of All We Know about the Vandalic Language (5th–6th centuries)', in *The Vandals and the Sueves*, ed. Giorgio Ausenda, Stephen Barnish and A. Rodolfi (forthcoming), p. 3; see <http://www.academia.edu/691311/Tracing_the_Language_of_the_Vandals> [accessed 1 January 2015].

of the tenth century; and *Becca*, who appears in the same general context in *Widsith*, line 115.³⁸ Other Vandal names are dithematic, like most Germanic names, as in *Frid-amal*, *Hoa-mer* and *Hoa-geis* or *Oa-geis*, although the obscurity of their elements shows that Vandalic developed in isolation from Old Scandinavian.

We find an unexpected name for the Vandalic language in *De conviviis barbaris* ('on barbarian guests'), Epigram no. 285 of the *Latin Anthology* (which appears just before the start of Symphosius' *Riddles*):³⁹

> Inter *eils!* goticum *scapia! matzia ia drincan!*
> Non audet quisquam dignos educere versus.
> Calliope madido trepidat se iungere Baccho
> Ne pedibus non stet ebria Musa suis.⁴⁰
>
> Between Gothic 'Hail! Waiter! Meat and drink!'
> No-one dares to produce any decent lines.
> Calliope is alarmed to join with matted Bacchus
> Lest a drunken Muse not stand on her feet.

After much debate on the vernacular morphology of the first of these lines, the most painstaking discussion of all four of them concludes that these 'Gothic' words are most likely Vandalic.⁴¹ They convey a Roman's scorn, or perhaps real horror, at the noise from another table in a crowded hall or restaurant. The poet may refer specifically to the Gothic regiment of one thousand which is said to have escorted Amalafrida, sister of King Theoderic of Italy, to her wedding with Thrasamund in Carthage in 500, but his word *goticum* may also be taken to refer to Vandalic on the evidence of contemporary hearsay.⁴² From the eastern Mediterranean the historian Procopius judged the languages of [Ostro-]Goths, Visigoths, Vandals and Gepids to be one and the same when he said: τῆς γὰρ Ἀρείου δόξης εἰσὶν ἅπαντες, φωνὴ τε αὐτοῖς ἐστι μία, Γοτθικὴ λεγομένη ('they are all of the Arian faith and their language is one, called Gothic', *Wars*, III. 2. 5).⁴³ The close kinship between the languages is confirmed by a third vernacular phrase, *froia arme*, which is held to be the Vandalic translation of *Domine miserere* ('Lord have mercy'), in the Turin manuscript of the *Collatio Beati Augustini cum Pascentio ariano* ('debate between

---

³⁸ *The Poetic Edda*, ed. and trans. Ursula Dronke, vol. 1: *Heroic Poems* (Oxford, 1969), p. 56 (n. 14/3).
³⁹ Riese, *Anthologia Latina*, p. 187.
⁴⁰ Magnús Snædal, 'The "Vandal" Epigram', in *Lingua e Cultura dei Goti*, ed. Fabrizio Raschellà, *Filologia Germanica* 1 (2009), 181–214.
⁴¹ Ibid., pp. 204–10.
⁴² Wolfram, *History of the Goths*, p. 308.
⁴³ Haury, *De Bellis*, p. 311.

the Blessed Augustine and Pascentius the Arian'), of the mid-fifth century.[44] The first word, *frōja*, resembles Gothic *fráuja* ('lord') from the surviving Gospels of Wulfila, as well as OE *frēa*, Old High German *frô* ('lord') and Old Norse *Freyr*. As we have seen, Vandalic is classified as East Germanic, of Scandinavian origin and closely related to the Ostrogothic of Italy and Visigothic of Spain.[45] These languages were distinct from the West Germanic language of the Suevi or Sueves, some of whom are known to have followed the Vandals to Carthage. The use of *goticum* for Vandalic may reflect the Goths' even greater numbers, their profusion of raids in the third century, their most spectacular irruption into the Roman Empire in 376, and the likelihood that Arian missionaries used Gothic on their Vandal converts in the later fourth century, when they first met them in the upper Danube valley.

With the language came an identity, but the evidence so far suggests that the Vandals of North Africa were not a nation until created one by Hasding princes a generation after they entered Africa Proconsularis in 435.[46] Although the Vandals began to Romanise themselves in North Africa from this time onwards (for instance, by building bath houses), they stayed aloof from their Roman subjects both in their Arian faith and by means of the Hasding name itself. With this name it seems that the ruling kindred traced its history to those lands on the far side of the Danube which they had once shared with the Goths. In the 470s this northern river appears unexpectedly in the *Medea* of Dracontius, who reshapes the old story of Jason carrying Juno (i.e. Hera) across the river Euhenus:

> Est nimis acceptus iuvenis mihi pulcher Iason
> Qui gelidum quondam mecum transnaverat Istrum.
>
> (lines 56–7)[47]

> Too pleasing to me is the young beautiful Jason
> Who once swam with me across the freezing Danube.

On the strength of Dracontius' use of folktale motifs in the same Classical story, as well as on that of his address to his teacher Felicianus in the preface to *Romulea* (his name for the larger collection), it has been suggested that Dracontius was a Vandal on his mother's side.[48] His allusion to the Danube reveals that, despite their acceptance of

---

[44] *PL* 33 (Paris, 1845), cols. 1156–62 (esp. col. 1162); Heinrich Tiefenbach, 'Das wandalische Domine miserere', *Historische Sprachforschung: Historical Linguistics* 104.2 (1991), 251–68.
[45] Francovich Onesti, 'Tracing the Language of the Vandals'.
[46] Andreas Schwarcz, 'The Settlement of the Vandals in North Africa', in *Vandals, Romans, and Berbers*, ed. Merrills, pp. 49–57 (esp. p. 54).
[47] Bright, *The Miniature Epic in Vandal North Africa*, p. 50.
[48] Ibid., pp. 67–8.

Roman ways, the Vandals of the late fifth century had not forgotten the river boundary of two to three centuries earlier. The remainder of my essay will search the kitchen of Germanic legend for any scraps concerning pigs in the lost Vandal ideology.

Pigs in Germanic Legend

Far to the north of the Danube lies the Baltic shore which the historian Tacitus, in his *Germania* of AD 98, presents as the homeland of the Suevi. These distant etymological forebears of the Sueves, allies of the Vandals and Alans in Spain, are cited only in passing as borrowers of Celtic ways:

> Ergo iam dextro Suebici maris litore Aestiorum gentes adluuntur, quibus ritus habitusque Sueborum, lingua Britannicae propior. Matrem deum venerantur. Insigne superstitionis formas aprorum gestant: id pro armis hominumque tutela securum cultorum etiam inter hostes praestat.[49]

> So, upon the right of the Suevian Sea, the Aestyan nations reside, who use the same customs and attire as the Suevians; their language more resembles that of Britain. They worship the Mother of gods. As the characteristic of their national superstition, they wear the images of wild boars: this alone serves them for arms, this is the safeguard of all, and by this every worshipper of the goddess is secured even in the midst of his foes.
>
> (*Germania*, ch. 45)

If Tacitus' source is to be trusted, his words tell us that the Baltic Suevi borrowed not only their ways and dress from their Celtic Aestyan neighbours, but also the cult of the *Mater deum* 'Mother of the gods' which lies behind the boar insignia that protect them in battle. That is, their pig serves both war and a great female deity. Here it is worth noting that Tacitus, listing four tribes descending from Mannus (son of Tuisto) near the start of *Germania*, puts Suebi and Vandilii together last.[50] A Celtic origin for the wider Germanic fascination with wild boars has been accepted on the strength of this passage.[51] As to how the boar images may have been worn, this was not on badges or pins: the poet of *Beowulf*, seven or eight centuries later in England, shows

---

[49] *The 'Germania' of Tacitus*, ed. Rodney P. Robinson (Middletown, CT, 1935), p. 332.
[50] Ibid., p. 273 (ch. 2).
[51] Heinrich Beck, *Das Ebersignum im Germanischen: Ein Beitrag zur germanischen Tier-Symbolik*, Quellen und Forschungen zur Sprach- und Kulturgeschichte der Germanischen Völker, N.F. 16 (140) (Berlin, 1965), pp. 58, 110–12.

a troop of Geats guarding themselves as they disembark in Denmark. On their heads they place helmets, and on these:

> Eoforlic scionon
> ofer hleorber<g>an   gehroden golde,
> fah ond fyrheard,   ferhwearde heold
> guþmod grimmon.

> Boar-images shone
> adorned with gold over cheek-guards,
> gleaming and fire-hardened, the war-spirited one
> kept life-watch for fierce men.
>
> (*Beowulf*, lines 303–6)

There appears to be some archaeological corroboration for the material existence of boar-images in this later period, as well as for the purpose which both Tacitus and the poet of *Beowulf* attribute to them, in the boar-emblems on the helmets engraved on the sixth-century Torslunda plates from Sweden, and in the boars fixed to the top of the Benty Grange and Pioneer helmets from eighth-century England.[52] The older Sutton Hoo helmet, probably from before *c.* 625, may also feature a boar in its ridge-like stylisation of a hair-crest bisecting the helmet from the forehead to the back. Still further back in history, since some Roman helmets may have been fashioned with similar purpose, it seems plausible that the boar motif circulated more widely among warriors of Germanic tribes.[53]

The boar also features in two versions of *Heiðreks saga ok Hervarar* ('the saga of Heiðrekr and Hervǫr'). This is a *fornaldar saga* 'legendary saga' which is thought to have been written in Iceland in the thirteenth century.[54] Along with other works in the genre, *Heiðreks saga* preserves the names and outlines of heroic legends which started with the decline and fall of the Roman Empire. The legends in *Heiðreks saga* are about the Goths and their enemies the Huns in the era before the Tervingi and Greuthungi famously crossed the Danube into the empire in 376.[55] Later these groups were respectively renamed as Visigoths and Ostrogoths. In the saga, the tribal name *Tervingi* from this period

---

[52] Helmut Roth, *Kunst der Völkerwanderungszeit* (Frankfurt am Main, 1979), pp. 262–3 and pl. 199a; *The Making of England: Anglo-Saxon Art and Culture, AD 600–900*, ed. Leslie Webster and Janet Backhouse (London, 1991), pp. 59–60 (Benty Grange); Richard Underwood, *Anglo-Saxon Weapons and Warfare* (Stroud, 1999), pp. 103–4 (Pioneer Helmet); Jennifer Foster, 'A Boar Figurine from Guilden Morden, Cambridgeshire', *MedArch* 21 (1977), 166–7.

[53] Guy Halsall, *Warfare and Society in the Barbarian West, 450–900* (London, 2003), pp. 170–1.

[54] *Hervarar saga ok Heiðreks*, ed. Christopher Tolkien, Viking Society for Northern Research, Text Series 2, 2nd edn (London, 1976), pp. xvii–xx.

[55] Peter Heather, 'The Crossing of the Danube and the Gothic Conversion', *Greek, Roman, and Byzantine Studies* 27 (1986), 289–318 (esp. pp. 314–16).

has a thirteenth-century reflex in *Tyrfingr* (ch. 1), the sword which belongs to Angantýr, the grandfather of two princes named Angantýr and Heiðrekr. The latter is said to become king of Reiðgotaland ('land of the *Reið*-Goths', ch. 7). Before that, the fourth-century tribal name *Greuthungi* is reflected in the byname of Heiðrekr's Odinic foster-father, Gizurr *Grýtingaliði* ('aid to the Grýtingar', ch. 5).⁵⁶ It is also worth noting that the fifth and sixth sons of the first Angantýr are referred to as *Haddingjar tveir* ('the two men each called Haddingr', ch. 1). This name, as the assimilated from of *Hardingr < *Hazdingaz, is formally identical with the word Ἄστιγγοι ('Astingoi' or *Hasdingi*), a name for the Vandals.⁵⁷ The double naming may recapture the existence of two Vandalic tribes in Spain, or the joint rule of Raptos and Raos, kings of the Ἄστιγγοι even earlier in the *History* of Cassius Dio.⁵⁸ Though imperfectly aware of the implications of its many names, *Heiðreks saga* represents the Vandals thus as kin to the Goths through a sister's son relationship between the men called Haddingjar, their sister Hervǫr, and her sons Angantýr and Heiðrekr.⁵⁹ Equally unfathomably, the Vandal seniority implicit in this genealogy recalls Pliny the Elder's *Natural History* (AD 77–9), which classifies *Gutones* ('goths') as a sub-group of *Vandili* ('Vandals').⁶⁰

In this light let us now return to Heiðrekr as a Gothic king at the height of his power. Shortly he will lose this power after a brush with the god Óðinn, disguised as Gestumblindi ('the blind guest'), whom he invites to a riddle contest, but whose last riddle he cannot solve. Before the entry of Gestumblindi in the *Hauksbók* manuscript, which is dated to *c*. 1302–10 (Reykjavík, AM 544 4°), King Heiðrekr is said to keep a gigantic boar for sacrifice, as part of his midwinter cult:

> Heiðrekr konungr blótaði Frey; þann gǫlt er mestan fekk, skyldi hann gefa Frey; kǫlluðu þeir hann svá helgan, at yfir hans burst skyldi sverja um ǫll stórmál ok skyldi þeim gelti blóta at sonarblóti; jólaaptan skyldi leiða sonargǫltinn í hǫll fyrir konung ok lǫgðu menn þá hendr yfir burst hans ok strengja heit.⁶¹

King Heiðrekr worshipped Freyr; that boar, the biggest he could get, he was obliged to give to Freyr; they considered the boar so holy that oaths should be sworn over its bristles in all cases of great importance, and it

---

⁵⁶ Tolkien, *Heiðreks saga*, p. 86 (n. 58/2).
⁵⁷ Ferdinand Holthausen, *Wörterbuch des altnordischen (altnorwegisch-isländischen) einschliesslich der Lehn- und Fremdwörter sowie der Eigennamen* (Göttingen, 1948), 103 ('Haddingr'); Alexander Jóhannesson, *Altisländisches etymologisches Wörterbuch* (Bern, 1956), p. 250 ('*haddr* < *hazda-*').
⁵⁸ Cary and Foster, *Dio's Roman History*, 14 (LXXI.12).
⁵⁹ Tolkien, *Heiðreks saga*, pp. 2 (ch. 1), 11–13 (ch. 4), 26 (ch. 6).
⁶⁰ *C. Plini Secundi Naturalis Historia*, ed. Karl Mayhoff, 4 vols. (Leipzig, 1892–1909), vol. 1, p. 347 (IV. 28).
⁶¹ *Heiðreks saga: Hervarar saga ok Heiðreks konungs*, ed. Jón Helgason (Copenhagen, 1924), pp. 54–5.

was that boar which was sacrificed at the pig-sacrifice; at Yule eve this boar from the sounder was to be led into the hall and before the king, and men then laid hands over his bristles, making a vow.

(ch. 10)

Sæhrímnir, the boar of Valhǫll in Old Norse mythology, is also sacrificed and eaten, but he (in a more Celtic way) regenerates himself.[62] In another version of *Heiðreks saga*, in Copenhagen GKS 2845 4°, from the early fifteenth century, the same scene is written without mention of Freyr, although the riddle contest with Óðinn continues in the same way:

> Heiðrekr konungr sezt nú um kyrrt ok gerist höfðingi mikill ok spekingr at viti. Heiðrekr konungr lét ala gölt mikinn. Hann var svá mikill sem öldungar þeir, er stærstir váru, ok svá fagr, at hvert hár þótti ór gulli vera. Konungrinn leggr hönd sína á höfuð geltinum, en aðra á burst ok sverr þess, at aldri hefir maðr svá mikit af gert við hann, at eigi skuli hann hafa réttan dóm spekinga hans, en þeir tólf skulu gæta galtarins, eða ella skal hann bera upp gátur þær, er hann gæti eigi ráðit. Heiðrekr konungr gerist ok nú inn vinsælasti.[63]

> King Heiðrekr settles down peacefully for a while and becomes a great chieftain and a sage of much wisdom. King Heiðrekr had a great boar bred and raised. He was as big as the largest bulls, and so fair that each hair seemed to be of gold. The king puts one hand on the boar's head, and the other on his bristles, and swears this, that no matter the magnitude of whatever a man had done against him, he should receive true justice from his wise men, and these twelve are to watch over the boar, or else this man shall have to propound those riddles which the king could not solve. And now Heiðrekr becomes the most popular king.

(ch. 9)

Despite Freyr's absence, in this version the boar of golden bristles is presented as the religious symbol on which Heiðrekr swears an oath (in this case, to deliver justice). Common to both passages is the motif of a Gothic king resting his hand on a boar in a public ceremony. Peculiar to one variant (*Hauksbók*) is the role of Freyr as the king's tutelary god, to whom the pig belongs and its body must go. Peculiar to the other (Copenhagen GKS 2845 4°) is the defendant's option of a riddle contest with the king as an alternative to accepting justice from the twelve men who look after the boar. In either case, whether that of court-room or riddle, the boar sanctifies the king's rule.

---

[62] *Snorri Sturluson: Edda: Prologue and Gylfaginning*, ed. Anthony Faulkes (Oxford, 1982), p. 32 (ch. 38); Matthias Egeler, *Celtic Influences in Germanic Religion: A Survey*, Münchner Nordistische Studien 15 (Munich, 2013), pp. 81–5 (3.12); Beck, *Das Ebersignum*, p. 58.
[63] Tolkien, *Heiðreks saga*, p. 36.

You Sexy Beast

The god Freyr is associated with a gold-bristled boar in other remnants of the Icelandic tradition. The skald Úlfr Uggason describes Freyr in his *Húsdrápa* ('Eulogy on the house'), for which a date of *c.* 995 may be worked out from the mention of this poem in the context of a wedding in *Laxdœla saga* (ch. 29, *c.* 1245).[64] In this poem Freyr rides to the funeral pyre of Baldr (recently slain by Hǫðr and the mistletoe) in a procession of Norse gods:

> Ríðr á borg til borgar   boðfróðr sonar Óðins
> Freyr ok fólkum stýrir   fyrst ok gulli byrstum.[65]

Rides in first place, and on a boar with bristles of gold,
Battle-wise Freyr to the fortress of Óðinn's son and he guides the peoples.

The poet's *borg* refers to the pyre as a wall of logs, but its guise here as 'fortress' also recalls European wars. This verse was quoted probably in the 1230s in illustration of kennings for Freyr within *Skáldskaparmál* ('poetics') by the mythographer Snorri Sturluson (1179–1241), who adds that the boar is called *Gullinbursti* ('golden-bristle', ch. 14).[66] In his preceding treatise, the *Gylfaginning* ('beguiling of Gylfi'), Snorri writes a prose version of the story of Baldr's funeral in which *Freyr ók í kerru með gelti þeim, er Gullinbursti heitir eða Slíðrugtanni* ('Freyr drove in a cart with that pig whose name is Golden-Bristle or Slice-Tooth', ch. 49).[67] Úlfr's heathen verse, on which Snorri relies for some of this information, also tells us that Freyr is *boðfróðr* ('battle-wise'), that he *fólkum stýrir* ('guides the peoples') and does so *fyrst* ('first'), at the head of the procession. These terms resemble Freyr's epithet in *Skírnismál* ('lay of Skírnir') as *fólkvaldi goða* ('field-marshal of gods', stanza 3).[68] They also match the warlike associations of boars which we have seen in *Germania* and *Beowulf*. It is as a god leading nations to war that Freyr rides his boar in this pre-Christian poem.

An association between the boar and the marching of nations lingers on in Cynewulf's *Elene*, his possibly ninth-century adaptation of a Latin text of the *Acta Cyriaci* ('acts of St Cyriac'). The story concerns the Invention of the True Cross by Empress Helena in Jerusalem, allegedly in 326. Helena was the mother of Emperor

---

[64] Richard North, 'Image and Ascendancy in Úlfr Uggason's *Húsdrápa*', in *Text, Image, Interpretation: Studies in Anglo-Saxon Literature and its Insular Context in Honour of Éamonn Ó Carragáin*, ed. Alastair Minnis and Jane Roberts, Studies in the Early Middle Ages 18 (Turnhout, 2007), pp. 369–404 (esp. pp. 370–7).
[65] *Snorri Sturluson: Edda: Skáldskaparmál*, ed. Anthony Faulkes, 2 vols. (London, 1998), vol. 1, p. 19 (verse 63). See also North, 'Úlfr's *Húsdrápa*', p. 391.
[66] Faulkes, *Gylfaginning*, p. 47.
[67] *The Poetic Edda*, ed. and trans. Ursula Dronke, vol 2: *Mythological Poems* (Oxford, 1997), pp. 377, 405 (n. 3/2).
[68] Text based on that in *Cynewulf's 'Elene'*, ed. P. O. E. Gradon, 2nd edn (Exeter, 1977), pp. 15–22, 26–30.

Constantine I (r. 306/324–37), whose early rise to power and battle against Maxentius for Rome in 312 has been blurred in the *Acta* with a number of other wars. The initial date of AD 233, which Cynewulf preserved in *Elene*, adds to the confusion, for although Constantine did campaign against the Franks in 310, the additional presence of Huns among the migrating hordes in the opening stage of this poem is reminiscent of Roman campaigns well after his time, in the late fourth and even fifth centuries. In this amalgam of wars, however, the source appears to reflect Constantine's treaty with the Goths in 332, the first of its kind ever recorded; possibly also the war of his son Constantius II (r. 337/350–61) against various tribes, including the Vandals.[69] In Cynewulf's adaptation, the hordes assemble thus:

> Garas lixtan,
> wriðene wælhlencan. Wordum ond bordum
> hofon herecombol. Þa wæron heardingas
> sweotole gesamnod ond eal <sib> geador;
> For folca gedryht.

> Spears glinted,
> mail-coats on the move. With words and shields
> they lifted war-standards. Barbarians now were
> manifestly gathered and all their kin together;
> a retinue of nations marched.
> (*Elene*, lines 23–7)

The final phrase recalls the movement of *fólk* ('nations') implicit in Freyr's warlike procession towards Baldr's funeral pyre, while also encapsulating the period now known as the 'Age of Migrations'. The word *heardingas* (here 'barbarians') also has a certain role to play. This word occurs only in *Elene* and in the Old English *Rune Poem* and is usually taken as a cypher for 'warriors' on the basis of *heard*, 'hard(ened)', with the attributive *-ing* attached.[70] Formally, however, with **hazd-* > **hard-*, we have a word identical with Ἀστιγγοι, *Hasdingi* and *Haddingjar*. On this evidence Cynewulf's word *heardingas* appears to descend from a name which refers to the Vandals. However, Cynewulf's word's meaning cannot be quite so specific in his time, for there is no mention of *heardingas* (or of the *Wendle*) in the tribal catalogue *Widsith*; the context, in which Constantine defends the empire, speaks for 'barbarians' as a generalised meaning in the word. Constantine's victory against them, of which the poet assures us through Constantine's vision of the cross the night before, further defines the *heardingas* as heathens:

---

[69] Wolfram, *History of the Goths*, pp. 62–4.
[70] C. W. Grein, *Sprachschatz der angelsächsichen Dichter* (Göttingen, 1861), p. 59 ('hearding: vir strenuus, Held').

> Hæðene grungon,
> feollon friðelease.   Flugon instæpes
> Huna leode,   swa þæt halige treo
> aræran heht   Romwara cyning,
> heaðofremmende.   Wurdon heardingas
> wide towrecene.
>
> Heathens were slaughtered,
> fell without ransom. As quickly as they fled,
> men of the Huns, so did the king of Romans
> order that the holy war-promoting tree
> should be raised. Barbarians found themselves
> driven far and wide.
>
> (*Elene*, lines 126–31)

In these lines it appears that *heardingas* is chosen in order to describe barbarians as a type. In the earlier scene of the vision which leads to their rout in this battle, Cynewulf takes care to show Constantine as a warlord not yet brought to the true faith. On the eve of the battle, an angel visits Constantine in a dream:

> Þuhte him wlitescyne   on weres hade
> hwit ond hiwbeorht   hæleða nathwylc
> geywed ænlicra   þonne he ær oððe sið
> gesege under swegle.   He of slæpe onbrægd,
> eofurcumble beþeaht.
>
> Dazzling fair in a man's form there appeared to him,
> white and brilliant of hue, some kind of man
> displayed more peerless than any, either now or before,
> he saw beneath the sun. From sleep he awoke,
> roofed by boar-banner.
>
> (*Elene*, lines 72–6)

The *eofurcumbel* appears to define the emperor as a Germanic heathen on a par with the *herecumbol*-wielding *heardingas* (line 25) whom he must fight the next day.[71] This and other parts of Cynewulf's militarisation of his king are additions to the Latin, which runs more briefly as follows:

> Ea vero nocte veniens vir splendidissimus suscitavit eum, et dixit: Constantine, noli timere, sed respice sursum in cœlom, et vide, et intendens in cœlom vidit signum Crucis Christi, ex lumine claro constitutum, et desuper litteris scriptum titulum, IN HOC VINCE.[72]

---

[71] Beck, *Das Ebersignum*, pp. 10–11.
[72] Quoted in Antonina Harbus, 'Text as Revelation: Constantine's Dream in *Elene*', *Neophilologus* 78 (1994), 645–53 (esp. p. 645).

That night, however, a man most radiant came and awakened him, and said: Constantine, fear not, but look up into heaven and see, and so looking up to heaven he saw the sign of the Cross of Christ made of bright light, and above it an inscription written with the letters CONQUER BY THIS.

In Cynewulf's addition to the Latin, the boar-image on a banner protects the sleeping king. This resembles the declared purpose of the gilded swine-emblems on Geatish helmets in *Beowulf*, lines 303–6.

A more complete analogue of *Húsdrápa*'s association between the golden boar, the god Freyr and a funeral may be seen in the '*Finnsburh* Episode' in *Beowulf*, lines 1063–160.[73] In this episode King Finn of the Frisians, son of *Folcwalda* ('commander of the people', *Beowulf*, line 1089), prepares to seal a treaty with his former enemies the Half-Danes, in a funeral following a battle in which his son and brother-in-law have fallen on opposite sides:

> Að wæs geæfned ond i<n>cgegold
> ahæfen of horde. Here-Scyldinga
> betst beadorinca wæs on bæl gearu.
> Æt þam ade wæs eþgesyne
> swatfah syrce, swyn ealgylden,
> eofer irenheard, æþeling manig
> wundum awyrded. Sume on wæle crungon!

> The oath was performed and Ing-gold
> lifted from the hoard. The best fighting man
> of raiding Scyldings was ready on the bier.
> At that pyre it was easy to see
> a blood-stained war-shirt, an all-golden swine,
> an iron-hard boar, many a prince sent by wounds
> to his maker. Distinguished men died in that slaughter!
>
> (*Beowulf*, lines 1107–13)

This context gives us a heathen king with both a golden boar-image and a father known as *Folcwalda*, whose name on line 1089 is like *fólkvaldi goða* ('field-marshal of gods'), an epithet reserved for Freyr in *Skírnismál*, stanza 3. In addition, the first element in the compound *i<n>cgegold* (line 1107, *icge gold* in the manuscript) has been read as identical with *incge*, a prefix which also appears on line 2577 in *incge laf*, referring to Beowulf's sword 'heirloom'; *incge* is identifiable as a formal cognate of *Ingvi*, *Yngvi* or *Ingunar*, three variants of a prefix to Freyr's name in Old Norse mythology.[74] The oldest example of these, *Ingvi-freyr* (literally, 'Ingvi-lord'), occurs in *Haustlǫng* ('harvest-long'),

---

[73] Richard North, 'Tribal Loyalties in the *Finnsburh Fragment* and Episode', *LSE* ns 21 (1990), 13–43 (esp. pp. 32–6).
[74] Christopher Ball, 'Incge Beow. 2577', *Anglia* 78 (1960), 403–10 (esp. pp. 409–10).

a shield-poem with pastoral elements which was composed by the Norwegian Þjóðólfr of Hvinir, probably *c.* 900.[75] This prefix is also known in Frisian, from runes carved on a seventh- or eighth-century bone amulet found in Wijnaldum, as *inguz*;[76] and in Gothic, in the rune-name *enguz*;[77] it has also been read into the damaged runic inscription on the Pietroasa ring of *c.* 450, as **gutani [i]ngwa hailag** ('holy to Enguz of the Goths'), although, more controversially,[78] **gutani [i]owi** ('to the Jove of the Goths') and **gutaniowi** ('to Gutaniowi [a woman's name, cognate with Old Icelandic Guðný]') have also been proposed.[79] Regardless of the difficulty of some of this detail, the same *Ing*-stem is fairly widespread in Germanic names from early to late in the first millennium. It also occurs in *Ingomar*, husband of Ermengon the Sueve in the aforementioned funerary inscription from Hippo in 474.[80] On these scraps of evidence, it is reasonable to suppose that there was a cult corresponding to that of Ingvi-freyr in the background of Vandals as well as Goths.

In this light it is worth revisiting the lines on 'Ing' in the eleventh-century Old English *Rune Poem*. This work survives in a 1705 printed transcription from a now-lost original in which George Hickes copied rune names in Roman letters and then in runic form on the left-hand margin.[81] The poem aims to memorialise, or even to teach, the *futhorc*, or runic alphabet, which lay in the Anglo-Saxon tradition. Where the Ing-rune, cognate with Gothic *enguz*, is concerned, the poet says:

> **ing** wæs ærest   mid East-Denum
> gesewen secgun,   oþ he siððan eft
> ofer wæg gewat,   wæn æfter ran;
> þus heardingas   ðone hæle nemdun.

---

[75] *The 'Haustlǫng' of Þjóðólfr of Hvinir*, ed. and trans. Richard North (Enfield Lock, 1997), pp. 6 (text), 43–4 (n. 10/6).

[76] Tineke Looijenga, *Texts and Contexts of the Oldest Runic Inscriptions* (Leiden, 2003), p. 325 ('?**ngz inguz ngz**').

[77] Franz Unterkircher, *Alkuin-Briefe und andere Traktate im Auftrage des Salzburger Erzbishofs Arn um 799 zu einem Sammelband vereinigt: Codex Vindobonensis 795 der österreichischen Nationalbibliothek Faksimileausgabe*, Codices Selecti 22 (Graz, 1969), pp. 10–13; René Derolez, *Runica Manuscripta: The English Tradition* (Bruges, 1954), pp. 52–63 (esp. p. 58). On evidence for the Gothic cult of Enguz, see Richard North, *Heathen Gods in Old English Literature*, CSASE 22 (Cambridge, 1997), pp. 143–53.

[78] C. J. S. Marstrander, 'De Gotiske Runeminnesmerker', *Norsk tidsskrift for sprogvidenskap* 3 (1929), 25–175 (esp. pp. 39–65).

[79] Richard Loewe, 'Der Goldring von Pietroasa', *Indogermanische Forschungen* 26 (1909), 203–8; followed by Wolfram, *History of the Goths*, pp. 109–10; Magnús Snædal, 'The Runic Inscriptions from Kovel and Pietroassa', in *'Unte boka usqimiþ, iþ ahma gaqiujiþ' (2 Cor. 3, 6): Giornate per Piergiuseppe Scardigli 1° e 2 ottobre 2009: Università di Siena, Facoltà di Lettere e Filosofia (di Arezzo)*, pp. 6–8; <https://www.academia.edu/758283/The_Runic_Inscriptions_from_Kovel_and_Pietroassa> [accessed 2 January 2015].

[80] Merrills and Miles, *The Vandals*, pp. 95–7.

[81] *The Old English Rune Poem: A Critical Edition*, ed. Maureen Halsall (Toronto, 1981), pp. 21–32; North, *Heathen Gods*, pp. 44–8.

> Ing was first among eastern Danes
> seen among men, until back again later he
> passed over the wave, the wagon ran after;
> thus did barbarians name that hero.
>
> (*Rune Poem*, lines 67–70)

Ing's circuit in this brief mnemonic is comparable with other wagon-tours, such as those of Nerthus in the first-century *Germania*, ch. 40, or of Freyr in the fourteenth-century *Gunnars þáttr helmings*.[82] These are usually treated as reflexes of a common Germanic cult ancestral to the Norse Vanir, Freyr, Freyja and their father Njǫrðr.[83] Of greater interest here, however, is the poet's use of *heardingas* for the people who first give this *hæle* ('hero') his name. Although the meaning of this passage is generalised, the association between Ing and *heardingas* may long precede the poem, from a time when the elements meant something more specific. If so, it appears that some Anglo-Saxons believed that the Vandals honoured Ing (their version of Ingvi-freyr) before anyone else did.

Conclusions

If we return to Carthage and Luxorius' pet pig in the 520s, these scraps of evidence and surmise from a reconstructed Germanic past may be used as a guide to the nativism of Vandal masters. As Arian Christians, the Hasdings were at least as hostile to paganism as the Catholics they persecuted. Yet Luxorius' use of pastoral in this *Archilochium*, as we have seen, gives him the freedom to engage with pagan culture on a ground which was free from questions of faith and heresy. If pastoral was a place where their own folklore might venture a role, we can read the opening words *Martis aper* ('a boar of Mars') as an allusion to Freyr and Gullinbursti in a lost Vandalic guise. Although, with *porticibus aureis* ('gilded colonnades') on line 3, it is the building and not the boar that is golden in this poem, Luxorius' use of *dominus* ('lord') for the pig's owner on the penultimate line returns us to Freyr. It has long been accepted that this name is the personification of a title for 'lord' which is better known from OE *frēa*, Old High German *frô*, Gothic

---

[82] Robinson, *Germania*, p. 317 (ch. 40); *Flateyjarbók*, ed. C. R. Unger, 3 vols. (Christiania, 1860–8), vol. 1, pp. 337–9 (chs. 277–8); North, *Heathen Gods*, pp. 19–25.

[83] Dieter Timpe, 'Tacitus' *Germania* als religionsgeschichtliche Quelle', *Germanische Religionsgeschichte: Quellen und Quellenprobleme*, ed. Heinrich Beck, Dietrich Ellmers and Kurt Schier, Ergänzungsbände zum Reallexikon der Germanischen Altertumskunde 5 (Berlin, 1992), pp. 434–85.

fráuja, and apparently Vandalic *frōja*, too.[84] The settled ideal of kingship, divine as well as mortal, in all these cases probably derived from an emulation of the Inguz god in whose honour the Scandinavians, the last Germanic heathens of Europe, transformed the 'lord' epithet into a proper name. Of the North African Hasdingi, moreover, it has been argued that *dominus* became the preferred appleation from Huneric (r. 477–84) onwards, that is, from the time Dracontius says that he endured arrest and imprisonment for having eulogised a *dominum ignotum* ('a long-forgotten lord').[85] Like a late Roman manifestation of the boar on whose bristles King Heiðrekr publicly lays his hand, Luxorius' pig is *domini placidam manum quietus appetens* ('the quiet one seeking his lord's calm hand'). Luxorius refers to himself as a puppy's *dominus* ('master') in Epigram no. 73, but his use of Vandal patrons, together with the role of Fridamal as a self-styled boar-slayer in no. 18, supports the notion that the *dominus* of the pig in no. 6 is a Vandal.[86] We do not know who he was, whether king or prince, but if it is true that he had tamed a wild boar, as the first line implies, this man had invested much in a creature not normally raised as a pet. The question to ask, therefore, is what this *frōja* saw in his pig.

Venus, whose cult, according to Luxorius, the Vandal boar seems recently to have joined, figures in this epigram as Mars' rival (rather his lover, as in some other sources). There is no Classical precedent for linking either deity to boars, but there is some evidence in the Germanic tradition by which make such a connection for Venus. In the first century, as we have seen, Tacitus associated the Celtic and Suevic *formas aprorum* ('images of wild boars') with the *Mater deum* ('Mother of gods') in *Germania* (ch. 45). This deity is thought to protect her warriors through the power of boar emblems which they display in battle, probably on their helmets. Our Old Norse analogues for Venus-pigs, which were composed more than a thousand years later, consist of two scenes: one from the likely eleventh-century *Helgakviða Hjǫrvarðssonar* ('lay of Helgi Hjǫrvarðsson'); the other from the composite poem *Hynduljóð* ('lay of Hyndla'), which, though extant only in *Flateyjarbók*, resembles *Heiðreks saga* in revealing some names and associations that are many centuries older.

In the first case, we are told a sad story of Heðinn, Helgi's brother, who meets an amorous *trǫllkona* ('demon woman') on his travels.[87] She *bauð fylgð sína Heðni* ('offered Heðinn her company'), but he turns her down, so she warns him that *Þess scaltu gialda at bragarfulli* ('You

---

[84] D. H. Green, *The Carolingian Lord: Semantic Studies in Four Old High German Words: Balder; Frô; Truhtin; Hêrro* (Cambridge, 1965), pp. 19–55.
[85] Merrills, 'The Perils of Panegyric', pp. 156–7.
[86] Rosenblum, *Luxorius*, pp. 154–5.
[87] *Edda: Die Lieder des Codex Regius nebst verwandten Denkmälern*, ed. Gustav Neckel and Hans Kuhn, 5th edn (Heidelberg, 1983), p. 147.

shall pay for this at the pledging cup'). The next story proceeds on the assumption that its audience understands the ceremony:

> Um qveldit óro heitstrengingar. Var fram leiddr sonargǫltr, lǫgðo menn þar á hendr sínar, oc strengðo menn þá heit at bragarfulli. Heðinn strengði heit til Svávo, Eylima dóttur, unnosto Helga, bróður síns, oc iðraðiz svá miǫc.

> In the evening vows were made. A boar from the sounder was led forward, men laid their hands on him, and then, with a toast from the pledging cup, made vows. Heðinn made a vow to win Sváva, Eylimi's daughter, the sweetheart of his brother Helgi, and regretted this so terribly.

Once again, the boar's bristles sanctify a vow, this one to do with love. In Scandinavia the leading goddess of love is known as Freyja, Freyr's sister. Although Freyja's name is missing in the story in *Helgakviða Hjǫrvarðssonar*, she has a lot to do with a boar in *Hyndluljóð*.

The story in this poem, the basis of which was probably composed in the twelfth century, is that Freyja wakens the seeress Hyndla from the dead so that they both may ride to Valhǫll (Óðinn's 'hall of the slain'): Hyndla on a wolf and Freyja on her pet boar *Hildisvíni* ('war-swine').[88] Freyja's aim is to make Hyndla reveal to her the full ancestry of her lover, Óttarr. As Hyndla suspects, the pig is really Óttarr, transformed by Freyja. The goddess at first denies this:

> Dulin ertu Hyndla, draums ætlig þér,
> er þú qveðr ver minn í valsinni,
> þar er gǫltr glóar, gullinbursti,
> Hildisvíni, er mér hagir gørðo,
> dvergar tveir, Dáinn oc Nabbi.

> You are muddled, Hyndla, I think you are dreaming,
> when you say my man is in company for Valhǫll
> in my boar where he glows with his golden bristles,
> War-Swine, whom, skilled, they made for me,
> the two dwarves Dáinn and Nabbi.
>
> (stanza 7)

Later Hyndla divines that Óttarr has indeed been turned into this golden boar named after the ferocity of a soldier (stanza 12). The names she produces, a who's who of heroes and their kindreds in the north, bring three familiars together from as early as the third century:

---

[88] Ibid., pp. 190–2.

> 'Búi oc Brámi,   Barri oc Reifnir,
> Tindr oc Tyrfingr   oc tveir Haddingiar;
> alt er þat ætt þín,   Óttarr heimsci.'

> 'Búi and Brámi, Barri and Reifnir,
> Tindr and Tyrfingr and the two Haddingjar;
> That's all your family, Óttarr the foolish.'

(stanza 23)

The wider list of twelve almost matches that of the berserker sons of Arngrímr and Eyfura at the start of *Heiðreks saga*, with the exception of Tyrfingr, there the name of a sword (ch. 1).[89] As we have seen, however, Tyrfingr and the two Haddingjar are Norse nominal reflexes of Tervingi and Hasdingi, respectively names for the kindreds of Visigoths and Vandals. Jǫrmunrekkr, reflex of the Greuthung Goth Ermanaric, follows in stanza 25, as well as the Burgundian Gunnarr and Hǫgni in stanza 27. Thus the three tribes of eastern Scandinavia, the Goths, Vandals and Burgundians, are still remembered together. After Hyndla is finished, Freyja admits that Óttarr is the boar when she compels Hyndla to bring him a potion by which he can learn the whole list (stanzas 46–9). The aim is to help him win a bet he has made with his bad brother, Angantýr. The lengths to which Freyja will go for her *Hildisvíni* ('war-swine') in this poem can thus be seen to bind him to her as a servant just as much as a lover. As in the last line of Luxorius' epigrams, where the boar of Mars *fit magis ut Veneris dicatus ille sit sacris* ('acts more as if assigned to Venus' rites)', the conceit of *Hyndluljóð* is Circean: a tame boar is a man in disguise.

The idea that Luxorius' pig in the villa may stand for the Vandals receives some support from his Carthaginian tendency to represent society types as freakish, foolish or perverted.[90] So, to conclude this essay's reading of Epigram no. 6, it seems likely that two things are going on. One is flattering, that the *dominus* in question is a Vandal who styles himself as a king of old, with a boar in residence to authenticate his race and ancestral cult. The other reading, less flattering but still consistent with my reconstruction of folklore, is that this pig represents all the Vandals in Carthage. On line 5, where the pig *nec Parios lapides revellit ore spumeo* ('neither tears down Parian stone with foaming mouth'), there may be an ironic reference to the spoliation of marbles from disused public buildings in order to build baths and private Vandal homes.[91] Luxorius' brief poem reads like a wry epitaph: once the Vandals were too fierce; now they are too civilised!

---

[89] Tolkien, *Heiðreks saga*, pp. 1–2 (ch. 1).
[90] George, 'Vandal Poets in their Context', p. 136.
[91] Leone, *The End of the Pagan City*, pp. 97–8.

When the war came, it did seem that the North African Vandals belonged to Venus. According to Procopius' account of Justinian's invasion, written some seventeen years later:

ἐθνῶν γὰρ ἁπάντων ὧν ἡμεῖς ἴσμεν ἁβρότατον μὲν τὸ τῶν Βανδίλων, ταλαιπωρότατον δὲ τὸ Μαυρουσίων τετύχηκεν εἶναι. οἱ μὲν γὰρ, ἐξ ὅτου Λιβύην ἔσχον, βαλανείοις τε οἱ ξύμπαντες ἐπεχρῶντο ἐς ἡμέραν ἑκάστην καὶ τραπέζῃ ἁπάσῃ εὐθηνούσῃ ὅσα δὴ γῆ τε καὶ θάλασσα ἥδιστά τε καὶ ἄριστα φέρει. ἐχρυσοφόρουν δὲ ὡς ἐπὶ πλεῖστον, καὶ Μηδικὴν ἐσθῆτα ἣν νῦν Σηρικὴν καλοῦσιν ἀμπεχόμενοι ἔν τε θεάτροις καὶ ἱπποδρομίοις καὶ τῇ ἄλλῃ εὐπαθείᾳ καὶ πάντων μάλιστα κυνηγεσίοις τὰς διατριβὰς ἐποιοῦντο. καὶ σφίσιν ὀρχησταὶ καὶ μῖμοι ἀκούσματά τε συχνὰ καὶ θεάματα ἦν ὅσα μουσικά τε καὶ ἄλλως ἀξιοθέατα ξυμβαίνει ἐν ἀνθρώποις εἶναι. καὶ ᾤκηντο μὲν αὐτῶν οἱ πολλοὶ ἐν παραδείσοις ὑδάτων καὶ δένδρων εὖ ἔχουσι· ξυμπόσια δὲ ὅτι πλεῖστα ἐποίουν, καὶ ἔργα τὰ ἀφροδίσια πάντα αὐτοῖς ἐν μελέτῃ πολλῇ ἤσκητο.[92]

> Of all the nations we know of, the Vandals have turned out the most luxurious, the Moors the most hardy. The Vandals, all of them from the time they gained Libya, would enjoy baths every day as well as a table abounding in all the sweetest and best things that the earth and sea provide. And they wore gold very generally, and dressing up in the Medic garments which are now called *Seric* ('silk'), passed their time in theatres and hippodromes and in other pleasurable pursuits, and in hunting most of all. And for them there were dancers and mimes as well as such musical or otherwise arresting things as are heard or seen among men. And most of them dwelt in parks which were well stocked with water and trees; and they held a great number of banquets and all the erotic acts were much performed among them.
>
> (*Wars*, IV. 6. 5–9)

For this claim of degeneracy Procopius may rely on Luxorius and other North African epigrams as much as on refugees, and it is worth noting that 'it was as soldiers that the Vandals were deported by Justinian and used in his Persian wars'.[93] On the other hand, the Vandals did not have Belisarius.

The outwitted Gelimer soon lost his advantage and brought down the Vandals for ever by retreating to a fort on Mount Papua with a retinue of Moors. In a letter to the besieging General Pharas of Byzantium, Gelimer wished disaster on Justinian. Being unable to avenge himself with violence, however, he achieved catharsis with a poem. In the pre-Christian *Sonatorrek* ('hard loss of sons', *c.* 960), Egill Skalla-Grímsson invokes Óðinn, god of poetry, as he mourns his son Bǫðvarr, drowned off Borg. Egill moves from the impossibility of violent revenge to the act of composition as an alternative means

---

[92] Haury, *De Bellis*, pp. 443–4.
[93] Schwarcz, 'The Settlement of the Vandals in North Africa', p. 57.

of relieving his grief.⁹⁴ In a similar way Gelimer requested a loaf, a sponge and a lyre. Although this part of his letter continues to puzzle scholars, the messenger explained to Pharas, according to Procopius, that the loaf was because Gelimer was hungry, the sponge to wipe away his tears, and the lyre, lastly, because:

κιθαριστῇ δὲ ἀγαθῷ ὄντι ᾠδή τις αὐτῷ ἐς ξυμφορὰν τὴν παροῦσαν πεποίηται, ἣν δὴ πρὸς κιθάραν θρηνῆσαί τε καὶ ἀποκλαῦσαι ἐπείγεται.

as a good player of the lyre Gelimer has made himself an ode on the present disaster, which he is in haste to sing at the lyre with lamenting and mourning.

(*Wars* IV. 6. 33).⁹⁵

If Gelimer was as indebted as Egill to a one-eyed god for his poem, we shall never know, but the story shows that the Vandals had their own elegiac tradition. Pig or no pig in a villa, Gelimer's ode for a lost nation ran deeper than the whole *Latin Anthology*, and through him the Vandals' last epitaph was composed not by Luxorius, but by the Vandals themselves.

---

⁹⁴ Richard North, 'The Pagan Inheritance of Egill's *Sonatorrek*', in *Atti del 12° Congresso internazionale di studi sull'alto medioevo*, ed. Teresa Pàroli, Seventh International Saga Conference (Spoleto, 1990), pp. 147–67 (esp. pp. 154–8).
⁹⁵ Haury, *De Bellis*, p. 447.

8

'For the Sake of Bravado in the Wilderness'[1]

Confronting the Bestial in Anglo-Saxon Warfare

Thomas J. T. Williams

'We are wise in our civilized knowledge, but our knowledge extends just so far [...]
Who knows what shapes earthly and unearthly may lurk beyond the dim circle of light our knowledge has cast?
Who knows what gods are worshipped under the shadows of that heathen forest, or what devils crawl out of the black ooze of the swamps?'
[...]
'There's nothing in the universe cold steel won't cut', answered Conan.[2]

The equation of the behaviour of men in war with the attributes of animals is ingrained in modern descriptions of violence: men 'fight like beasts', 'crawl like worms', 'die like dogs'. The imagery is old and surprisingly stable over time and place. In the *Iliad*, Odysseus fights like a boar in a thicket, just as Alfred is said to have done at the battle of Ashdown, or Caradawg at Catraeth.[3] It is therefore not at all surprising to encounter a bestial dimension to the conceptualisation of Anglo-Saxon warfare. Animal imagery finds rich expression in the material culture of the Anglo-Saxon military elite in the seventh and eighth centuries,[4] as well as in later literature, a fact to which many

---

[1] *Guthlac A*, line 208, in *Anglo-Saxon Poetry*, trans. S. A. J. Bradley (London, 1982), p. 255; unless otherwise stated all line references and untranslated Old English poetry are from *The Anglo-Saxon Poetic Records: A Collective Edition*, ed. Elliot van Kirk Dobbie, 6 vols. (New York, 1931–53).

[2] Robert E. Howard, 'Beyond the Black River', *Weird Tales* (May/June 1935), republished in *The Complete Chronicles of Conan*, ed. Stephen Jones (London, 2006), pp. 442–3.

[3] Homer, *Iliad* 11.413–420, in *Homer: The Iliad*, trans. Robert Fitzgerald (Oxford, 1974), p. 191; Asser, *Vita Alfredi*, ch. 38, in *Alfred the Great: Asser's Life of King Alfred and Other Contemporary Sources*, ed. and trans. Simon Keynes and Michael Lapidge (Harmondsworth, 1983), p. 79; Aneirin, 'Y Gododdin', lines 30–3, in *The Earliest Welsh Poetry*, trans. Joseph P. Clancy (London, 1970).

[4] For a recent general survey and references, see Aleks Pluskowski, 'Animal Magic', in *Signals of Belief in Early England: Anglo-Saxon Paganism Revisited*, ed. Martin O. H. Carver, Alexandra Sanmark and Sarah Semple (Oxford, 2010), pp. 118–20.

of the papers in this book and elsewhere have drawn attention.⁵ This chapter will briefly survey some of the ways in which the beast was represented, encountered, and conceptualised in the warfare of early medieval England, before moving to a consideration of the battlefield as wilderness: a place that was imagined as an appropriate forum for expressing, testing and containing the bestial energies that were imagined to be unleashed in the conduct of violence.

The general reluctance of people to kill each other in conflict has been frequently observed in modern contexts, and it has long been recognised that in pre-state societies even exceptionally war-like groups engage in artificial rituals designed to induce a state of heightened aggression in which lethal violence is made possible.⁶ An early medieval version of this phenomenon has been suggested as a key aspect of the magical–military axis in Viking-age Scandinavia. Through a comparison between medieval Scandinavian literature, traditional circumpolar religious practice, and the archaeology and iconography of the Scandinavian iron-age and Viking period, Neil Price has suggested that references to *berserkir* ('bear-' or 'bare-shirts') and *ulfheðnar* ('wolfskin-wearers') in Old Norse poetry and saga writing may be reflective of a war-cult that channelled aggression through the use of 'shamanic' rituals and a belief in shape-shifting.⁷ Whether or not the thesis can be accepted in its entirety, there can be little doubt that a belief in beast-warriors (whatever the precise nature of that belief) was current during the second half of the first millennium in northern Europe.⁸ Seen in this light, the donning of boar-crested helmets or the girding on of war-gear decorated with serpents or raptors can be imagined as part of a transformative process that involved the adoption of a 'bestial' identity intended in part to facilitate the killing of others.⁹ The animals employed in relation to elite activity – warfare in particular – are usually those associated with predatory or aggressive roles – raptors, wolves, eagles, boars,

---

⁵ See, for example, North on the currency of boar imagery, Chapter 7 in this volume; Brunning on the role of the serpent in military contexts, Chapter 2 in this volume; and Tania M. Dickinson, 'Symbols of Protection: The Significance of Animal Ornamented Shields in Early Anglo-Saxon England', *MedArch* 49 (2005), 109–63.

⁶ For example, out of 400 actively deployed American soldiers surveyed after WWII, only between 15% and 25% reported ever having used their weapons in combat; see Clark McCauley, 'Conference Overview', in *The Anthropology of War*, ed. Jonathan Haas (Cambridge, 1990), pp. 26–55; Napoleon A. Chagnon, *Yanomamö: The Fierce People* (New York, 1968); I. J. N. Thorpe, 'Anthropology, Archaeology, and the Origin of Warfare', *World Archaeology* 35.1 (2003), 145–65.

⁷ Neil Price, *The Viking Way: Religion and War in Late Iron Age Scandinavia* (Uppsala, 2002), esp. pp. 366–78.

⁸ See Introduction to this volume, pp. 1, 3–4; for the evidence of shamanism in Anglo-Saxon England, see Stephen Glosecki, *Shamanism and Old English Poetry* (New York, 1989).

⁹ See the discussions in this volume by Brunning and North.

aquatic predators, threatening serpents – perhaps reflecting, as Aleks Pluskowski has argued, the self-identification of a warrior class with an animal 'otherness' encountered most frequently at or beyond the margins of managed agricultural landscapes.[10] This inverts the way in which the legitimisation of violence is traditionally viewed: rather than conceiving of an enemy as the 'other', such a process transforms the self into something 'else' in order to enable the adoption of behaviours otherwise considered antisocial.

One can perhaps also see, as Pluskowski suggests, a deliberate social distinction being drawn between warrior and farmer in the focused adoption of the symbolism of 'wild' animals for military purposes, with the image of the wild beast standing for an elite status that encompassed violence, predation and the freedom to roam beyond the limits of a society rooted in agricultural activity.[11] These identities do not necessarily need to have been static, as the animal symbolism of war-gear could perhaps express a transformation from one social role to the other (although the centuries which witnessed the adoption of a more extravagant material expression of warrior identity seem to correspond to the development of an increasingly exclusive aristocratic fighting caste).[12]

The observable characteristics of specific animals and the context of their representation in material and literary culture can shed some light on how different beast-identities were perceived. For instance, the use of the boar in helmet decoration can be taken alongside the characteristic aggression of the animal when threatened to suggest that the boar was considered a particularly appropriate symbol of defensive attributes.[13] By contrast, the wolf is invoked in more ambiguous contexts as an icon of violence and power, with sinister predatory associations that enabled it to be used as a descriptor for

---

[10] Pluskowski, 'Animal Magic', pp. 117–18.
[11] Aleks Pluskowski, *Wolves and the Wilderness in the Middle Ages* (Woodbridge, 2006), p. 141.
[12] Ibid., pp. 135–6; Guy Halsall, *Warfare and Society in the Barbarian West, 450–900* (London, 2003), pp. 53–70; Andrew Reynolds, 'Archaeological Correlates for Anglo-Saxon Military Activity in Comparative Perspective', in *Landscapes of Defence in Early Medieval Europe*, ed. John Baker, Stuart Brookes and Andrew Reynolds (Turnhout, 2013), pp. 1–38. As Adams makes clear in Chapter 1 of this volume, the use and adoption of animal imagery could also relate to Classical and Continental referents, and this in turn can be suggested to signify ethnic and political affiliations that reached beyond a 'Germanic' and 'pagan' Anglo-Saxon cultural paradigm. For the wider context and implications of these arguments, see Guy Halsall, *Barbarian Migrations and the Roman West* (Cambridge, 2007), pp. 455–82. I agree with these positions, and do not consider them incompatible with either Pluskowski's ideas or those set out in the rest of this chapter. By the seventh century it in any case seems likely that the political vocabulary of Roman-derived symbology had lost some of its earlier significance; Guy Halsall, *Worlds of Arthur* (Oxford, 2013), pp. 253–99.
[13] See North, Chapter 7 in this volume; and, for a survey of the relevant material that exercises caution over the interpretation, William Chaney, *The Cult of Kingship in Anglo-Saxon England* (Manchester, 1970), pp. 121–7.

monsters (Grendel in *Beowulf*), heathen cannibals (the Mermedonians of *Andreas*), pagan marauders (Asser's Vikings) and criminals.[14] The way that the two animals were employed by Asser in his *Life of Alfred* is instructive: whereas the Vikings are described as being 'like wolves' when they 'burst out of all the gates and joined battle' before their camp at Reading, Alfred – at their next meeting at Ashdown – is described as 'acting courageously, like a wild boar, supported by divine counsel and strengthened by divine help'.[15] In some ways the strategic circumstances described were similar, both protagonists having been forced into an offensive action from what should have been a position of strength – the Vikings from their fortified encampment, and the West Saxons confronting an invader on home territory. What differentiates the two confrontations is the moral context as seen from the writer's perspective. Unlike the Viking army, Alfred is seen to be acting in defence of his people and his patrimony (and explicitly with divine support), and as such the boar is an appropriate metaphor.

The explicit self-identification of the warrior with predatory beasts and monstrous creatures through material culture and naming traditions may also have given the bestial dimension of conflict some sense of reality in practice, as men on the battlefield would have encountered opposition from others who thought of and presented themselves in similar ways.[16] The presence of wild animals on or near the Anglo-Saxon battlefield may have compounded these associations. A survey of ethological approaches to the behaviour of the so-called 'beasts of battle' – the wolf, raven and eagle – encountered frequently in Anglo-Saxon and Scandinavian battle poetry has led to the suggestion by Eric Lacey that the motif may have its origins in the observed behaviour of these beasts in relation to incidents of violent conflict.[17] Most importantly, Lacey draws attention to studies that demonstrate the close cooperation of wolves and ravens in scavenging for carrion and, most startlingly, anecdotal evidence of their ability to recognise and follow groups of armed men.[18] The gathering of such groups in the early medieval period may have been sufficiently

---

[14] Grendel is described as *heorowearh* ('blood-wolf', *Beowulf*, line 1267); the Mermedonians as *wælwulfas* ('wolves of slaughter', *Andreas*, line 150); the Vikings behave in 'lupine fashion' (*lupino more*, *Vita Alfredi*, ch. 36); for the lupine terminology applied to criminals and social deviants see Pluskowski, *Wolves and the Wilderness*, p. 186 and references. See also Bintley, Chapter 9 in this volume.

[15] *Vita Alfredi*, ch. 36, 38, p. 79.

[16] Halsall, *Worlds of Arthur*, pp. 287–8; Gale R. Owen-Crocker, 'Beast Men: *Wulf* and *Eofor* and the Mythic Significance of Names in *Beowulf*', in *Myth in Early Northwest Europe*, ed. Stephen Glosecki (Turnhout, 2007), pp. 257–80; Pluskowski, *Wolves and the Wilderness*, p. 142.

[17] Eric Lacey, 'Birds and Bird-Lore in the Literature of Anglo-Saxon England' (unpublished PhD thesis, University College London, 2013), esp. pp. 114–19.

[18] Ibid.

frequent and distinguishable from other forms of assembly to trigger behavioural adaptations among groups of wild animals seeking a convenient source of protein in the form of fresh corpses: as Lacey puts it, 'it is very probable that ravens and wolves learned to associate groups of armed men with food, and that they appeared before the fighting broke out.'[19] If this is so, it is worth considering how animals may learn to recognise military activity. While the combination of unusual dress, weaponry and a male gender bias in the group is a potential factor, it is likely that the repeated use of certain places (or types of landscape) for mustering or battle can also help to explain adaptations in animal behaviour. Indeed, as the rest of this chapter will seek to explore, there is ample evidence that the landscape of Anglo-Saxon conflict was structured according to symbolic or traditional patterns of thought and behaviour, and that certain sites may have been reused for military activity over several centuries.[20]

The popularity of the 'beasts of battle' motif – alongside the material and conceptual expressions of beast-identities in war – makes it reasonable to suppose that the battlefield, haunted by the image and perhaps the reality of predatory animals, might have come to be seen as emblematic of wilderness: a place of bestial passions and behaviours beyond the limits of ordinary social discourse. It is, therefore, worth asking whether it is possible to see any wider connection between the perception of the environment in Anglo-Saxon England and the practice and conceptualisation of warfare. It should be stressed at the outset that this is only one perspective from which one can look at the phenomena of violence in early medieval Britain; strategic, political or economic concerns were also important factors in the locational characteristics of conflict.[21] However, by approaching warfare in the light of symbolic and cosmological considerations, I

---

[19] Ibid., p. 116.

[20] On the landscape of conflict and military assembly in Anglo-Saxon England, see John Baker and Stuart Brookes, 'Explaining Anglo-Saxon Military Efficiency: The Landscape of Mobilisation', in *The Danes in Wessex*, ed. Ryan Lavelle and Simon Roffey (Oxford, 2015); Kerry Cathers, '"Markings on the Land" and Early Medieval Warfare in the British Isles', in *Fields of Battle: Terrain in Military History*, ed. Peter Doyle and Matthew R. Bennett (Dordrecht, 2002), pp. 9–18; Guy Halsall, 'Anthropology and the Study of Pre-Conquest Warfare and Society', in *Weapons and Warfare in Anglo-Saxon England*, ed. Sonia Chadwick Hawkes (Oxford, 1989), pp. 155–78; Thomas J. T. Williams, 'Landscape and Warfare in Anglo-Saxon England and the Viking Campaign of 1006', in *Early Medieval Europe* (forthcoming); Thomas J. T. Williams, 'The Place of Slaughter: Exploring the West Saxon Battlescape', in *The Danes in Wessex*, ed. Ryan Lavelle and Simon Roffey (Oxford, 2015).

[21] For a case study that brings all these factors into focus, see Williams, 'Landscape and Warfare in Anglo-Saxon England'; for wide-ranging discussion of military issues, see Halsall, *Warfare and Society*; Ryan Lavelle, *Alfred's Wars: Sources and Interpretations of Anglo-Saxon Warfare in the Viking Age*, Warfare in History (Woodbridge, 2011); John Baker and Stuart Brookes, *Beyond the Burghal Hidage: Anglo-Saxon Civil Defence in the Viking Age* (Leiden, 2013).

hope to reframe some aspects of how that warfare might have been understood.

Ongoing research by this author has been concerned primarily with the locations of warfare that can be identified in written sources and analysed through an investigation of landscapes, place-names and other evidence.[22] The approach is underpinned by the fundamental premise that the decisions people make about where to fight battles are not determined by functional logic alone.[23] It is therefore necessary to consider the various religious, cultural, mythological and cosmological ideas that informed or were shaped by violent events. After all, these were moments that saw the boundary between life and death crossed by multiple individuals in quick succession, accompanied by an uninhibited outpouring of aggression that went well beyond the norms of day-to-day social discourse. At the core of the research project is a quantitative survey of battlefield locations recorded in historical sources, and an analysis of the landscape types those locations represent. Much of the sense of place necessarily derives from place-names, as chronicle entries are often short and lacking in detail.[24] The creation of this data-set has made it possible to enhance and expand the exploratory study published by Guy Halsall in 1989 that suggested a strong representation of certain landscape categories – most notably water-crossings and ancient monuments – in the record of early Anglo-Saxon conflict.[25] Although Halsall did posit the suggestion that these locations were chosen for their symbolic resonance, the reasons why certain types of landscape may have been considered more appropriate than others has not yet been explored in any detail.[26]

Table 8.1 derives from the complete data-set, and lists all those battles recorded in the *Anglo-Saxon Chronicle* and Bede's *Ecclesiastical History* that were believed to have occurred between 429 (the date

---

[22] For an overview of the project, see Landscape and Warfare in Early Medieval Britain <https://tjtwilliams.wordpress.com/landscape-and-warfare/early-medieval-britain/> [accessed 1 March 2015].

[23] Or, rather, by 'functional logic' as defined from a twenty-first-century perspective, which is clearly different from what an early medieval warrior (or chronicler) might have judged to be rational and effective, as any number of examples will attest. For this argument, see Halsall, *Warfare and Society*, pp. 6–7. For battlefields as socially constructed landscapes, see, *inter alia*, John Carman and Patricia Carman, *Bloody Meadows: Investigating Landscapes of Battle* (Stroud, 2006).

[24] There are a few notable exceptions: see, for example, Asser's description of the battle of Ashdown (*Vita Alfredi*, ch. 38), Bede's description of the prelude to the battle of Chester, and the poetic treatments of the battles of Maldon and Brunanburh.

[25] Halsall, 'Anthropology and the Study of Pre-Conquest Warfare and Society'.

[26] Although the idea has been touched on; in addition to papers by the author see Reynolds, 'Archaeological Correlates for Anglo-Saxon Military Activity'; Sarah Semple, *Perceptions of the Prehistoric in Anglo-Saxon England: Religion, Ritual and Rulership in the Landscape* (Oxford, 2013), pp. 96–100; Howard Williams, *Death and Memory in Early Medieval Britain* (Cambridge, 2006), pp. 207–11.

Table 8.1 The toponymy of early medieval battles in English sources to AD 860

Conflict name	Place-name/description*	Date in sources†	Sources‡	Non-topographical features (place-name)	Topographical features (place-name)	Topographical features (described in sources)
			Monumental and memorial			
Pevensey Castle	Andredescester	491	ASC [A]	personal name	fortification	–
Salisbury	Searobyrg	552	ASC [A]	other	fortification	–
Bera's Fort	Beranbyrg	556	ASC [A]	personal name	fortification	–
Wibba's Hill	Wibbandune	568	ASC [A]	personal name	hill	–
Woden's Barrow (1)	Woddesbeorge	592	ASC [A]	supernatural	barrow / mound	–
Degsa's Stone	Degsastan (Degsa lapis); 'in loco celeberrimo'	603	HE i.34	personal name	standing stone(s)	–
Chester	'Ciuitatem Legionum, quae a gente Anglorum Legacaestir, a Brettonibus autem rectius Carlegion appellatur'	606 [c. 616]	HE ii.2; ASC [A]	military	fortification	–
Bea's Hill	Beandune	614	ASC [A]	personal name	hill	–
Cirencester	Cirenceastre	628	ASC [A]	other	fortification	–
Bamburgh	'Urbem usque regiam, quae ex Bebbae quondam reginae uocabulo cognominatur'ª	c. 650	HE iii.16	personal name	fortification	fortification
Wilfar's Hill	'Uilfaresdun, id est Mons Uilfari'	651	HE iii.14	personal name	hill	–

Confronting the Bestial in Anglo-Saxon Warfare

Conflict name	Place-name/ description*	Date in sources†	Sources‡	Non-topographical features (place-name)	Topographical features (place-name)	Topographical features (described in sources)
Posent's Fort	Posentesbyrg	661	ASC [A]	personal name	fortification	–
Bieda's Head	Biedanheafde	675	ASC [A]	personal name	hill	–
Woden's Barrow (2)	Woddesbeorge	715	ASC [A]	supernatural	barrow/mound	–
Edwin's Cliff	Eadwinesclife	761	ASC [D]	personal name	hill/mountain	–
Wicga's Barrow	Wicganbeorge	851 [850]	ASC [A]	personal name	barrow/mound	–

Coastal, riverine and wetland

Conflict name	Place-name/ description*	Date in sources†	Sources‡	Non-topographical features (place-name)	Topographical features (place-name)	Topographical features (described in sources)
Alleluia Battle	'uallem circumdatam mediis montibus intuetur'	[429 or c. 440][b]	HE i.20	–	–	hills; valley; river/stream[c]
Aylesford	Ægelesþrep[d]	455	ASC [A]	personal name	ford	–
Crayford	Crecganford	457	ASC [A]	–	river/stream; ford	–
Wipped's Creek	Wippedesfleote	465	ASC [A]	personal name	wetland	–
Mearcred's Brook	Mearcredesburnan stede	485	ASC [A]	personal name	river/stream	–
Cerdic's Shore (1)	Cerdicesora	495	ASC [A]	personal name	coastal	–
Cerdic's Shore (2)	Cerdicesora	514	ASC [A]	personal name	coastal	–
Charford	Cerdicesford	519	ASC [A]	personal name	ford	–
Bedcanford	Bedcanforda	571	ASC [A]	other	ford	–
River Idle	'ad orientalem plagam amnis, qui vocatur Idlæ'	617	HE ii.12	–	–	river/stream
Bradford on Avon	Bradanforda be Afne	652	ASC [A]	–	river/stream; ford	–

Conflict name	Place-name/description*	Date in sources†	Sources‡	Non-topographical features (place-name)	Topographical features (place-name)	Topographical features (described in sources)
Winwaed	prope fluuium Uinued	655	HE iii.24	–	–	river/stream; wetland
Two Rivers	'duo flumina cadaveribus mortuorum replentes'	[671]	VSW xix	–	–	hills/mountain; river/stream
River Trent	Iuxta fluuium Treanta	679	HE iv.21	–	river/stream	–
Nechtansmere	'in angustias inaccessorum montium' [HE] 'Nechtanesmere (quod est stagnum Nechtani)' [SD]	685	HE iv.26; SD i.9	personal name	wetland	hills/mountains
Otford	Ottanforda	773 [776]	ASC [A]	personal name?	ford	–
Kempsford	Cynemæresforda	800 [802]	ASC [A]	personal name	ford	–
Tax Fords	Gafulforda	823 [825]	ASC [A]	other	ford	–
Southampton	Hamptune	837 [840]	ASC [A]	–	settlement/enclosure	coastal
Parret	Pedridan muþan	845 [848]	ASC [A]	–	–	river/stream; coastal
Thanet	Tenet	853	ASC [A]	other	–	coastal; island

Trees and woodland

Conflict name	Place-name/description*	Date in sources†	Sources‡	Non-topographical features (place-name)	Topographical features (place-name)	Topographical features (described in sources)
Cerdic's Wood	Cerdicesleaga	527	ASC [A]	personal name	woodland	–
Battle Wood	Feþanleag	584	ASC [A]	military	woodland	–
Penselwood	Peonnum	658	ASC [A]	other	woodland	–

Conflict name	Place-name/description*	Date in sources†	Sources‡	Non-topographical features (place-name)	Topographical features (place-name)	Topographical features (described in sources)
Whalley	Hwælleage	798	ASC [D]	–	hill; woodland	–
Ellandun	Ellendune	823 [825]	ASC [A]	–	tree; hill	–
Aclea	Aclea	851	ASC [A]	–	woodland	–
Bestial						
Dyrham	Deorham	577	ASC [A]	beast	settlement/enclosure	–
Other						
Mount Badon	'Badonici montis'	<c. 500	HE i.16	other	hill/mountain	–
Hatfield	'campo qui vocatur Haethfelth'	633	HE ii.20	–	moor/heath; field	–
Maserfield	Maserfelth	642	HE iii.9	other	field	–
Bensington	Benesingtun	777 [779]	ASC [A]	personal name	settlement	–
Dore	Dore	827 [829]	ASC [A]	other	–	–
Carhampton (1)	Carrum	833 [836]	ASC [A]	–	stones/rocks	–
Portland	Port	837 [840]	ASC [A]	other	–	–
Carhampton (2)	Carrum	840 [843]	ASC [A]	–	stones/rocks	–
Winchester	Wintanceaster	860	ASC [A]	–	fortification	settlement

Conflict name	Place-name/ description*	Date in sources†	Sources‡	Non-topographical features (place-name)	Topographical features (place-name)	Topographical features (described in sources)
Multiple features						
Cymen's Shore	*Cymenesora*	477	ASC [A]	personal name	coastal	coastal; woodland^e
Cerdic's Ford - Netley	*Natanleaga oþ Cerdicesford*	508	ASC [A]	personal name	ford; wetland; woodland	–
Wihtgar's Fort	*Wihtgar[a]byrg*	530	ASC [A]	personal name	fortification	island
Deniseburn/ Heavenfield	'*Deniseshurn, id est Riuus Denisi* [...] *Hefenfeld, quod dici potest latine Caelestis Campus*'	[634–5]	HE iii.1–2	supernatural; personal name	field; river/stream	field; fortification
Beorgford	*Beorgf(e)orda*	752	ASC [A]	–	barrow/mound; ford	–
Hengest's Hill	*Hengestdune*	835 [838]	ASC [A]	personal name/ beast	hill	–

* For brevity and clarity, only the earliest known reference to the battle is included in this table.

† Dates given are those that appear in the primary source material. Where these have been reconstructed or rectified, they have been given in square brackets. Rectified dates for Chronicle entries follow those provided in *The Anglo-Saxon Chronicles*, ed. and trans. Michael Swanton (London, 1996).

‡ Abbreviations in this column refer to the following sources and editions:

ASC [A] Manuscript 'A' of the Anglo-Saxon Chronicle; *The Anglo-Saxon Chronicle: A Collaborative Edition*, vol. 3: *MS. A*, ed. Janet M. Bately (Cambridge, 1986).

ASC [D] Manuscript 'D' of the Anglo-Saxon Chronicle; *The Anglo-Saxon Chronicle: A Collaborative Edition*, vol. 6: *MS D*, ed. Geoffrey T. Cubbin (Cambridge, 1996).

HE Bede's *Historia Ecclesiastica*; *Bede the Venerable Saint, 673–735: Bede's Ecclesiastical History of the English People*, ed. Bertram Colgrave and Roger A. B. Mynors (Oxford, 1969).

SD Symeon of Durham's *Libellus de Exordio*; *Symeon of Durham: Libellus de Exordio atque Procursu istius, hoc est Dunhelmensis, Ecclesie / Tract on the origins and progress of this the Church of Durham*, ed. and trans. David W. Rollason (Oxford, 2000).

VSW Stephen's *Vita Sancti Wilfrithi*; *The Life of Bishop Wilfrid by Eddius Stephanus*, ed. and trans. Bertram Colgrave (Cambridge, 1927).

a ASC [A] sub anno 547 supplies the OE place-name *Beb'b'anburh*.

b The battle is supposed to date to one of the two visits of St Germanus to Britain, which were recorded in the life of the saint written by Constantius of Lyons in c. 480 and from which Bede derived his account.

c Although Bede's narrative places the first phase of the battle in 'a valley surrounded by hills', the subsequent route is dominated by a description of the vanquished army drowning in a river.

d All manuscripts of the *Anglo-Saxon Chronicle* give a version of this place-name that retains the uncertain second element 'prep'. In this form, the place-name is unidentifiable. However, Aylesford, Kent, is known from charters of the tenth century (S 1211, S 1212) and a later entry in the *Anglo-Saxon Chronicle* (CDEF manuscripts, s.a. 1016) as Æglesford (and variant spellings thereof). Place-name authorities identify this with the *Chronicle*'s *Ægþesþrep*: see Johannes K. Wallenberg, *Kentish Place-Names* (Uppsala, 1931), pp. 286–8; and Johannes K. Wallenberg, *The Place-Names of Kent* (Uppsala, 1934), p. 145; Wallenberg's position is the one adopted here, though it is not immune to criticism. For the charters, see *The Electronic Sawyer: Online Catalogue of Anglo-Saxon Charters* <http://www.esawyer.org.uk> [accessed 2 January 2015].

e The full reference describes the victory of Ælle and his three sons over the British and their subsequent flight into the Weald.

of the earliest recorded battle) and 860 (the date of the last battle to occur before the advent of the 'great' Viking army in 866, an event which can reasonably be taken to mark a significant – if not absolute – shift from traditional modes of warfare in early medieval Britain).[27] Those encounters for which insufficient details survive to provide any meaningful data are excluded. The evidence of chronicles and saints' lives composed outside the zone of 'Anglo-Saxon' ethnic influence has also been excluded – not because these sources lack interest, but because they introduce a self-consciously external (and often hostile) view that brings us no closer to understanding cultural traditions that can broadly, if problematically, be described as 'Anglo-Saxon' by around AD 600.[28] It perhaps goes without saying that the earliest recorded conflicts, particularly those of the fifth and sixth centuries, cannot be taken at face value as a reflection of real historical events.[29] What they do show, however, is a sense of how the battlefield landscape was imagined, and thus the sorts of places that were considered appropriate for the business of fighting by the latter half of the period covered.

Given these parameters and caveats, fifty-nine battles remain in the list. These have been attributed landscape characteristics deriving from their place-names and other descriptive details provided by the documentary record. It is immediately evident that a number of features are disproportionately represented, and that these largely correspond to the similar groupings proposed by Halsall (although selection criteria are slightly different in this case).[30] The category headings that I have used to organise the material are as follows: 'Monumental and memorial', 'Coastal, riverine and wetland landscapes', and 'Trees and woodland'. Presentation of this data is complicated by the fact that several entries have characteristics that place them in more than one of these categories. Where this is the case, I have clarified them under the heading 'Multiple features'. In addition, two conflict sites specifically refer to animals in their toponymy (here under the headings 'Bestial' and 'Multiple features'). I would once again stress that this is only one way of sorting this data, and does not directly take into account other important groupings or landscape

---

[27] Guy Halsall, 'Playing by Whose Rules? A Further Look at Viking Atrocity in the Ninth Century', *Medieval History* 2:3 (1992), 2–12.

[28] For an introduction to debates on early medieval ethnicity, Patrick J. Geary, *The Myth of Nations: The Medieval Origins of Europe* (Princeton, 2002).

[29] Patrick Sims-Williams, 'The Settlement of England in Bede and the Chronicle', *ASE* 12 (1983), 1–41; Heinrich Härke, 'Material Culture as Myth: Weapons in Anglo-Saxon Graves', in *Burial and Society: The Chronological and Social Analysis of Archaeological Burial Data*, ed. Claus Kjeld Jensen and Karen Høilund Nielsen (Aarhus, 1997), pp. 119–27; Barbara Yorke, 'Fact or Fiction? The Written Evidence for the Fifth and Sixth Centuries AD', *ASSAH* 6 (1997), 45–50.

[30] Halsall, 'Anthropology and the Study of Pre-Conquest Warfare and Society'.

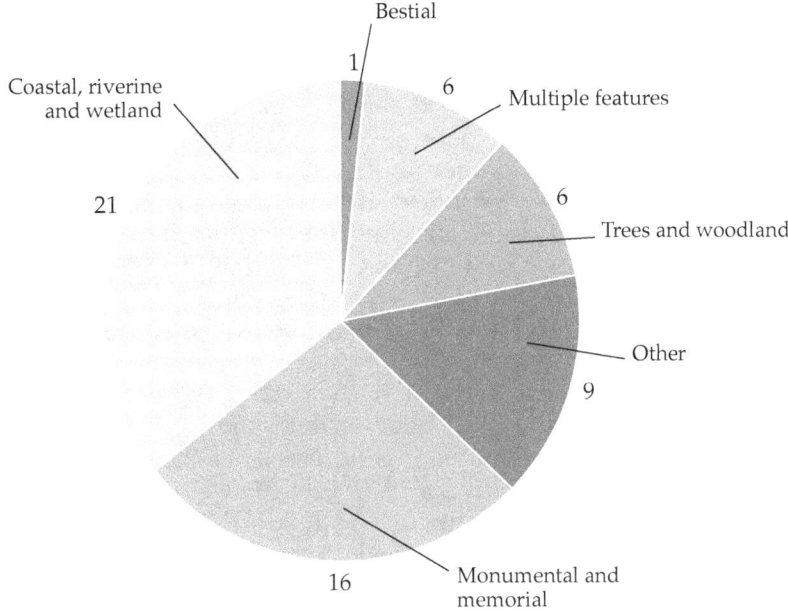

Fig. 8.1 Predominant landscape attributes of conflict sites, AD 429–860

categories (e.g. the presence of personal names, fortifications, or 'feld'-type place-names), or the much richer characterisation of landscape made possible by the direct study of identifiable landscape (Fig. 8.1).[31]

The categories highlighted are, however, significant groupings, and can all be interpreted as possessing liminal or outlandish qualities – either as boundaries or as the home of wild or monstrous creatures explicitly associated with warfare in poetic and archaeological contexts. By considering these associations in the broader context of poetic and hagiographic texts, it is possible to flesh out the relationship between warfare, wilderness and the bestial as it may have been seen from an Anglo-Saxon perspective of the seventh to ninth centuries and beyond.[32]

[31] For the potential of this approach, see Williams, 'Landscape and Warfare in Anglo-Saxon England'; and Williams, 'The Place of Slaughter'.
[32] There are clear methodological problems raised by any attempt to project onto earlier periods evidence gleaned from an eclectic corpus of texts that are often of uncertain date. Although space constraints preclude a systematic justification for the approach taken here, it is worth briefly noting that in this chapter I have simply sought to highlight common ideas that can be identified across time and in different kinds of evidence. Where these commonalities exist, I have tried cautiously to suggest that this *may* indicate a slowly evolving and generally conservative cultural milieu that preserves (perhaps unwittingly) attitudes of thought and behaviour which might have had currency in earlier centuries. Much of what follows must remain speculative, and I hope it is read in the spirit of creative enquiry in which it was written. I have argued elsewhere that,

Monumental and Memorious Landscapes

This category is the most diverse, encompassing a range of reused ancient sites alongside natural features that may have been used in a similar way as anchors for specific legendary or memorial purposes. Thus, this category includes hill-forts, Roman military/urban sites, burial mounds, a single standing stone, and a number of individual hills or mounds with compound names that include personal names (some with a legendary or ancestral significance) in a way which implies they may have been perceived as incorporating funerary monuments or memorials.[33]

It is evident that, viewed from a later Anglo-Saxon perspective, the burial mound was a haunted and sinister, but also numinous, location.[34] In particular, the mound is seen as the haunt of monstrous creatures, dragons and demons in particular – an association that has enjoyed a long and distinguished folkloric legacy. Literary sources, especially *Beowulf* and the poetic treatment of the *Life of St Guthlac*, make these connections very clearly. The landscapes of *Beowulf* confirm the view presented in *Maxims II* that *Draca sceal on hlæwe* ('the dragon belongs in its mound'), by repeatedly emphasising the dragon's choice of dwelling place: he is the 'barrow guardian' – the *beorges hyrde*.[35] The mound around which the action of Guthlac is focused is described in an even more menacing light, as the former home of a troop of devils, and the text claims that similar locales can equally be expected to harbour sinister forces:

> Wide is this wilderness and the multitude of fugitive settlements and the secret dwellings of wretched spirits, and those who inhabit these lodging-places are devils.[36]

Significantly, for both Guthlac and Beowulf the mound itself becomes a place of conflict, in which the hero is forced to fight against its occupant. The mound, therefore, can be seen perhaps as emblematic of heroic action in the landscape – a symbol of wilderness to be tamed through violence.

---

despite the undoubted changes to warfare that occurred from the ninth century onward, the landscape of battle in England retains features that can be described as 'traditional' right up until the Norman Conquest (and possibly beyond); see Williams, 'The Place of Slaughter'.

[33] Williams, 'The Place of Slaughter'; Semple, *Perceptions of the Prehistoric*, pp. 74, 88, 96–100.
[34] Sarah Semple, 'A Fear of the Past: The Place of the Prehistoric Burial Mound in the Ideology of Middle and Later Anglo-Saxon England', *World Archaeology* 30.1 (1998), 109–26.
[35] *Maxims II*, line 27; *Beowulf*, line 2304. See also the discussions by Symons and Bintley in this volume, Chapters 3 and 9, respectively.
[36] *Guthlac A*, lines 297–8, trans. Bradley, *Anglo-Saxon Poetry*, p. 257.

The use of such monuments in the context of judicial execution and the burial of social outsiders offers archaeological corroboration for this aspect of the Anglo-Saxon thought-world, and the recurrent description of these sites as 'heathen burials' in Old English charter bounds compounds the sinister association.[37] In particular, the use of the barrow as an execution site demonstrates the extent to which this fear conditioned social behaviour in the later Anglo-Saxon period, and reinforces the idea that this type of location could be considered particularly appropriate for violence directed towards social deviants. The conceptual similarities that made it appropriate for criminals, monsters and Vikings all to be described using the same lupine metaphors imply that dealing with transgressive behaviour could blur the distinction between 'judicial' and 'military' violence. These spheres of action were not necessarily clearly drawn in the Anglo-Saxon period, an age when the judicial ordeal brought God's justice directly to the mortal world through corporal trauma.[38] Perhaps, in this light, the use of mounds as battlefields might suggest that armed aggression could, in some cases, be regarded as a moral and social aberration that could be dealt with most appropriately through the application of quasi-judicial violence.[39]

It is surely also significant that a large number of battles recorded in Bede and in the *Anglo-Saxon Chronicle* are associated with barrows or with hills and mounds compounded with personal names that imply a relationship to memorial monuments. Some of these – such as Hengest's Hill (*Hengestdun*) – may have been thought to contain burials even if they were not barrows *per se*. The presence of ancestral figures such as Hengest and Woden in Anglo-Saxon royal genealogies implies that at least some of these places had more positive connotations in the pre- and early Christian period, which in some cases survived as late as the eleventh century.[40] The presence of powerful, even divine, ancestral occupants alongside dragons or other monstrous inhabitants would have characterised these places as dangerous and otherworldly even without the demonic associations they later accrued, and it is possible that the mound could also have operated as a focal point from which supernatural power could be drawn in the context of warfare. One can, for example, read the late

---

[37] Andrew Reynolds, *Anglo-Saxon Deviant Burial Customs* (Oxford, 2009).
[38] Morton W. Bloomfield, 'Beowulf, Byrhtnoth, and the Judgment of God: Trial by Combat in Anglo-Saxon England', *Speculum* 44.4 (1969), 545–59.
[39] Williams, 'The Place of Slaughter'; Williams, 'Landscape and Warfare in Anglo-Saxon England'.
[40] Sarah Semple, 'In the Open Air', in *Signals of Belief in Early England*, ed. Carver *et al.* (Oxford, 2010), pp. 33–9; Williams, *Death and Memory in Early Medieval Britain*, pp. 207–11.

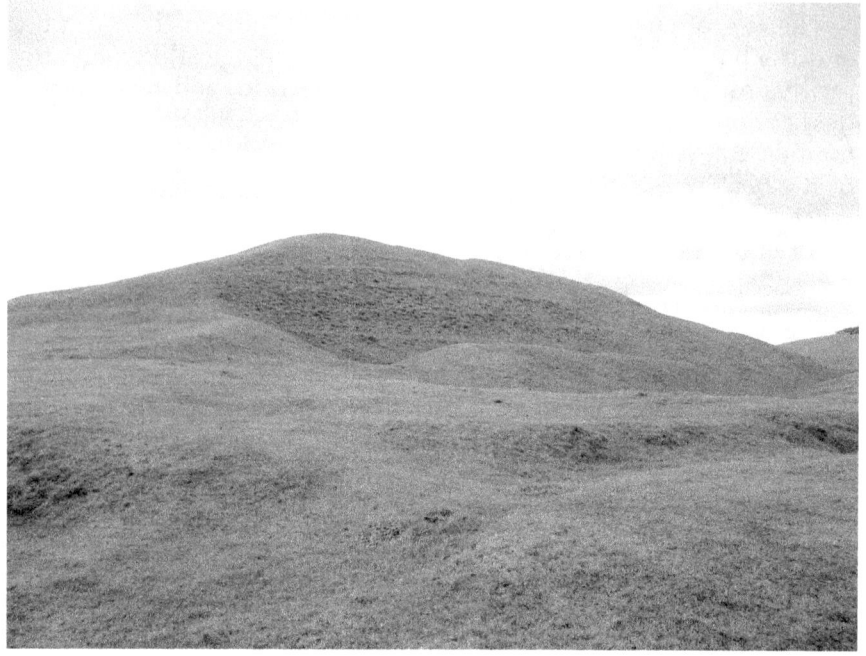

Fig. 8.2 The Neolithic long-barrow known as Adam's Grave
(formerly *Woddesbeorg*), Wiltshire

chronicle account of the approach to Cwichelm's Barrow by the Viking army in 1006 in this light.[41]

The two battles recorded as having been fought at Woden's Barrow (*Woddesbeorg*) in Wiltshire may imply something similar. While it is perfectly possible to regard Woden purely in the light of his ancestral significance in the Anglo-Saxon genealogies, it is tempting to see this repeated use of a particular landscape in the light of other associations the figure may have had as a god connected with death and battle, ravens and wolves.[42] Richard North has made the intriguing suggestion that Woden's Barrow may have derived its name from associations gained through the presence of carrion birds in the aftermath of battles fought there.[43] If, as Lacey suggests, the 'beasts of battle' topos has its roots in observed animal behaviours and habitats,[44] it follows that mythological associations specific to place and preserved in place-names may have grown similarly from the

[41] Williams, 'Landscape and Warfare in Anglo-Saxon England'.
[42] Pluskowski, 'Animal Magic', p. 116.
[43] Personal communication.
[44] Lacey, 'Birds and Bird-Lore', pp. 114–19.

combination of ethological phenomena and human activity. If this is true of Woden's Barrow, it might equally apply to other theophoric place-names of similar character. Woden's Barrow sits in close relation to a number of other Woden place-names, including the defensive earthwork of Wansdyke (Woden's ditch). A battle against the Vikings was also fought further afield at *Wodnesfeld* ('Woden's Field', modern Wednesfield, Wolverhampton) in 911. It is possible to imagine these as places set aside for violence, frequented by the beasts of battle and hallowed through blood and sacrifice (Fig. 8.2).

There is no simple way to characterise the mound in the Anglo-Saxon thought-world but, however it is approached, the presence of otherworldly power is a common theme. The metrical charm *Wið Forstice* describes the warlike and threatening non-human forces that might be unleashed at the burial mound (*hlæw*): gods, elves, witches, smiths. One can easily imagine that this projection of supernatural power with unmistakeably martial overtones might preserve a memory of the spirits that once inhabited the Anglo-Saxon battlefield, just as they may have stalked the Viking warrior's imagination.[45] This sense of the mound as a reservoir of supernatural power that could be tapped for military purposes is strikingly illustrated in the eighth-century *Life of St Wilfrid.* Having been blown towards the unknown lands of the South Saxons, the eponymous bishop is confronted by a wizard leading 'a great horde of pagans' hell-bent on murdering and robbing Wilfrid's entourage:

> The chief priest of their idolatry set himself up on a high mound like Balaam and started to curse God's people, trying to bind their hands by his magic art.[46]

The story continues, with a touch of bathos, to recount how a stone thrown by one of the bishop's companions felled this fearsome sorcerer. Inevitably (and this is clearly the point of the episode within the narrative), much is made of the obvious parallel with the Old Testament story of David and Goliath, and we are thus encouraged to see the South Saxons as emblematic of a monstrous paganism overthrown through the work of a Christian saint. Significantly, however, the action is described as occurring in the context of a battle couched in explicitly heroic terms (the Christians agree that 'no one should turn his back and flee in battle, but that each should either die with honour or live in triumph').[47] In this anecdote the mound plays a central role as both a source of supernatural power for the practice

---

[45] Price, *The Viking Way*, pp. 393–5.
[46] 'Life of Wilfrid', ch. 13, trans. J. F. Webb, in *The Age of Bede*, ed. D. H. Farmer, 4th edn (London, 1998), p. 121.
[47] Ibid.

of heathen battle magic, and also as an appropriate environment for heroic action that symbolises the semi-human savagery of pagan antagonists.

Mounds and barrows are not the only ancient monuments to occur in the conflict landscape. Prehistoric earthworks (especially iron-age hillforts) and Roman ruins appear frequently, and these also seem to have been associated with superhuman or monstrous creators – at least by the later Anglo-Saxon period when the vernacular poetry was committed to its surviving written form. Most famously, the remains of decaying masonry walls are in several poems described as the 'work of giants' (*enta geweorc*), and place-name evidence also suggests an association of earthwork structures with Woden or 'Grim'.[48] It is perhaps no coincidence that the most prominent of monumental remains – dykes, walls and earthen banks – are explicitly liminal structures marking landscape boundaries. Old English poetry and prose, such as *Beowulf* and *Genesis*, present an image of the world in which the confines of hearth and home (represented by the image of the hall) are juxtaposed with what lies 'outside' or on the margins – a threatening and dangerous wilderness, literally 'monster-world' (*fifelcynnes eard*).[49] Perhaps the remains of *enta geweorc* implied a symbolic boundary beyond which the attributes of dangerous, non-human, literally 'outlandish' adversaries could be projected.

Coastal, Riverine and Wetland Landscapes

No topographical transition implies a boundary so profoundly as that between land and water, whether it be the sudden break caused by a river or pool, or the termination of the land itself at the ocean's edge. Water is disproportionately represented in the conflict landscape, and can be seen in the light of the above discussion as a topographical manifestation of the theme of boundaries. Rivers and the coast are, of course, a primary means of demarcating political geography. Northumbria – 'the land north of the river Humber' – is defined literally in relation to a riverine boundary. However, when approached from a literary perspective, water can be found symbolising the wilderness in a more general sense as a place bereft of joy, the antithesis of the hall.[50] The wilderness against which both the

---

[48] Audrey L. Meaney, 'Woden in England: A Reconsideration of the Evidence', *Folklore* 77:2 (1966), 105–15. References to *enta geweorc* can be found in *The Ruin* (line 2), *The Wanderer* (line 85) and *Beowulf* (line 2717).
[49] *Beowulf*, line 104.
[50] Alvin A. Lee, *Gold-Hall and Earth Dragon: Beowulf as Metaphor* (Toronto, 1998).

hall of Creation in Cadmon's *Genesis* and the hall of Heorot in *Beowulf* are contrasted is described explicitly as an encircling ocean, and poems such as *The Seafarer* and *The Wanderer* present the ocean as a wasteland which contrasts with the splendours of lost human culture. This theme is developed in other conflict narratives that feature remote locations bounded by water (some of which also include barrows). Cuthbert's battle with the demons of Farne Island is simultaneously a physical and a moral struggle, and the place is deliberately chosen as somewhere appropriate for spiritual combat against the monstrous inhabitants of the wild. Guthlac's mound is set amid fens, a dreadful focal point of wetland wilderness; Wilfrid's battle occurs on the shores of the ocean. In each case, the theme of physical/spiritual combat is played out at the water's edge. The idea of wetland being connected with moral struggle would explain the predominance of this sort of landscape in legendary Anglo-Saxon invasion narratives (especially *Anglo-Saxon Chronicle* accounts of battles in the fifth and early sixth centuries, and the Northumbrian wars recounted by Bede). Bede's history, in particular, was structured in order to demonstrate the providential nature of the English 'conquest'. The British are situated within the history as deserving of divinely ordained destruction, and the repeated choice of riverine landscapes for battle makes sense in light of the wider Anglo-Saxon cosmological perspective outlined above. Britons in this reading are equated with the sub-human inhabitants of other wetland settings, destined for annihilation.[51]

This association between water and monsters is frequently repeated. The whale which gave up its bones to the Franks casket is described in that object's runic inscription as the 'king of terror', Beowulf is described as a slayer of ocean dwelling *nicor*, and *Maxims II* presents us with the commonplace *þyrs sceal on fenne gewunian ana innan lande* ('the monster must abide in the fen, alone in its domain').[52] No wetland

---

[51] Bede's template for many of his later riverine battles seems to have been the Hallelujah battle recounted in the first part of his *Ecclesiastical History* (Bede, *Ecclesiastical History of the English People*, I. 20). Here it is the pagan Saxons who are drowned trying to flee from the pious dramatics of St Germanus, and the Britons who are painted as God's party. The moral paradigm was reversed by Bede's day, largely due – as Bede would have understood from his reading of Gildas – to the moral backsliding and sinful error of the British church. The theme of a watery death in the aftermath of battle is repeated several times in Bede's history, and may ultimately derive from Old Testament stories of Flood and Exodus, as well as allusions (clearly drawn both in St Germanus' victory and in Oswald's victory at Heavenfield/Denisebrun) to the victory of Constantine I at the Milvian Bridge; for Oswald as a new Constantine, see Alan Thacker, '*Membra Disjecta*: The Division of the Body and the Diffusion of the Cult', in *Oswald: Northumbrian King to European Saint*, ed. Clare Stancliffe and Eric Cambridge (Stamford, 1995), pp. 97–127 (p. 112).

[52] *Maxims II*, lines 42–3.

landscape, however, is so unambiguously wild and monster-haunted as the lair of the Grendel-kin:

> [...] The water was infested
> with all kinds of reptiles. There were writhing sea-dragons
> and monsters slouching on slopes by the cliff,
> serpents and wild things such as those that often
> surface at dawn to roam the sail-road.[53]

It is into this water that the hero must plunge in order to take the battle to Grendel's mother; indeed, it is the measure of the hero that he is willing to enter this daunting environment to confront danger. The mere, like the dragon's mound later in the poem, becomes a battlefield that amplifies the strength and moral courage of Beowulf – his steadfast adherence to a heroic ethic is demonstrated by the lack of anxiety he shows for his own safety, while nevertheless making careful provision for his lord, his retainers, and those who have shown him generosity.[54] On a similar note, though the battle in the year 508 at *Cerdices ford/Natanleaga* (probably Charford/Netley Marsh in Hampshire) was later provided with a false etymology that connected it to the fictional King Nazaleod,[55] the place-name ('wet-wood', or 'marshy clearing') preserves the memory of a landscape similar to the monster-mere described by the Beowulf poet. It may be that this sort of place lent a romantic atmosphere to warfare (or the literary memories of warfare), which assisted warrior elites to perpetuate a constructed heroic self-image.

It is therefore possible that in the apparent popularity of rivers and wetlands as sites of conflict in the written record one can perceive an echo of a mentality that saw such locations as particularly appropriate settings for violent encounters with human adversaries conceived of as 'monstrous'. Like the mound, however, the picture remains ambiguous. Water was undeniably a source of power – dangerous indeed, but imbued with qualities that demanded respect. Cult practice with explicitly military symbolism is spectacularly attested in the Anglo-Saxon 'homelands',[56] and is implied in England by a long continuity of weapon depositions at water crossings – a practice that seems to have started during the conversion period and lasted

---

[53] *Beowulf*, lines 1425–30; in *Beowulf: A New Translation*, trans. Seamus Heaney (London, 1999), p. 47.
[54] *Beowulf*, lines 1442–54.
[55] Sims-Williams, 'The Settlement of England', p. 29.
[56] *The Spoils of Victory: The North in the Shadow of the Roman Empire*, ed. L. Jørgensen, B. Storgaard and L. G. Thomsen (Copenhagen, 2003); Julie Lund, 'At the Water's Edge', in *Signals of Belief in Early England*, ed. Carver, pp. 49–66.

into the later Middle Ages.⁵⁷ It is perhaps also significant that – in the seventh and early eighth centuries especially – the bearing of shields and weapons decorated with the images of aquatic monsters became an important component of martial preparation.⁵⁸ Perhaps in some contexts the symbolism of the water-dwelling predator could be adopted and turned outwards, towards the enemy, drawing power from an older sense of the wetland landscape as a source of supernatural assistance.

Trees and Woodland

Hugh Magennis has argued that in Icelandic saga literature, the *Myrkviðr* (the 'dark forest', or 'mirkwood') is generally presented as menacing and vast.⁵⁹ For the hero to enter the trackless forest is to show a courage that is analogous to that required for battles against trolls or dragons, and overcoming fear of the forest is not only the measure of a hero, but also a moral victory in a wider human struggle against the overwhelming and threatening forces of the wilderness – the shapeless 'out there', in which all manner of threats and horrors can be imagined. It is the woodland setting, no less than the water, that contributes to the sinister aspect of the Grendel mere in *Beowulf*, and which characterises the environment as an appropriately marginal setting for the physical aspect of heroic struggle.⁶⁰ It is unsurprising, therefore, that trees and woodland occur with some frequency in the landscape of conflict, and in poetic treatments of warfare more generally. In particular, the forest is the environment that is most explicitly associated with the 'beasts of battle' topos – particularly the wolf – thus establishing a conceptual relationship between warfare and the woodland wilderness.⁶¹

Like other wild places, however, the forest is also an appropriate setting for the expression of savage urges, in which the warrior may release the bestial energies implicit in his identity. This idea is brought forcefully to life by the description in *Beowulf* of the battle in *Hrafne-wudu* ('ravenswood', line 2925).⁶² The association of the

---

⁵⁷ Lund, 'At the Water's Edge'; Semple, 'In the Open Air'; Andrew Reynolds and Sarah Semple, 'Anglo-Saxon Non-Funerary Weapon Depositions', in *Studies in Early Anglo-Saxon Art and Archaeology: Papers in Honour of Martin G. Welch*, ed. Stuart Brookes, Susan Harrington and Andrew Reynolds (Oxford, 2011), pp. 40–8.
⁵⁸ Dickinson, 'Symbols of Protection'; Pluskowski, 'Animal Magic', pp. 108–12.
⁵⁹ Hugh Magennis, *Images of Community in Old English Poetry* (Cambridge, 1996).
⁶⁰ See Bintley, Chapter 9 in this volume; also Michael D. J. Bintley, 'Cain's Kin and Abel's Blood: *Beowulf* 1361–4', *Opticon1826* 9 (2010), online at <http://www.opticon1826.com/article/view/opt.091005> [accessed 2 January 2015].
⁶¹ For this relationship, see Pluskowski, *Wolves and the Wilderness*.
⁶² *Beowulf*, lines 2919–78.

raven with battlefields and death, discussed above and elsewhere in this volume,[63] defines this particular woodland as a wilderness setting appropriate for violent action. These associations are compounded by the appearance of the two Geatish brothers Wulf ('wolf') and Eofor ('boar'), who are introduced as Ongentheow's slayers in the context of Hygelac's feud with the Swedish king. The brothers' names heighten the sense of a bestial environment where human identity is indistinct, compromised or mutable, and that impression is strengthened by the half-formed characters the poet presents: neither Wulf nor Eofor has any role in the poem beyond the violence for which he is responsible, and neither one of them speaks. They appear only as semi-human actors who exist to 'embody the savagery that is associated with their names'.[64] The only differentiation between them is in the animal archetypes that they embody. Although it is Eofor who strikes the deadly blow, it is Wulf who strikes first, hacking at the king's silver head as he sinks to his knees. Eofor strikes in defence of Wulf when Ongentheow strikes back against him. Thus the boar is presented as violent and deadly, but still heroic in defence of his companion; the wolf is impulsive, savage and unrestrained. This juxtaposition of animal imagery can be compared to Asser's use of the same animal metaphors.[65] Perhaps the poet's purpose in introducing Wulf and Eofor was to allow Hygelac to claim glory for the death of Ongentheow without wielding the sword in person – they represent bestial 'masks' that enable the release of violence, and are in this sense analogous to the donning of a boar-crested helm or raptor-embossed shield.

Thus, here as elsewhere, one can perhaps see a tension between the presentation of the battlefield as a forum for heroic action, a wilderness against which a warrior can be tested, and its presentation as a place set aside for monsters, where men become beasts. It is notable that all the categories of landscape discussed thus far also have potential resonances as places of power, of ancestral significance or pertaining to pre-Christian cults. The trees and woodland of the Anglo-Saxon conflict landscape are no exception, and although there is not the space in this chapter for a detailed consideration of their role,[66] it is significant that in two cases the names of early battle-sites are compounded with the term *leah/leag* ('woodland clearing'), which also seems to have had a significance in the location of pre-Christian

---

[63] See the discussion by Lacey, Chapter 5 in this volume, though see also Osborn, Chapter 4 in this volume, for an alternative view; Pluskowski, 'Animal Magic', p. 116.
[64] Owen-Crocker, 'Beast Men', p. 277.
[65] See above, pp. 178–9.
[66] John Baker, Stuart Brookes and Thomas J. T. Williams, 'The Battle of Penselwood, AD 1016 and the Landscape of Anglo-Saxon Warfare' (in preparation).

cult sites.⁶⁷ Taken alongside other evidence, including the presence of ancestral and theophoric place-names and the implications of the 'beasts of battle' topos, this might imply a cult dimension to the places and practice of warfare in the early Anglo-Saxon period.⁶⁸

Bestial Landscapes

Only two battles in this sample reference beasts directly in their toponymy. *Hengestdun* (either Hingston Down, Cornwall, or Hingsdon Down, Devon)⁶⁹ might mean either 'Hill of the Stallions' or 'Hill of Hengest', the legendary founder of the Kentish royal dynasty who appears in the genealogies of the kings of Kent and Wessex with his brother Horsa ('horse', 'mare'), and whose own name means 'horse' or 'stallion'. It has very plausibly been suggested that these names should be linked to pre-Christian deities euhemerised as ancestral figures,⁷⁰ and the presence of the name in the ninth-century conflict register would be extremely interesting even without the equine association. However, it seems probable that the West Saxons would have recognised the ambiguity in the name, and that a 'hill of Hengest' would have carried multiple associations. It has been emphasised that the horse had a particularly privileged place in the repertoire of animal symbols used by Anglo-Saxon elites.⁷¹ Horses are found in high-status graves, and their prominent use in warfare is highly probable.⁷² A battlefield that brought these associations to mind would have made this a symbolically charged location, where ideas of elite identity coalesced around the memory of an important military victory. It is also entirely plausible that the place was named in memory of the battle (rather than vice versa), perhaps recalling the use of cavalry. In much the same way as the Woden landscapes, *Hengestdun* may have simultaneously expressed mythic/ancestral symbolism and the presence of beasts.

---

⁶⁷ See Table 8.1. See also the discussion in Michael D. J. Bintley, *Trees in the Religions of Early Medieval England* (Woodbridge, 2015).
⁶⁸ For a brief exploratory discussion see: <https://www.academia.edu/1854404/Landscapes_of_Ritual_Warfare_in_Early_Medieval_Britain_poster_2010> [accessed 2 January 2015].
⁶⁹ See Oliver J. Padel, *Cornish Place-Name Elements*, 2 vols., EPNS 56–7 (Nottingham, 1985); John E. B. Gover, Allen Mawer and Frank M. Stenton, *Place-Names of Devon*, EPNS 8–9 (Cambridge, 1931–2); Craig Weatherhill, 'Where was Hengestesdun?', *Cornish World Magazine* (October 2007).
⁷⁰ Yorke, 'Fact or Fiction?'.
⁷¹ Chris Fern, 'Horses in Mind', in *Signals of Belief*, ed. Carver *et al.*, pp. 128–57.
⁷² Chris Fern, 'Early Anglo-Saxon Horse Burials of the Fifth to Seventh Centuries AD', *ASSAH* 14 (2007); for the best recent surveys of the use of horses in warfare in Anglo-Saxon England, see Halsall, *Warfare and Society*, pp. 180–5; and Lavelle, *Alfred's Wars*, pp. 281–6.

Dyrham (*Deorham*) is generally interpreted as 'deer-enclosure' and left at that.[73] This seems to be an association that has been reinforced by the presence of a deer-park in the grounds of Dyrham Manor, near to the probable location of the battle.[74] The element 'ham' is probably in this case derived from OE *hamm*, 'land hemmed in by water or marsh (perhaps also by high ground); a river-meadow; cultivated plot on the edge of woodland or moor'.[75] The term is difficult to define with precision, but probably in its earliest sense was used to designate an area bounded by distinctive topography.[76] The Old English word *deor*, meanwhile, has a more general sense than specifically 'deer', and may be used to mean 'wild beast'.[77] The name Dyrham, therefore, can perhaps be interpreted more loosely as 'place of wild beasts'/'wilderness'. The presence of an iron-age hillfort in the vicinity of the likely battle-site reinforces a sense of the landscape as being in some sense 'outlandish'.[78] In the tradition recorded in the *Anglo-Saxon Chronicle*, this battle was also at the front line of the Anglo-Saxon advance into regions under Romano-British domination. As a boundary associated with the doomed and morally contemptible Britons, a landscape that emphasised 'wilderness' would have been entirely appropriate to historical traditions of the Anglo-Saxon conquest as they were remembered in later centuries.

The word *deor*, however, also has the adjectival sense of 'brave' or 'bold', suggesting firstly that 'beast-like' behaviour could have praiseworthy aspects, and secondly that – like *Hengestdun* – the place-name *Deorham* may have signified more than is implied by a bald translation. Twice in *Beowulf* the compound *hilde-deore* ('war-brave [men]') is used as a plural noun,[79] so it seems likely that *deor* could also have the sense of a 'brave man/warrior'. This raises the possibility of a second understanding of the place-name Dyrham, as '*hamm* of the brave warrior'. Although this is a speculative reading and does not conform to recognised Old English naming patterns, it remains possible that – as with *Hengestdun* – the depth of meaning

---

[73] A. H. Smith, *The Place-Names of Gloucestershire*, 4 vols., EPNS 38–41 (Cambridge, 1964–5).
[74] For the traditional location of the battle, see T. G. P. Hallett, 'The Battle of Deorham', *Transactions of the Bristol and Gloucestershire Archaeological Society* 8 (1883–4), 62–73; and W. St. C. Baddeley, 'The Battle of Dyrham A.D. 577', *Transactions of the Bristol and Gloucestershire Archaeological Society* 51 (1929), 95–101.
[75] Margaret Gelling and A. Cole, *The Landscape of Place-Names* (Stamford, 2000), pp. 46–55.
[76] University of Nottingham, *Key to English Place-Names: Alphabetical List of Elements in the KEPN Data* (hosted by the University of Leicester) <http://halogen.le.ac.uk/kepn/kepn_elements/> [accessed 2 January 2015].
[77] ASD.
[78] See above, p. 194; the univallate hill-fort is known as Dyrham Camp (NMR ST 77 NW 5).
[79] ASD.

contained in the name would have been readily apprehended by a culture accustomed to visual and linguistic polysemy.[80] It may be that the name was a way of memorialising both the wildness of the place and the heroic violence of the events that were believed to have occurred there, a reading which situates it very comfortably alongside the presentation of conflict landscapes in poetry and hagiography discussed elsewhere in this chapter.

Wolves Beyond the Border[81]
Anglo-Saxon Warfare in Cosmological Perspective

Tim Ingold has suggested that what we often mean by 'nature' is really 'what lies "out there". All kinds of entities are supposed to exist out there, but not you and I.'[82] This conceptualisation, perceived from 'inside' looking out, is reflected in the landscapes of *Beowulf*. All kinds of entities *do* dwell in the wilderness landscape beyond Heorot, and they are typically monstrous and unfriendly. Denis Cosgrove describes the wilderness of mythological landscapes as 'the wild wood, the moor and waste, the mountain fastness and the trackless desert or marsh'.[83] In this description he could almost be quoting from the *Beowulf* poet's description of the haunts of the monster Grendel:

> Wæs se grimma gæst Grendel haten,
> Mære mearcstapa, se þe moras heold,
> Fen ond fæsten.

> So was the grim ghoul Grendel named,
> Famed prowler of borders who held the moors
> The fen and fastness.[84]

The foregoing consideration of the conflict landscape has sought to show that there is a broad equivalence between the imaginative

---

[80] See, *inter alia*, Leslie E. Webster, 'Encrypted Visions: Style and Sense in the Anglo-Saxon Minor Arts, A.D. 400–900', in *Anglo-Saxon Styles*, ed. Catherine E. Karkov and George H. Brown (Albany, NY, 2003), pp. 11–30, and Sarah L. Keefer, '"Either/And" as "Style" in Anglo-Saxon Christian Verse', in ibid., pp. 179–200.

[81] This subheading, and the title of the original conference paper that it preserves, are ultimately derived from Robert E. Howard, 'Wolves Beyond the Border (draft)', published in *The Complete Chronicles of Conan*, ed. Stephen Jones (London, 2006), p. 862. Howard's fiction, though naïve and politically incorrect by modern standards, is interesting for the way in which it routinely presents wild places as monster-haunted environments ideal for heroic action.

[82] Tim Ingold, 'The Temporality of the Landscape', in *Interpretive Archaeology: A Reader*, ed. Julian Thomas (London, 2000), pp. 510–30 (p. 511).

[83] D. Cosgrove, 'Landscapes and Myths, Gods and Humans', in *Landscapes: Politics and Perspectives*, ed. B. Bender (Oxford, 1993), pp. 281–305 (p. 297).

[84] *Beowulf*, lines 102–4, author's translation.

spaces prowled by the monsters of later Anglo-Saxon thought and the settings assigned to earlier conflicts. Perhaps this represents a general tendency to imagine warfare as an activity confined to those places already set aside as marginal, haunted, at the borders – a symbolic attempt to keep that which belongs 'out there' from coming 'in'. It is perhaps significant that close investigation of locatable conflicts reveals that a significant number – around two thirds – were fought explicitly on political boundaries, while many more took place at points of topographical transition or water-crossings.[85] However, monsters do not simply inhabit the wilderness or the borderland; they also embody it, and the landscape itself can therefore stand as a metaphor for the savage or the sinister.[86] In this context, to take battle to an enemy in a landscape conceived of in monstrous terms is peculiarly appropriate to the testing of heroic identity.[87] Christine Rauer has stressed the similarities between the hero Beowulf confronting the monster in his lair and the numerous analogues that describe Christian saints who braved similar dangers (dragon and all), albeit for more explicitly spiritual ends.[88] Although this may not be primarily, or even predominantly, a Christian concept, the Christian emphasis on spiritual struggle in environments perceived as demon-haunted – mediated through the lives of desert fathers and the tale of St Anthony and given insular expression in the lives of Cuthbert, Wilfrid and Guthlac – is particularly important for perceiving the moral/ethical dimensions of warfare and its locales.[89]

This is not to say that warriors could not consciously adopt bestial attributes when cast, or when casting themselves, in a predatory or belligerent role. It is instructive that – as has often been remarked upon – the identities of heroic warrior and monstrous creature are equivocal and frequently linked semantically in poetic texts.[90] 'Terrible' deeds are the preserve of the mightiest warriors and the most horrendous of demon-spawned adversaries, who are thus linked through their capacity for outrageous violence. (Beowulf himself notably crushes a man to death with his bare hands; *Beowulf*, lines 2498–2508.)[91] No less unsettling is the frequently sympathetic light in which the case for violence is put on behalf of these monsters,

---

[85] PhD research data, unpublished.
[86] Andy Orchard, *Pride and Prodigies: Studies in the Monsters of the Beowulf Manuscript* (Cambridge, 1995).
[87] Magennis, *Images of Community*; we still talk in these terms: in sports and exploration, deserts, jungles and mountains are 'conquered' or 'overcome'.
[88] Christine Rauer, *Beowulf and the Dragon: Parallels and Analogues* (Cambridge, 2000).
[89] See also Bintley, Chapter 9 in this volume.
[90] Orchard, *Pride and Prodigies*, pp. 28–34.
[91] Ibid.

whether by Guthlac's demons, Grendel's mother or the dragon.[92] It is tempting to speculate that these ambiguities reflect unease regarding the role of the warrior in a Christian world. Even during the sixth and seventh centuries – when martial elites seem to have enjoyed particular power and prestige – ostentatious barrow burials (such as Asthall barrow in Oxfordshire, or Taplow in Buckinghamshire) can be found isolated from community cemeteries and without satellite graves, possibly reflecting anxiety about the subversive threat inherent in warrior identities.[93] It would be precisely this sort of location that would come to be regarded as unwholesome in the later Anglo-Saxon period,[94] a time when society was increasingly looking to legal and religious legitimacy mediated through anointed kingship.[95] Perhaps it was becoming recognised that bestial power could all too easily go astray, and the hero swiftly become the monster.

The topography of early Anglo-Saxon battles suggests that the relationship of beasts to warfare was more than a simple poetic trope or apotropaic device. Conflict landscapes conceived of as 'bestial' – in so far as they might have been regarded as the natural haunts of supernatural or wild forces – could function as fora for the performance of cosmological and ethical constructs that saw the actors taking turns to challenge or adopt a bestial identity. However, as indicated in the introduction to this volume, it is impossible to impose on the Anglo-Saxon mind the modern conceit of a binary distinction between wild nature and human culture. While hagiographic texts stress the presence of the demonic in landscapes both ancient and wild, there are hints that some of these same landscapes may have originally been associated with supernatural forces that had an ambiguous or even positive relationship to the exercise of power in pre-Christian communities. The pervasive imagery of bestial predators in the accoutrements of a warrior aristocracy can be taken as supportive of the idea that warfare was an activity that picked at the edges of human culture, unravelling threads that could easily become snared in the primeval tangle of predator and prey. In later centuries, Old Norse skaldic verse – some of it composed in England – would routinely praise kings for their open-handed feeding of ravens, wolves and eagles with the corpses of the slain. Frequently taken as a generic device expressing

---

[92] Ibid.
[93] Reynolds, 'Archaeological Correlates for Anglo-Saxon Military Activity'.
[94] Semple, 'A Fear of the Past'.
[95] Janet L. Nelson, *Politics and Ritual in Early Medieval Europe* (London, 1986), pp. 283–308.

bloodthirsty triumphalism,[96] the possible presence of these animals on the early medieval battlefield lends a visceral reality to the sentiment. Perhaps warfare, as understood in a pre- or semi-Christian world, was part of a wider symbiosis with the rest of the cosmos; perhaps to slaughter one's enemies was to feed the gods.[97]

---

[96] Judith Jesch, 'Eagles, Ravens and Wolves: Beasts of Battle, Symbols of Victory and Death', in *The Scandinavians from the Vendel Period to the Tenth Century*, ed. Judith Jesch (Woodbridge, 2002), pp. 251–71.

[97] This paper is partly based on research conducted at UCL with funding provided by the Arts and Humanities Research Council. Warm thanks to my wife, Zeenat, and my father, Geoffrey, for all their help.

9

Where the Wild Things Are in Old English Poetry

Michael D. J. Bintley

This chapter focuses on the apparent opposition in Old English poetry between those places which are occupied by humans, and those which are the domain of wild beasts. The aim is to demonstrate that there is in fact no clear binary opposition between the two; they cannot, for example, be defined simply by distinguishing the rural from the urban, or civilisation from the 'natural' world. To consider landscape in these flexible terms is ultimately Augustinian, in so far as no place is presented as being irredeemably evil; certain places are tarnished through the transgressions of those with rational capacity, but the potential of these landscapes (and their inhabitants) for redemption is often eminently achievable. Bede, drawing on Isaiah in his *Historia Ecclesiastica*, exhorted missionaries to seek out isolated, inhospitable, and rural places in which to establish hermitages and other ecclesiastical outposts. In these locations, where the 'dragons' of pagan ignorance once lay, the green shoots of Christian recovery might then spring forth. These efforts are most obviously reflected in the *Guthlac* poems, in which the warrior-saint expels a horde of demons from his fenland hermitage, but are equally visible in less obviously didactic Old English poetry, such as *Beowulf*.

It was not only rural places that required redemption. Places that had been built to house human communities could be inhabited by people who were as wild and bestial as Guthlac's demons and Grendel – those who had rejected God. The city of Mermedonia in *Andreas*, whose description evokes a ruinous Roman city, is presented as a realm of satanic cannibalism until its conversion to Christianity, when a church is constructed at its heart; the glory of Babylon leads Nebuchadnezzar into seven years of bestial madness when he vainly interprets that glory as proof of God's blessing. Elsewhere, this moral interplay between 'natural' and consciously manipulated landscapes finds a comfortable point of balance. In the Exeter Book *Phoenix*, the eponymous avian builds a nest in the forest from twigs that represent the souls of the virtuous. Similarly, in King Alfred's preface to the Old English *Soliloquies*, timbers are chosen from the forest to build a homestead in ways that have generally been thought to reflect the gathering of Latin wisdom, yet may equally reflect urban regeneration at the end of the ninth century. In this preface, the reassembly of the forest's best trees parallels the process through which any landscape can be reclaimed as a good Christian place. Finally, the early twelfth-century *Durham* presents a town whose natural and human-made features work in harmony to ensure its steadfastness and fame throughout Britain. Brought together, these examples indicate that it was rational action within landscapes, rather than their inherent characteristics, which was thought to determine whether or not they were places of human and divine order, or of bestial chaos.

Bede and the Augustinian Tradition

'Nature', as Augustine and his readers in early medieval England understood it, included humans, but was also something from which they were set apart. Humans were believed to have been created with a rational capacity for moral choice, and were therefore capable of performing good or evil actions.[1] In contrast, Augustine writes in his *De civitate Dei*, there is little sense in condemning the faults of *pecorum et arborum* ('beasts and trees'), for they are without *intellectu uel sensu uel uita* ('intelligence, or senses, or life'), and their sustenance and death are governed by God in order to ensure the *pulchritudinem temporum* ('beauty of the seasons').[2] The 'natural' world and its 'beasts', under these terms, were distinct from humans. Those with moral choice might corrupt them, but they were not in themselves evil. Given this received wisdom, it is understandable that early English poets and authors did not present any landscape as irredeemable, or any place as incapable of being befouled by sin.[3] Britain, as Bede presented it, had been defiled by the transgressions of its increasingly marginal inhabitants, the Romano-British, whose moral failings had led to the divine punishment of invasion by the heathen English. Despite this, Bede's depiction of Britain as a *locus amoenus* at the beginning of his *Historia ecclesiastica* certainly suggests that he saw it as Edenic in certain respects, and its people as primed to receive the word of

---

[1] See further discussion concerning this distinction in the Introduction to this volume.

[2] *Sancti Aurelii Augustini: De Civitate Dei XI–XXII*, ed. B. Dombart and A. Kalb, Corpus Christianorum, Series Latina 48 (Turnhout, 1955), xii.4 (p. 358). The same issue is also discussed in the *Enchiridion*; see *Sancti Aurelii Augustini: De Fide Rerum Invisibilium etc.*, ed. M. P. J. van den Hout *et al.*, Corpus Christianorum, Series Latina 46 (Turnhout, 1969), iv.12 (p. 54).

[3] Earlier discussion of Augustinian influence on *Beowulf* is usefully summarised in Alvin A. Lee, 'Symbolism and Allegory', in *A Beowulf Handbook*, ed. Robert E. Bjork and John D. Niles (Lincoln, 1977), pp. 232–54 (esp. p. 241); also Stephen C. Bandy, '*Beowulf*, the Defense of Heorot', *Neophilologus* 56 (1972), 86–92.

God. This conversion might most easily be achieved by rebuilding the faith in those places where Roman Christianity had previously been established, as attested by the large number of churches constructed on, or near to, Roman architecture.[4] More difficult, and to some more laudable, was establishing ecclesiastical communities in places less obviously suited to human habitation: Lindisfarne is an obvious example.[5]

Bede's enthusiasm for missionary work in isolated and remote places is evident throughout his writings. In 734, shortly before his death, he wrote to Bishop Egbert of York complaining that some such communities were subject to episcopal taxation without receiving the benefit of regular ecclesiastical ministration:

> multae uillae ac uiculi nostrae gentis in montibus sint inaccessis, ac saltibus dumosis positi, ubi nunquam multis transeuntibus annis sit uisus antistes qui ibidem aliquid ministerii aut gratiae caelestis exhibuerit; quorum tamen ne unus quidem a tributis antistiti reddendis esse possit immunis.[6]

> Many of the villages and hamlets of our people may be situated in mountains that are inaccessible, or in dense forests, where over the course of many years a bishop has never been seen performing his ministry and revealing his heavenly grace. However, not one of these places is immune from paying the tributes which are due to that bishop.

Given his concern here, it is unsurprising that Bede reserved special praise for those who devoted their attention to the spiritual needs of those living in wild and secluded places. In his *Historia*, praising St Cuthbert (c. 634–87), Bede wrote the following about the holy man's devotion to his ministry:

> Solebat autem ea maxime loca peragrare, illis praedicare in uiculis, qui in arduis asperisque montibus procul positi aliis horrori erant ad uisendum, et paupertate pariter ac rusticitate sua doctorum arcebant accessum.

---

[4] Tyler Bell, 'Churches on Roman Buildings: Christian Associations and Roman Masonry in Anglo-Saxon England', *MedArch* 42 (1998), 1–18; Tyler Bell, *The Religious Reuse of Roman Structures in Early Medieval England*, BAR British Series 390 (Oxford, 2005).

[5] Bede draws attention to the inaccessibility of Lindisfarne when it is first introduced in the *Historia*. When Oswald had sent for Bishop Aidan, with the aim of establishing a Northumbrian see, he gave him Lindisfarne in accordance with his wishes. All references to the *Historia Ecclesiastica* (*HE*) are from *Bede the Venerable Saint, 673–735: Bede's Ecclesiastical History of the English People*, ed. Bertram Colgrave and R. A. B. Mynors (Oxford, 1969), iii.3 (pp. 218–21). Colgrave and Mynors suggest that Lindisfarne may have had special appeal for Aidan because of its similarity to Iona (in certain respects), and its proximity to Oswald's royal seat at Bamburgh.

[6] *Venerabilis Baedae: Historiam ecclesiasticam gentis Anglorum, Historiam abbatum, Epistolam ad Ecgberctum, una cum Historia abbatum auctore anonymo*, ed. Charles Plummer, vol. 1 (Oxford, 1896), p. 410.

Now he used especially to make for those places and preach in those villages that were far away on steep and rugged mountains, which others dreaded to visit and whose poverty and ignorance kept other teachers away.[7]

Bede's words in both the *Historia* and his letter to Egbert emphasise the practical difficulties of preaching to those separated from the ebb and flow of social currents by mountains or forests. In a landscape where conversion had only recently taken place, or may even have been ongoing, Bede's celebration of individuals devoted to maintaining Christianity among the geographically marginalised elements of English society is entirely understandable.

Communities like these that were particularly likely, in *tempore mortalitatis* ('times of plague'), to neglect Christian practices and resort to idolatry, pagan incantations, and the use of amulets.[8] Thus, Bede praised Wilfrid (*c.* 633–709) for making a special effort to minster to apostates in such isolated communities. After King Ecgfrith expelled him from his see in Northumbria, Wilfrid assisted in converting the South Saxons. By the time he arrived, according to Bede, these heathens had endured three years of famine and drought. On what was to become the day of their baptism, Wilfrid overturned *prisca superstitione* ('ancient superstitions') and *idolatria* ('idolatry') in a rather telling fashion, by demonstrating the superiority of his god's power over the weather, as well as effecting a symbolic baptism. On this occasion *descendit pluuia serena, sed copiosa, refloruit terra, rediit uiridantibus aruis annus laetus et frugifer* ('a gentle yet ample rain fell; the earth revived, the fields once more became green, and a happy and fruitful season followed').[9] Undertaking missionary work like this was probably more important to the Church in Bede's England than he fully admits, especially given that he was attempting to write the ecclesiastical history of a people who acutally had very little such history for him to record. When the *Historia* was completed *c.* 731, an organised Christian infrastructure had not yet been achieved in Sussex. At the time of writing, Bede notes that the kingdom of the South Saxons, *iam aliquot annis absque episcopo manens ministerium sibi episcopale ab Occidentalium Saxonum antistite quaerit* ('having been for several years without a bishop, receives episcopal ministrations from the bishop of the West Saxons').[10] There was evidently still much work to be undertaken in rural locales such as these, perhaps primarily in terms of improving regular ministry.

---

[7] *HE* iv. 27 (pp. 432–3).
[8] Ibid.
[9] Ibid., iv. 13 (pp. 374–5).
[10] Ibid., v. 23 (pp. 558–9).

Establishing an effective ecclesiastical presence in rural, mountainous, and otherwise remote places also required fixed positions in the landscape, of the kind that Lindisfarne had become for those ministering to the Northumbrians. The third book of the *Historia ecclesiastica* describes how Oswald's son Æthelwald gave Cedd a grant of land so that he could build a monastery at which Æthelwald might pray, hear the word of God, and ultimately be buried. Bede describes the place in which Cedd chose to build the monastery at Lastingham as being:

> in montibus arduis ac remotis, in quibus latronum magis latibula ac lustra ferarum quam habitacula fuisse uidebantur hominum; ut, iuxta prophetiam Isaiae, 'in cubilibus, in quibus prius dracones habitabant, oriretur uiror calami et iunci', id est fructus bonorum operum ibi nascerentur, ubi prius uel bestiae commorari, uel homines bestialiter uiuere consuerant.

> amid some steep and remote hills, which seemed better fitted for the haunts of robbers and the dens of wild beasts than for human habitation; so that, as Isaiah says, 'In the habitations where once dragons lay, shall be grass with reeds and rushes', that is, the fruit of good works shall spring up where once beasts dwelt or where men lived after the manner of beasts.[11]

Bede quotes from Isaiah 35:7 here, but does so without indicating that the biblical reeds and rushes flourish because of such baptismal waters as Wilfrid brought to the South Saxons. What ousts the dragons in these places, and nurtures the fruits of good works, is the presence of the monastery and the good Christian practices of those within it. Also significant is the alignment of wild beasts with sinful humans in these habitats. Bede clearly regards wild places as fitting places for wild beasts and wild people. Deprived of Christian reason, the two categories might as well be one and the same – both of them mired in pagan ignorance, and awaiting the cleansing waters of baptism.

Cleansing Rural Landscapes in Guthlac and Beowulf

This approach to distinguishing between humans and non-humans, and environments correspondingly hospitable and inhospitable to human life, is evident throughout Anglo-Saxon literature. This essay, however, focuses largely on Old English poetry, rather than either the Latin texts less well known to vernacular audiences, or the more overtly didactic works of homilists. The discussion begins by

---

[11] Ibid., iii. 23 (pp. 286–8).

considering two of the best-known examples in Old English poetry of wild and inhospitable environments that are morally 'cleansed' by heroic actions. The first of these, from *Guthlac A*, is more obviously connected with Bede, and concerns events which had taken place in the generation following the foundation of the monastery at Lastingham. Guthlac had been a warrior in his youth, fighting in the retinue of Æthelræd of Mercia, son of Penda and brother of Wulfhere and Peada, before he entered a monastery in 697.[12] Two years later he set out to establish his hermitage in the Lincolnshire fens, adopting various aspects of the *miles Christi* in his battle against demonic assailants.[13] According to Felix's eighth-century *Vita sancti Guthlaci* and the two Guthlac poems, Guthlac established his hermitage on a *beorg on bearwe* ('barrow in a wood', line 148), *þæt lond gode fægre gefreoþode* ('that he might justly watch over that land for God', lines 151–2).[14]

Guthlac's decision to take up residence in a *beorg*, as Reichardt and Sharma have rightly observed, connects his actions with those of others within the eremitic tradition who sought out holy mountains for solitude and 'interior spiritual achievement'.[15] However, Reichardt's argument sidesteps both the critical discourse which has long understood the *beorg* to be not a mountain, but a barrow,[16] and the more obvious fact that the audience of this poem is likely to have known that the landscape of the Lincolnshire fens does not include mountains (as Sharma points out).[17] Sarah Semple, in her discussion of Anglo-Saxon perceptions of burial mounds, notes that Guthlac's choice of a barrow, a 'lonely, unholy and despised place', was part

---

[12] Bertram Colgrave, *Felix's Life of Saint Guthlac: Introduction, Text, Translation and Notes* (Cambridge, 1956), pp. 3–4, 84–5 (ch. 20); Jane Roberts, *The Guthlac Poems of the Exeter Book: Edited with an Introduction and Commentary* (Oxford, 1979), pp. 4–5.

[13] Joyce Hill, 'The Soldier of Christ in Old English Prose and Poetry', *LSE* ns 12 (1981), 57–80 (p. 65).

[14] References to *Guthlac A* from *The Exeter Anthology of Old English Poetry: An Edition of Exeter Dean and Chapter MS 3501*, ed. Bernard J. Muir, 2 vols., 2nd edn (Exeter, 2000), pp. 108–36. For references to Guthlac's fenland barrow amid a grove of trees, see Colgrave, *Felix's Life of Saint Guthlac*, pp. 88–9 (ch. 25), 92–5 (ch. 28).

[15] Paul F. Reichardt, '*Guthlac A* and the Landscape of Spiritual Perfection', *Neophilologus* 58 (1974), 331–8 (p. 335). For Sharma, see below.

[16] For one of the most recent and comprehensive arguments to this effect, see Alaric Hall, 'Constructing Anglo-Saxon Sanctity: Tradition, Innovation and Saint Guthlac', in *Images of Sanctity: Essays in Honour of Gary Dickson*, ed. Debra Higgs Strickland, Visualising the Middle Ages 1 (Leiden, 2007), pp. 207–35.

[17] Manish Sharma, 'A Reconsideration of the Structure of *Guthlac A*: The Extemes of Saintliness', *JEGP* 101.2 (2002), 185–200 (p. 195). Sharma also notes earlier discussion of this feature by Shook, who equated the *beorg* with a tumulus (or burial mound), Wentersdorf, who saw it as a site of pagan worship, and Roberts, who finds its use in *Guthlac A* (but not *Guthlac B*) ambiguous; see Laurence K. Shook, 'The Burial Mound in Guthlac A', *Modern Philology* 58 (1960), 1–10 (pp. 4–9); Karl P. Wentersdorf, '*Guthlac A*: The Battle for the *beorg*', *Neophilologus* 62 (1978), 135–42; Roberts, *The Guthlac Poems of the Exeter Book*, p. 132.

of a tradition that drew initially on connections between heathens and barrows, and later upon the fear of those criminals who had been executed and interred within them.[18] This grim locale is paralleled by the evil of Guthlac's demonic adversaries:

> Oft þær broga cwom
> egeslic ond uncuð,   ealdfeonda nið,
> searocræftum swiþ.   Hy him sylf hyra
> onsyn ywdon,   ond þær ær fela
> setla gesæton.   Þonan sið tugon
> wide waðe,   wuldre byscyrede,
> lyftlacende.

Often terror came there, terrible and strange, the hostility of the ancient enemy, powerful in its machinations. They revealed their shape before him, and had previously established many lairs in that place. From there they took to the wing, flying through the air, wandering widely, shorn of glory.

(*Guthlac A*, lines 140–6)

The wanderings of these creatures (here in flight, but elsewhere threatening to crush Guthlac with their feet) are in keeping with the landscape they inhabit, characterised by a lack of evident fixity or purpose, and an inability to return to the fastness of the heavenly kingdom.[19]

Guthlac's victory over the demons is a question of faith and perseverance, in which he endures every trial and threat to which he is subjected. With the appearance of Bartholomew, and his command that the tormentors leave the saint alone, Guthlac's victory over both them and their inhospitable domain is ensured, and the grim fenland is made beautiful. As Sievers has observed, the perception within 'modern scholarship' that the Anglo-Saxons' descriptions of 'nature' were always in some way alienated and distanced from those of their Continental contemporaries is clearly contradicted by the beauty of the landscape following Guthlac's defeat of his assailants,[20]

---

[18] Sarah Semple, 'A Fear of the Past: The Place of the Prehistoric Burial Mound in the Ideology of Middle and Later Anglo-Saxon England', *World Archaeology* 30.1 (1998), 109–26 (pp. 112–13, 115, 123); Sarah Semple, 'Recycling the Past: Ancient Monuments and Changing Meanings in Early Medieval Britain', in *Antiquaries and Archaists: The Past in the Past, the Past in the Present*, ed. Megan Aldrich and Robert J. Wallis (Reading, 2009), pp. 29–45; Howard Williams, 'Ancient Attitudes to Ancient Monuments', *British Archaeology* 29 (1997).

[19] This also connects the demons with Satan, as tormentor, in Job 1:7, where he tells God that he has come *ait circuivi terram et perambulavi eam* ('from roaming throughout the earth, going back and forth on it').

[20] Alfred K. Siewers, 'Landscapes of Conversion: Guthlac's Mound and Grendel's Mere as Expressions of Anglo-Saxon Nation-Building', *Viator* 34 (2003), 1–39 (p. 1).

a landscape which, as Catherine Clarke has noted, exhibits many traditional features of the *locus amoenus*:[21]

> Smolt wæs se sigewong   ond sele niwe,
> fæger fugla reord,   folde geblowen;
> geacas gear budon.   Guþlac moste
> eadig ond onmod   eardes brucan.
> Stod se grena wong   in godes wære;
> hæfde se heorde,   se þe of heofonum cwom,
> feondas afyrde.

Peaceful was that plain of victory and that hall anew, and fair the voices of the birds, as the earth blossomed; and the cuckoos greeted the year. Blessed and resolute, Guthlac could enjoy his dwelling place. That green place stood under the protection of God; that guardian, he who had come from the heavens, had put the demons to flight.

(*Guthlac A*, lines 742–8)

Where once there were demons, flitting on the wing, there are now tree-dwelling birds (Guthlac's substitute for human society), whom he nourishes with food from his own hands, like a human counterpart to the life-sustaining cross which he set on the barrow as his battle-standard. Although there are no other people in this place to undergo conversion, its reclamation through these good Christian actions makes it a demonstrably pleasant location, whose potential for good Christian works is heralded by reassuring birdsong that brings an end to the poem's horror.

The harrowing of Grendel's lair follows a similar pattern, and cleansing is an important theme throughout *Beowulf* when it comes to purifying the habitats of humans and their adversaries. Beowulf personally promises Hrothgar that he will *Heorot fælsian* ('cleanse Heorot', line 432); the narrator later uses the same word to explain that Beowulf has fulfilled his vow (lines 825, 2352), as does Wealhtheow in her speech (line 1176) before Grendel's mother attacks the golden hall. The word is employed once more to describe the cleansing of the mere (line 1620), but is not used of the dragon's barrow, perhaps because of some ambiguity regarding Beowulf's motives in confronting this enemy. It is necessary for Heorot to be cleansed, as, like Eden, it was originally created as a *folcstede* ('people's place', line 76), through Hrothgar's cosmogonic act of speech.[22] As Halverson observed, Heorot is a world in itself, built by the word of Hrothgar, and within its boundaries serves to represent a

---

[21] Catherine Clarke, *Literary Landscapes and the Idea of England, 700–1400* (Cambridge, 2006), p. 50.
[22] Edward B. Irving, *Rereading Beowulf* (Philadelphia, 1989), p. 150.

'principle of harmony'.[23] Similarly, Helena Hamerow described how the organisation of space within Anglo-Saxon and other Germanic hall buildings, as attested by their archaeology, both reflected and reinforced social organisation.[24] Expanding upon this terrestrial symbolism, Jennifer Neville has observed that Bede's commentary *In Genesim* compares the construction of a building to the creation of the cosmos, in terms reminiscent of an Anglo-Saxon vision of the universe as 'a structure with a timbered roof'.[25] As long as Heorot is home to those good practices which bind society together, then all shall be well, though it is clear from the poet's first allusion to the Heathobards that the collapse of these social bonds will one day doom Hrothgar's hall to inevitable destruction (lines 81–5), like everything made by human hands, and indeed everything mundane.[26]

In much the same way as Guthlac's hermitage in Crowland, Grendel's mere is a place on the outskirts of society, held at arm's length from the consciously and humanly ordered wooden world of Heorot.[27] This construction from wood is worth emphasizing, as it is a feature which Heorot shares with Beowulf's own, less celebrated, hall later in the poem – both of them spaces in which humans carry out those activities that serve to bind their society together.[28] By contrast, the monster habitats to which these halls stand in opposition, and which threaten the lives of humans throughout the poem, are defined principally by their stone construction and subterranean location. In this way, wood and stone become part of a dichotomy between the worlds of humans and monsters. In contrast with Heorot, Grendel's mere is a place of *harne stane* ('grey stone', line 1415) and *neowle næssas, nicorhusa fela* ('rainy headlands, and many nicor-houses', line 1411), to which the Danes and the Geats travel from Heorot after the attack by Grendel's mother, and where they find sea monsters basking on the rocky *holmclifu* ('sea-cliffs', line 1421) and *næshleoþum* ('headland

---

[23] John Halverson, 'The World of *Beowulf*', *English Literary History* 36.4 (1969), 593–608 (p. 594).
[24] Helena Hamerow, *Early Medieval Settlements: The Archaeology of Rural Communities in North-West Europe, 400–900* (Oxford, 2002), p. 12.
[25] Jennifer Neville, *Representations of the Natural World in Old English Poetry*, CSASE 27 (Cambridge, 1999), p. 67 (also pp. 147–8); *Bedae Venerabilis Opera: Pars 2.1, Opera Exegetica*, ed. C. W. Jones, Corpus Christianorum, Series Latina 118a (Turnhout, 1967), pp. 10–17. See also Martin Green, 'Man, Time, and Apocalypse in *The Wanderer, The Seafarer*, and *Beowulf*', in *Old English Shorter Poems: Basic Readings*, ed. Katherine O'Brien O'Keefe (London, 1994), pp. 281–302 (p. 290).
[26] Norman E. Eliason, 'The Burning of Heorot', *Speculum* 55.1 (1980), 75–83 (p. 83).
[27] Irving, *Rereading Beowulf*, p. 149. On the specificity of the terms used to describe the landscape of *Beowulf*, see Margaret Gelling, 'The Landscape of *Beowulf*', *ASE* 31 (2002), 7–11.
[28] Michael G. Shapland, 'Meanings of Timber and Stone in Anglo-Saxon Building Practice', in *Trees and Timber in the Anglo-Saxon World*, ed. Michael D. J. Bintley and Michael G. Shapland (Oxford, 2013), pp. 21–44.

slopes', line 1427) on which Æschere's head is discovered.[29] The lair itself, referred to no fewer than three times as a hall, is nevertheless an underwater cave in a natural landscape setting.[30] Admittedly, it is described in extreme, exaggerated and fantastical terms, but this is entirely in keeping with the extreme, exaggerated and fantastical events that take place within it.[31] Beowulf, though possessed of extraordinary strength and power, is still a man, just as the cave, otherworldly and terrible as it is, is still a cave. The narrator refers to it as a hall because it is the place that the Grendels call home, and thus still a 'hall' in this sense, complete with the conventional Germanic domestic trappings of hearth, bedding, and weapon-adorned walls.[32] The natural stone construction of this monstrous hall thus emphasizes its opposition to Heorot, a 'man-made world' carved from wood, which 'represents the imposition of order and organisation on chaotic surroundings'.[33]

The hellish pedigree of Grendel's mere is well known. Andy Orchard has demonstrated analogues in a number of traditions, including a motif which Donald Fry termed the 'Cliff of Death', a vernacular version of the *Visio S. Pauli* (and Blickling Homily XVI), insular depictions of hell, Virgil's *Aeneid*, and *Alexander's Letter to Aristotle*.[34] These relationships contribute to the mere's sinister character, and our sense that it lies beyond what we would expect to encounter in nature. This is further illustrated by the overhanging trees, whose vitality is suspended by the bonds of frost:

> Nis þæt feor heonon
> milgemearces þæt se mere standeð;
> ofer þæm hongiað hrinde bearwas,
> wudu wyrtum fæst wæter oferhelmað.

It is not far hence in a measure of miles that the mere stands; over it hang frosty trees, a wood fast in its roots overshadows the water.

(*Beowulf*, lines 1361–4)

---

[29] All references to *Beowulf* are from *Klaeber's Beowulf and the Fight at Finnsburg*, ed. R. D. Fulk, Robert E. Bjork and John D. Niles, 4th edn (Toronto, 2008).

[30] Although described as a *nipsele* ('hostile hall', line 1513), *hrofsele* ('roofed hall', line 1515), and *hofe* ('hall', line 1507), it is difficult to see how the Grendel's lair might be a 'roofed building in the plain at the bottom of the mere [...] roofed against the water of the mere', as George Clark suggested in *Beowulf*, Twaynes English Authors Series 477 (Boston, 1990), p. 100.

[31] See discussion in Richard Butts, 'The Analogical Mere: Landscape and Terror in *Beowulf*', *ES* 68 (1987), 113–21 (pp. 114–16).

[32] Irving, 'Rereading *Beowulf*', p. 150.

[33] Halverson, 'The World of *Beowulf*', p. 601.

[34] Donald K. Fry, 'The Cliff of Death in Old English Poetry', in *Comparative Research in Oral Traditions: A Memorial for Milman Parry*, ed. John Miles Foley (Columbus, OH, 1987), pp. 213–34; Andy Orchard, *Pride and Prodigies: Studies in the Monsters of the Beowulf Manuscript*, rev. edn (Toronto, 2003), pp. 41–7.

Though the wood is secure in its roots, the ice that binds these trees recalls the frost-fetters that cover the earth in *The Wanderer*, and ensnare the sailor in *The Seafarer*, emphasising the hostility of the waters that lie below. That other non-humans equally shun the mere is evident in the behaviour of the stag which (in Hrothgar's description) would rather lay down its life at the water's edge than risk leaping into its depths (lines 1368–72).

The cleansing of the mere is described in no uncertain terms. Grendel's blood melts the blade of the giants' sword, with which Beowulf beheads his corpse, *ise gelicost, ðonne forstes bend fæder onlæteð* ('like ice, when the Father unlooses the bonds of frost', lines 1608–9). This indicates that the bonds of unnatural evil have been undone by the hero's virtuous actions:

> Sona wæs on sunde se þe ær æt sæcce gebad
> wighryre wraðra, wæter up þurhdeaf;
> wæron yðgebland eal gefælsod
> eacne eardas þa se ellorgast
> oflet lifdagas ond þas lænan gesceaft.

Then he was immediately in the water, who before endured combat, the slaughter of evil ones. He dove up through the water; the surging currents were entirely cleansed, the vast depths, when the alien spirit left the days of life and this temporary creation.

(*Beowulf*, lines 1618–22)

When at last Beowulf reaches the surface, *lagu drusade, wæter under wolcnum, wældreore fag* ('the lake subsided, the water under the clouds, stained with battle gore', lines 1630–1). Although the mere is not suddenly transformed into a *locus amoenus*, as are the surroundings of Guthlac's hermitage, the reader of *Beowulf* is in no doubt that the mere is no longer a seat of evil, and poses no further threat to the Danes.

Cities of Sin in Daniel and Andreas

Guthlac and *Beowulf* both offer examples of rural, 'natural' environments from which evil is expelled by heroes who impose divine or human societal order upon them. Alfred Siewers has persuasively argued that the conquest of these places formed part of an Anglo-Saxon 'ideological project', of 'superimposing a new cultural landscape on Britain's most fertile areas', in ways that emphasised the sense of Anglo-Saxon culture as 'God-chosen and hegemonic'.[35] The same can also be said of the approach to urban

---

[35] Siewers, 'Landscapes of Conversion', p. 3.

environments in Old English poetry, of which Babylon in *Daniel* and Mermedonia in *Andreas* are good examples. Significantly, in both of these works the sinfulness of evildoers is emphasised through their association with beasts.

Daniel opens with the sack of Jerusalem by the *wulfheort* ('wolf-hearted one', line 116), Nebuchadnezzar, and the violent subjection of the Israelites. Following this conquest, Nebuchadnezzar dreams of the violent end of every empire and every human pleasure (lines 104–20), the exegesis of which is patiently given by Daniel, and promptly ignored by the Babylonian king, who is busy building a golden statue for his subjects to worship. In addition to this arrogance (the primary reason for his punishment), Nebuchadnezzar attempts to burn three virtuous youths who refuse to worship his golden idol, though divine intervention preserves them from harm.[36] Nebuchadnezzar's second dream is of a great tree that represents himself and his empire, which is subsequently felled and has its stump bound. This too is interpreted by Daniel, but the king ignores him again and, in his vaunting pride, interprets his city's greatness as proof of God's favour:

> Ongan ða gyddigan þurh gylp micel
> Caldea cyning þa he ceastergeweorc,
> Babilone burh, on his blæde geseah,
> Sennera feld sidne bewindan,
> heah hlifigan; þæt se heretyma
> werede geworhte þurh wundor micel,
> wearð ða anhydig ofer ealle men,
> swiðmod in sefan, for ðære sundorgife
> þe him god sealde.[37]

Then the Chaldean king began to boast with great arrogance, when in his prosperity he looked upon the fortress, the city of Babylon, broadly stretching about the plain of Shinar, and towering tall; the warrior king had built it as a great wonder for the multitude, and become stubborn over all men, proud in spirit, as a result of the privilege that God had granted him.

(*Daniel*, lines 598–606)

The city itself is not presented as a realm of evil deeds, because its idol-worship is largely Nebuchadnezzar's fault. It is appropriate, as a result, that Nebuchadnezzar is punished with seven years of bestial madness befitting the ungodly practices he has promoted:

---

[36] See discussion in Graham D. Caie, 'The Old English *Daniel*: A Warning Against Pride', *ES* 59.1 (1978), 1–9 (esp. pp. 7–9); also Manish Sharma, 'Nebuchadnezzar and the Defiance of Measure in the Old English *Daniel*', *ES* 86 (2005), 103–26 (p. 103).

[37] All references to *Daniel* are from G. P. Krapp, *The Junius Manuscript* (London, 1931), pp. 110–32.

> Seofon winter samod   susl þrowode,
> wilddeora westen,   winburge cyning.
> Ða se earfoðmæcg   up locode,
> wilddeora gewita,   þurh wolcna gang.
> Gemunde þa on mode   þæt metod wære,
> heofona heahcyning,   hæleða bearnum
> ana ece gast.

For seven years altogether the king of the wine city suffered misery, and the wastes of wild beasts. Then that suffering one looked up, the intellectual equal of the wild beasts, through the passing of the clouds. He then remembered in his mind that the creator, the high king of the heavens, was, for the sons of men, the sole eternal spirit.

(*Daniel*, lines 620–6)

Here, as elsewhere, the *Daniel* poet remains close to the source in describing Nebuchadnezzar's fate. There is a tidy alliterative binding in the first line here of the king to his seven-year punishment, followed by an unravelling as the king of the *winburg* ('wine town') finds himself cast out into the *wildeora westen* ('wilderness of wild beasts'). His salvation comes from looking up out of this place, and seeking to be elevated from the status of *wilddeora gewita* to the seat of the *heofona heahcyning*.

After Nebuchadnezzar has regained his wits and his throne, the reader is reminded once again of his former alignment with wild beasts, though the exact nature of these creatures is never explicit, and their habitat is never described as anything more than a wilderness. The poet treats them as one homogenous group, with an apparently common lack of reason. Nebuchadnezzar himself is redeemed from this state because of his faith in God:

>   Siððan deora gesið,
> wildra wærgenga,   of waðe cwom,
> Nabochodonossor   of niðwracum,
> siððan weardode   wide rice,
> heold hæleða gestreon   and þa hean burh,
> frod, foremihtig   folca ræswa,
> Caldea cyning,   oðþæt him cwelm gesceod,
> swa him ofer eorðan   andsaca ne wæs
> gumena ænig   oðþæt him god wolde
> þurh hryre hreddan   hea rice.

After the companion of wild beasts, and the friend of the savage ones – Nebuchadnezzar – returned from his wandering, from his severe punishments, he afterwards governed the wide kingdom, watched over the public purse and that high city, as a wise and mighty leader of the people, the king of the Chaldeans, until death destroyed him, so that to him no man on earth was an adversary, until God wished to relieve him of that high kingdom in death.

(*Daniel*, lines 661–70)

These lines reflect Nebuchadnezzar's transition from inhumanity to humanity in terms that emphasise his former state, not simply his separation from human society – the king was the *deora gesið* ('companion of beasts'), and *wildra wærgenga* ('friend of the savage ones'). This suggests that Nebuchadnezzar actively sought these friends through his rejection of the divine instruction he received in dreams. However, God is good enough to maintain Babylon throughout the king's madness, so that when he does return home, it is still a functioning city, and not a wild ruin. The *hean burh* over which Nebuchadnezzar holds power until his death-day, keeping a steward's watchful eye upon the *hæleða gestreon*, is thus preserved in keeping with God's will. Robert Finnegan went so far as to suggest that Babylon even becomes, after Nebuchadnezzar's conversion, 'the physical type of the heavenly Jerusalem'.[38]

Though Babylon was an archetypal city of sin in the Middle Ages, and its king the companion of beasts, it is not the only city in Old English poetry to have been inhabited by humans who were decidedly bestial, even though capable of reason. The most dramatic example in Old English poetry of an urban place inhabited by bestial humans is Mermedonia in *Andreas*, with its anthropophagic Mermedonian inhabitants. The narrative of *Andreas* is thought to have adhered fairly closely to its source: a now-lost Latin version of the Greek *Praxeis*, which is a life of St Andrew closely related to the Latin *Casanatensis* and to an Old English translation of another Latin version now partly preserved in the Blickling Homilies, and more fully represented in Cambridge, Corpus Christi College MS 198.[39] The *Andreas* poet is also thought to have drawn upon *Beowulf*, which makes comparison between these poems and their monstrous environments all the more appropriate in the context of this chapter.[40]

---

[38] Robert Emmett Finnegan, 'The Old English *Daniel*: The King and his City', *NM* 85 (1984), 194–211 (p. 195).

[39] See discussion in *Andreas*, ed. Richard North and Michael D. J. Bintley (forthcoming); *The Acts of Andrew in the Country of the Cannibals*, trans. Robert Boenig, Garland Library of Medieval Literature 70.B (New York, 1991), pp. v–ix; *The Vercelli Book*, ed. George P. Krapp, ASPR 2 (New York, 1932), p. xxxvi; Hugh Magennis, *Images of Community in Old English Poetry*, CSASE 18 (Cambridge, 1996), p. 173.

[40] Andy Orchard, *A Critical Companion to 'Beowulf'* (Cambridge, 2003), pp. 164–6. This same issue is also discussed in Anita R. Riedinger, 'The Formulaic Relationship between *Beowulf* and *Andreas*', in *Heroic Poetry in the Anglo-Saxon Period: Studies in Honor of Jess B. Bessinger Jr.*, ed. Helen Damico and John Leyerle, Studies in Medieval Culture 32 (Kalamazoo, MI, 1993), pp. 283–312; also Tom A. Shippey, *Old English Verse* (London, 1972), p. 115. Arguments to the contrary have generally failed to consider material shared by the two poems in context, e.g. Leonard J. Peters, 'The Relationship of the Old

Although the Mermedonians' monstrosity matches Grendel's in many respects (of which their cannibalism is only one), they surpass him in the planning and forethought that goes into the execution and consumption of their victims:

> Eal wæs þæt mearcland morðre bewunden,
> feondes facne, folcstede gumena,
> hæleða eðel; næs þær hlafes wist
> werum on þam wonge, ne wæteres drync
> to bruconne, ah hie blod ond fel,
> fira flæschoman, feorrancumenra,
> ðegon geond þa þeode. Swelc wæs þeaw hira
> þæt hie æghwylcne ellðeodigra
> dydan him to mose meteþearfendum,
> þara þe þæt ealand utan sohte;
> swylc wæs þæs folces freoðoleas tacen,
> unlædra eafoð, þæt hie eagena gesihð,
> hettend heorogrimme, heafodgimmas,
> agetton gealgmode gara ordum.
> Syððan him geblendan bitere tosomne,
> dryas þurh dwolcræft, drync unheorne,
> se onwende gewit, wera ingeþanc,
> heortan on hreðre, (hyge wæs oncyrred),
> þæt hie ne murndan æfter mandreame,
> hæleþ heorogrædige, ac hie hig ond gærs
> for meteleaste meðe gedrehte.[41]

All bound in murder was that border country, with devil's crime, that men's habitation, homeland of heroes; it was not loaf food there, or drink of water that men in that country had for their use, but blood and skin, flesh of men come from far, on which they in that nation dined. Such was their custom, that each man from a nation of foreigners did they make, when needing food, into meat, of those who sought that land by water from abroad; such was the people's uncivilised character, violence of the wretched, that gallows-minded, they would with spear-points dispatch the eyesight, enemies blood-thirsting, the head-jewels. For them together then mordantly wizards would mix with witchcraft a drink monstrous which overturned the wits, the intellect of men, heart in the breast; their reason was overthrown, so that they did not mourn men's pleasures, heroes ravenous, but hay and grass would vex them when weak for want of food.

(Andreas, lines 19–39)

English *Andreas* to *Beowulf*', *Proceedings of the Modern Language Association* 66.5 (1951), 844–63; David Hamilton, 'The Diet and Digestion of Allegory in *Andreas*', *ASE* 1 (1972), 147–58 (p. 147); David Hamilton, '*Andreas* and *Beowulf*: Placing the Hero', in *Anglo-Saxon Poetry: Essays in Appreciation for John C. McGalliard*, ed. Lewis E. Nicholson and Dolores Warwick-Frese (Notre Dame, IN, 1975), pp. 81–98.

[41] All references to *Andreas* are from North and Bintley.

The Mermedonians are comparable with Nebuchadnezzar in so far as they are lowered to the level of beasts, being described as *wælwulfas* ('wolves of slaughter', line 150), though it is their conscious rejection of God and acceptance of Satan which has led to their present state in *Andreas*, in contrast with the pride of the Babylonian king.[42] Most notable here is the Mermedonians' consumption of hay and grass (which the biblical Nebuchadnezzar also ate) when they are unable to lay their hands on human flesh, and their ability to stupefy their victims using a poisonous draught that deprives them of *wera ingeþanc*.[43] This draws attention to their lack of human reason, implying a sense of contagious immorality that leaves the victims as morally decrepit as their captors.

Much of the action in *Andreas* takes place within an urban environment, dilapidated though it seems to be; like Guthlac, Andrew is fighting to control a piece of land.[44] The 'development of place and setting' in *Andreas*, as Magennis has noted, marks one of the Old English poet's most significant additions to his source material, through the borrowing of 'features derived from the vernacular poetic traditions'.[45] As I have previously argued, the *Andreas* poet may have been deliberately engaging with these conventions in an effort to facilitate an ideological transition between the way in which Roman urban ruins had been viewed previously, and their subsequent reoccupation.[46] The Mermedonians would thus have been recognised by a contemporary audience as inhabiting an urban foundation of the sort that was ubiquitous throughout the early English landscape, and the city is presented in terms familiar to us from elsewhere in the corpus. When Andrew first encounters it, Mermedonia is described in a way that evokes the Roman settlement in *The Ruin*:

> Onwoc þa wiges heard, wang sceawode
> fore burggeatum; beorgas steape,
> hleoðu hlifodon, ymbe harne stan
> tigelfagan trafu, torras stodon,
> windige weallas.

---

[42] John Casteen, '*Andreas*: Mermedonian Cannibalism and Figural Narrative', *NM* 75 (1974), 74–8.
[43] Brian Shaw, 'Translation and Transformation in *Andreas*', in *Prosody and Poetics in the Early Middle Ages: Essays in Honour of C. B. Hieatt*, ed. M. J. Toswell (Toronto, 1995), pp. 164–79.
[44] Fabienne L. Michelet, *Creation, Migration and Conquest: Imaginary Geography and Sense of Space in Old English Literature* (Oxford, 2006), p. 164; see also Heather Blurton, *Cannibalism in High Medieval English Literature* (Basingstoke, 2007), p. 22.
[45] Magennis, *Images of Community*, p. 173.
[46] Michael D. J. Bintley, 'Demythologising Urban Landscapes in *Andreas*', *LSE* ns 40 (2009), 105–18. See also discussion in North and Bintley, *Andreas*.

Awoke then the war-hardened, saw the lie of the land before the town's gates; steep mountains, cliffsides rose up, around the hoary rock stood shacks adorned with tiles, towers, windswept walls.

(*Andreas*, lines 839–43)

Following Andrew's brutal torture at the hands of the Mermedonians, he summons a baptismal deluge from a pillar in his jail cell by appealing to God's mercy, whereupon the imminent threat of the flood forces the Mermedonians into a hasty conversion.[47] Once *Godes tempel* ('God's temple', line 1634) has been constructed within the city walls, the settlement becomes a place of 'admirable community'.[48] What was described once as a *hæðnan burg* ('heathen stronghold', line 111), and twice as a *mæran byrig* ('infamous/famous town', lines 287, 973), becomes a *beorhtan byrig* ('bright city', line 1649), a *goldburg* ('golden city', line 1655), and a *winbyrig* ('wine city', line 1672).[49]

Constructing loci amoeni in The Phoenix, the Soliloquies, and Durham

So far this chapter has shown that Old English poetry preserves examples of both rural and urban environments that are regarded as the habitats of wild beasts, either because beasts dwell in them, or because the humans who live there act in a sinful and bestial fashion. Each of these locations, however, has potential for redemption through the actions of the virtuous. As well as being discovered in the landscape, such places could also be constructed by humans to serve as seats of good works. The final part of this chapter considers three instances in which 'nature' outside of human society is drawn upon in human constructions to promote the growth of various communities: the allegorical abstraction of the nest in the *Phoenix*; Alfred's exhortations in the preface to the Old English *Soliloquies*; and the glorious city described in *Durham*, which harmoniously combines the natural world with one which has been built by human hands.

In preparation for its process of regeneration in *The Phoenix*, the bird flies to a secluded woodland grove in Syria. Here, the Old English

---

[47] Marie Michelle Walsh, 'The Baptismal Flood in the Old English *Andreas*: Liturgical and Typological Depths', *Traditio* 33 (1977), 137–58.

[48] Magennis, *Images of Community*, p. 174; also Hugh Magennis, *Anglo-Saxon Appetites: Food and Drink and their Consumption in Old English and Related Literature* (Dublin, 1999), p. 25; also Michelet, *Creation, Migration and Conquest*, p. 175.

[49] 'Infamous' is probably the most appropriate translation of *mæran* in both cases, as this is how God and the sailors describe it on their way to Mermedonia.

author expands on his (probable) Latin source, the *De Ave Phoenice* of Lactantius, writing that:[50]

> Him se clæna þær
> oðscufeð scearplice,   þæt he in scade weardað
> on wudubearwe,   weste stowe,
> biholene ond bihydd   hæleþa monegum
> Ðær he heanne beam   on holtwuda
> wunað ond weardað   wyrtum fæstne
> under heofum hrofe,   þone hatað
> Fenix on foldan,   of þæs fugles noman.[51]

That pure one then flies rapidly away from [the Syrians] to live in seclusion in a woodland grove, a deserted place, holed up and hidden from the multitudes of men. There he dwells and nests in a high tree, in a holt-wood, a tree fast in its roots under the roof of heaven, which men on earth call the Phoenix, after the name of that bird.

(*Phoenix*, lines 167–74)

In this place the phoenix constructs its nest from twigs retrieved from the forest. These are identified as the souls of the virtuous, in ways that draw appropriate vegetal parallels with Isaiah and the intended growth of reeds and rushes.[52]

> þa æþelan sind
> wyrta wynsume,   mid þam se wilda fugel
> his sylfes nest   biseteð utan,
> þæt hit færinga   fyre byrneð,
> forsweleð under sunnan,   ond he sylfa mid,
> ond þonne æfter lige   lift eft onfehð
> edniwinga.

these are the noble and joyful plants with which that wild bird constructs his nest, so that it immediately burns up in fire, is consumed under the sun, and he himself with it, and then after the flames returns to life renewed.

(*Phoenix*, lines 528–34)

The allegory presented in these passages also draws a parallel between the construction of the bird's nest and the development of

---

[50] *Sources and Analogues of Old English Poetry: The Major Latin Texts in Translation*, trans. Michael J. B. Allen and Daniel G. Calder (Cambridge, 1976), pp. 113–20 (p. 115); Daniel G. Calder, 'The Vision of Paradise: A Symbolic Reading of The Old English *Phoenix*', *ASE* 1 (1972), 167–81 (pp. 167–70); Carol Heffernan, 'The Old English *Phoenix*: A Reconsideration', *NM* 83 (1982), 239–54 (p. 239); Brian A. Shaw, 'The Old English *Phoenix*', in *Medieval Translators and their Craft*, ed. Jeannette Beer, Studies in Medieval Culture 25 (Kalamazoo, MI, 1989), pp. 155–83 (p. 157).

[51] References to *The Phoenix* are from Muir, *The Exeter Anthology of Old English Poetry*, pp. 164–87.

[52] Shaw, 'The Old English *Phoenix*', p. 169.

the Christian Church explored by Bede in his *De Templo* (*c*. 729–31). Bede adopts a long-established metaphor connecting the individuals who made up the Church with the building materials which made up physical churches – an idea that is evident throughout his writing, but perhaps nowhere more so than in this text.[53] Here he explores the idea of the Temple of Jerusalem as a metaphor for numerous figures: not only the body of Christ, the body of the Church, and the soul of the individual, but also the relationship between all of these and more besides, a series of connections that was already well established in the New Testament:[54]

> Post fundamentum uero talibus ac tantis lapidibus compositum aedificanda est domus praeparatis diligentius lignis ac lapidibus ac decenti ordine collocatis quae olim de prisco suo situ uel radice fuerant abstracta quia post prima fidei rudimenta post collocata in nobis iuxta exemplum sublimium uirorum fundamenta humilitatis addendus est in altum paries operum bonorum quasi superimpositis sibi inuicem ordinibus lapidum ambulando ac proficiendo de uirtute in uirtutem.

> But after the foundation which is made up of stones of such quality and size, the house must be built with wood and stones very carefully dressed and laid in the proper arrangement, <wood and stones> which had once been removed from their original position and roots, because, after the first rudiments of the faith and after the foundations of humility have been laid in us after the example of men of high virtue, there remains to continue upwards the wall of good works, superimposing on each other, as it were, courses of stones by the life we lead and by advancing from virtue to virtue.[55]

Part of what Bede demonstrates here is that the structure of the Church is made up of many different elements, as those responsible for its construction and maintenance should recognise. The temple must be constructed out of appropriate timbers, just as the Phoenix's nest must be made from appropriate twigs, both of which serve as metaphors for the various human elements essential to the structure of the Church. *De Templo* and *The Phoenix* thus both offer examples of locations in which humans are represented as plant-life, and in which those humans contribute to the creation of virtuous environments whence the fruits of good works may spring forth.

Similar ideas also appear in the King Alfred's preface to the Old English translation of Augustine's *Soliloquies*, albeit in terms which

---

[53] Seán Connolly and Jennifer O'Reilly, *Bede: On the Temple* (Liverpool, 1995), p. xvii.
[54] Ibid., p. xxxiii.
[55] *Bedae Venerabilis Opera: Pars II Opera Exegetica; 2a, De Tabernaculo, De Templo, In Ezram et Neemiam*, ed. D. Hurst, Corpus Christianorum, Series Latina, 1991 (Turnhout, 1969), pp. 155–6 (lines 334–70); Connolly and O'Reilly, *Bede: On the Temple*, i. 4.4 (p. 16).

may refer to both the reassembly of Christian wisdom, and the development of the burghal system under Alfred and his successors.[56] The production of the *Soliloquies*, a relatively obscure choice for translation, probably took place after the translation of the *Cura Pastoralis* and the *Consolation* (if that was an Alfredian production), since it refers to these texts retrospectively.[57] Unsurprisingly, this work and its preface have predominantly been written about by literary scholars. As a consequence, the critical tendency has been to interpret the words of its speaker as largely pertaining to the production of literature. The speaker describes himself as a woodsman on his way through the forest, looking up into its overhanging branches, and taking whatever he needs to manufacture the tools and materials:

> Gaderode me þonne kigclas, and stuþansceaftas, and lohsceaftas, and hylfa to ælcum þara tola þe ic mid wircan cuðe, and bohtimbru and bolttimbru to ælcum þara weorca þe ic wyrcan cuðe, þa wlitegostan treowo be þam dele ðe ic aberan meihte. Ne com ic naþer mid anre byrðene ham, þe me ne lyste ealne þane wude ham brengan, gif ic hyne ealne aberan meihte. On ælcum treowo ic geseah hwæthwugu þæs þe ic æt ham beþorfte.[58]

> I gathered then cudgels and pillars, and beams, and handles for all those tools with which I knew how to work, and bow timbers and beams for each of those buildings which I knew how to construct, the fairest trees of all that I might carry. I did not come home with a single burden, without wanting to bring all of that wood homewards, if I could have borne it. In every tree I saw something I had need of at home.

Numerous commentators on this passage have noted that the uncharacteristically sudden opening of the work must either be an idiosyncrasy of this preface, or, as seems rather more likely, an indication that it has somehow been truncated.[59] There is no preamble to suggest that the persona voicing these thoughts is the same as the

---

[56] Although this is obviously not a work of Old English poetry, the *Preface* to the *Soliloquies* evidently belongs to the idea complex found in *The Phoenix* and *De Templo*, and its inclusion in this discussion as a vernacular text reflecting similar attitudes is hopefully more acceptable than its exclusion would have been.

[57] This ordering is referred to in Nicole Guenther Discenza, *The King's English: Strategies of Translation in the Old English 'Boethius'* (Albany, NY, 2005), p. 1; also Paul E. Szarmach, 'The Meaning of Alfred's *Preface* to the *Pastoral Care*', *Mediaevalia* 6 (1982), 57–86 (p. 70); Paul E. Szarmach, 'Alfred's *Soliloquies* in London, BL, Cotton Tiberius A. iii (art. 9g, fols. 50v–51v)', in *Latin Learning and English Lore*, ed. Katherine O'Brien O'Keeffe and Andy Orchard (Toronto, 2005), vol. 2, pp. 153–79 (p. 160).

[58] References to the preface to the *Soliloquies* are from *King Alfred's Old English Version of St. Augustine's Soliloquies*, ed. Henry L. Hargrove, Yale Studies in English 13 (New York, 1902), pp. 1–2.

[59] Milton McCormick Gatch, 'King Alfred's Version of Augustine's *Soliloquia*: Some Suggestions on its Rationale and Unity', in *Studies in Earlier Old English Prose*, ed. Paul E. Szarmach (Albany, NY, 1986), pp. 17–45 (p. 17).

one in the earlier prefaces, though the tone is similar. In one respect, this process of gathering wood and timber from the forest for use at home recalls the accumulation and translation of the wisdom of the Church Fathers.[60] But this reading has been questioned by Gatch, who points out that it is unlikely to refer solely to the works that 'Alfred' had translated (i.e. texts by Augustine, Gregory, and Jerome), particularly as 'there is no direct, necessary connection between this list of Western Fathers and the text that follows.'[61] Gatch has argued that the 'unified structure' that was being created out of this Augustinian wood 'is at once an integral structure made of materials gathered from the forest of patrology and a collection of flowers and sayings'.[62]

It would be a mistake not also to consider this passage in terms of the practical concerns of Alfred and other kings in the late ninth century,[63] namely, the practical reorganisation of Anglo-Saxon society, and the fortified places of human community that were being established in the landscape for the defence of the kingdom:

> Forþam ic lære ælcne ðara þe maga si, and manigne wæn hæbbe, þæt he menige to þam ilcan wuda þar ic ðas stuðansceaftas cearf, fetige hym þar ma, and gefeðrige hys wænas mid fegrum gerdum, þat he mage windan manigne smicerne wah, and manig ænlic hus settan and fegerne tun timbrian þara, and þær murge and softe mid mæge on eardian ægðer ge wintras ge sumeras.

> Therefore I advise each of those who is able, and has many wagons, that he think on that same wood where I carved these pillars, and fetch himself there more, and loads his wagons with fair timber, that he may twist together many fair walls, and establish many a noble house and timber a fair town thereof, and there with merriment and comfort prevail both in winters and summers.

The sense here, as in *The Phoenix*, is of a figure gathering those building materials most necessary for the construction of an ideal dwelling-place, but the ways in which this can be interpreted in the preface to the *Soliloquies* are manifold. On one level, the bounty

---

[60] Allen J. Frantzen, *King Alfred* (Boston, 1986), pp. 71–2; also Antonia Harbus, 'Metaphors of Authority in Alfred's Prefaces', *Neophilologus* 91 (2007), 717–27 (p. 725). Rackham notes an important distinction to be made between wood and timber: wood, or underwood, is material gathered by taking cuttings from 'coppice stools, pollards, or small suckers', or from the branches of trees felled for timber. Timber, by contrast, is 'big stuff suitable for making planks, beams and gateposts' – in other words building material for things like houses and ships. See Oliver Rackham, *Trees and Woodland in the British Landscape*, 3rd edn (London, 1996), p. 10.
[61] Gatch, 'King Alfred's Version of Augustine's *Soliloquia*', p. 25.
[62] Ibid.
[63] Ruth Waterhouse, 'Tone in Alfred's Version of Augustine's *Soliloquies*', in *Studies in Earlier Old English Prose*, ed. Paul E. Szarmach (Albany, NY, 1986), pp. 47–85 (p. 49).

of the forest can be seen as the wisdom of the patristic fathers. On another, these timbers can also be understood as the many different types of individual, all with diverse skills, that were necessary to the preservation of England in the late ninth century, thus paralleling the need for appropriate individuals in *The Phoenix* and *De Templo*. Finally, the wood of these trees may also represent, in a quite literal sense, the physical material utilised in the institution of the burghal system under Alfred, and continued by his successors.

Both *The Phoenix* and Alfred's preface suggest that pleasant places for community and good works need not occur naturally, but can also be consciously constructed. The Old English poem *Durham*, which dates from the post-Conquest period, suggests that by this point the distinction between urban and rural locales had become blurred, if not lost, in terms of the reciprocal relationship between the two. A town like Durham is one whose prosperity and holiness are bolstered by the relationship between elements of 'natural' and human construction.[64] Dobbie noted that the *terminus post quem* of *Durham* is established by its reference to the relics of St Cuthbert, which were not moved to Durham until 1104, while a *terminus ante quem* of 1109 is provided by a reference to the poem itself in Symeon's *Historia Dunelmensis Ecclesiae*.[65] Schlauch concluded that *Durham* is the only extant example in the Anglo-Saxon vernacular of the *encomium urbis*, a literary form of rhetoric dating to ancient times that catalogued various aspects of a city.[66] The first eight lines of this poem are of particular relevance:

> Is ðeos burch breome   geond Breotenrice,
> steppa gestaðolad,   stanas ymbutan
> wundrum gewæxen.   Weor ymbeornad,
> ea yðum stronge,   and ðer inne wunað
> feola fisca kyn   on floda gemonge.
> And ðær gewexen is   wudafæstern micel;
> wuniad in ðem wycum   wilda deor monige,
> in deope dalum   deora ungerim.[67]

---

[64] This English *encomium urbis* is paralleled in the Norman tradition by Orderic Vitalis's description of the landscape surrounding Rouen in his *Ecclesiastical History*. For further discussion of this landscape see Leonie V. Hicks, 'Through the City Streets: Movement and Space in Rouen as Seen by the Norman Chroniclers', in *Society and Culture in Medieval Rouen, 911–1300*, ed. Elma Brenner and Leonie V. Hicks, Studies in the Early Middle Ages 39 (Turnhout, 2013), pp. 125–49 (pp. 136–7).

[65] *The Anglo-Saxon Minor Poems*, ed. Elliott van Kirk Dobbie, ASPR 6 (New York, 1942), pp. xliii–xlv.

[66] Margaret Schlauch, 'An Old English *encomium urbis*', *JEGP* 40 (1941), 14–28; also Shippey, *Old English Verse*, p. 176; Calvin B. Kendall, '"Let Us Now Praise a Famous City": Wordplay in the OE *Durham* and the Cult of St. Cuthbert', *JEGP* 87 (1988), 507–21 (p. 507); Dobbie, *Anglo-Saxon Minor Poems*, p. xlv. Dobbie also notes the existence of a long Latin poem by Alcuin, written *c.* 780–2, 'in praise of the city and church of York' (p. xlv).

[67] Dobbie, *Anglo-Saxon Minor Poems*, p. 27.

> This city is famous throughout Britain, established on steep slopes and wondrously constructed with stones all about. There runs past it a strong flowing river, enclosed by weirs; there dwell therein many kinds of fish in that teeming flood; also there has grown up a great woodfastness. In that place dwell many wild beasts in the deep dales, countless creatures.
>
> (*Durham*, lines 1–8)

Steep slopes, water, stone, and woodland are united in the defence of the city. John Baker has noted that the word *fæsten*, used here in conjunction with *wuda*, is a term that seems to have been used in 'an almost metaphorical way' to describe places which, among other things, 'could serve as strongholds of a sort'.[68] *Durham* thus presents the city as a place for both beasts and humans; a place of human construction at peace with the natural world outside its walls, the implication perhaps being that human mastery over the river and woodfastness has enabled human mastery over the population of beasts. Whoever the author of *Durham* may have been, his or her conception of the relationship between the city and its hinterland shows that these bestial spaces are attendant upon the world of humans.

Conclusions

Old English poetry broadly reflects the Augustinian tradition, in so far as there is no place, rural or urban, that is free from the potential for evil, nor any place that cannot be redeemed from this fallen state. In Bede's mid-Saxon context, in a landscape where conversion had only recently been effected through the baptism of the aristocracy, those places where the dragons of pagan ignorance still lurked, and where humans were still likely to live in the manner of beasts, were those which lay far from the centres of human society. Accordingly, Bede reserved special praise for those who sought to promote Christian community in these places. It is fitting that two of the most prominent examples of landscapes whence evil is driven out are situated in fenland wilderness. In *Beowulf*, both Heorot and Grendel's mere are cleansed by heroic deeds, just as Guthlac rids the barrow in the fens of its winged demons. Landscapes where 'men lived in the manner of beasts' are not only to be found in the wastelands. They exist in urban settings, too – like Mermedonia in *Andreas*, which is initially presented as a realm of satanic cannibalism, and does not become a place of

---

[68] John Baker, 'Old English *fæsten*', in *A Commodity of Good Names*, ed. O. J. Padel and David N. Parsons (Donington, 2008), pp. 333–44 (esp. p. 314).

profitable community until its conversion to Christianity, when a church is constructed within its walls. Babylon, comparably, may be a mighty city, but this is no proof of divine favour. As punishment for pride, Babylon's ruler, Nebuchadnezzar, finds himself driven out to share in the company of beasts; when he submits to the power of God, his wits are restored, and he regains his kingdom. Elsewhere, in works like the *Phoenix* of the Exeter Book and the preface to the Old English *Soliloquies*, there is a clear sense that places of Christian community can be actively constructed by those who wish to promote good works.

Each of these examples presents certain difficulties. The dragon's barrow in *Beowulf* is never 'cleansed', Guthlac's assailants are often unthreatening to the point of insubstantiality, the Mermedonians convert only on pain of death, and Babylon is never punished – only its lord, Nebuchadnezzar. These are all ambiguities and concerns with which the poets engage to some degree. This is quite revealing, especially when the instabilities are considered in the context of the three texts explored at the end of this chapter, all of which are concerned with constructing moral centres through human action. It is reasonable to conclude that the approach to landscapes in these examples, in which human agency determines whether a place is viewed in a positive or negative light, is broadly reflective of the Judaeo-Christian philosophical tradition. What is particularly interesting about this, in terms of the division between rational humans and irrational beasts, is that the line of separation can in fact be crossed quite easily.[69] This is part of the reason why the line must be drawn so clearly in the first place. The effects of transgression affect not only the human perpetrators, but also have consequences for the world around them. To act against the divine order of things, and against one's God-given reason, is to become bestial, and to make bestial all of one's surroundings.

---

[69] See discussion in Stephen C. Bandy, 'Cain, Grendel, and the Giants of *Beowulf*', *Papers on Language and Literature* 9 (1973), 235–49 (esp. p. 237).

10

Entomological Etymologies

Creepy-Crawlies in English Place-Names

John Baker

Domestic livestock was a central part of the Anglo-Saxon agricultural economy, both pastoral and arable; wild birds and mammals, too, could be a source of food, provide heroic imagery, and possess mystical associations; exotic and mythical creatures stirred the medieval imagination; and beasts of burden were a mainstay of overland transport. This should be clear from the other chapters in the present volume. It is easy, in such a context, to overlook the less visibly or physically striking parts of the animal kingdom, inhabited by those creatures that are small in stature but vast in number: the tiny beasts and bugs that buzz, creep, crawl and wriggle. Invertebrates often seem too small to concern us; too mundane to arouse interest; too unpleasant even to contemplate. Yet 'creepy-crawlies' are fundamentally important to the natural cycles of life and landscape. Some provide us with important resources, while others help to break down the waste products of farming and domestic activity. Others, though, can menace crops and threaten the wellbeing of livestock. These small creatures are an ever-present aspect of human existence, and although they may not often inspire poetic outpourings or the interest of bureaucrats, they must have occupied a certain space in the early medieval consciousness, as they still do today. Their imprint on all forms of evidence may be slight, but is detectable, and their influence on life is just as important as that of the other beasts discussed in this book.

The study of insect remains has certainly proved profitable in archaeological discussion of animal-husbandry,[1] while written texts

---

[1] Peter J. Osborne, 'An Insect Fauna of Late Bronze Age Date from Wilsford, Wiltshire', *Journal of Animal Ecology* 38.3 (1969), 555–66; Peter J. Osborne, 'Insect Remains', in *Fisherwick: The Reconstruction of an Iron Age Landscape*, ed. C. Smith, BAR British Series 61 (Oxford, 1979), pp. 85–7; Peter J. Osborne, 'Insects', in *Wilsford Shaft: Excavations, 1960–2*, ed. Paul Ashbee, Martin G. Bell and Edwina V. Proudfoot, English Heritage Archaeological Report 11 (London, 1989), pp. 96–8; David N. Smith, 'Insect Remains', in *A Prehistoric and Romano-British Landscape: Excavations at Whitemoor Haye Quarry, Staffordshire, 1997–1999*, ed. Gary Coates, BAR British Series 340 (Oxford, 2002), pp. 67–72.

and artefacts can tell us something about the medieval understanding of insects.[2] This chapter explores the remains invertebrates have left in the toponymic record, and examines the potential of place-names to contribute, in various ways, to our knowledge of the Anglo-Saxons' relationship with these creatures. Invertebrates are referred to in a reasonably large number of English place-names, though Smith's observation that '[i]nsect names (some of which may have been used as nicknames) are frequent in p[lace-]n[ame]s' requires some qualification: many of them are minor rather than major names, and some examples are now lost.[3] Despite the relative frequency of insect place-names, however, Field's discussion of '[c]reatures great and small' in English field-names went no smaller than rabbits,[4] suggesting that invertebrates are seldom the centre of attention even at the microtoponymic level. Smith's parenthetical comment serves as a reminder, moreover, that the corpus is far from straightforward. Nevertheless, the study of invertebrate place-names may provide an important means of studying Anglo-Saxon and medieval perceptions of, and attitudes towards, this class of creatures, and in turn allow insights into other aspects of medieval society and economy, including agricultural and pastoral arrangements and preoccupations. The following discussion addresses some of the challenges attached to the study of invertebrates in place-names, and assesses their value in three important areas: first, as a contribution to our knowledge of the semantics of Old English invertebrate names; second, as a reflection of the importance of invertebrates to everyday life in Anglo-Saxon England; and third, as a source of information on Anglo-Saxon perceptions and exploitation of the landscape.

In order to assemble the material for such an analysis a number of problems must be confronted. It is impossible here to provide complete coverage of all toponymic occurrences of invertebrate terminology, many of which (as noted above) are found in field-names. These microtoponymic instances tend to be first recorded only in modern documents, and this can make unequivocal identification of their constituent elements very difficult without detailed case by case evaluation. Indeed, to make the material manageable, the present analysis is based predominantly, though not exclusively, on place-names with attested medieval forms, and certainly makes no claim to be fully comprehensive in scope. Even so, interpretation of

---

[2] E.g. Mildred Budny and Dominic Tweddle, 'The Maaseik Embroideries', *ASE* 13 (1984), 65–96 (p. 86); Marilina Cesario, 'Ant-Lore in Anglo-Saxon England', *ASE* 40 (2011), 273–91.
[3] Albert H. Smith, *The Place-Names of Gloucestershire*, part 2, EPNS 39 (Cambridge, 1964), p. 207.
[4] John Field, 'Creatures Great and Small: Excursions among English Field-Names', *Nomina* 13 (1990), 91–108.

place-names with medieval spellings can still be difficult. For example, the Old English element *pēo*, which is of uncertain etymology but probably denotes an insect, perhaps 'a fly, a gnat',[5] can result in similar late medieval spellings to the Old French and Middle English element *pie* ('magpie'). In the case of Pyon in Herefordshire (recorded as *Pionie*, *Peune* in 1086, and as *Pyone* in 1292), attestations are early enough almost certainly to rule out ME *pie*, which cannot have arisen before the late eleventh century. This name seems likely therefore to consist of OE *pēo* with *ēg* ('island').[6] On the other hand, Pymore in Cambridgeshire (recorded as *Pymoor* in 1497) is not on record before the last decade of the fifteenth century, so might easily contain either OE *pēo* or ME *pie* (in this case with OE *mōr*, 'moor, marsh').[7]

With attestations as late as this, a further problem arises. Many of the Old English elements discussed here have Middle English and Present Day English (PDE) descendants. Therefore, in cases where eleventh-century or earlier spellings are lacking, it can be impossible to say with certainty that the place-names were coined in the Old English period rather than the Middle English, and that they consequently reflect Anglo-Saxon rather than later medieval perceptions. For example, the lost field-names *Bitelfelde* (1462) in West Yorkshire and *Bittlewell* (1684; *Bittewell* 1610) in Rutland[8] may have been coined in either period,[9] and may therefore tell us something about perceptions of invertebrates in either early or late medieval England. These questions are very difficult to answer, and for that reason the chronological significance of this chapter is hard to pinpoint. Much of what is discussed certainly or probably relates to the Anglo-Saxon period, but some of the material will reflect later medieval perceptions, and so this chapter is intentionally broad in its temporal sweep.

Of course, sometimes the *terminus post quem* for the emergence of an English place-name element can be accurately ascertained, and the difficulty in establishing the period of coining reduced. The lost West Yorkshire field-name *Papilyonholm*, *Papilionholm* (1310, 1323), *Pampellion Holm* (1316), *Pamplyonholme* (1323) might contain a Middle

---

[5] Eilert Ekwall, *Studies on English Place-Names* (Stockholm, 1936), pp. 102–4; Albert H. Smith, *The Place-Names of the East Riding of Yorkshire and York*, EPNS 14 (Cambridge, 1937), p. l.
[6] Ekwall, *Studies on English Place-Names*, p. 103; Albert H. Smith, *English Place-Name Elements*, part 2: *JAFN–YTRI*, EPNS 26 (Cambridge, 1956), p. 62; *contra* Arthur T. Bannister, *The Place-Names of Herefordshire: Their Origin and Development* (Cambridge, 1916).
[7] Percy H. Reaney, *The Place-Names of Cambridgeshire and the Isle of Ely*, EPNS 19 (Cambridge, 1943), p. 224.
[8] David N. Parsons and Tania Styles, with Carole Hough, *The Vocabulary of English Place-Names (Á–BOX)* (Nottingham, 1997), p. 107; Albert H. Smith, *The Place-Names of the West Riding of Yorkshire*, part 2, EPNS 31 (Cambridge, 1961), p. 245; Barrie Cox, *The Place-Names of Rutland*, EPNS 67–9 (Nottingham, 1994), p. 100.
[9] In the second case the name could even have arisen in the early modern period.

English element derived from OFr *papilion* ('butterfly');[10] but such an element is only likely to have entered English from the second half of the eleventh century, when Anglo-Norman vocabulary became part of England's linguistic makeup. It is relevant to Anglo-Saxon perceptions of invertebrates in the landscape only insofar as late medieval interpretations of the environment can be projected backwards. It is possible to extrapolate from it, but not to push the coining of the name itself further into the past. In any case, no claim is made here to be uncovering an exclusively Anglo-Saxon interaction with invertebrate life; the analysis and conclusions are applicable more broadly to the medieval period.

Medieval Perceptions of Invertebrates

All of these complications notwithstanding, possible reference to invertebrates can be identified in a substantial corpus of probably early place-names, a body of data which might be able to contribute to our understanding of creepy-crawlies in the medieval consciousness. In this regard, unfortunately, perceptual and semantic obstacles arise. Anglo-Saxon perceptions of invertebrates could be very different from our own, and the line between observable and mythical characteristics might have been blurred, or even nonexistent.[11] Modern scientific taxonomy, moreover, inevitably influences and constrains today's vernacular usage, so that PDE invertebrate vocabulary is often defined by entomological classification – almost, indeed, glossing zoological terminology. So to the modern observer, 'beetle' normally denotes a class of insects, albeit a wide one, of the *Coleoptera* order, defined by the specialised development of its upper wings; and sometimes, more specifically those that are black and relatively large.[12] The Latin *coleoptera* is from a Greek word meaning, appropriately, 'sheath-winged'.[13] We cannot be sure that Anglo-Saxon classifications followed similar lines. PDE *beetle* is derived from OE *bitela*, which must originally have meant 'thing which bites' or the like (cf. the OE verb *bitan*, 'to bite'),[14] and is equated with Latin *mordiculus* 'little biter' in glosses. To an Old English speaker, then, the defining characteristic of a *bitela* might have been its propensity for biting (although the precise etymology may have been obscure from an early

---

[10] Smith, *Place-Names of the West Riding of Yorkshire*, part 2, p. 173.
[11] See, for instance, Cesario, 'Ant-Lore', esp. fig. 7, for an Anglo-Saxon view on ants.
[12] *OED*, s.v. 'beetle', n. 2
[13] *OED*, s.v. 'Coleoptera', n.
[14] *OED*, s.v. 'beetle', n. 2; *DOE*, s.v. 'bitela', 'bītan'.

date).[15] That group might have included insects that today would be called beetles, but the word also glosses Latin *blatta*, which can mean 'cockroach'. Cockroaches (*Dictyoptera* order) would not, today, be classified with beetles.[16] OE *ceafor*, which survives as PDE *chafer*, is a very similar case in point. This word, too, is regularly rendered as 'beetle' when identified in place-names, but its Proto-Germanic root is **kafroz*, from the stem **kaf-* ('to gnaw'), and it can also gloss Latin *bruchus* ('locust' or 'caterpillar').[17] Perhaps the characteristic that defined a *ceafor* in the eyes of an Anglo-Saxon was the tendency to nibble or gnaw at things, especially vegetation. OE *wicga*,[18] another of the terms that seems to cover the modern meaning 'beetle', probably denotes literally 'something which wiggles',[19] and could presumably refer to a wide range of wriggling creepy-crawlies, some of which are not even insects, let alone beetles. That kind of categorisation would not map very neatly onto modern entomological typologies.

Another problem concerns the transferred application of invertebrate terminology. Words that probably, or even clearly, denote invertebrates in certain contexts might sometimes be used with other meanings: metaphorically, in reference to topographical features that supposedly resemble the creature in question; metonymically, where the defining characteristic of the invertebrate might as aptly define another feature; or in the coining of personal names. An instance of the first of these is OE *lūs*, the ancestor of PDE *louse*, an element found particularly in compounds with words denoting mounds or hills, including OE *berg* and *dūn*, and ON *haugr*. Forsberg believed it unlikely that such features would regularly be thought of as lousy, and thought the first element might have been chosen in order to connote louse-like characteristics,[20] such as extreme smallness – the mounds in question were so tiny, or were shaped in such a way, that they were metaphorically lice. Compounds of this kind are recurrent in English place-names and charter boundary clauses, and have close parallels in other Germanic languages. Gelling wondered whether

---

[15] Parsons *et al.*, *Vocabulary of English Place-Names (Á–BOX)*, p. 107, gloss the word 'insect, grub, beetle'.
[16] Eugene F. Linssen, *Insects of the British Isles*, 3rd edn (Harmondsworth, 1987), pp. 70, 152.
[17] *DOE*, s.v. 'ceafer'; *OED*, s.v. 'chafer'.
[18] Sometimes given as **wigga*; cf. *docga/dogga* ('dog'), *frocga/frogga* ('frog'), where the velar geminate [gg] is represented orthographically as <cg> or <gg>, apparently indifferently (Alistair Campbell, *Old English Grammar* (Oxford, 1959), p. 27 (§64 and n. 2); Richard M. Hogg, *A Grammar of Old English*, vol. 1: *Phonology*, pbk edn (Chichester, 2011), pp. 34 (2.61), 42–3 (2.78(3)).
[19] Margaret Gelling with H. D. G. Foxall, *The Place-Names of Shropshire*, part 1, EPNS 62–3 (Nottingham, 1990), pp. 314–15.
[20] R. Forsberg, *A Contribution to a Dictionary of Old English Place-Names* (Uppsala, 1950), pp. 182–8; followed by Albert H. Smith, *The Place-Names of Gloucestershire*, part 1, EPNS 38 (Cambridge, 1964), p. 209; Albert H. Smith, *The Place-Names of Gloucestershire*, part 4, EPNS 41 (Cambridge, 1965), p. 152.

OE *lūs* might, consequently, have come to serve as a hill-name on its own, although simplex instances have not been identified.[21] Forsberg's reasoning seems sound, since lice are parasitic and unlikely, therefore, to frequent a mound; however, the argument might be challenged nonetheless, given that the medieval understanding of the invertebrate kingdom does not map perfectly onto our own. It is very difficult to be sure that a creature denoted by *lūs* would have been incompatible with the habitat in which the barrow was situated, and it is therefore impossible to be certain that the compound *lūs-berg* did not mean 'barrow swarming with *lūs*-type creatures'. A similar question surrounds the recurrent compound *ǣmette-hyll*, and whether it actually denotes 'an ant-hill' (either literally, or, in a topographical application, 'hill shaped like an ant nest'), or 'a hill that swarms with ants'.[22]

The problem of metonymy can be illustrated by *wicga* ('something which wiggles'). As well as being a description appropriate to more than one type of invertebrate, an argument has been made for its application in a compound noun descriptive of a certain type of terrain. The element occurs several times with the same generic OE *mōr* ('marsh, moor').[23] Gelling noted that Wigmore Castle 'overlooks an unstable marsh in which wet mounds erupt and disappear', and that the Shropshire examples were in marshy environments. She suggested that OE **wicga-mōr* might be a term for such a 'wiggling' marsh.[24] Certainly the recurrence of the compound suggests a specialised meaning, but two instances of Pymore, one in Cambridgeshire the other in Dorset, if taken to be compounds of OE *pēo* ('a fly, a gnat') and *mōr*, suggest that marshland could be thought of as infested or swarming with insects of one kind or another.[25]

---

[21] Margaret Gelling with H. D. G. Foxall, *The Place-Names of Shropshire*, part 6, EPNS 89 (Nottingham, 2012), pp. 65–7.

[22] Allen Mawer and Frank M. Stenton, *The Place-Names of Bedfordshire and Huntingdonshire*, EPNS 3 (Cambridge, 1926), pp. 67–8; Reaney, *Place-Names of Cambridgeshire and the Isle of Ely*, p. 78; Albert H. Smith, *The Place-Names of the West Riding of Yorkshire*, part 6, EPNS 35 (Cambridge, 1961), p. 88; Albert H. Smith, *English Place-Name Elements*, part 1: Á–IW, EPNS 25 (Cambridge, 1956), p. 3; Parsons et al., *Vocabulary of English Place-Names (Á–BOX)*, p. 29.

[23] Margaret Gelling, *The Place-Names of Berkshire*, 3 vols., EPNS 49–51 (Cambridge, 1973–6), p. 916; Gelling with Foxall, *Place-Names of Shropshire*, part 1, pp. 314–15; John McNeal Dodgson, *The Place-Names of Cheshire*, part 4, EPNS 47 (Cambridge, 1972), p. 55; A. D. Mills, *The Place-Names of Dorset*, part 3, EPNS 59–60 (Cambridge, 1989), p. 127.

[24] Smith notes its use in two instances of the place-name Wig Stones (1840; 1858), where it may denote 'moving stones, logan stones'. See Albert H. Smith, *The Place-Names of the West Riding of Yorkshire*, part 5, EPNS 34 (Cambridge, 1961), p. 217; Smith, *Place-Names of the West Riding of Yorkshire*, part 6, p. 80.

[25] Anton Fägersten, *The Place-Names of Dorset* (Uppsala, 1933; republished Wakefield, 1978), p. 255; Reaney, *Place-Names of Cambridgeshire and the Isle of Ely*, pp. 78, 244; Ekwall, *Studies on English Place-Names*, p. 103.

Entomological Etymologies

A personal name Wicga has also been suggested as the first element of several place-names (e.g. Wigfield, West Yorkshire; Wiggie, Surrey; Wigborough, Essex),[26] and this name is recorded as that of a householder in eleventh-century Colchester.[27] Some analyses of place-names containing OE *wibba* take this element also to be a personal name. In early discussion, the second of these was based on the mistaken belief that an Old English personal name *Wibba was on record, when in fact that was due to a misreading of the initial P of Pibba as a Þ (wynn). Even so, the possibility of *Wibba as a short form of dithematic names such as Wigbald or Widbald has been proposed.[28]

The complexities involved in identifying genuine references to invertebrates are perhaps best exemplified by OE *wifel*, the origin of PDE *weevil*. Fellows-Jensen notes that *wifel* glosses a range of Latin terms, such as *papila*, *panpila*, *cantarus*, *gurgulio* and *scarebius*, 'and would seem to have denoted insects of many kinds in much the same way as does the modern word "beetle"'.[29] Nevertheless, the idea that an invertebrate could be the most characteristic aspect of a landscape feature or settlement may well have seemed absurd early in the twentieth century, and a putative personal name *Wifel appears regularly in early place-name discussion.[30] Kitson, however, demonstrated that the generics with which the element is compounded, and the frequency of its occurrence in the names of features in charter boundary clauses (while remaining absent from the Anglo-Saxon onomasticon), more or less precluded this explanation.[31] He suggested rather that it denoted the insect; a conclusion Fellows-Jensen also prefers in most cases.[32] Derivation from a personal name

---

[26] Albert. H. Smith, *The Place-Names of the West Riding of Yorkshire*, part 1, EPNS 30 (Cambridge, 1961), p. 293; John E. B. Gover, Allen Mawer, Frank M. Stenton and Arthur Bonner, *The Place-Names of Surrey*, EPNS 11 (Cambridge, 1934), p. 306; Percy H. Reaney, *The Place-Names of Essex*, EPNS 12 (Cambridge, 1935), p. 323.

[27] *Domesday Book: Essex*, ed. Alexander Rumble (Chichester, 1983), B3 105a.

[28] E.g. Bannister, *Place-Names of Herefordshire*, pp. 201–2; Mats Redin, *Studies on Uncompounded Personal Names in Old English* (Uppsala, 1919), pp. 107–8; Mawer and Stenton, *Place-Names of Bedfordshire and Huntingdonshire*, p. 142; Albert. H. Smith, *The Place-Names of Gloucestershire*, part 3, EPNS 40 (Cambridge, 1964), p. 267; Smith, *Place-Names of Gloucestershire*, part 4, p. 208.

[29] Gillian Fellows-Jensen, 'The Weevil's Claw', in *Namenwelten: Orts- und Personennamen in historischer Sicht*, ed. Astrid van Nahl (Berlin, 2004), pp. 76–89 (p. 78).

[30] E.g. Allen Mawer and Frank M. Stenton, *The Place-Names of Buckinghamshire*, EPNS 2 (Cambridge, 1925), p. 260; Allen Mawer and Frank M. Stenton, in collaboration with Frederick T. S. Houghton, *The Place-Names of Worcestershire*, EPNS 4 (Cambridge, 1927), p. 247; Allen Mawer, Frank M. Stenton and John E. B. Gover, *The Place-Names of Sussex*, 2 vols., EPNS 6–7 (Cambridge, 1929–30), pp. 298, 305; John E. B. Gover, Allen Mawer and Frank M. Stenton, *The Place-Names of Wiltshire*, EPNS 16 (Cambridge, 1939), p. 326.

[31] Peter Kitson, 'Quantifying Qualifiers in Anglo-Saxon Charter Boundaries', *Folia Linguistica Historica* 14.1–2 (1993), 29–82 (pp. 75–7).

[32] Fellows-Jensen, 'The Weevil's Claw'.

persists nonetheless,[33] especially where the generic is a habitative element or the place-name is an *ingas* formation;[34] in the Danelaw the Scandinavian personal name *Vífill* may lie behind some place-names that otherwise look as though they belong here.[35] Other possibilities have also been advanced. Wallenberg, in discussing Wilsley in Kent, posited a river-name **Wifel(e)* or similar, denoting a winding stream, and noted an apparent coincidence of *wifel* place-names with streams of that kind;[36] Insley proposes the existence of an OE **wīfel*, cognate with Old Swedish **vívil(l)* ('pagan priest'), which may lie behind the place-name Vivilsta in Uppland, Sweden.[37] Fellows-Jensen notes a meaning 'dart' that could have been used in a transferred sense to describe a pointed piece of land;[38] and Hough draws attention to the OE word *wifel*, a variant of *wifer* ('spear'), and discusses Wilsill in West Yorkshire (*Wifeles healh c.* 1030) as possibly analogous with the recurrent place-name compound OE **lutegāres-halh* ('hollow with a trapping spear').[39] Whatever view is taken, interpretation of this group of place-names is certainly challenging.

It is clear that identification of genuine references to invertebrates in English place-names is far from straightforward, but two observations can be made. Firstly, in view of the difficulty in getting to the heart of Anglo-Saxon perceptions of invertebrates, and the rather unusual portrayal of certain insects in some Anglo-Saxon texts,[40] it seems hard to rule out the possibility that words denoting invertebrates were also used as given names. Secondly, given the likely disjuncture between some modern and Anglo-Saxon definitions, place-names ought to offer a means of refining the meanings and dialectal context of Old English invertebrate terms. At the very least, distributional maps of the different terms for, say, 'beetle' might reveal regional variation in their occurrence.

---

[33] E.g. Kenneth Cameron, *A Dictionary of Lincolnshire Place-Names* (Nottingham, 1998), pp. 139–40; Mills, *Place-Names of Dorset*, part 3, pp. 23–4, 288; M. Gelling with H. D. G. Foxall, *The Place-Names of Shropshire*, part 5, EPNS 82 (Nottingham, 2006), pp. 104–5.

[34] Fellows-Jensen, 'The Weevil's Claw', pp. 80–1, 83.

[35] Ibid., pp. 84–5.

[36] Johannes K. Wallenberg, *The Place-Names of Kent* (Uppsala, 1934), pp. 96–7.

[37] John Insley, 'Gumeningas', in *Reallexikon der germanischen Altertumskunde*, 2nd edn, vol. 13, ed. H. Beck *et al.* (Berlin, 1999), pp. 191–3; Kenneth Cameron and John Insley, *The Place-Names of Lincolnshire*, part 7: *Lawress Wapentake*, EPNS 85 (Nottingham, 2010), p. 141; see also Gunter Müller, *Studien zu den Theriophoren Personennamen der Germanen* (Cologne, 1970), pp. 90–1.

[38] Gillian Fellows-Jensen, *Scandinavian Settlement Names in the East Midlands* (Copenhagen, 1978), p. 383; Fellows-Jensen, 'The Weevil's Claw', p. 80.

[39] Carole Hough, 'Wilsill in Yorkshire and Related Place-Names', *Notes & Queries* 248.3 (2003), 253–7.

[40] In the *Liber monstrorum*, for example, ants have six feet and run very fast, while in the Old English *Wonders of the East* they are as big as dogs; in both they are associated with gold, see Cesario, 'Ant-Lore'. See also Chardonnens, this volume, pp. 142–5.

This is unlikely, however, to be a straightforward exercise. For example, Old English had a wide range of terms to denote 'a beetle', including *bitela, budda, ceafor, wibba, wifel, wicga*. Of all of these, *wifel* and *wicga* are the most common in place-names, each occurring more than forty times in place-names attested in medieval documents and in Anglo-Saxon charter boundary clauses. Allowing for the possibility that some of these place-names might contain personal names, and that those with habitative generics or *ingas* constructions are the more likely candidates for this, an analysis that excludes those might help us to understand something about the application of these beetle words (Tables 10.1 and 10.2). Both *wifel* and *wicga* seem to be compounded frequently with water-related generics,[41] and with generics denoting woodland, clearings or trees.[42] It might also be noted that both have a similar distribution nationally. On the face of it, *wifel* seems to occur predominantly in the south-west Midlands and the South – thirty-four times in all – while some of the few occurrences further north might be explained as the Old Norse personal name *Vífill*. Twelve of those thirty-four examples survive only in Anglo-Saxon charter boundary clauses, while no such instances occur further north and east. Instances of OE *wicga* are similarly numerous in the south-west Midlands and the South, though of these only one example has a pre-Conquest boundary clause as its sole witness. The only major difference is in the number of occurrences in the northernmost counties of the Midlands, and north of the Humber. More than a quarter of the sample of OE *wicga* place-names occur there, compared with just under one eighth of the *wifel* names. The samples are too small to draw firm conclusions from this, but if anything it might suggest that some names in northern England currently taken to contain the Old Norse personal name *Vífill* (and therefore absent from Table 10.1) would be better interpreted as containing OE *wifel*, their later spellings perhaps influenced by association with the personal name. In this example we may have evidence of two terms for invertebrates, with a relatively general application, and a similar national distribution.

The generics with which invertebrate terms are compounded might enhance understanding of the habitats frequented by those creatures. Ekwall noted that names of insects 'are frequently combined with words for "valley", "wood" or the like'.[43] It is not entirely clear what he meant by this statement, since he illustrated his point with

---

[41] *Wifel* with OE *ēg, ford* (×3), *lacu, mere* (×2), *pōl, welle* (×3); *wicga* with *brōc, mere, pōl* (×2), *rið, sik, twisla, welle* (×2) (and of course several times with OE *mōr* ('moor, marsh'), discussed above). Note also several occurrences with OE *hamm*, which can denote land hemmed in by a river.

[42] *Wifel* with OE *hangra, hyrst, lēah* (×3), **rodu, þorn; wigga* with OE *(ge)fall, fyrhþe, lēah* (×4), *pyrige, stubb, wald*.

[43] Ekwall, *Studies on English Place-Names*, p. 101.

Table 10.1 OE *wifel* place-names attested in the medieval period, excluding those with habitative generics

Place-name*	County	Early spellings and dates (or date of lost name)	Other elements
Great Wilsey	Oxfordshire	*Wiveleseia*, 1199; *Wylsey mede alias Wynelsey*, 1541	ēg
Uuibeles uuelle	Gloucestershire	780 (11th C)	welle
Wavering Lane	Dorset	?*Wynelynglane(forlang)* (probably from *Wyuel-*), 1313	ing, lanu
wifæles mere	Hampshire	973×4 (12th C); 979 (12th C)	mere
Wifelescumb	Somerset	*juxta terminos wifelescumb*, *Wifelescumbes gemere*, 854 (12th C)	cumb
wifeles cumbes heafod	Somerset	941 (12th C); 972 (12th C)	cumb
Wifelesham	Wiltshire	961 (12th C)	hamm
wifeles lace	Oxfordshire	*Wifeles lace*, 904 (11th C); *Wifeleslace*, 1004 (1307–27), 929 (11th C)	lacu
wifeles stigele	Hampshire	900 (11th C); 960 (12th C)	stigel
Wifelinge	Kent	*Wifelinge*, 949	ing
Wiflingfalod	Wiltshire	931 (early 10th C)	ing, fald
Wiflahirst	Kent	*Wiflahirst*, 804 (13th C)	hyrst
Wilden	Worcestershire	*Wineladuna*, 1182 (17th C); *Winelduna*, 1182 (18th C); *Wybeldone*, 1275; *Wiveldon*, 1299	dūn

Entomological Etymologies

Place-name*	County	Early spellings and dates (or date of lost name)	Other elements
Wilkesley	Cheshire	Wiuelesde, 1086 Winclestle, c. 1130 (1479) Wivelescle, 1230	clēa
Willesborough	Kent	Wifeles berge, 863 Wifeles beorge, 993 for 996 (14th C) Wyuellesberg', 1243	berg
Willesey/Wilsey	Cambridgeshire/ Essex	Wilnesle, 1275 Wylsey Hall, 1553; cf. Humphrey de Wyuelesley, 14th C	(ge)hæg
Willesley	Derbyshire [Leicestershire since 1897]	Wivoleslei(e), 1086	lēah
Willesley	Wiltshire	Wyvelesleye, c. 1207	lēah
Willspoole	Leicestershire	Wylspole, 1467×84 Willspoole, 1625	pōl
Wilmire	Durham	Wiflesmer, c. 1280 Wyuesmere, 1316 Whyuelesmer, 1325	mere
Wilsbury	Gloucestershire	Wyuelesburi, 1282	burh
Wilsford	Lincolnshire	Wivolesforde, 1086	ford
Wilsford	Wiltshire	Wifeles ford, 892 (13th C), 933 (14th C) Wivlesford, 1086 Wiuelesford, 1185	ford
Wilsford	Wiltshire	Wiflesford(e), 1086	ford

239

Place-name*	County	Early spellings and dates (or date of lost name)	Other elements
Wilsill	West Yorkshire	Wifeles healh, c. 1030 Wifles-, Wiueshale, 1086 Wiueleshale 1154–91	halh
Wilsley	Kent	de Wiueleslegh', 1226	lēah
Wilstone	Hertfordshire	Wivelestorn(e), 1220	þorn
Wimsell Lane	Dorset	on hean wifeles hylle, 933 (12th C), cf. William de Wyuelleshill', 1244	hyll
Winswell or Willeswell	Devon	Wiveswilla, 1086	welle
Wivelesdale	Cambridgeshire	Wivelesdale, 1360	dæl
Wiveleshangre	Wiltshire	1272–1307	hangra
Wivelisconbe	Somerset	Wyuelesconet hund', 1084 Wivelescumbe, 1178	cumb
Wivelridge	Sussex	Wyueregg', 1248 Wyuelerugg', 1332 Wyueleregge, 1344	hrycg
Wivelrod	Hampshire	Wivelrod, 1236	*rodu
Wivelsfield	Sussex	Wifelesfeld, c. 765 (c. 1300) Wiuelesfeud, Wyvelesfeld, 1235	feld
Woolridge	Gloucestershire	Wiv-, Wiu-, Wyoelrugge, 12th, 13th C Wolleruge, 1270	hrycg
Wyfeleshille	Oxfordshire	Wyfeleshille, 1004 (1307–27)	hyll
Wynelsland	Kent	Wynelsland, 1327 Wyvelisland, 1360 Wevelysland, 1433	land

Entomological Etymologies

Place-name*	County	Early spellings and dates (or date of lost name)	Other elements
Wyueledenesheuede	Gloucestershire	*Wyueledenesheuede*, 1236	denu, heafod
Wyuelesgate	Buckinghamshire	*Wyuelesgate*, 14th C	geat
Wyueleshell'	Rutland	*Willeshulles*, 1346 *Wyueleshell'*, *Wyueleshelleyes*, 1363	hyll
Wyueles ho	Oxfordshire	(*into*) *Wyueles ho*, 1005–12 (c. 1325–50)	hōh
Wyvelesden	Hampshire	*Wyvelesden*, 1403	denu
Wyvelesdene	Hampshire	*Wyvelesdene*, 1379	denu
Wyvils	Berkshire	*Wifeles wyll(e)*, 1007 (c. 1240) (*Hither*) *Wyvils*, 1840	welle

* Lost place-names are given in italics.

Sources: Olof S. Anderson, *The English Hundred-Names: The South-Western Counties*, vol. 2, Lunds Universitets Årsskrift 35.5 (Lund, 1939). p. 63; Cameron, *Place-Names of Derbyshire*, p. 712; CDEPN, p. 682; Cox, *Place-Names of Rutland*, 37, p. 434; Barrie Cox, *The Place-Names of Leicestershire*, part 4, EPNS 84 (Nottingham, 2009), p. 72; Paul Cullen, 'The Place-Names of the Lathes of St Augustine and Shipway, Kent' (unpublished PhD thesis, University of Sussex, 1997), pp. 132, 341; Jonh McNeal Dodgson, *The Place-Names of Cheshire*, part 3, EPNS 46 (Cambridge, 1971), p. 93; Fellows-Jensen, 'The Weevil's Claw'; Margaret Gelling, *The Place-Names of Oxfordshire*, 2 vols., EPNS 23–4 (Cambridge, 1953–4), pp. 167, 181–2; Gelling, *Place-Names of Berkshire*, pp. 638–9; John E. B. Gover, 'Hampshire Place-Names', unpublished manuscript held at the Institute for Name-Studies, University of Nottingham (n.d.), pp. 130, 233, 256; John E. B. Gover, Allen Mawer and Frank M. Stenton, *The Place-Names of Devon*, 2 vols, EPNS 8–9 (Cambridge, 1931–2), p. 686; John E. B. Gover, Allen Mawer and Frank M. Stenton, *The Place-Names of Hertfordshire*, EPNS 15 (Cambridge, 1938), pp. xli, 53, 248; Gover, Mawer and Stenton, *Place-Names of Wiltshire*, pp. 110, 326, 372; Kitson, 'Quantifying Qualifiers', p. 75; Allen Mawer, *The Place-Names of Northumberland and Durham* (Cambridge, 1920), p. 217; Mawer and Stenton, *Place-Names of Buckinghamshire*, p. 260; Mawer and Stenton, with Houghton, *Place-Names of Worcestershire*, p. 247; Mawer, Stenton and Gover, *Place-Names of Sussex*, pp. 305, 532–3; Mills, *Place-Names of Dorset*, part 3, pp. 23–4, 288; L. W. H. Payling, 'The Place-Names of Kesteven (South-West Lincolnshire) (unpublished PhD thesis, University of Leeds, 1936), pp. 514–15; Reaney, *Place-Names of Cambridgeshire and the Isle of Ely*, pp. 102–3, 309, 318; Reaney, *Place-Names of Essex*, p. 572; Smith, *Place-Names of the West Riding of Yorkshire*, part 5, p. 150; Smith, *Place-Names of Gloucestershire*, part 1, p. 182; part 3, pp. 156, 244; Johannes K. Wallenberg, *Kentish Place-Names* (Uppsala, 1931), pp. 96–7, 283; Wallenberg, *Place-Names of Kent*, p. 324; Victor Watts, *The Place-Names of County Durham*, part 1: *Stockton Ward*, ed. Paul Cavill, EPNS 83 (Nottingham, 2007), p. 32.

Table 10.2 OE *wicga* place-names attested in the medieval period, excluding those with habitative generics

Place-name*	County	Early spellings and dates (or date of lost name)	Other elements
le wyʒesike	Rutland	1399–1413	sīk
Rigery Farm	Hertfordshire	Wygefriʒe, 1278; Wyggefrith, 1304	fyrhðe
Viggory Mead	Surrey	Wygerythebregge, 1412; Wygeryythbrigge, 1430; Wygrethe, 1474	rið
Wellpool's Farm	Surrey	Wighepole, 1216–72; Wigepol, 1241	pōl
Wicgan dic	Oxfordshire	1002 (13th C)	dīc
Widbrook	Wiltshire	Wyggebrok, 1279	brōc
Widgerley	Wiltshire	Wiggele, 1257	lēah
Wigborough	Essex	Wicgheberga, 1086; Wigheberga(m), -ā, 1086; Wyg(h)eberg(h)e, 1206	berg
Wigdon	Devon	Wyggedon, 1458	dūn
Wigeflat	Derbyshire	c. 1240	flat
Wigfield	West Yorkshire	Wigefall, 13th C	(ge)fall
Wiggadon	Devon	Wigedon, 1249	dūn
Wiggedal'	Derbyshire	1272–1307	dæl or dāl
Wiggelonde (now Wighill?)	Surrey	Wiggelonde, c. 1240	land
Wigger Dale	Derbyshire	Wi-, Wyggewalledale, 1226	wælle, dæl

Entomological Etymologies

Place-name*	County	Early spellings and dates (or date of lost name)	Other elements
Wiggie	Surrey	Wygehaye, 1332	(ge)hæg
Wiggold	Gloucestershire	Wigge, Wyggewald, 1109	wald
Wiggonlee Farm	Derbyshire	Wyggeleg', 1255	lēah
Wigham	Devon	Wygeham, 1330	hamm
Wightwizzle	West Yorkshire	Wygestwysell, c. 1280	twisla
Wigland	Cheshire	Wiggelaunde, 1208–29	land
Wigley	Derbyshire	Wi-, Wyggeley(e), -leg', -lay, -le, 1254	lēah
Wigmoor	Devon	Wyggemere, 1292; Wygemore, 1333	mere
Wignall	Lancashire	de Wygnale, 1323	halh
Wignall Street (Foxash Farm)	Essex	Wyggenhale, 1255	halh
Wignam Meadow	Oxfordshire	Wigenham, 1278–9	hamm
Wigperry	Sussex	Wyggepyrye, c. 1296; Wygepirie, 1298	pyrige
Wig Pool	Gloucestershire	Wi-, Wyggepol, 1282; Wigpoole, 1692	pōl
Wigside	Durham	Wygesyde, 1382	sīde
Wigwell Grange	Derbyshire	Wi-, Wyggewall(e), early 13th C, 1229	wælle
Witpit Copse	Gloucestershire	Wygeput, 1327; Week Pitt, 1771	pytt

Place-name*	County	Early spellings and dates (or date of lost name)	Other elements
Wyegate Hill	Gloucestershire	*Uuiggangeat*, 972 (10th C) *Wigheiete*, 1086 *Wyget*, 1337	geat
Wyggedal(hull)	West Yorkshire	14th C	dāl, hyll
Wyggeleuam	Oxfordshire	c. 1250	hlāw
Wyggeleye	Worcestershire	1182	lēah
Wyggenhill	Berkshire	*Wyggenhill*, mid-13th C	hyll
Wyggepet (now Rockell's Farm)	Essex	*Wicgepet, Wigghepet*, 1086 *Wuggefosse*, 1228 *Wyg(g)eputt'*, 1231	pytt, fosse
Wyggestubbe	Oxfordshire	c. 1210-20	stubb
Wygginham	Berkshire	*Wygginham*, mid-13th C *Wiginghame, Wiggenhame, Wigginghamfelde, Wiggynhame*, 1548	hamm
Wyghtfeld	Herefordshire	1341	feld

* Lost place-names are given in italics.

Sources: Bannister, *Place-Names of Herefordshire*, p. 207; Cameron, *Place-Names of Derbyshire*, pp. 34, 207, 222, 415, 428, 515, 762; Cox, *Place-Names of Rutland*, p. 298; Dodgson, *Place-Names of Cheshire*, part 4, p. 50; Eilert Ekwall, *The Place-Names of Lancashire* (Manchester, 1922), p. 138; Gelling, *Place-Names of Oxfordshire*, pp. 131, 191, 255, 357, 480; Gelling, *Place-Names of Berkshire*, p. 23; Gover, Mawer and Stenton, *Place-Names of Devon*, pp. 39, 116, 131, 410, 686; Gover, Mawer, Stenton and Bonner, *Place-Names of Surrey*, pp. 67, 130, 289, 306; Gover, Mawer and Stenton, *Place-Names of Hertfordshire*, pp. 198, 248; Gover, Mawer and Stenton, *Place-Names of Wiltshire*, pp. 118, 343; Mawer, *Place-Names of Northumberland and Durham*, p. 216; Mawer and Stenton, with Houghton, *Place-Names of Worcestershire*, p. 399; Mawer, Stenton and Gover, *Place-Names of Sussex*, p. 269; Reaney, *Place-Names of Essex*, pp. 323, 342, 526-7; Albert. H. Smith, *English Place-Name Elements*, part 2: *JAFN-YTRI*, EPNS 26 (Cambridge, 1956), p. 122; Smith, *Place-Names of the West Riding of Yorkshire*, part 1, pp. 153, 229, 293; Smith, *Place-Names of Gloucestershire*, part 1, pp. 49, 81; part 3, pp. 220, 244.

examples including Dronfield in Derbyshire (OE *drāna-feld*, 'open land of the drones'),⁴⁴ and Midgehall in Wiltshire (OE *mycg-halh*, 'midge nook'), the second element of which does not necessarily mean 'a valley';⁴⁵ perhaps the combination with topographical generics was the implication. Detailed analysis of these generics might allow a clearer understanding of the habitats associated with particular invertebrates, but it will have to proceed with considerable care. For one thing, the semantic problems outlined above mean that a definitive corpus of invertebrate place-names will be very hard to establish, even if those with habitative generics are omitted, while the inclusion of wrongly identified instances would dilute the analysis. For another, the corpus of individual invertebrate terms in place-names recorded before the end of the medieval period can be very small. A statistically robust sample would probably require the inclusion of many more minor names, and this would introduce the problems associated with interpreting late spellings, outlined in the introduction.

Invertebrates as a Resource

This paper began with the assertion that invertebrates, though small in stature, were an extremely important part of the animal kingdom in Anglo-Saxon times, and should not be underestimated. In a few cases, the importance of insects to humans is easily demonstrable – some can be such a valuable resource that they are cultivated. This is most obviously true of honey bees, which provide both honey and wax. Place-names provide important evidence of medieval apiculture, most explicitly in the occurrence of the element **bīcere* (gen.pl. **bīcera*, 'bee-keeper').⁴⁶ This is often compounded with woodland terms: OE *lēah* ('woodland clearing') in the field-name *le Bykereslegh* (1384, Cheshire),⁴⁷ and possibly Bickley (Worcestershire; *Bykelege, Bikele, Bykeley, Bikerly* 1240);⁴⁸ OE *sceaga* ('wood') in Bickershaw, Lancashire (*Bikersah Bikesah* c. 1200);⁴⁹ ON *þveit* ('clearing') in the field-name

---

⁴⁴ Kenneth Cameron, *The Place-Names of Derbyshire*, 3 vols., EPNS 27–9 (Cambridge, 1959), p. 243.
⁴⁵ Gover et al., *Place-Names of Wiltshire*, p. 275.
⁴⁶ Eilert Ekwall, 'Names of Trades in English Place-Names', in *Historical Essays in Honour of James Tait*, ed. John G. Edwards, Vivian H. Galbraith and Ernest F. Jacob (Manchester, 1933), pp. 79–89 (p. 84); Smith, *English Place-Name Elements*, part 1: *Á–ĪW*, pp. 34–5; Klaus Dietz, 'AE. *Bēocere* "Imker", ME *bike* "Bienennest" und die Ortsnamen auf *Bick*', *Anglia*, 103 (1985), 1–25; Parsons et al., *Vocabulary of English Place-Names (Á–BOX)*, pp. 97–8; Della Hooke, *The Landscape of Anglo-Saxon England* (Leicester, 1998), pp. 28–9; Mary Higham, 'The Problems of the Bee-Keepers', *JEPNS* 34 (2001–2), 23–8.
⁴⁷ John McNeal Dodgson, *The Place-Names of Cheshire*, part 1, EPNS 44 (Cambridge, 1970), p. 147.
⁴⁸ Mawer et al., *Place-Names of Worcestershire*, p. 53.
⁴⁹ Ekwall, *Place-Names of Lancashire*, p. 102.

Bickerthwaite in Knaresborough, West Yorkshire (*Bekerystwayt* 1428);[50] and OE *wudu* ('wood') in Vicar Wood in Kedleston, Derbyshire (*Bikerwode c.* 1220).[51] Such references are in keeping with the attested use of woodland locations for apiculture,[52] but it is worth remarking also on the recurrence of compounds involving **bīcere* and generics denoting habitative sites or enclosures. The lost field-name *Le Bikersegh* (1371) in Cheshire,[53] *bycera fald* in a charter of 972 for Acton Beauchamp in Herefordshire,[54] and Bickers Court in Tanworth, Warwickshire (cf. *Bikeruscroft* 1357),[55] contain OE *(ge)hæg, fald* and *croft* – all types of enclosure. OE *tūn* ('farm, settlement') is the generic in Bickerston in Norfolk, and in five instances of Bickerton, in Cheshire, Herefordshire, Northumberland and West Yorkshire (twice, one now lost).[56] These latter might be thought of as specialised honey- and wax-producing settlements.

The element that denotes the honeybee, OE *bēo*, has sometimes been mistakenly identified when other etymologies are more likely,[57] but is also found compounded with terms for settlements and enclosures. These include ON *bý* ('settlement' – e.g. Beeby in Leicestershire),[58] OE *cot* ('cottage' – e.g. Beckett in Berkshire),[59] *croft* (a lost *Becroft(a)* 1154–9 and *c.* 1180 in Derbyshire),[60] *wīc* ('specialised settlement' – e.g. Bewick, Northumberland and East Yorkshire),[61] and *worþ* ('enclosure' – e.g. Beauworth, Hampshire),[62] but not, it seems, OE *tūn*. *Bēo* is also compounded with references to woodland or trees: OE *lēah* in Beoley in Worcestershire,[63] Beaulieu in Dorset,[64] Billow in Gloucestershire,[65] and Beeleigh in Essex;[66] and with *orceard* ('orchard')

---

[50] Smith, *Place-Names of the West Riding of Yorkshire*, part 5, p. 106.
[51] Cameron, *Place-Names of Derbyshire*, p. 580.
[52] Higham, 'The Problems of the Bee-Keepers'.
[53] Dodgson, *Place-Names of Cheshire*, part 1, p. 158.
[54] Peter Sawyer, *Anglo-Saxon Charters: An Annotated List and Bibliography*, Royal Historical Society Guides and Handbooks 8 (London, 1968), charter no. 786; Ekwall, 'Names of Trades', p. 84.
[55] John E. B. Gover, Allen Mawer and Frank M. Stenton, with Frederick T. S. Houghton, *The Place-Names of Warwickshire*, EPNS 13 (Cambridge, 1936), p. 378.
[56] Smith, *English Place-Name Elements*, part 1: *Á–ĪW*, p. 33; Albert H. Smith, *The Place-Names of the West Riding of Yorkshire*, part 4, EPNS 33 (Cambridge, 1961), p. 247; Smith, *Place-Names of the West Riding of Yorkshire*, part 5, p. 56; Dietz, 'AE. *Bēocere*'; Parsons *et al.*, *Vocabulary of English Place-Names (Á–BOX)*, p. 96.
[57] Parsons *et al.*, *Vocabulary of English Place-Names (Á–BOX)*, p. 82.
[58] Barrie Cox, *The Place-Names of Leicestershire*, part 3, EPNS 81 (Nottingham, 2004), p. 42.
[59] Gelling, *Place-Names of Berkshire*, p. 376.
[60] Cameron, *Place-Names of Derbyshire*, p. 722.
[61] Mawer, *Place-Names of Northumberland and Durham*, p. 19; Smith, *Place-Names of the East Riding of Yorkshire and York*, p. 59.
[62] Richard Coates, *Hampshire Place-Names* (Southampton, 1993), p. 31.
[63] Mawer *et al.*, *Place-Names of Worcestershire*, p. 186.
[64] Mills, *Place-Names of Dorset*, part 3, p. 241.
[65] Smith, *Place-Names of Gloucestershire*, part 2, p. 214.
[66] Reaney, *Place-Names of Essex*, p. 219.

in the lost field-name *le Byorchard* (1447), in Charlton Marshall, Dorset.[67] OE *bēo* place-names may then also hint at specialised bee-keeping in some instances.

Other insects may also have provided a resource for the medieval population. Leeches had medical applications, so that names such as Latchmere in Surrey, Latch Moor in Dorset (both OE *lǣce + mere*, 'leech lake') and Lashbrook in Oxfordshire (*lǣce + brōc*, 'leech stream'), may have encoded practical information. Other invertebrates might have formed part of the medieval diet. Snails (OE *snægl*), certainly part of the medieval diet in some regions,[68] are recorded in Snailcroft and Snailwell in Cambridgeshire,[69] Snailham in Sussex,[70] Snailslinch in Surrey,[71] and Snailsbreach in Dorset.[72] Reaney objected to Ekwall's interpretation of Snailwell (*Sneillewelle c.* 1050 (*c.* 1350),[73] *Snegeluuelle, Snelleuuelle* 1086) as 'stream frequented by snails', preferring a metaphorical reference to a slow-moving stream;[74] but it is not impossible that the stream was renowned as an especially good place from which to procure snails.

Invertebrates as a By-Product of Human and Animal Activity

The lifecycle of many invertebrates is dependent on proximity to larger animals, and it may be that some toponymic references to insects are an indirect reflection of farming practices. Analysis of invertebrate remains has certainly become an important and profitable element in archaeological assessment of the historical landscape. Since different habitats give rise to very specific assemblages of fauna, the study of fossilised invertebrate remains can help to build a detailed and nuanced picture of the makeup of the physical environment, identifying likely levels of woodland cover or grassland, the presence of standing water or human habitations, and so on.[75] Types of farming activity can also be interpreted archaeologically by consideration of the associated by-products. In the case of pastoralism, for instance,

---

[67] A. D. Mills, *The Place-Names of Dorset*, part 2, EPNS 53 (Cambridge, 1980), p. 13.
[68] Melitta Weiss Adamson, *Food in Medieval Times* (Westport, CT, 2004), pp. 44–5.
[69] Reaney, *Place-Names of Cambridgeshire and the Isle of Ely*, pp. 78, 195–6, 274.
[70] Mawer et al., *Place-Names of Sussex*, p. 510.
[71] Gover et al., *Place-Names of Surrey*, p. 173.
[72] Mills, *Place-Names of Dorset*, part 2, p. 62.
[73] Sawyer, *Anglo-Saxon Charters*, charter no. 1051.
[74] Eilert Ekwall, *The Concise Oxford Dictionary of English Place-Names*, 4th edn (Oxford, 1960), p. 428; Reaney, *Place-Names of Cambridgeshire and the Isle of Ely*, pp. 78, 195–6.
[75] E.g. Osborne, 'Insect Remains', *Fisherwick*; Mark A. Robinson, 'The Insects', in *Sacred Mound, Holy Rings: Silbury Hill and the West Kennet Palisade Enclosures: A Later Neolithic Complex in North Wiltshire*, ed. Alasdair Whittle, Oxbow Monograph 74 (Oxford, 1997), pp. 36–47; Smith, 'Insect Remains'.

concentrations of fly puparia are regarded as indicative of cattle husbandry,[76] while the presence of dung-beetle remains may also signal the long-term presence of livestock.[77] This approach should perhaps be extended to place-names – indeed, Cullen and Jones have already discussed the importance of place-names containing elements denoting manure.[78] Old English words for 'dung-beetle' include *scearnbudda, scearnwibba, scearnwifel* and *tordwifel*,[79] but these seem to be absent from place-names attested in the medieval period. While it may be that some of the examples of *scearn* ('dung, filth') and *tord* ('a turd, dung') place-names cited by Cullen and Jones are reduced compounds originally containing *scearnbudda* or the like, it is also possible that *budda*, *wibba*, *wifel* and other 'beetle' words on their own sometimes signified dung-beetles.

For an example of the potential significance of such place-name elements, the excavation of Wilsford Shaft, Wiltshire, is worth considering. Here, specialists have identified vast numbers of dung-beetle remains in the fills of the Bronze Age shaft, indicating that this was once open grassland frequented by grazing animals. Although the dung-beetles could indicate the presence of other animals, including sheep, the concentration of large numbers of beetles (and therefore, presumably, large quantities of animal waste) around the shaft suggests that it may have acted as a source of water around which cattle congregated, their dung creating an attractive habitat for the beetles.[80] It is at least noteworthy that Wilsford is first recorded as *Wiflesford(e)* (1086),[81] from OE *wifeles-ford* ('weevil's ford'). Now, the place-name was obviously coined many hundreds of years after the digging of the shaft, and refers to a feature – a river crossing – that was perhaps 2 or 3 kilometres to the west-south-west. It is not the intention here to suggest a direct connection between the archaeological site and the place-name. However, the archaeological evidence is a clear indication that livestock grazed extensively in the vicinity, and it seems likely that this use of the area persisted long after the shaft had been filled. Seasonal movement of stock may well have necessitated use of the nearby ford by large numbers of cattle, year after year, and such activity might well have given rise to increases in manure in

---

[76] Edith Schmidt, 'Remains of Fly Puparia as Indicators of Neolithic Cattle Farming', *Environmental Archaeology* 11 (2006), 143–4.
[77] E.g. Harry Kenward and Allan Hall, 'Dung and Stable Manure on Waterlogged Archaeological Occupation Sites: Some Ruminations on the Evidence from Plant and Invertebrate Remains', in *Manure Matters: Historical, Archaeological and Ethnographic Perspectives*, ed. Richard Jones (Farnham, 2012), pp. 79–95.
[78] Paul Cullen and Richard Jones, 'Manure and Middens in English Place-Names', in *Manure Matters*, ed. Jones, pp. 97–108.
[79] *OED*, s.v. 'sharnbud', 'turd', 'weevil'; *ASD*, s.v. 'scearnwibba', 'scearnwifel', 'tordwifel'.
[80] Osborne, 'An Insect Fauna', pp. 562–4; Osborne, 'Insects', *Wilsford Shaft*.
[81] Gover *et al.*, *Place-Names of Wiltshire*, p. 372.

close proximity to the crossing, and frequent infestation with beetles. Place-names are unlikely to provide anything like the nuanced analyses of invertebrate remains achieved by palaeoentomologists, but it is at least worth considering that a place-name such as Wilsford might reflect the importance of the river-crossing for pastoralist communities.

Another example relates to place-names containing references to insects that might be considered pests. Several place-name elements refer to flies or gadflies. One of these, OE *bēaw*, is found, for example, in Bowcombe, Devon (with OE *cumb* ('valley'); *Bocumb* 1219–20, and *Baucumb* 1238);[82] in Beauford, Cambridgeshire (with OE *feld* ('open land') or *ford* ('river-crossing'): *Beufeld* 1299, and *Beauford* 13th C);[83] and in Beausale, Warwickshire (with OE *halh* ('nook'): *Beoshelle* 1086, and *Beausala* 12th C).[84] OE *brēosa*, another term meaning 'gadfly', is the first element of Brisley, Norfolk (with OE *lēah* ('woodland clearing'): *Bruselea c.* 1105, and *Brisele* 1199),[85] of Braiseworth, Suffolk (with OE *worð* ('enclosure'): *Briseworde* 1086),[86] and of Bricett, Suffolk (with OE *(ge)set* ('dwelling'): *Brieseta* 1086, and *Brisete* 1198).[87] OE *flēoge* ('fly') is the first element of Fly Hill, Derbyshire (with OE *hyll* ('hill'): *Fleghull'* 1343).[88]

While flying insects of these kinds are a nuisance to all humans, they can be a real scourge to pastoral farmers, because of the ways in which they interact with livestock. Some gadflies are blood-suckers whose bites can cause discomfort to cattle, while others are more aggressively parasitic: eggs of the common botfly, for example, find their way into the stomachs of horses, where they pass through the larvae stage.[89] The Sheep Botfly, endemic to southern England and Wales, deposits its larvae in the nostril, usually that of a sheep or goat (although other mammals can sometimes serve as hosts), where they develop for up to nine months, causing discomfort at the very least, and at worst a loss of appetite and more serious complications, resulting occasionally in death.[90]

---

[82] Ibid., p. 284; Reaney, *Place-Names of Cambridgeshire and the Isle of Ely*, pp. 78, liii.
[83] Reaney, *Place-Names of Cambridgeshire and the Isle of Ely*, pp. 78, 267.
[84] Gover et al., *Place-Names of Warwickshire*, p. 200.
[85] Ekwall, *Studies on English Place-Names*, p. 101; *CDEPN*, p. 88; John McNeal Dodgson, *The Place-Names of Cheshire*, part 5 (I:i), EPNS 48 (Cambridge, 1981), p. 114.
[86] *CDEPN*, p. 78; Dodgson, *Place-Names of Cheshire*, part 5 (I:i), p. 114.
[87] Ekwall, *Studies on English Place-Names*, p. 101.
[88] Cameron, *Place-Names of Derbyshire*, p. 32; Smith, *English Place-Name Elements*, part 1: *Á–IW*, p. 176.
[89] Linssen, *Insects of the British Isles*, pp. 125, 129.
[90] Kenneth J. Capelle, 'The Occurrence of *Oestrus Ovis* L. (diptera: Oestridae) in the Bighorn Sheep from Wyoming and Montana', *The Journal of Parasitology* 52.3 (1966), 618–21 (p. 618).

Where place-names make reference to such creatures, it may once again be a reflection of long-term pastoral activity in the vicinity. A prevalence of parasitic insects might be symptomatic of high levels of stock-rearing in the area. In this respect, the two place-names *Clay Brook* (*Cleybroke* 1488; *Cle(y)-, Clegbroke* 1492) and *Cleggcliffe* (*Clegclyve* 1274, 1275; *-clif* 1308; *Clegeclif* 1285; *Gleg Clyff* 1307) in Southowram, West Yorkshire, may be relevant. Both are now lost, but Smith placed the former near to Shibden Hall,[91] while the latter may well have been adjacent to Beacon Hill, if Goodall is right in assigning the (apparently corrupt) 1553 form *Gletclif* to this place.[92] Since Beacon Hill is immediately to the south-west of Shibden Hall, it seems likely that the two names were in very close proximity and should be considered together. The second elements are clearly OE *brōc* ('stream') and *clīf* ('steep slope'), respectively, but the first has been interpreted variously as ON **klegg* ('clay') or OE *clǣg* ('clay'), ON **kleggi* ('a haystack, a hill'),[93] or even an ON byname *Kleggr*, cognate with ON *kleggi* ('gadfly, cleg').[94] It seems just as likely that the first element is simply ON *kleggi* ('gadfly, cleg') – association with OE *clǣg* perhaps influencing the later development – and that these place-names thus denote a 'stream/steep slope infested with gad-flies'. Shibden, the name of the hall adjacent to which both Clay Brook and Cleggcliffe lie, is recorded as *Scypedene* in 1240–6, which seems to consist of OE *scēap* with *denu* ('sheep valley'). It may well be that a valley grazed by sheep provided a habitat suitable for an infestation of gadflies.

Bewsborough (*Bevsberg(e)* 1086; *Beuesb'ge* 1161–2) and Beauxfield (*Bewesfeld* ?10th C (13th C);[95] *Bevesfel* 1086; *Beauffeld'* 1199), both in Whitfield, Kent, may also contain the element *bēaw*. The element is apparently difficult to distinguish from a personal name of the same form,[96] and both Anderson and Wallenberg have cast doubt on the likelihood of gadflies providing the specific either for these two place-names or for the name of the wider district perhaps denoted by Beauxfield.[97] However, Bewsborough was the meeting-place of an Anglo-Saxon administrative district or hundred. Such sites are sometimes closely associated with place-names indicative of pastoral

---

[91] Albert. H. Smith, *The Place-Names of the West Riding of Yorkshire*, part 3, EPNS 32 (Cambridge, 1961), p. 91.
[92] Armitage Goodall, *Place-Names of South-West Yorkshire* (Cambridge, 1913), p. 104.
[93] Smith, *Place-Names of the West Riding of Yorkshire*, part 3, p. 91; Bertil Ejder, 'Notes on Yorkshire Place-Names', *ES* 46.1–6 (1965), 110–13 (p. 110).
[94] Smith, *Place-Names of the West Riding of Yorkshire*, part 3, p. xii.
[95] Sawyer, *Anglo-Saxon Charters*, charter no. 140.
[96] Smith, *English Place-Name Elements*, part 1: *Á–IW*, p. 23; Parsons *et al.*, *Vocabulary of English Place-Names* (*Á–BOX*), p. 67.
[97] Olof S. Anderson, *The English Hundred-Names: The South-Eastern Counties*, vol. 3, Lunds Universitets Arsskrift 37.1 (Lund, 1939), pp. 141–3; Wallenberg, *Kentish Place-Names*, pp. 52–3.

Entomological Etymologies

activity, and may often have been venues to which livestock was brought. Some may indeed have their origins in the regulation of rights over common land among pastoralist communities.[98] Infestation by gadflies might have been a characteristic of sites of this kind.

Discussion and Conclusions

Outlined above are just a few examples of the important ways in which people – including of course the Anglo-Saxons – have interacted with invertebrates. Many more examples could be found. Not all bees produce honey, but other species carry out a crucial role in the pollination of crops. Names such as Dorney (*Dornei* 1086; *Dorney* 1209–19) in Buckinghamshire,[99] and the lost *dorendale gate* in Leicestershire (late 13th C),[100] which may well be compounds of OE *dora* ('bumblebee') with OE *ēg* ('island') and ON *dalr* ('valley'), respectively, may recognise an invertibrate population that would have been particularly favourable for, say, fruit or vegetable crops. Conversely, place-names such as Hamsterley in Durham (*Hamsteleie* c. 1190; *Hamsterley* 1242), perhaps a compound of OE *hamestra* ('a corn-weevil') and *lēah* ('woodland clearing'),[101] or the field-name *Hoppehull* in Cranborne, Dorset, recorded in 1280 and probably containing OE *hoppa* ('grass-hopper') and *hyll* ('hill'),[102] might have carried warnings about insects that can destroy grain-stores or crops. Some insects can spread disease, most obviously mosquitos, which carry malaria. This was endemic at least to the East Anglian Fenland from the sixteenth to nineteenth centuries, and perhaps also in the medieval period, though this is not known.[103] Place-names such as Gnatham (*Gnattham* 1301) in Cornwall, Gnatham (*Gnatham* 1311) in Devon, and the lost field-name *Natmarethorne* (1330) in Great Longstone, Derbyshire,[104] may therefore have served as a useful caution, being derived from OE *gnætt-hamm* ('hemmed-in land infested with gnats') and *gnætt-mere-þorn* ('gnat-pool thorn-tree') respectively. In general, however, the significance of place-name references to invertebrates

---

[98] John Baker, 'The Toponymy of Communal Activity: Anglo-Saxon Assembly Sites and their Functions', in *Els noms en la vida quotidiana: Actes del XXIV Congrés Internacional d'ICOS sobre Ciències Onomàstiques: Annex, secció 7*, ed. Joan Tort I Donada, published online (2014), http://www.gencat.cat/llengua/BTPL/ICOS2011/cercador.html, 1498–1509.
[99] Mawer and Stenton, *Place-Names of Buckinghamshire*, p. 228; Ekwall, *Studies on English Place-Names*, p. 101.
[100] Barrie Cox, *The Place-Names of Leicestershire*, part 3, EPNS 81 (Nottingham, 2004), p. 65.
[101] Ekwall, *Studies on English Place-Names*, p. 102.
[102] Mills, *Place-Names of Dorset*, part 2, p. 216.
[103] Oliver Rackham, *The History of the Countryside*, pbk edn (London, 1987), pp. 389–90.
[104] Gover *et al.*, *Place-Names of Devon*, p. 245; Cameron, *Place-Names of Derbyshire*, p. 141.

for study of the landscape probably lies in what they reveal about farming practices and management of resources.

It is so easy to be struck by the elegance and beauty of large beasts and birds, or distracted by the danger and excitement they offer, that we overlook the smallest creatures. Early place-name scholars may sometimes have found it extraordinary that such apparently unimportant things as invertebrates might help to define a feature of the landscape. Wallenberg disliked the idea that place-names such as Wilsley, Kent, could contain the etymon of PDE *weevil* simply because he considered the creature so 'insignificant'; it could not, he felt, 'have attracted the fancy of the settlers to such an extent that the name of the insect became a component of pl[ace]-n[ame]s in so many cases'.[105] Yet the work of Gelling and Cole,[106] among others, has highlighted the Anglo-Saxons' nuanced appreciation of their environment, and it should not be a surprise if this included an understanding of the significance of invertebrates within their landscape.

It goes almost without saying that invertebrates of one kind or another must have figured strongly in medieval lives, even if they were not always at the forefront of consciousness. Sometimes their presence would have been unobtrusive, at other times unwelcome, but nonetheless significant. Invertebrates could be a potentially important resource, a hazard for domestic beasts or a side-effect of their husbandry, a help or a danger to crops, and a vector of disease. If the habitat in which they lived remained, if suitable systems of land- and livestock-management persisted, if the beasts that served as hosts continued to be present, then certain invertebrates might have become just as constant a feature of the landscape as the trees, ponds and plants they frequented. Further research into the place-names that record their presence will involve very detailed and careful considerations, and must confront a number of obstacles, but it certainly has the potential to reveal something significant about medieval use of the landscape and perceptions of invertebrates themselves.

---

[105] Wallenberg, *Place-Names of Kent*, pp. 96–7.
[106] Margaret Gelling and Ann Cole, *The Landscape of Place-Names* (Stamford, 2000).

A version of this paper was presented at the 'Beasts in the Anglo-Saxon World' conference in June 2011, and I am grateful to all who have provided feedback and suggestions, including Dr Richard Jones, Dr Paul Cullen and Professor John Insley, and especially to Dr Jayne Carroll, who read and commented on an earlier draft.

11

Beasts, Birds and Other Creatures in Pre-Conquest Charters and Place-Names in England

Della Hooke

There are occasional references to the creatures of legend and folklore in the names of places and boundary landmarks, but in general these sources seem to reveal a close local knowledge of the place being described, especially in pre-Conquest boundary clauses. While the material can be difficult to handle, given uncertainties of translation, and confusion surrounding Anglo-Saxon personal names and some locally known names for particular trees, names referring to animals can reveal much about the concerns of those living in early medieval England. Domestic stock such as pigs, cattle, horses and sheep are noted, and details of animal husbandry are revealed. Terms used for cattle, sheep or horses, for instance, may indicate how they were managed; names may show the location of stalls, byres, and studfolds, or elaborate upon the use of seasonal pastures. The animals of the hunt regularly appear in some regions, and many other wild creatures are noted in particular locations. Even birds are frequently named in both place-names and charters. Some charter boundary clauses are particularly rich in animal and bird names. Importantly, such names provide an intimate view of how local people viewed their countryside.

Mythological Creatures

There is a great deal of information about mythological creatures in Old English literary sources but, on the whole, Anglo-Saxon charters and place-names are very much more down to earth.[1] Monsters *do*

---

[1] This paper is not a comprehensive survey of all the names recorded, and this study is currently being extended as a research project exploring the subject further. Here 'early' place-names means those recorded by 1086, to be found in the place-name volumes of the English Place-Name Society unless otherwise indicated. Old Norse names often tend to be later recordings, due to the scarcity of charters surviving for northern and eastern England, and the meagre covering of Domesday Book. Space does not allow

appear, but they seem to be more often mythical 'humanoid-beasts' rather than 'animal-beasts'. Giants and goblins may be associated with pits – like the *þyrspytt* on the boundary of Poden, Worcestershire – or barrows: a *scuccanhlaw*, 'demon's or goblin's barrow', occurs as an early name for Warren Farm in Buckinghamshire, while Shobrooke in Devon is 'demon's brook' or 'haunted brook'.[2] An 'elf's seat' (*on elfaledes*) is referred to on the boundary of Corse, Gloucestershire, while *brogan gate* in Wytham, North and South Hinksey, Berkshire, may be 'monster/terror gate'.[3] The belief in pits, meres or ponds providing a link with the underworld finds expression, of course, in the popular Anglo-Saxon poem *Beowulf*, and a sprinkling of minor place-names recorded in charters seem to refer to this and especially to the monster Grendel, 'a notorious prowler of the borderlands, who held the wastelands, swamps and fastness'.[4] He is associated, for instance, with a pit in Abbot's Morton, Worcestershire, with an unlocated mere in Old Swinford in the same county, and another at Ham, Wiltshire.[5] The names of heathen gods also, of course, appear in place-names; and Wayland's smithy, a charter boundary landmark on the boundary of Compton Beauchamp in the Vale of the White Horse, refers to a Neolithic chambered tomb.[6]

Dragons

In contrast with 'humanoid' monsters, dragons are presumably to be included in the animal world. While the *Anglo-Saxon Chronicle* notes fiery dragons seen over Northumberland in AD 793, heralding famine and the first Viking attack on Lindisfarne,[7] there are very few dragons in the charters (Fig. 11.1). As they are in *Beowulf* or the *Gnomic Verses*, these mostly appear to be associated with tumuli. In South Damerham near Fordingbridge (historically Wiltshire, now Hampshire), a tenth-century boundary clause describes how the bounds run *þonne to þes drakenhorde* ('thence to the dragon's hoard' – OE *draca*, 'dragon', with *hord*, 'treasure').[8] Although Grundy suggests

---

all the variant spellings of Old English terms to be included here. Terms found only in glossaries are not included here either, as they can be misleading.

[2] In order: P. H. Sawyer, *Anglo-Saxon Charters: An Annotated List and Bibliography* (London, 1968), S 1591; Della Hooke, *Worcestershire Anglo-Saxon Charter-Bounds* (Woodbridge, 1990), pp. 882–3; S 138; S 387; and *CDEPN*.
[3] S 1551; S 663, and Margaret Gelling, *The Place-Names of Berkshire*, part 3, EPNS 51 (Cambridge, 1976), p. 728.
[4] Michael Swanton, *Beowulf, Edited with an Introduction, Notes and a New Prose Translation* (Manchester, 1978), pp. 38–9, 94–5.
[5] S 78, S 579, and Hooke, *Worcestershire Anglo-Saxon Charter-Bounds*, pp. 43–6, 162–7; S 416.
[6] S 564, and Gelling, *The Place-Names of Berkshire*, part 3, pp. 692, 694.
[7] *The Anglo-Saxon Chronicle*, ed. and trans. Michael Swanton (London, 1996), pp. 54–6.
[8] S 513. A later, similar name occurs as a field-name in Yanworth, Gloucestershire, in 1222. Smith suggests that this may allude 'to the folk-belief in dragons guarding treasures and

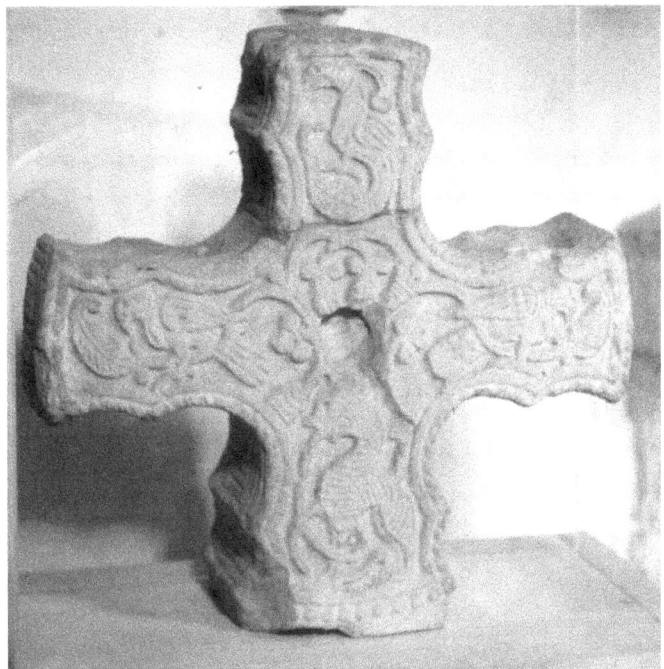

Fig. 11.1 A dragon depicted on an early
ninth-century cross at Cropthorne, Worcestershire

that this was 'probably a place where coins had been found', there is a distinct possibility that this represents a formerly opened barrow that had contained precious artefacts. Grundy also notes how the site gave rise to an otherwise modern name Drake North, a piece of woodland in West Park.[9] Drakelow in Derbyshire, recorded as a place-name in a charter of 942,[10] is indeed 'dragon's mound or tumulus', and other such names are recorded later – like the Drakelow name in Wolverley, Worcestershire, recorded in 1240 (*Brakelowe* 1240, *Drakelow* 1582), and the later Drakelow in Cheshire (*Drakelow(e)* 1310). Rhinoceros fossils found in fluvio-glacial deposits may also have been referred to as dragons.[11]

There is another charter reference to a *wyrm*, a term sometimes used as another name for a dragon, as in *Beowulf* (lines 3131–2) and other literary sources. However, OE *wyrm* can also simply mean 'snake', and Wormsley, Herefordshire (*Wermeslai* 1086), is translated by Watts

---

barrows': A. H. Smith, *The Place-Names of Gloucestershire*, part 1, EPNS 38 (Cambridge, 1964), p. 191.

[9] G. B. Grundy, 'The Saxon Land Charters of Hampshire with Notes on Place and Field Names', *Archaeological Journal* 2nd series 31 (1924), 69.

[10] S 484, though this is not necessarily a reliable document.

[11] David Horovitz, *The Place-Names of Staffordshire* (Brewood, 2005), pp. 235–6.

as 'the snake's wood or clearing'.[12] A charter reference to a *wurmstealle*, on the boundary of woodland belonging to Sandford in Devon, is translated by Finberg as either 'the snake-pit' or 'the dragon's lair'. However, the word actually referred (for some uncertain reason) to a 'cattle shelter'.[13] If a location was known to be frequented by real snakes, it does not seem unlikely that they would feature in its name; there are, indeed, a number of place-names which may contain the term *wyrm*. However, as so often with Old English place-names, it can be difficult to distinguish between an animal and a personal name. Thus, while the place-names Wormley in Hertfordshire, Worminghall in Buckinghamshire, or Wormhill in Derbyshire (and so on), are likely to incorporate a personal name Wyrma, Worminster in Somerset (*Wormester* 946, *Wuormestorr* 1065) may be either 'Wyrm's tor' or 'the dragon's tor', and Wormley, Hertfordshire (*Wrmeleia* c. 1060), could be 'Wyrma's wood' or 'snake infested wood'.[14]

Problems of Identification

As shown above, one of the greatest problems encountered in investigating animal names is that so many were adopted as personal names. Understandably, Anglo-Saxon men seem happy to have called themselves names such as Hengest (OE *hengest*, 'stallion'), Bār (OE *bār*, 'male pig'), Eofer (OE *eofor*, 'wild boar'), or Wulf (OE *wulf*, 'wolf') – names which might have been considered to have a certain cultural cachet – but Ceafor ('beetle') or Mycg ('midge') are harder to explain unless they were adopted as nicknames. Similar problems arise over many other personal names: for example, confusion between *Catta and OE *catt* ('cat'), as *on cattan ege* in Newnham Murren, Oxfordshire; between *Hroc and OE *hrōc* ('rook'), as in a *roces æcere*, a boundary landmark of an estate at Beckley, Oxfordshire; and between *Otta and *otor* ('otter') in *ottanmere*, another boundary landmark on the same estate.[15] In the past, place-name scholars have tended to favour personal names when referring to settlement names, though there has been some retreat from this position in recent years. In charter boundary clauses where the name is associated with a specific topographical feature there is perhaps more chance that the name might refer to an actual creature. The number of terms that are recognised has also been augmented in recent years, though some still

---

[12] *CDEPN*, p. 701.
[13] S 890; H. P. R. Finberg, *West-Country Historical Studies* (Newton Abbot, 1969), pp. 38–42; Gelling, *The Place-Names of Berkshire*, part 3, p. 918.
[14] S 509, S 1042; *CDEPN*, pp. 700–1.
[15] S 738, S 943.

remain uncertain.¹⁶ Names incorporating what may be **pohha/*pocca* ('fallow deer'), or **bagga* ('badger') have been interpreted as topographical, personal or possibly animal names, but many are more common in post-Conquest minor names.¹⁷ There are few charters for the north of England, and many place-names there are later recordings, so Old English names will inevitably predominate over those in Old Norse as far as this study is concerned.

Another hurdle is presented by certain tree names incorporating terms for animals: a *lusþorn* ('louse thorn') recorded in Worcestershire may refer to the spindle tree, *Euonymus europaeus*, whose berries were known as 'louse-berries' in the Midlands because they were baked, powdered and sprinkled on the hair to kill nits and lice, but this tree was also known in Midland dialects as the cat-tree or dog-tree/dogwood tree, and a *doggi þorn* is recorded in Olveston, Gloucestershire.¹⁸ The other dogwood or cat-tree was the dogwood itself, *Cornus sanguinea* – a very similar tree but with black rather than red berries – the vernacular names apparently implying, like *lūs*, some derogatory meaning or something small (goats, too, sometimes later implied a derogatory association). Given the reference to thorns, however, dog-rose is another possibility here. The *crawan þorn* of Chilcomb in Hampshire, and that of Badbury in Wiltshire, may have been *Rhamnus catharticus*, purging buckthorn.¹⁹ However, on other occasions trees may have been associated with the real birds that were seen often to perch upon them.

Since Old English spellings can often be corrupt in the documents, especially in Domesday Book, etymological rules do not always apply or are not always reliable. It can, for instance, be difficult to be certain that references to OE *wrænna* are indeed to a wren and not to OE **wræna* ('stallion'). It can similarly be difficult to distinguish between OE *swan*¹ and *swān*² ('swan' and 'swain'). OE *putta* ('kite, bittern') is not only the personal name Putta, the name of one bishop of Rochester, but also gets confused with OE *pytt* ('pit') in several charters, as in the pits constructed to catch wild animals. Other

---

¹⁶ See, for instance, Carole Hough, 'Place-Name Evidence for Old English Bird-Names', *JEPNS* 30 (1998), 60–9. Most 'creature' names are also listed in A. H. Smith, *English Place-Name Elements*, 2 vols., EPNS 25, 26 (Cambridge, 1956), which also includes later recorded examples.

¹⁷ See Carole Hough, 'OE *wearg* in Warnborough and Wreighburn', *JEPNS* 237 (1995), 14–20 (p. 18); Carole Hough, 'Place-Name Evidence for an Anglo-Saxon Name: OE **pohha/*pocca* ('fallow deer')', *ASE* 30 (2001), 1–14; and Carole Hough, 'Ælfric of Eynsham, Pucklechurch, and Evidence for Fallow Deer in Anglo-Saxon England', *Nomina* 35 (2012), 103–30.

¹⁸ Geoffrey Grigson, *The Englishman's Flora* (St Albans, 1975), p. 131; S 664; and Della Hooke, *Trees in Anglo-Saxon England* (Woodbridge, 2010), p. 242.

¹⁹ S 376; S 568; J. K. Wallenberg, *Kentish Place-Names*, Uppsala Universitets Årsskrift (Uppsala, 1931); Smith, *The Place-Names of Gloucestershire*, part 1, p. 48.

similar forms are *puttoc and *pytell, the latter perhaps referring more specifically to the buzzard, though bird species are not always easy to identify from the terms used.

Creatures in the Landscape

Reference to animals in literature is not considered here. These tend to be to animals that had some iconic role, such as the horse associated with the warrior elite, or the wolf that inhabited the dangerous wilds on the edges of the settled world. Charters and place-names tend to reveal the everyday world of those inhabiting it at a time when almost everyone was closely attached to the soil and intimately aware of their surroundings. Consequently, one hears primarily about the domestic animals upon which the population depended or the wild ones they either hunted or saw around them. Because of problems of identification a statistical analysis of this kind of name distribution, such as that carried out by the author with regard to the names of tree species,[20] would be unhelpful, but location can still offer valuable pointers towards the regional use of the rural countryside. Although infrequent visitors might on occasion give rise to a place-name, in general it seems that a place-name referring to an animal, bird, etc. 'tended to describe the landscape in terms of persistent and familiar features'.[21]

Domestic Animals

Although there were obviously regional differences, mixed farming predominated in early medieval England. The names of most domestic animal species are found in place-names and charters in a form familiar to farmers today. However, some animal names are obviously more frequent than others, and recur in different regions that shared a common characteristic. Among these are the animals that were pastured on the seasonal grazing offered in regions of wood-pasture.

---

[20] Hooke, *Trees in Anglo-Saxon England*.
[21] Richard J. Evans, Lorcán O'Toole and D. Philip Whitfield, 'The History of Eagles in Britain and Ireland: An Ecological Review of Placename and Documentary Evidence from the Last 1500 Years', *Bird Study* 59.3 (2012), 335–9 (p. 336), drawing upon the work of Margaret Gelling, *Place-Names in the Landscape* (London, 1984), and Margaret Gelling and Ann Cole, *The Landscape of Place-Names* (Stamford, 2000).

Animals in wood-pasture

An animal particularly characteristic of the author's home region in the Midlands is the pig (Fig. 11.2). This animal occurs more often than any other in the charters of Worcestershire because much of the region was well wooded and noted as a valuable wood-pasture resource. Wood-pasture is found throughout the country, except in the intensively cultivated region to the south east. While all kinds of domestic stock might be pastured within woodland it was the pig that was pre-eminent, herds being driven into the woods in the summer and early autumn both to remove them from the main crop-growing regions and to fatten them on acorns (in the south of England beech-mast was an equally important food). The presence of the pigs themselves helped to determine the open character of much of the woodland, which in turn led to better crops of acorns (Fig. 11.3).

Wood-pasture was one of the most important resources available in Anglo-Saxon England and played a fundamental role in the rural economy. Indeed, this use of woods was so important that in some circuits the Domesday surveyors recorded the value of woodland according to the number of pigs it could support or might render as tax. Ine of Wessex's laws of 688×694 illustrate the importance of the wood-pasture trees, stipulating that 'if … anyone cuts down a tree that can shelter thirty swine, and it becomes known, he shall pay 60 shillings.'[22] In charters, the seasonal swine-pastures are named as *denbære*, *wealdbære*, *pascua porcorum*, or even *fearnleswe*, etc. (*læs* is 'pasture', hence 'fern pasture'). They often lay some considerable distance from the home estates, and were approached by clearly delineated drove roads.[23]

The Kentish charters contain the most detail, sometimes referring to the size of herds permitted in the seasonal pastures, the dens. Thus, Ickham and Palmstead had pasture for fifty pigs in one area of woodland, Wouldham pasture for 120 pigs at *Horshyrste* (in Yalding), and various estates of Christ Church, Canterbury, had swine-pastures for 120 pigs in the woods of *Ægylbyrhtingahyrst* and *Hostringedenne* (probably Ashenden in Tenterden, Kent) in the ninth century.[24] Domesday Book records that the amassed woods of Stoneleigh in the Warwickshire Arden could support 2,000 swine.[25] These charters, too, refer to the other stock that might be pastured in the dens, including

---

[22] Ine, 43–4: F. L. Attenborough, *The Laws of the Earliest English Kings* (Cambridge, 1922), pp. 50–1.
[23] Della Hooke, '*Wealdbæra & swina mæst*: Wood Pasture in Early Medieval England', in *Life in Medieval Landscapes: People and Places in the Middle Ages: Papers in Memory of H. S. A. Fox*, ed. Sam Turner and Bob Silvester (Oxford, 2012), pp. 32–49.
[24] S 123; S 885; S 1623.
[25] *Domesday Book, 23, Warwickshire*, ed. J. Plaister (Chichester, 1976), 1, 4.

Della Hooke

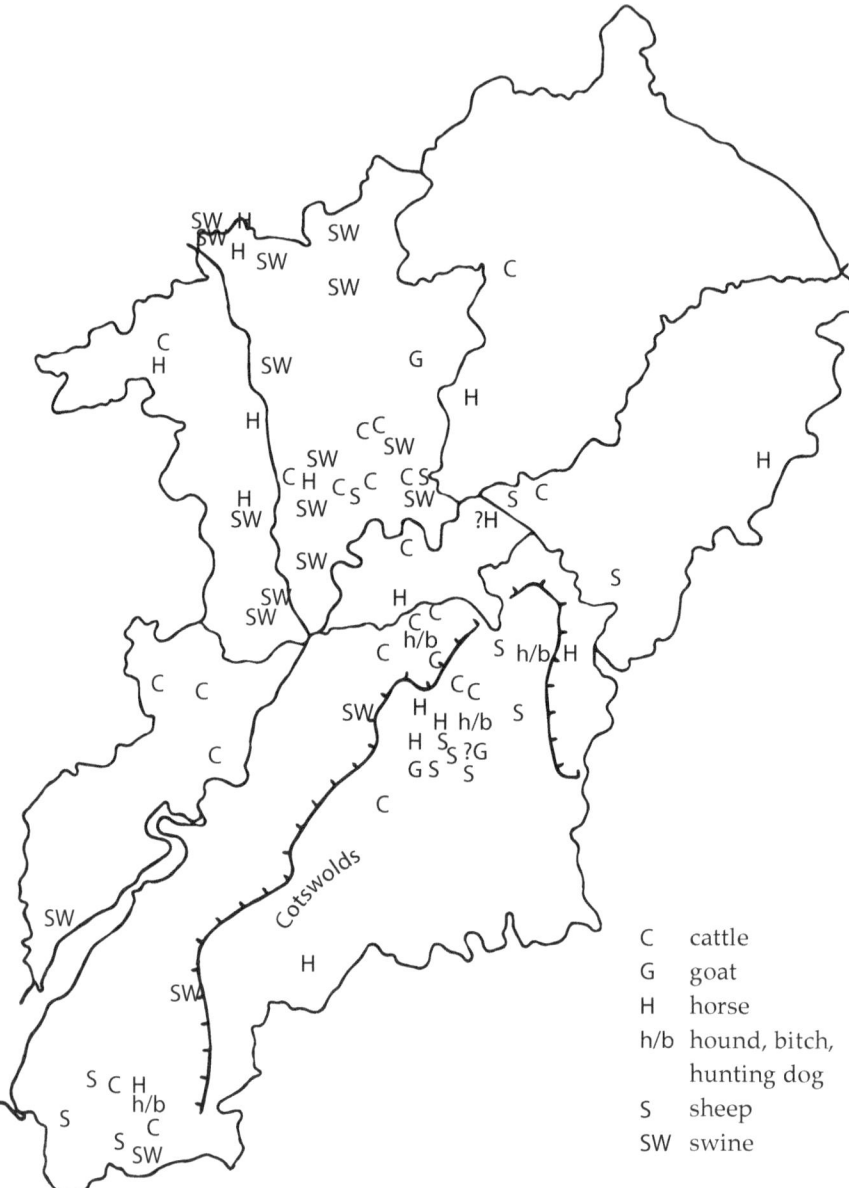

Fig. 11.2 Domestic animals noted in charters and early place-names in the West Midlands (noting regions discussed in the text)

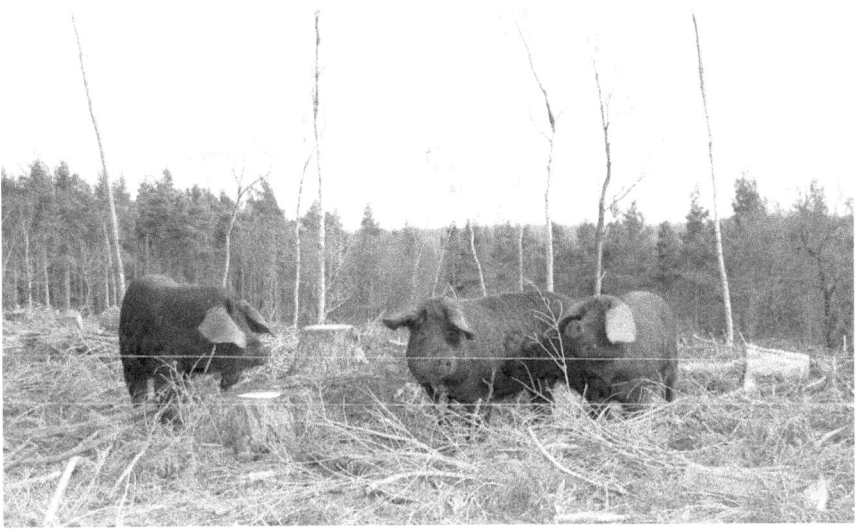

Fig. 11.3 Pigs being used by conservators to clear woodland above an early enclosure in the Wyre Forest, Worcestershire

cattle, sheep, and occasionally goats. In Worcester charters, too, rights could be granted to pasture a certain number of pigs, and one also finds disputes over how many animals could legally be pastured, for example in the ninth century between the king and the Church of Worcester over the right to mast in the woods below the Malverns.[26] A considerable number of *swīn*-names also appear across the wooded uplands of south Staffordshire.[27] There are occasional references to *swin-hagan* ('swine enclosures or fences'), as in the South Hams of Devon or Wrington in Somerset, on the hill above Evesham, and in the Malvern foothills in Worcestershire.[28]

In charters and place-names the reference is usually to OE *swīn*, with *bār* used for the male boar, whether wild or domestic. Various records refer to other terms for pigs, including OE *sugu* ('sow'), *fearh*/ *fōr* ('piglet, hog'), and **hogg*, which are mostly found in later place-names, though Farfield in Belbroughton, Worcestershire (*Forfeld* 817), appears to be *fōr* with *feld* ('hog open land'). Sometimes pigsties (OE *hlōse*) are also mentioned, as in the seasonal Sussex den of *Hlos dionu* belonging to *Derantune* (?Durrington), or a wood called *hlos leage* in Sandford, Devon, while a *hlos mere* is noted on the boundary

---

[26] S 1437; Hooke, *Worcestershire Anglo-Saxon Charter-Bounds*, p. 96.
[27] Della Hooke, 'The landscape of the Staffordshire Hoard', *Staffordshire Archaeological and Historical Society Transactions* 45 (2011), 1–12.
[28] Whether these were intended to keep pigs in or out is unclear, though it was probably the former. S 298, and Hooke, *Pre-Conquest Charter-Bounds of Devon and Cornwall* (Woodbridge, 1994), pp. 105–12; S 371; S 80, and Hooke, *Worcestershire Anglo-Saxon Charter-Bounds*, pp. 46–7.

of Taunton estates in Somerset.[29] Other names refer to the *swān* or swine-herd, such as *swanan dionu* in Sussex, another den belonging to *Derantune* in AD 934, or *swana croft* ('swine/herdsman's croft'), a boundary landmark in Eynsham, Oxfordshire, in 1005; a Swinford is also recorded in the same parish, and *ðone swan weg* ('the swineherd's/ herdsman's way') appears in Wootton, Berkshire.[30] Stock were often moved to seasonal pastures via well-recognised routes, and some of the 'ford' names may indicate where these crossed rivers and streams. Fords are associated in this way with swine, oxen and other cattle, horses, goats, deer and hunting dogs.

Horses were frequently pastured in woods, and 'horse' with *lēah*, a term indicating wood-pasture, is found in charters and place-names, as *horsan leah* at Crux Easton, Hampshire, or the place-name East and West Horsley, Surrey (*Horsalæge* 9th C).[31] There are also many references to studfolds in the charters (places where horses would be bred and reared), which are again often compounded with *lēah*. References to horse crofts, probably enclosed fields where the animals were being pastured, are also found in charters (as in Seckley and Wick, Worcestershire), as are roads that were used by horses (such as a 'horse path' in Bishop's Lydiard, Somerset). The implication of the 100 wild horses bequeathed by Wulfric to Burton Abbey in Staffordshire between 1002 and 1004 is also of interest with respect to wood-pasture, because these animals could have been left to roam free within the woods of Needwood, just as they do in the New Forest today, with surplus foals being rounded up annually, probably to be broken in for riding.[32] Churchmen, especially, might need to travel regularly around their *parochiae*.

Other domestic animals

Most domestic animals appear regularly in place-names and in the minor names of boundary clauses. Looking at one county alone, Oxfordshire, one finds animal place-names referring to cattle (Rotherfield Greys and Rotherfield Peppard in the Chilterns), swine (Swyncombe in the Chilterns and Swinbrook in Wychwood), horses (Horspath), and sheep (Shifford and Shipton on Cherwell), perhaps including tegs or young sheep (Tackley: either OE *tacca*, *tagga*, or

---

[29] S 425; S 405, and Hooke, *Pre-Conquest Charter-Bounds of Devon and Cornwall*, pp. 117–22; S 443.

[30] S 425; S 911; Margaret Gelling, *The Place-Names of Oxfordshire*, part 2, EPNS 24 (Cambridge, 1954), pp. 260, 264; S 858.

[31] Della Hooke, 'Early Medieval Woodland and the Place-Name Term *lēah*', in *A Commodity of Good Names: Essays in Honour of Margaret Gelling*, ed. O. J. Padel and David N. Parsons (Donington, 2008), pp. 365–76.

[32] Ibid.

a personal name *Tæcca*, with *lēah*), the latter two on the Cotswold limestone hills beside the River Cherwell. In Gloucestershire, there are references to cows (Cowley), bulls (Bulley), horses (Horsley), sheep (Shipton Oliffe and Shipton Solers), neat cattle (Natton), oxen (Oxenton), and pigs (Swindon). Indeed, most of the creatures named in charter boundary clauses also gave rise to early place-names. Charters add the cat, deer, and otter.[33]

Horses were valuable animals, used in warrior culture as gifts and for general riding.[34] In wills they were usually (but not always) bequeathed to the king, often along with battle gear, as in the tenth-century will of Ælfgar which bequeathed *tueye suerde fetelsade and tueye bege ayther of fifti mancuses goldes. and þre stedes. and þre scheldes. and þre speren* ('two swords with sheaths, and two armlets, each of fifty *mancuses* of gold, and three stallions and three shields and three spears'), or the will of Wulfgeat of Donington, Shropshire, c. 1000, who bequeathed to his lord '2 horses and 2 swords and 4 shields and 10 mares with 10 colts'.[35] The will of the Ætheling Æthelstan in 1015 included bequests of two horses to his father: one had been a gift from Thurbrand; the other is described as *þæs hwitan horses* ('the white horse') that he had obtained from Leofwine. Æthelstan's will also leaves *anne blacne stedan* ('a black stallion') to Bishop Ælfsige.[36] Some such bequests describe the horses, as with the *four hors so ic best habb* ('four horses, the best that I have'); others specify whether the animals were supplied with or without harness: *feower hors. twa gesadelode. 7 twa ungesadelode* ('four horses, two saddled and two unsaddled').[37] The terms used may differentiate between categories of these animals, from working horses (OE *hors*) to steeds or stallions (*hengest*) or mares. OE *hyrse* ('mare') is found in a reference to *on hyrs leaghe/on ers lege* in West Overton, Wiltshire,[38] a name surviving as Hursley Bottom, while OE *stot* refers to 'a poor horse'. The horse is, however, generally referred by the Old English term *hors, horsa*, as in the place-name Horsey in Norfolk (*Hors(h)eia* 1086), probably here referring to an area of higher ground in the coastal marshes where wild horses would have grazed. At Henstridge in Somerset (*Hengesteshrege* 10th C, *Hengesterich* 1086) stallions (OE *hengest*) were probably pastured on the ridge overlooking Henstridge Marsh.[39] OE *mūl* may either have referred to mules or been used as a personal name.

---

[33] Gelling, *The Place-Names of Oxfordshire*, parts 1 and 2.
[34] Jennifer Neville, 'Hrothgar's Horses: Feral or Thoroughbred?', *ASE* 35 (2006), 3–157.
[35] S 1483, S 1534; Dorothy Whitelock, *Anglo-Saxon Wills* (Cambridge, 1930), nos. 2 and 19.
[36] S 1503.
[37] S 1526, S 1536.
[38] S 449, S 784.
[39] *CDEPN*, pp. 317, 298.

Cattle were valued for their meat, milk and hides as well as being draught animals. The ox (OE *oxa*, and often also *hryðer*) was essential for ploughing and also as a beast of burden (draught-cattle, OE **weorf*, appear in later place-names), while other cattle are referred to as calves (OE *cælf, calf, cealf*), cows (OE *cū*), bulls (OE **bula*), bullocks and heifers (OE **steorce, styrc, stirc, steorc*), neat cattle, and Cornish **bryn* ('cattle'). Very often the references are to places where the cattle were stalled or pastured, but in Himbleton, Worcestershire, the charter-bounds refer to the *eapland eal swa ðe oxa went* ('ploughland as the ox turns').[40] Names for animal houses appearing in charters include *scypen*, like *ðes cincges scypene* ('the king's cowsheds') at Kingston Lisle, Berkshire,[41] or the place-name Shippon in the same county.

These terms are obviously related to husbandry practices. Sheep, too, may be referred to in charters, by the terms *scēap* and its regional variants, *eōwu* ('ewe'), *lamb* ('lamb'), **tacca* and its variants ('young sheep'), *ram* (sometimes difficult to differentiate from OE *hramsa*, 'wild garlic'), and *weðer* ('castrated ram'), the latter perhaps indicated in the *wether stoche* of Purton, Wiltshire.[42] Sheep pasture is indicated by the Old English term **slæget*, recorded in a charter landmark *on þæt slæget* in Horton, Dorset, and in *his sceapa læse* ('pasture for his sheep') in Alton Priors and Patney, Wiltshire.[43] Places where sheep were washed are recorded in Hampshire, as in the *sceap wæscan* ('sheepwash') on the boundary of East Woodhay and Highclere, and in the *uadum nomine Scepesuuasce* ('ford named "Sheep-wash"') on the River Stour at Shipston-on-Stour, Warwickshire, which gave its name to the parish (*Scepwestun* 1086: OE *scēap*, with *wæsce* and *tōn*).[44] Sometimes, sheep were associated with the hill-slopes and valleys where they were pastured, and 'Shipton' and related place-names often indicate regions where they were particularly important. In Gloucestershire a concentration of such names in the valley of the River Coln implies that this part of the Cotswolds, at least, was sheep country (Fig. 11.2).[45] Here also, Yanworth (*Janew(o)rth(e)* 1043–66) may be from OE *(ge)ēan* ('in lamb'). By the eighth century the abbess of St Peter's, Gloucester, had acquired land at Pinswell in Colesbourne in the same region to use as a sheep-walk for bringing in her flocks,[46] and in Offa and Charlemagne's time England was noted for its export

---

[40] S 219 and Hooke, *Worcestershire Anglo-Saxon Charter-Bounds*, pp. 129–34.
[41] S 713.
[42] S 1586.
[43] S 969; S 1403.
[44] S 680, S 565, S 383, S 258; S 61.
[45] Della Hooke, 'Early Cotswold Woodland', *Journal of Historical Geography* 4.4 (1978), 333–41 (pp. 340–1).
[46] S 1782; H. P. R. Finberg, 'Some Early Gloucestershire Estates', in *Gloucestershire Studies*, ed. H. P. R. Finberg (Leicester, 1957), pp. 1–16 (pp. 12–14).

of woollen cloaks. In medieval times the Cotswold region was to grow immensely wealthy on the back of its wool trade, a prosperity reflected in the richness of its churches.

The goat also appears frequently. OE *gāt* is normally a nanny goat, the most frequently mentioned, but *ticce*, **tige* ('kid') also occurs, as in *tichan stedes hagan* ('the enclosure at the kid's place or homestead') at Wokefield and Sulhamstead Bannister, Berkshire; *gātbucca* ('billy goat') features in *buccan crundel* ('the goat's quarry/ravine') in a charter of Leckhampstead, Berkshire.[47] The term *bucca* also occurs in an enigmatic reference to the execution of a *ceorl* at [Broad] Chalke, Wiltshire, described in AD 955 as being *for þan buccan* ('because of the goat').[48] *Bucca* ('buck'), could also refer to a male deer, and another explanation for this execution might have been because the person hanged there had illegally taken a deer or goat.

Some charters note the kind and number of domestic animals belonging to a particular estate. In the late eighth century the minster of Westbury on Trym, Gloucestershire, was called upon to pay render to the king which included *vii hriðru 7 six weðeras* ('seven cattle/oxen and six wethers').[49] When Oswald, Bishop of Worcester and Archbishop of York, leased Compton Greenfield and Marsh, Gloucestershire, in AD 990, it included *xxx. euwna mid hiora lambum. 7 IIII. oxan 7 twa cy 7 an hors* ('thirty ewes with their lambs, and four oxen and two cows and a horse');[50] Luddington, in the Avon valley of Warwickshire, was leased in the early eleventh century by the community at Worcester on the understanding that the lessee should return the estate three years later with its *xii. þeowe men. 7 .II. gesylhðe oxan. 7 .I. hund sceapa. 7 half hundred forðra cornes* ('twelve slaves and two teams of oxen and 100 sheep and fifty fothers of corn').[51] Wills also frequently bequeathed the domestic stock associated with a particular estate. Thus Æthelgifu made bequests to various churches *c*. 980×990, which included *XXX. boues, XX. de Getesdene, et x. de Acersce, et XX. uaccas, X. de Getesdene, et X. de Acersce* ('thirty oxen [?and bulls: Lat. *boves*], twenty from Gaddesdon [Hertfordfire], and ten from *Acersce*, and twenty cows, ten from Gaddesdon and ten from *Acersce*'), plus sheep, including ewes with their lambs, from an estate at Langford, Buckinghamshire.[52] It seems that even in intensively cultivated regions mixed farming predominated, with sheep mentioned alongside working oxen.

---

[47] S 578; S 491, and Gelling, *The Place-Names of Berkshire*, part 3, p. 662.
[48] S 582.
[49] S 146.
[50] S 1362; A. J. Robertson, *Anglo-Saxon Charters*, 2nd edn (Cambridge, 1956), no. 65, pp. 134–5.
[51] S 1421; Della Hooke, *Warwickshire Anglo-Saxon Charter-Bounds* (Woodbridge, 1999), p. 108.
[52] S 1497; Dorothy Whitelock and Neil R. Ker, *The Will of Æthelgifu* (Oxford, 1968).

Animal bone assemblages seem to bear this out, for example at *Hamwic*, where the most common bones were those of sheep/goats and cattle, closely followed by domestic pigs (although animals had been brought into the town from outlying estates). At Fishergate, York, the eighth-century fauna was again dominated by cattle and sheep, with smaller numbers of pig; similar evidence appears at West Stow in Suffolk.[53]

Several names of hundreds appear to refer to a place where an animal's head had been placed upon a stake. Those referring to swine include *Swinesheafde* Hundred 974, the site of a court leet of Oswaldslow Hundred, Worcestershire, and Swineshead Hundred, Gloucestershire, in 1086. As Smith notes: 'the allusion may be to the heathen custom of setting up an animal's head on a post as part of sacrificial rites'.[54] Several such names also appear among charter boundary landmarks: two boundary clauses of Bishops Cleeve and adjacent lands in Gloucestershire refer to landmarks that include a stallion's head (*hengestes heafod*), beside a major *herepað* route linking Cirencester and Winchcombe, and close to an Iron Age hillfort (see Fig. 11.6).[55] Watts, however, following the view of Gelling and Cole, states that 'the theory that this class of name was literally meant and referred to the ritual exposure of animal heads in pagan times is no longer accepted'; many other place-name scholars now follow Gelling and Cole in preferring to see such names as originating as descriptions of local topographical features. This applies especially to Swineshead names, which Gelling and Cole see as 'an appellative for projecting ridges in low ground' that resemble a 'swine's snout'.[56] However, it is not always easy to identify the local topographical feature that was being described, especially when charters and early place-names refer in this way to pigs, horses and badgers. Certainly the heads of felons appear on occasion to have been impaled on stakes after execution, sometimes to be displayed beside routeways; an example is the *heafod stocce* of Donnington in the north Gloucestershire Cotswolds, which stood beside the Roman Fosse Way. In this busy and accessible spot, at the end of a spur of high ground, the severed head may have served

---

[53] The statistics are summarised in Derek Yalden, *The History of British Mammals* (London, 1999), pp. 136–40. For West Stow, see Stanley West, *West Stow, The Anglo-Saxon Village*, vol. 1: *Text*, East Anglia Archaeology Report 25 (Suffolk, 1985), pp. 89, 169; for *Hamwic*, see Jennifer Bourdillon and Jenny Coy, 'The Animal Bones', in *Excavations at Melbourne Street, Southampton, 1971–6*, ed. P. Holsworth, CBA Research Report 33 (York, 1980), pp. 79–121; for Fishergate, see Terry P. O'Connor, *Bones from 46–54 Fishergate*, Archaeology of York 15/4 (London, 1991).

[54] A. H. Smith, *The Place-Names of Gloucestershire*, part 3, EPNS 40 (Cambridge, 1964), pp. 74–5, and part 4, EPNS 41 (Cambridge, 1965), p. 3.

[55] A *beranheafde* in Abbots Morton, Worcestershire, might be a either a bear's head or, perhaps more likely, 'barley headland'. S 441, S 1549; S 78.

[56] *CDEPN*, p. 595; Gelling and Cole, *The Landscape of Place-Names*, pp. 175–6.

as an eye-catching reminder of the punishment meted out to criminals, as there are other references to thieves in this region.[57] Hundreds, too, had recognised judgement and execution sites. However, this does not explain the reason for displaying an animal's head, if that did indeed happen.

Animals of the Hunt: Deer and Other Game Animals

Deer were valued as a source of venison long before the Normans arrived in England, and were often caught by being driven into nets by huntsmen with dogs. The hart, a mature red deer usually past its fifth year, and stronger than the female hind, was the favoured quarry. The wallowing place of the hart is noted in Stoke Prior and Alvechurch in Worcestershire (along with, in the latter boundary clause, a 'roe-deer's lair'); there is also a hart ford in Oldberrow, Warwickshire, and a hart hill, coomb, spring and brook in the Evenlode valley of north-east Gloucestershire, a county with many other 'deer' names (Fig. 11.4).[58] Such references are common, especially compounded with *lēah*, but a hind leap, perhaps a leap-gate, is noted in Bishop's Cleeve on the Gloucestershire Cotswolds and in the south-east of the county, and in the place-name Hindlip in Worcestershire (*hindehlyp* in 966); a 'leap-gate' is also recorded in the charter of Cold Ashton in south-east Gloucestershire.[59] The north Cotswolds were noted as hunting country, and in AD 855 Blockley minster was freed by King Burgred of Mercia from dues which included *pastu. et ab refectione omnium ancipitrum et falconum in terra Mercensium et omnium uenatorum regis uel principis nisi ipsorum tantum qui in prouincia Hwicciorum sunt* ('the feeding and maintenance of all hawks and falcons in the land of the Mercians, and of all huntsmen of the king or ealdorman except only those who are in the province of the Hwicce').[60]

The hart or stag is frequently encountered from the north of England down to Kent, associated with springs, fords, islands and streams, hills, woods and coastal headlands. By medieval times, at least, the Normans had reintroduced the fallow deer (which may already have been introduced in small numbers in Roman times, and was introduced again in the later part of the early medieval period), and this rapidly became the favourite animal of the chase, hunted best

---

[57] S 115; Della Hooke, *Anglo-Saxon Landscapes: The Charter Evidence*, BAR British Series 95 (Oxford, 1981), p. 200. The *drakenhorde* landmark at South Damerham (S 513, above) follows a reference to such a 'headstake' which must have stood at a high point beside the Rockbourne–Damerham road.

[58] S 60; S 1272; S 79; S 1238, S 1548 and S 109.

[59] S 141, S 1549; S 414.

[60] S 202.

on horseback. An early reference that may be to fallow deer (OE *fealu*, referring to the colour) can be noted in a charter boundary of land at Badby, Dodford and Everdon, Northamptonshire, referring to *fealuwes lea* (preserved in the parish name Fawsley), which Johansson translates as 'forest frequented by fallow deer'.[61] The animal possibly appears in several other place-names, too, such as Fawley, Berkshire. Hough questions whether some early references in place-names might not be to OE **pohha/*pocca* ('pock, pustule'), alluding to the distinctive spots of the fallow deer.[62] It is arguable that fallow deer bucks may have been brought in during the tenth and eleventh centuries as visually attractive animals, but the evidence is not wholly convincing and requires further archaeological evidence.[63] In the late tenth-century *Colloquy* attributed to Ælfric, the Old English terms *rann* and *rægan* ('roe-buck' and 'does') are used to translate the *dammas* ('fallow deer') of Classical sources, which may indicate that the author was unfamiliar with fallow deer in Anglo-Saxon England. However, Hough suggests that this is a mistranslation, and so proves no such thing; he also notes that *dā* ('doe') was already in use, thus strengthening the case for the presence of fallow deer in late-Saxon England.[64] The roe was a less valuable animal, and in central Worcestershire a roe-deer hedge was almost certainly meant to try to keep these away from crops, as was another in Bishop's Cleeve where there was also a *rahhlinc* or slope below. In place-names, too, deer are referred to in the name of Durford in Sussex and Deerhurst in Gloucestershire.

The hare (OE *hara*) was not particularly valued as game, but places hares frequented are referred to in charter landmarks – including a spring in Worcestershire, a mere in Gloucestershire and a hill in Wiltshire, although the hare is usually an animal of field and heath, though again the term can be difficult to distinguish in place-names from OE *hār* ('grey, hoar'). Some of the hounds, dogs and bitches noted are likely to have referred to hunting dogs, which could also be indicated by OE *ræcc*; Rochford, Worcestershire (*Recesford* 1086),

---

[61] S 495; Christer Johansson, *Old English Place-Names Containing Lēah* (Stockholm, 1975); Eilert Ekwall, *The Concise English Dictionary of English Place-Names*, 4th edn (Oxford, 1960), p. 176.

[62] Hough, 'Place-Name Evidence for an Anglo-Saxon Animal Name', pp. 2–3; Carole Hough, 'Deer in Sussex Place-Names', *Antiquaries Journal* 88 (2008), 43–7. This is not an interpretation favoured by Watts (*CDEPN*), who notes that the Old English term also means 'pouch' and for Poughill in Devon could have been used in a topographical sense.

[63] N. Sykes and R. F. Carden, 'Were Fallow Deer Spotted (OE **pohha/*pocca*) in Anglo-Saxon England? Reviewing the Evidence for *dama dama dama* in Early Medieval Europe', *Med Arch* 55 (2011), 139–62 (p. 142).

[64] Sykes and Carden, 'Were Fallow Deer Spotted?', p. 142; *Ælfric's Colloquy*, ed. G. N. Garmonsway, Exeter Medieval Texts & Studies (Exeter, 1991), p. 24; Carole Hough, 'Ælfric of Eynsham, Pucklechurch, and Evidence for Fallow Deer in Anglo-Saxon England', *Nomina* 35 (2012), 103–30.

for instance, may be 'hunting-dog's ford'.⁶⁵ Deer seem to have been recorded most often in semi-wooded areas, as shown on Fig. 11.4 (though the distribution here is influenced by charter coverage).

Another quarry, the *bār* ('boar') is noted in charters in Savernake Forest, Wiltshire, in references to a *bares stige/bares anstige* ('boar's uphill path'); in a thicket at Crondall (*baran fyrhðe*); and in a wood in North Stoneham (both in Hampshire).⁶⁶ Place-names add, among others, Barwell, Leicestershire (*Barwalele* 1043, *Barewell(e)* 1086). In these cases, however, the references may be to male domesticated pigs. *Eofor* ('wild boar') is more common in place-names, often compounded with *lēah* as in the name Everley, North Yorkshire (*Eurelai* 1086), or Everleigh, Wiltshire (*Eburlea(g)h* 8th C). The term *bār* is easily confused with *bere* or *bær* ('barley'), and either is a possibility in the Domesday place-name Barlow in Derbyshire; *bār* may even be confused with *bera* ('bear'), the latter having still been present in Britain in Roman times, though there is no clear evidence in place-names indicating their survival in this period (see above).

The British beaver was hunted to extinction early in the medieval period, but place-names such as *beferburnan*, close to Worcester, show that beavers were present there in the early tenth century, although perhaps already in reduced numbers (unless the name referred to earlier circumstances).⁶⁷ The lynx (OE *lox*) was also present in northern Britain until about 1200, and may be referred to in a later Shropshire place-name Lostford, recorded in 1121, which Gelling translated as 'lynx ford'.⁶⁸ As dangerous predators of domestic stock, wolves were often captured in pits, such as those noted to the east and west of Worcester (*wulf*, 'wolf', with *seað*, 'pit') at Broadwas and Bredicot, and others found in the compound *wulfputt/wulfputte* ('wolf-pit') in the bounds of Olveston, Gloucestershire, and Crondall and Itchell, Hampshire.⁶⁹ A *wulfhaga* may have been a strong barrier protecting game reserves from wolves, as at Longdon, Worcestershire.⁷⁰ Other

---

⁶⁵ *CDEPN*, p. 504.
⁶⁶ S 336, S 416; S 418.
⁶⁷ Yalden, *The History of British Mammals*, p. 134, fig. 5.2; S 1280 (AD 904), S 1596, S 401). For a discussion of the place-name Bevereley, see Richard Coates, 'Beverley: A Beaver's Lodge Place', *JEPNS* 33 (2002), 17–22.
⁶⁸ Margaret Gelling, *The Place-Names of Shropshire*, part 5, EPNS 82 (Nottingham, 2006), p. 153; the lynx may also be noted in the bounds of a spurious charter, allegedly of AD 975, for Bleadon, Somset, in a landmark *usque loxanwode warūtreen* ('as far as *lox* ?lynx wood' with ?*weargtrēow* 'gallows') (S 804).
⁶⁹ S 126, S 1369, and Hooke, *Worcestershire Anglo-Saxon Charter-Bounds*, pp. 87–90, 311–14; S 664, S 1558. Another wolf pit is recorded in a post-Conquest boundary clause of *Horselege* in Wolverley, Worcestershire (plus a hen's wood and a studfold); see *Hemingi Chartularium Ecclesiae Wigorniensis*, ed. Thomas Hearne (Oxford, 1723), pp. 429–30 – not shown on Fig. 11.2.
⁷⁰ Della Hooke, 'Pre-Conquest Woodland: Its Distribution and Usage', *Agricultural History Review* 37 (1989), 113–29; Della Hooke, 'Royal Forests – Hunting and Other Forest Use in

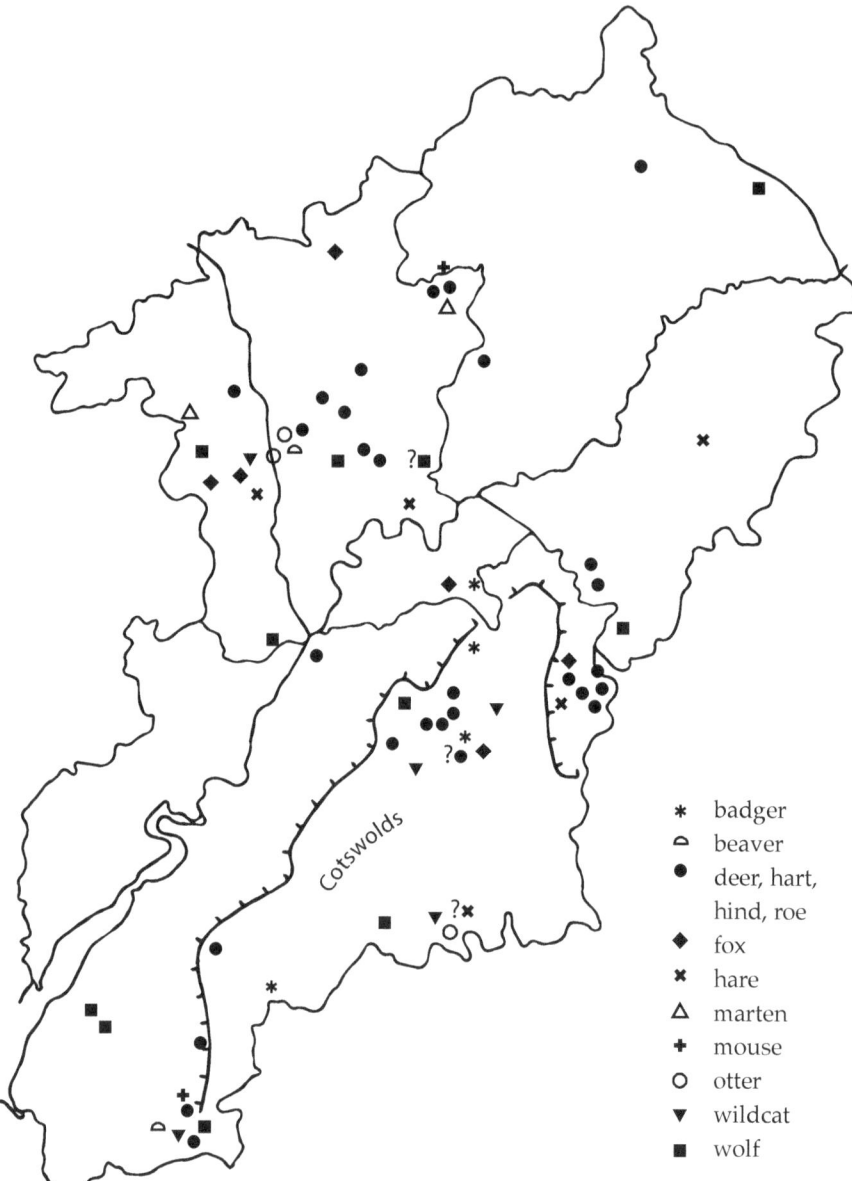

Fig. 11.4 Wild Animals noted in charters and early place-names in the West Midlands

places were noted as being frequented by wolves in both charter-bounds and place-names – such as hills, ridges and slopes, coombs, woods, watery locations like springs, brooks and meres, and barrows. Pits for catching wolves are noted in charter-bounds only a few miles each side of the town and burh of Worcester, and strong boundary to keep them out of deer reserves features in the woods in the south-west of the same county.[71] Wolford in Warwickshire (*Volwarde*, *Worwarde* 1086) appears to have been the 'place to watch for wolves' (OE *wulf*, *weard*). The wolf was still present in England in medieval times, but had been hunted to extinction by the sixteenth century.[72]

Other wild animals

There are many other kinds of wild animal mentioned in charters and early place-names. Apart from those game animals already noted, one frequently finds foxes (and vixen), and otters in rivers. Less common, but still recorded, are seals beside the sea; martens or weasels in woods (as in *forð to mearðes (le)age* in the charter-bounds of *Bedintun*, Pillaton, Staffordshire, or Martley, Worcestershire);[73] wildcats; and badgers (OE *brocc*; possibly too OE **bagga*, from its bag-like shape), to name just a few. One can even encounter tiny animals such as voles, mice (OE *mūs* in Moseley, Warwickshire), or shrew-mice (OE *screāwa* in Stoke Canon, Devon).[74]

Birds in Charters and Place-Names

It is references to birds that are perhaps most surprising as charter boundary landmarks – one might expect these to be rather ephemeral as landmarks, but in association with topographical features the list of bird species recorded is remarkably long.[75] It may be significant that wildlife habitats were particularly rich in the less intensively cultivated environment of the Anglo-Saxon period, and that birdsong is likely to have been much more noticeable (as it is in less densely

---

Medieval England', in *New Perspectives on People and Forests*, ed. Eva Ritter and Dainis Dauksta (London, 2011); S 786.

[71] Ibid.
[72] Aleks Pluskowski, *Wolves and the Wilderness in the Middle Ages* (Woodbridge, 2006), p. 97.
[73] S 879, and Della Hooke, *The Landscape of Anglo-Saxon Staffordshire: The Charter Evidence* (Keele, 1983).
[74] S 389.
[75] For a linguistic study of bird-names, see Peter R. Kitson, 'Old English Bird-Names', *ES* 78:6 (1997), 481–505; and Peter R. Kitson, 'Old English Bird-Names (ii)', *ES* 79.1 (1998), 2–22. These are not, however, confined to the early medieval period or to charter and place-name evidence.

settled parts of Europe today), especially given that most people lived close to the land.

It is not difficult to see why meres and ponds might be characterised by the presence of birds or fowl – *fugel mere* is a not uncommon landmark, occurring, for instance, in Alderminster, Warwickshire; Willersey and Evenlode, Gloucestershire; and Ham, Wiltshire.[76] These wetland birds are not the seagulls and Canada geese we see so often today, but other species, including cranes (the term *cran, cron, cranoc* probably also covering the heron, together with **corn* – a metathesised form of *cron*); these frequented, for instance, the *cranmere* of Wormleighton, Warwickshire; Pendock, Worcestershire; and Edington, Wiltshire, as well as numerous other meres scattered across Midlands and southern England.[77] The Anglo-Saxon interest in cranes may be revealed in the reference to a *cranhunteresstone* at Butleigh in Somerset;[78] indeed, the crane was virtually exterminated about 400 years ago, and is only now being re-introduced. Apart from cranes and herons, other birds associated with meres, brooks and springs (and sometimes pits) include ducks, hens and cocks, doves, geese and swans, crows and rooks, diving birds (OE *dūfedoppa*), a blackbird, a wren, and possibly seagulls. OE *snīte* ('snipe'), a bird now much less common than in former times, is found in *snitan ige* ('snipe island') in the bounds of Shellingford, Berkshire.[79]

Hawks (OE *hafoc*), on the other hand, were often noticed circling over high ground such as hills, ridges, slopes or barrows, just as they are today: such places include ridges at Bentley, Holt, Worcestershire, and Acton Beauchamp in Herefordshire; and barrows at Uffington in Berkshire, Witney in Oxfordshire, and on the Deerhurst estates in Gloucestershire (this bird was apparently common over the Gloucestershire Cotswolds: Fig. 11.5).[80] Hawks, described as 'big' and 'small', were used by the Anglo-Saxon fowler, after being taken from the wild in autumn to be tamed and trained for falconry. The eyries of the native hawks are, of course, sometimes noted in Domesday Book, and possibly also included those of the much-prized peregrine falcon – not a member of the *Accipitrodae* but of the *Falconidae*. This species is powerful, bold, and fast, and was later described in the fifteenth-century *Boke of St Albans* (1486) as the hawk for an earl, though this is not a work to be taken too literally. Others like the true hawks included the goshawk (described as fit for a yeoman) and the

---

[76] S 786, S 1599, S 1325, S 416.
[77] S 588, S 1314, S 765.
[78] S 270a.
[79] S 1546; S 1546, Gelling, *The Place-Names of Berkshire*, part 3, pp. 696–7.
[80] S 1301, S 776, S 561, S 771 and S 1001, S 1551.

Beasts, Birds and Other Creatures in Charters and Place-Names

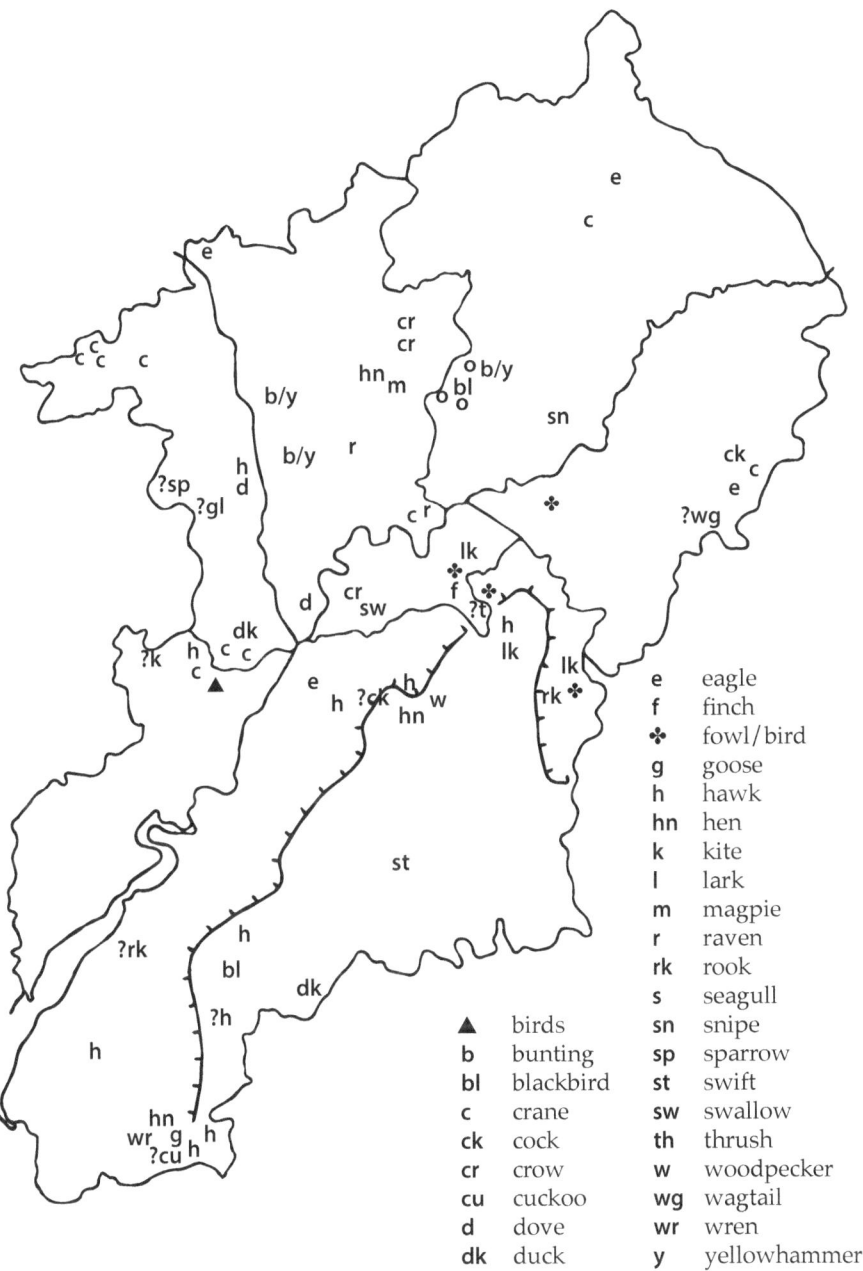

Fig. 11.5 Birds noted in charters and early place-names in the West Midlands

female sparrowhawk ('fit for a priest'),[81] but the charter hawks may have included a wide array of birds such as buzzards and kestrels, although OE *wrocc*, as in Wroxton, Oxfordshire, or Wroxhall, Isle of Wight, may explicitly refer to a buzzard or even a marsh harrier.[82] Another term for a hawk was OE *pyttel*, possibly referring to the kestrel, which is found associated with a valley in East Overton, Wiltshire, where the bounds run *on pytteldene* (this term may also have referred to the marsh harrier in Dorset).[83] The kite, OE *cyte, cȳta, cēta*, may be referred to in Wytham, North and South Hinksey, in Berkshire where the boundary ran *wið utan cytan igge* ('outside the island of the kite'), and at Welford in the same county, where a boundary ran *on cyta sihtes ford/Cytan seohtresford* ('to the kite's drain ford').[84] Eagles are also noted in charters, often in association with high places such as hills and ridges, as in *on earnes hricg* in Crediton, Devon, and *on earnes hlingc/hlince* in Cearn (?Charmouth, Dorset), but sometimes with specific trees such as *earnes beame* in Bromley, Kent (assuming these do refer to the bird rather than an individual named person).[85]

Various species apart from hawks were associated with barrows, whose elevation perhaps made birds particularly noticeable. In charter boundary clauses one finds barrows associated with larks (OE *lāwerce*), as near Evesham, Worcestershire; Cutsdean on the high Cotswolds, Gloucestershire; and Uffington, Berkshire. Swallows (OE *swealwa*) are noted on Bredon Hill, Worcestershire; swifts (OE *swift*) in a landmark *on swiftan beorh* at Calmsden, Gloucestershire; and crows in Winterbourne Monkton, Wiltshire.[86]

Ravens and crows, apart from frequenting certain locations, woods, or particular trees, tended to have sinister connotations – as scavengers of the battlefield – and were perceived in many northern European cultures as ill omens, along with magpies. The *crowanstaple* of Uplyme in Devon[87] could conceivably have been a gibbet – all members of the *Corvidae* family (which includes the magpie), were ever ready to feed on carrion. The crow is a common bird in charters, found associated not only with thorns and an oak, but also with such diverse landscape features as hills and coombs, quarries or ravines, woods, and even watery locations such as meres, brooks and fords. OE *crāwa/e* may incorporate ravens and jackdaws, but a raven (OE *hræfn*) seems to

---

[81] John Cummins, *The Hound and the Hawk: The Art of Medieval Hunting* (New York, 1988), p. 188.
[82] Gelling, *The Place-Names of Oxfordshire*, part 2, p. 409; *CDEPN*, p. 705; Kitson, 'Old English Bird-Names (ii)', p. 10.
[83] S 449; W. B. Lockwood, *The Oxford Book of British Bird-Names* (Oxford, 1984).
[84] S 663, and Gelling, *The Place-Names of Berkshire*, part 3, pp. 729–30; S 622, and Gelling, *The Place-Names of Berkshire*, part 3, pp. 663–4.
[85] S 255, S 443, S 331, and S 864.
[86] S 202.
[87] S 442.

be distinguished in *hrefnes pytt* ('the ravens' pit') on the boundary of Poden, Worcestershire; rooks (OE *hròc*) are mentioned specifically in *hroces ford* at Sandford, Devon, and jackdaws (OE **cā,*cādac*) in *cadaca hrygc*.[88]

These birds also appear in early place-names: *Cronuchomme* (*cranoc* with *hamm*) was an early name for Evesham, an estate and minster site located within a loop of the River Avon in Worcestershire. Cranes are particularly common in other early place-names, including Cransford, Suffolk; Cranford, Greater London; Great Cransley, Northamptonshire; Cranmore, Somerset; and Cranwell, Lincolnshire. Many of these are naturally associated with watery locations such as meres, springs and fords, although Great Cransley, Northamptonshire, is 'crane's wood', and Cornwood (*corna wudu*, Worcestershire, *c*. 957), may also be **cron* ('crane') wood.[89] Cranoe, Leicestershire, is 'crow's hill-spur', and Crawley, Hampshire, 'crow wood'. The hawk is also commonly found in place-names like Hawkesbury, Gloucestershire, but many more are medieval recordings, and *Hafoc* could be adopted as a personal name.[90] It was eagles (OE *earn*) that were noted at Upper Arley, Staffordshire; Crediton, Devon; Earnley, Sussex; and Taunton estates in Somerset. OE *pyttel* ('hawk or kestrel') is found in the place-name Pudleston, Herefordshire (*Pillesdvne* 1086).

The magpie seems to be referred to in the place-name Tardebigge, Worcestershire (*æt tærdebicgan c*. 1000, and *Tyrdebicgan* 11th C boundary clause), a name that has recently been seen as of British derivation – *Ardd-y-Big* in modern Welsh – and translated as 'height of the magpie'.[91] This was a place that may have been of pagan significance: a series of crucifixes once stood beside roads approaching the hill upon which the present church stands, and the church itself is dedicated to St Bartholomew, the 'caster-out of devils'.[92] OE *agu* for magpie does not seem to appear in the charters, but *higera, higra*, which might refer to the jay, magpie, or jackdaw, seems to be referred to in the landmark *on hingran hongran* ('to the magpie's hanger/hanging wood') in Cholsey and Moulsford, Berkshire; a later name,

---

[88] For ravens, see S 1591a, and Hooke, *Worcestershire Anglo-Saxon Charter-Bounds*, pp. 382–3; for rooks, S 890, and Hooke, *Pre-Conquest Charter-Bounds of Devon and Cornwall*, pp. 181–4; for jackdaws, S 293.

[89] S 1185; A. Mawer and F. M. Stenton, *The Place-Names of Worcestershire*, EPNS 4 (Cambridge, 1927), p. 54. For a study of crane place-names (of all periods), see S. Boisseau and D. W. Yalden, 'The Former Status of the Crane *Grus grus* in Britain', *Ibis* 140 (1998), 482–500, drawing upon Gelling, *Place-Names in the Landscape*.

[90] CDEPN, p. 288.

[91] S 1534 and S 1598; A. Breeze 'The Celts and Tardebigge', *Transactions of the Worcestershire Archaeological Society* 3rd ser. 20 (2006), 75–6. This interpretation has not been accepted by all place-name scholars, however, as the syntax is that of a Welsh-speaking population rather than being a British survival.

[92] Della Hooke, 'Christianity and the "Sacred Tree"', in *Trees and Timber in the Anglo-Saxon World*, ed. Michael D. J. Bintley and Michael G. Shapland (Oxford, 2013), pp. 228–50.

Harlow Hill, Northumberland (13th C), may also incorporate this term with *hlāw*, hence 'magpie hill'.⁹³ Other birds recorded with *lēah* represent a wide range of species, the commonest being the crow and the eagle, but also including the raven, wren, crane, goose, woodcock and cuckoo, the latter (OE *gēac*), in the place-name Yaxley, Suffok (*Jacheslacheslea, Lachele(i)a* 1086). Storrington, Sussex, is 'the storks' farm' (*Storgetune* 1086; OE **storc*). As with some animal names, place-names referring to certain bird species have been the subject of several studies attempting to ascertain historical distribution, but these are not confined to Old English sources, and rarely distinguish or concentrate upon names recorded before the Norman Conquest.⁹⁴

Other birds may find their way into the charters and early place-names by being associated with locally known places or landmarks: *pincan dene* in Childswickham, Worcestershire, may be a valley frequented by finches (OE *finc*, by-form *pinca*), as may be the post called *finces stapole* at Meon, Hampshire;⁹⁵ finch place-names include Finchhampstead, Berkshire (*Fincham(e)sted(e)* 1086). A landmark *turtlingcford* in Wick Episcopi, Worcestershire, may refer to the turtle-dove, noted at a ford there; pigeons or doves may have given their name to the *culverþorne* of Norton, Wiltshire (OE *dūfa* and *culfre* refer to this bird).⁹⁶ Other birds that appear are **succa* and variants, perhaps a reference to the wagtail (as in a pit in Kineton, Warwickshire); *fina*, a woodpecker (a meadow in Bishop's Cleeve, Gloucestershire; Fig. 11.6); wren, found with *lēah* in *on wrænnan leage* ('wood frequented by wrens') in Pucklechurch, Gloucestershire; OE *māse* ('the tit, tit-mouse'), as in *on masan mere* ('to the pond frequented by the tit-mouse', at Hawkridge Wood, Berkshire); and *þrostle* ('thrush' – a name surviving in dialect as 'throstle'), as in *þrostle well* ('thrush's spring') at Bleadon, Somset. Similarly, **þryscele* (also *þristling, þrysce*), another term for 'thrush', is found in the place-name Thrushelton, Devon (*Tresetone* 1086), meaning 'thrush farm or settlement'. In contrast, *þristlinga dene* in Broadway, Worcestershire, may be either 'bold person's valley' or 'thrush's valley' – such are the pitfalls of interpreting these terms.⁹⁷ OE *ōsle* ('blackbird') may be found in the place-name Ozleworth, Gloucestershire (*Oslan wyrÿ* 940, *Osleuueorde* 1086), though this could be the personal name Ōsla; *fiscere* may refer

---

[93] S 354; Gelling, *The Place-Names of Berkshire*, part 3, p. 757; *CDEPN*, p. 280.
[94] Evans *et al.*, 'The History of Eagles'; Margaret Gelling, 'Anglo-Saxon Eagles', *LSE* 18 (1987), 173–81; P. G. Moore, 'Ravens (*Corvus corax corax* L.) in the British Landscape: A Thousand Years of Ecological Biogeography in Place-Names', *Journal of Biogeography* 29 (2002), 1039–54.
[95] S 1370; S 1585.
[96] S 811.
[97] In order, S 773; S 1549; S 553; S 607; S 804; S 786.

to the kingfisher *oþ fisceres dene* in Buckland, Berkshire;[98] *pūr* ('dunlin', and perhaps 'bittern' or 'snipe') appears in *to pures fenne* at Rollington in Bulbridge, in *besuðan pur wuda* in Easole, Kent, and also in Purleigh, Essex (*Purlea* 988, *Purlai* 1086);[99] *snīte* ('snipe'), noted above, features in Snitterfield, Warwickshire (*Snitefeld* 1086 – 'the open land of the Snipe'). The term **wōp* in *wopig hangran*? may relate to an unidentified bird associated with a hanger (a wood on a slope) in Welford, Berkshire. *Cocc*² ('cock, ?woodcock') appears in *cocbroc* in Watchfield, Berkshire, and OE *hrucge* ('woodcock') in *on hrucgan cumbes ford* in Crediton, Devon.[100] A landmark *on omer lond* in Cudley, Worcestershire,[101] may be a reference to land frequented by the yellowhammer (a bird of the bunting family, OE *omer, amer*), and the place-name Amberley, Sussex (*Ambrelie* 1086), may be 'yellowhammer/bunting wood'. Oldberrow in Warwickshire, an estate within the once well-wooded Arden, may be *ūle* 'owl hill or barrow'; the charter also refers to an *ulan wyllan* ('owl spring') and an *osland mere* (?blackbird mere'), a *buntinge dic* (? 'buntings' dyke' – *bunting* being a term found in later place-names), and a hart ford.[102] Other 'owl' names include Ulley in Treeton, South Yorkshire (*Ollei(e)* 1086, 'owl wood'); Ulcombe in Kent (*Uulacumb* 941, *Olecūbe* 1086) 'owls' coomb'; and, with *ūf*, Ousden in Suffolk (*Vuesdana* 1086), 'owl's valley'.

Other small birds also find their way into early place-names: in addition to those noted above, *stint* ('stint', and possibly 'sandpiper or dunlin') appears in the name of Stinsford, Dorset (*Stincteford* 1086 – 'sandpiper ford'),[103] and *gēac* ('cuckoo') in Yaxley, Cambridgeshire, Yaxley, Suffolk, and Yaxham, Norfolk; Iffley, Oxfordshire, may recall plovers (*Gifetelea* 1004, cognate with MHG *gîbitz*).[104] The rare OE *pāwa, pāwe* ('peafowl') is found in Peamore, Devon (*Peumera* 1086). Some Old English bird names do not appear to find their way into early names, and are often recorded as minor names only later. Among these are *hrāgra* ('heron') and *hulfestre* ('plover').[105] So many birds appear in charters and place-names that it may be asked why some are missing: the robin, for instance, OE *rædda* or *rudduc* (found in glossaries), a

---

[98] S 639.
[99] S 493; S 1434.
[100] In order, S 552; S 413; S 255.
[101] S 1329.
[102] S 79; Hooke, *Warwickshire Anglo-Saxon Charter-Bounds*, pp. 30–6.
[103] 'Sandpiper' is not recorded before the seventeenth century but OE *pipere* could also indicate a wading-bird; Hough, 'Place-Name Evidence for Old English Bird-Names', pp. 64–5.
[104] Gelling, *The Place-Names of Oxfordshire*, part 1, p. 33, citing Ekwall, *The Concise Oxford Dictionary of English Place-Names*, p. 262.
[105] See, too, Hough's discussion of bird names for interpretations of place-names that may refer to OE **dunnoc* ('hedge-sparrow'), nightingales, and other birds; Hough, 'Place-Name Evidence for Old English Bird-Names'.

distinctive small bird, has not so far been noted in early place-names. Gelling, in her study of Oxfordshire place-names, notes the following bird names recorded in 1086: crows, as in Crowmarsh (*Cravmares*), Crowell (*Clawelle*), Crowmarsh Preston and Crowmarsh Bittle Farm in Benson (*Cravmeres*); woodpeckers, as in Finmere (*Finemere*); herons or cranes, in Cornbury (*Corneberie*); buzzards, in Wroxton (*Werochestan*); and possibly plovers, in Iffley (*Givetelei*). Charters, apart from references to birds in general, add hawks (*on hafoces hlew*); a *dufedoppa* ('diving water fowl', ?dabchick), found in the charter bounds of Witney (*into dufan dope*, referring to the Norton Ditch or Highmoor Brook); and possibly rooks (**Hroc* or OE *hrōc*, 'rook'), in *to roces æcere* in Beckley, Oxfordshire.[106]

Other Creatures: Amphibians and Reptiles and Insects

Although fewer in number, references to lesser creatures (even including insects – see Baker, Chapter 10 in this volume), are found in charters and place-names, though insect names have tended to be regarded as people's nicknames: thus, Loppa from *loppe*, 'spider', in the Shropshire place-name Loppington (*Lopitone* 1086), which could also be interpreted as 'place infested with spiders' with *tŭn*; and Ceafor, from *ceafor* ('chafer beetle'), though chafer beetles are associated with woods in Upton Snodsbury, Worcestershire, and Tichborne, Hampshire.[107] Similarly, *wigga* ('beetle') and *wifel* ('beetle, weevil') may be difficult to differentiate from the personal names Wicga and Wifel. Midgehall in Lydiard Tregoze, Wiltshire, may refer to OE *mycg* ('midge'), thus being a 'corner of land (*halh*) frequented by midges'.[108] OE *brēosa*, *brīosa* ('gadfly') may have given its name to a folk-name Bressingham in Norfolk and to Braiseworth 'gadfly enclosure' in Suffolk (*Briseworde* 1086), while OE *gnætt* ('gnat') appears in some later place-names. In Cornwall one even meets references to ants (*fonton morgeonec*, a spring noted in a charter landmark of Grugwith).[109] OE *lūs* ('louse') has been noted above. Bees, OE *bēo*, as in the Worcestershire place-name Beoley (*Beoleah* 972, *Beolege* 1086), were valuable as the source of honey, whether this was gathered from wild bees or from bees kept in hives, and 'honey brooks' or 'honey woods' are not uncommon.

Toads and frogs are not often referred to, although Tadmarton in

---

[106] Gelling, *The Place-Names of Oxfordshire*, parts 1 and 2; with special reference to S 1001 and S 943. For dabchick, see Lockwood, *The Oxford Book of British Bird-Names*.
[107] *CDEPN*, p. 382; S 786 and Hooke, *Worcestershire Anglo-Saxon Charter-Bounds*, p. 186; S 385.
[108] Midgehall is recorded as *(to) micghæma gemære* in 983 (S 846), 'to the bounds of the people of Midgehall', the latter *Mighal* in 1165. See discussion in Baker, p. 245 in this volume.
[109] S 1027.

Oxfordshire (*Tademærtun* and other forms in 956), is possibly OE **tádemere* ('toad or frog pool') with *tūn*, and a landmark *in to paddebyrig* in a boundary clause of Uffington, Berkshire, may also contain OE *padde* ('toad, frog') with *burh* (?'frog camp').[110] In *pocalege broc*, a landmark in the bounds of Arley, Warwickshire, the reference may be to OE **poc(c)e* ('frog').[111] OE *wyrm* ('snake') has been discussed above, and Netherfield, in Battle, Sussex (*Nedrefelle* 1086), may be the 'snake-infested open space', the first element here OE *næd(d)re* ('adder, snake'). In Cambridgeshire even snails are recorded in the place-name Snailwell (*Snelleuuelle* 1086, OE *snægel*).

Fish

Fishing rights were often noted among the appurtenances of estates granted or leased by charter, while weirs, constructed to enable fish to be caught, gave rise to some place-names and have also been identified archaeologically.[112] Although rivers, streams and meres noted for their fish are not uncommon in place-names and charter boundary clauses, particular kinds of fish are rarely specified. The exception is the eel: a gift from King Edgar to Ely Abbey in AD 970 included *tyn þusenda elfixa ælce geare þam munecum* ('ten thousand eels yearly for the monks') from the people at *Well*.[113] Eels were especially plentiful in the fenlands of eastern England before drainage and obstacles in rivers damaged their habitat: Ely, Cambridgeshire (*Elge c.* 731, *Elige c.* 900, *Elyg* 1086), for instance, is 'eel district'. Also in eastern England, a charter concerning fenland acquired in AD 1020×1023 by Ælfsige, abbot of Peterborough, in exchange for land at Orton, Huntingdonshire, notes the inland mere of Whittlesey, then a vast stretch of inland water with many named fisheries, marshes and waters.[114] Ælfric's *Colloquy* mentions river fishing in inland waters for *ælas 7 hacodas, mynas 7 æleputan, sceotan 7 lampredan, 7 swa wylce swa on wætere swymmaþ. Sprote.* ('eels, pike, minnows, burbot, trout and lampreys together with whatever swims in the water. Sprats.'), as well as sea fishing in coastal waters for fish including herrings, salmon, plaice and flounders.[115] However, references to particular kinds of fish

---

[110] S 1208 and Gelling, *The Place-Names of Berkshire*, part 3, pp. 686–8.
[111] S 898.
[112] Della Hooke, 'Uses of Waterways in Anglo-Saxon England', in *Waterways and Canal-Building in Medieval England*, ed. John Blair (Oxford, 2007), pp. 37–54.
[113] S 779.
[114] S 1463.
[115] Garmonsway, *Ælfric's Colloquy*, pp. 2–9; *Anglo-Saxon Prose*, ed. and trans. Michael Swanton (London, 1975), p. 110. The *ælpūte* ('eelpout') was, however, most likely to have been the burbot rather than the turbot (as translated by Swanton). It is a freshwater fish that may now be extinct in the United Kingdom.

are rare in place-names and charters. An undated survey of Tidenham, Gloucestershire, an estate where the River Wye drains into the Severn estuary, not only notes basket and hackle weirs on both rivers, but also names some of the fish paid to the lord of the estate, among them *styria 7 mereswyn. healic oðer sæfisc* ('sturgeon and porpoise, herring or sea fish' – although, according to Gelling, OE *styria* might refer to 'various fishes').[116] A *stirigan pole* (? 'sturgeon's pool') is also recorded on the boundary of Cumnor.[117] Again in AD 1061×1065 it was stated that the estate of Tidenham, then leased by Abbot Ælfwig and the community at Bath to Archbishop Stigand for his lifetime, was to revert to the monastery with the proviso that *.I. marc. goldes toeacan. 7 .VI. merswun 7 .XXX. þusenda hæringys .ælc eare.* ('1 mark of gold and six porpoises and 30,000 herrings [shall be given] annually').[118] The render of herrings in such vast numbers from this estate clearly indicates that fish were being taken from the sea as well as from rivers. OE *pīc* in the place-names Pickburn (*Pickeburne* 1086) and Pickmere, Cheshire, may also be to a type of fish (? the pike).

Particular Boundary Clauses Referring to Animals

Certain clauses seem to have been drawn up by surveyors particularly aware of the plants and creatures of the countryside. In my recent book, *Trees in Anglo-Saxon England*, I noted how many trees appeared in the boundary clause of the Crediton estate in Devon, whose bounds also contain numerous references to animals and birds. There are mentions of a wolf pit and a wolf coomb, a fox coomb, a swine coomb, a *deor* mere and a sheep brook, as well as an eagle ridge (or a personal name Earna?), possibly two hawk coombs, and a ford at a woodcocks' coomb (Fig. 11.5).[119] The Gloucestershire Bishop's Cleeve charters (Fig. 11.6), which include the present parishes of Stoke Orchard, Gotherington, Woodmancote and Southam and Brockhampton, as well as Bishop's Cleeve itself (in the eighth century known as *Timbingctun*, and later as *Wendles Clife* – the latter probably referring to the high land of Cleeve Cloud), also refer to a number of landmarks related to animals. These include a horse pool (*hors pole*) beside the River Swilgate on the boundary of Stoke Orchard; a stallion's head (*hengestes heafod*);[120] the hind-leap (*hindehlypan*), where a narrow valley

---

[116] S 1555; Gelling, *The Place-Names of Berkshire*, part 3, p. 725; S 1426.
[117] S 757.
[118] S 1426.
[119] Hooke, *Trees in Anglo-Saxon England*, p. 179; S 255, Hooke, *Pre-Conquest Charter-Bounds of Devon and Cornwall*, pp. 86–99.
[120] Perhaps a rather pagan object set beside a major routeway leading towards Winchcombe, a royal centre which became a shire town in the tenth century, and is close to an Iron Age

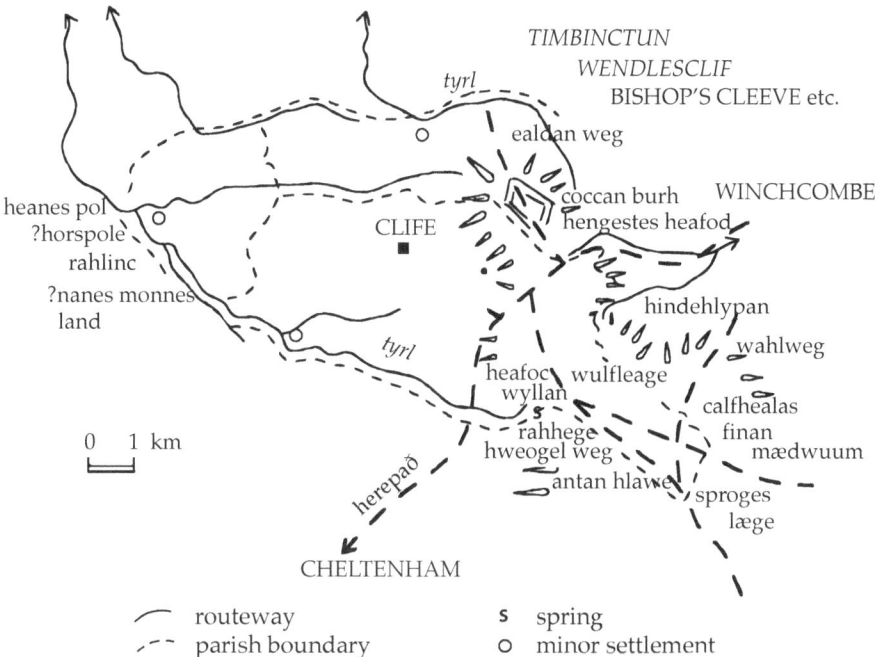

Fig. 11.6 The boundary landmarks of Bishop's Cleeve and adjacent lands, Gloucestershire, in a charter of AD 768×779 (S 141) and an undated boundary clause (S 1549)

cuts into the escarpment; a wolf wood (*wulfleage*), where woodland is still found at the head of another tributary valley; a calf's hollow or hill (*cealfeshealas* and *cælf hyl*), and ?woodpecker meadow (*fina mæde*) on the eastern boundary of Southam; the roe-deer hedge (*þan rahhege*), where the Southam boundary turns south-westward towards the hawk spring (*heafoc wyllan*) at the head of the Hyde Brook, here called the *suð Tyrl*, which flows into the Swilgate.[121] These estates lay on the Cotswold escarpment, taking in the high ground formed of Oolitic limestone, and the valley below to the west, floored by Lower Lias clays; the references to wolves and deer indicate that it was a rather wilder and more heavily wooded landscape than that of later times. The same animals are noted again along the scarp to the south in Cold Ashton and Pucklechurch, with wolves also in Olveston in the Vale (Fig. 11.4).

hillfort – see above.
[121] S 141, S 1549.

Conclusions

This account is by no means exhaustive. Though these are not, except in a very few cases, references to mythical creatures, in one sense they are certainly 'magical': they provide an insight into the Anglo-Saxon landscape that we can recognise and delight in. Moreover, the charter landmarks, unlike many place-names, reveal how local people actually saw their countryside. Wildlife was plentiful, and many habitats survived in a semi-wild state, inhabited by creatures whose populations have since dwindled drastically, or even vanished (like the wolf). People seem also to have been familiar with the names of species of birds, fish, and insects, and to have known the local places where they were most commonly found. All this produces an intimate picture of the early medieval countryside, a rich tapestry preserved for us through local place-names and charter landmarks which cast light upon how the Anglo-Saxons saw and experienced their surroundings. This was a landscape not entirely dominated by human agency, but shared with other creatures, both wild and domestic. Domestic stock was obviously essential to life, and reference to such animals can tell us something about the nature of early medieval farming practices. On the other hand, some wild animals, like the wolf, were seen as posing a danger to humans and to stock (something that can be explored further through literary sources, which encompass 'cultural' as opposed to 'scientific/factual' viewpoints);[122] other wild animals were considered more benign; and still others were used as a source of food and sport. The fact that such animals, birds and other creatures gave rise to place-names shows that they were by no means ignored, and suggests that humans may even have enjoyed their familiarity with at least some of these creatures.[123]

---

[122] E.g. Pluskowski, *Wolves and the Wilderness*.
[123] The author would like to thank Professor Richard Coates for reading this chapter and for his helpful suggestions.

Index

Abingdon, Berkshire, 28n
acid marks, 59
acorns, 259
Acta Cyriaci, 165
Adam and Eve, 68
Adam's Grave, see Woden's Barrow
adders, 55, 60–5, 86–7, 279
administration, 11, 250
adolescence, 106, 112
Adonis, god, 156
Ælfric of Eynsham, abbot, 133–4
  Colloquy, 268, 279
Ælfsige, abbot of Peterborough, 279
Ælfsige, bishop of Winchester, 263
Aeneid, see Virgil
Aesop, 148
Æthelgifu, will of, 265
Æthelred, king of Mercia, 210
Æthelred II, king of England, 98–100
Æthelstan, ætheling, 263
Æthelwald, king of Deira, 209
Æthicus Ister, 84
Africa, 45, 151–75
Africa Proconsularis, 152–3, 160
Age of Migrations, 166
Agnatic succession, 153
Agnus Dei, 98–100
agricultural year, 4
agriculture, 13n, 132, 137–40, 145–6, 178, 229, 229–82
Aidan, saint and bishop, 207
ailments, see illness
Alans, 153, 157, 161
Aldgate, London, 38
Aldhelm, abbot of Malmesbury, bishop of Sherborne, 144
Alexander's Letter to Aristotle, 214
Alfred the Great, king of Wessex, 48n, 104n, 176, 179, 181n, 221–6
Alsøy, Norway, 63
Altuna stone (U1161), 89
ambiguity, 1, 10, 14, 70–1, 92, 105, 108, 114, 117–25, 130, 178, 199, 203, 201n, 212, 228
amphibians, 15, 147, 233n, 278–9
amulets, 65, 68, 94, 98, 101, 169, 208
ancestry, ancestors, ancestral cults, 154, 172–3, 190–2, 198–9
Andalusia, Spain, 158
Andreas, 178–9, 215–21
Andrew, saint, see *Andreas*
Angar kyfyndawt, 123
angels, 103–4, 167

Angles, 50
Anglo-Norman, 232
Anglo-Saxon Chronicle, 76, 104n, 131, 181–7, 191–2, 195, 200, 254
animal husbandry, see husbandry
Anthony, saint, 202
ants, 142–9, 234, 236n, 278
anxiety, 145, 147, 203
apiculture, 245–7
Apollo, god, 36n, 98
apotropaism, 68, 70, 203
arable, see agriculture, farming
Argos, Greece, 43
Arians, Arianism, 153–60, 170
arm rings, 68
Armagh, Book of, 40
armrests, 96
Arrian: *Cynegetica*, 13, 21n, 22n
Årsunda stone (Gs9), 89
Artemis, see Diana
ash (tree), 67
Ashdown, battle of, 176, 179, 181
assemblies, 179–80, 250–1
Asser, bishop of Sherborne: *Vita Alfredi*, 176, 179, 181, 198
asses, 131, 146, 148
Asthall barrow, Oxfordshire, 203
Athena, goddess, 98
Atlakviða, 158–9
Attila, ruler of the Huns, 158–9
augury, 110, 118n, 113–30
Augustine of Hippo, saint, 159–60
  De civitate Dei, 206–7
  Enchiridion, 206n
  Soliloquia, 223–25
autumn, 259, 272
avian motifs, see bird motifs
avians, see birds
avifauna, see birds

Babylon, 216–20
Bacchus, god, 159
badgers, 149, 257, 266, 270–1
Balaam, diviner, 193
Baldr, 165–6
Balearic Islands, 153
Baltic, 158, 161
Bamburgh, Northumberland, 182, 207n
banners, 104–5, 124, 167–8
baptism, 127, 142, 208–9, 221
barbarians, 157–9, 166–7, 170
barking, 146

283

Index

barrows, 7, 9, 11, 77, 86, 182–3, 186, 190–5, 203, 210–12, 234, 254–5, 271–2, 274, 277
Bartholomew, saint, 211, 275
Basil I, emperor, 100n
baskets, 280
battles, battlefields, 11, 22, 38–9, 43, 49, 51, 56–8, 63–4, 66–8, 70–2, 104–5, 108, 112–15, 118, 122, 125, 128–9, 131, 153, 161, 166–8, 171, 176–204, 210–12, 215, 274
battle magic, 193–4
Battle of Brunanburh, The, 181n
Battle of Maldon, The, 181n
beaks, 1, 14, 95, 104
bears, 25n, 146, 152, 177, 269
beasts of battle, 11, 108n, 114–15, 128, 131, 179–80, 192–3, 197, 199
beavers, 269–70
Bede, saint
  De Templo, 222–4
  Historia Ecclesiastica, 87, 138, 181–7, 191, 195, 205–9
  In Genesim, 213
bee keeping, *see* apiculture
beech (tree), 259
beech mast, 259
bees, 245–7
beetles, 232–3, 235–7, 247–8, 256, 278
beheading, 89, 109, 215
Belisarius, count, 151–2, 174
belts, 1, 14, 26–7, 32, 48, 66, 69
Benty Grange helmet, 162
Beowulf, 2, 7, 9, 10, 17, 59, 67, 73–93, 94n, 106n, 107–9, 113–30, 158, 161–2, 168–9, 178–9, 190, 194–7, 200–03, 206n, 209–15, 218, 254–5
berserkers, 173, 177
bills (weapons), 46n
bird-angel, 104
birdmen, 101–05
bird motifs, 22, 98
birds, 9–10, 14, 19n, 21, 24, 26–7, 30, 34, 36–43, 46, 48, 49n, 51, 89, 94–131, 146, 152, 192, 212, 221–2, 229, 252, 253, 257–8, 271–8, 280–2
birdsong, 113–30, 212, 271
Birka, Uppland, Sweden, 62
bishops, 15n, 21, 104, 193, 207–8, 257, 263, 265
bitches, 260, 268
bites, 57, 67, 71n, 232
bitterns, 257, 277
Bjørnsholm, Sønderso, Denmark, 61
black, 108–9, 114–15, 119–23, 129
black grouse, 114–15
Black Sea, 39
blackbirds, 272–3, 276–7
blades, 53–72, 215
Blickling Homilies, 214, 218

blood, 57, 59, 63, 122, 133–4, 152, 168, 193, 215, 219, 249
bloodletting, 133–4
boar banners, 167–8
boar cults, 151–75
boars, 11, 14, 18, 19n, 23n, 24, 25n, 40, 47–9, 51, 151–79, 198, 256, 261, 269
Bodleian MS Harley, 585: 86
Boke of St Albans, 272
bone, bones, 7, 14, 169, 195, 266
Bonifatius, general, 152
borderlands, 201–4, 202, 219, 254
borders, 47–8, 88–9
botflies, 249
boundaries, 2–4, 8, 11, 18, 53, 71, 161, 181, 189, 194, 200, 202, 212–13
boundary clauses, 233, 235, 237, 253, 254–6, 261–81
bowls, 22n, 23–4, 40, 45, 50
bracteates, 14, 17, 19, 39, 96, 101–02
Bragi inn gamli Boddason: *Ragnarsdrápa*, 55
Bran, god, 109
bread, 87, 107n, 111
breakfast, 108, 111
bristles, 163–5, 171–2
Britain, British, 12, 14–15, 19–21, 25, 29, 50–1, 109, 134–5, 138, 146, 149, 161, 180, 188, 195, 200, 206, 215, 226–7, 269, 275
Britons, *see* Britain, British
Bromeswell shield, 36–8
brontology, 139–41, 145
brooks, 254, 267, 280
Brot af Sigurðarkviðu, 59
Brunanburh, battle of, 181
Brynhild, valkyrie, 59, 81
buckets, 24–5
buckles, 15, 26–7, 29, 40, 47
bucks, 268
buckthorn (tree), 257
bugs, *see* invertebrates
buildings, 67, 74, 96, 107–8, 110, 113–14, 118, 120, 124, 172, 194–5, 212–15
bullock, 264
bulls, 15n, 25, 104n, 146, 164, 263–5
bumblebee, *see* bees
bunting, 273, 277
burbots, 279
Burgred, king of Mercia, 267
Burgundy, Burgundians, 104, 158, 173
burial, burials, 29, 46, 50, 122, 124, 190–1, 193, 203, 210–11
burial mounds, *see* mounds
butter, 147
butterflies, 15, 232
buzzards, 258, 274, 278
byres, 253
Byzantium, Byzantines, Byzantine, 8, 20–3, 36n, 38–40, 43–5, 49, 99–100, 145, 151–4, 157, 174

284

Cædmon's Hymn, 195
Caesar, Julius, 17
calendars, 133
California, 106
Calliope, muse, 159
calves, 104n, 139–40, 264, 281
Cambridge, Corpus Christi College MS 198: 218
camel lore, 144
camels, 131, 134, 142–9
Canada geese, 272
canines, 14, 15n, 18, 32, 46–9
cannibals, cannibalism, 178, 205, 218–20
Canterbury, Kent, 259
Caradawg, 176
Carolingia, Carolingians, Carolingian, 40, 50n, 98n, 103n
carrion, 108n, 122, 126–7, 179, 192, 274
Carthage, Tunisia, 151–75
Casanatensis, 218
Cassiodorus, 59, 67
cat-tree, 257
caterpillars, 233
Catholics, Catholicism, 153–6, 170
Catraeth, battle of, 176
cats, 152, 256–7, 263
cattle, 14, 48n, 131, 134–5, 137–40, 143–9, 248–9, 256, 259–66
cavalry, 199
caves, 214
Cedd, saint, 209
Celtic mythology, 50, 104, 109
Celts, Celtic, 9, 13–15, 19, 31, 50, 104, 109, 134, 161, 164, 171
chafer beetle, 233, 278
chairs, 94–6, 98, 102
chaos, 70, 206
chariots, 26, 151
Charlemagne, king of the Franks, 264
charters, 187, 253–82
cheese, 137
Cheriton, Hampshire, 29
Cherwell, river, 263
chevrons, 59–60, 63, 65
chickens, 131, 146
chicks, 146
Chilterns, 262
chip-carving, *see* metalwork
Christ, 40–2, 46n, 47, 98–104, 154, 167–8, 223
Christ Church, Canterbury, 259
Christianity, 7–8, 54, 68, 98, 153–5, 205, 207–8
Christmas, 135–6, 141
Church, Christian, 13, 15, 49, 208, 223
Church Fathers, 110n, 225
Church of Worcester, 261
churches, 76, 89, 100, 127, 154, 205, 228, 275
circuses, 22, 25, 151
cities, 39, 99, 151–2, 155, 205, 216–21, 226–7

Claudian, *De apro et leone*, 156
claws, 21n, 30–2, 147
clerics, 104
cliffs, 108, 196, 214
cloisonné, 13, 15, 38n
Clonmacnoise Plaque, 103
clothing, 1, 99, 111
Cnut, *see* Knútr the Great
coast, 183–6, 188–9, 194–7, 263, 267, 279
cocks, cockerels, 14, 272–3
cockroaches, 233
Codex Amiatinus, 100, 103
Codex Regius, 55
coins, coinage, 19, 24, 39, 40n, 68, 97n, 98–102, 110n, 254–5
Collingbourne Ducis, Wiltshire, 28n
colonnades, 151, 156, 170
colours, 61–2, 69, 114, 119–22, 129–30, 143, 268
combat, 22, 38, 72, 113, 146, 168, 176–204, 210, 215, 220
Conan, 176
concealment, 73–7, 83–6, 88, 91–2
Consolation of Philosophy, Old English, 224
Constantine I, emperor, 165–8, 195n
Constantius II, emperor, 166
coombs, 271, 274, 280
corn-weevils, *see* weevils
corpses, 105, 108n, 114n, 127, 180, 203
corvids, 95, 105, 107, 121, 274
cosmos, cosmology, 11, 67, 70, 121, 204, 213
Cotswolds, 263
cottages, 246
cows, 3, 48n, 263–5
cowsheds, 264
craftsmen, 8, 15, 29, 62
cranes, 272–8
creepy-crawlies, *see* invertebrates
cremation, 14, 29
criminals, 178–9, 191, 211, 266–7
crofts, 246–7, 262
Cropthorne cross, Worcestershire, 255
crosses, 40, 99, 103–4, 165–8, 212, 255, 275
Crowland, Lincolnshire, 213
crows, 95n, 107n, 127–8, 273–6
croziers, 104
crucifixes, *see* crosses
crucifixion, 103
crusaders, 50–1
cubs, 152
Cuchullain, 97n
cuckoos, 212, 273, 276–7
cults, 94, 96, 151–75, 177, 196, 198–9
Cura Pastoralis, Old English, 224
Cuthbert, saint, 109n, 195, 202, 207, 226
Cwichelm's Barrow, 192
Cybele, goddess, 156
Cynegetica, 13, 20n, 21, 30n, 46n
Cynewulf: *Elene*, 63, 122, 165–8

285

Index

Dæghrefn, 106n, 115, 128–9
Daniel, 215–21
Daniel, prophet, 46, 145
Danube, river, 160–2
dark ecology, 6
David, king of Israel and Judah, 95n
dawn, 106, 108–10, 118–19, 121, 123, 126, 129, 196
De diebus malis, 133–5
De inventione litterae, 84–5
De tonitruis libellus ad Herefridum, 140–1
Dean and Shelton, Bedfordshire, 36–7
Dean, Hampshire, 31
deep ecology, 6n
deer, 3, 6, 14, 15n, 27, 49n, 131, 149, 200, 257, 262–3, 265, 267–81
demons, 108, 171, 191, 195, 202–3, 205, 210–12, 227, 254
denarii, 99
Denmark, Danes, Danish, 9, 38n, 47, 61, 65, 68, 74–5, 88, 94, 95n, 102n, 108n, 157–8, 162, 169–70, 213, 215
dens, 209, 259, 261–2
deor, 6, 131, 139, 200–1, 217–18, 226–7, 280
Deorham, 185, 200
deserts, 109, 201–2
Devon, 104n, 280
dew, 122–3
diamond (shape), 60–5
Diana, 25
Dio, Cassius: *History of Rome*, 157, 163
disease, 251–2
divination, 84–5, 148–9
diving birds, 272, 278
does, 268
dog burials, 50
dog-rose, 257
dogs, 13, 15n, 21, 48n, 49n, 50–1, 97n, 152, 233, 260
dogwood (tree), 257
dolphins, 26–7, 39
Domesday Book, 253n, 257, 259, 272
domestic animals, domestication, 7, 11, 14–15, 48, 105, 131–2, 229, 252–3, 258–67, 269, 294
Domitian, emperor, 151
Doorty Cross, Kilfenora, Country Clare, Ireland, 104
doves, 14, 30, 104, 146, 156, 272, 276
Dracontius, Blossius Aemilius
 De laudibus Dei, 154–5
 Medea, 160
dragons, 3, 7, 38–9, 43, 49, 53n, 67, 53–93, 104n, 131, 145–6, 190–1, 196–7, 202–3, 205, 209, 212, 254–6
Drävle stone (U1163), 89
dream books, 145–50
dreams, 132, 145–50, 216, 218
drink, 50, 87, 102, 125, 133, 159, 217, 219–21

drones, 245
drove roads, 259
ducks, 14, 43–6, 49–50, 272–3
dung-beetles, 248
dunlin, 277
Durham, 226–7
dykes, 193–4, 277
Dyrham, *see* Deorham

eagles, 15n, 22, 27, 36–44, 48–9, 98–100, 104–5, 108n, 110, 115, 122–3, 127, 131, 147, 177, 179, 203, 273–6, 280
ears, 24, 27, 30–2, 96, 104, 131, 140
earthworks, 193–4
East Germanic, 157–60
Ecgfrith, king of Northumbria, 208
Ecgtheow, 78, 92
ecology, ecocriticism, eco-philosophy, 5–8
Eddic poetry, 17, 42, 55–60, 67–71, 78, 105, 121–3, 126–7, 171
Eden, 212
Edgar, king of England, 279
Eels, 279
Egbert of York, bishop, 207–8
eggs, 37–9, 146, 249
Egill Skalla-Grímsson, 55–6
 Sonatorrek, 174
 Lausavísa, 58
Egypt, 134
Egyptian Days, 133–5
Einarr Helgason: *Lausavísa*, 58
Ekkisax, 59
Elbe, river, 27
Elene, see Cynewulf
elephants, 14, 131, 145, 147–8
elves, 193
Ely, Cambridgeshire, 279
Ely Abbey, 279
embroidery, 100
enamel, 31
enclosures, 12, 184–5, 200, 246, 249, 261, 265, 278
encomium urbis, 226
Enguz, *see* Ing
entomology, 229–52
equestrian equipment, 13, 31–2, 49, 63–4, 263
equestrianism, 21, 24, 47, 51, 122, 147, 199, 262–3, 267–8
Esdras, prophet: *Revelatio Esdrae*, 135–6
esoteric, 111
Eudoxia, princess, 153
Euhenus, river, 160
eunuchs, 146
Eve, *see* Adam and Eve
evil, 15, 68, 70, 78, 106, 108, 114, 116–17, 118n, 120, 124, 146–7, 158, 205–28
evil days, 133
evil women, 147–8

286

ewes, 265
Exeter Book, 7, 205, 210
Exodus, 122
experimentation, 133–4
eyes, 1, 67, 69–70, 98, 102, 131, 136–7, 219
eyries, 272
Eyvindr skáldaspillir Finnsson
   Hákonarmál, 57
   Háleygjatal, 68n
   Lausavísa, 65
Ezra, *see* Esdras

Fáfnir, 69, 77–9, 81–2, 88–9, 91
Fairford, Gloucestershire, 14–15
faith, 159–60, 167, 170, 207, 211, 217–18, 223
falconry, 46, 49, 51, 267, 272
falcons, 43, 45, 46n, 48, 51, 267, 272
fallow deer, 257, 267–8
fame, 64, 92, 113–14, 206
families, family trees, 19, 81–3, 112, 172–3
fanaticism, 154
fangs, 46, 57
farm ravens, 106–12
farms, farming, 97n, 106–12, 118, 137–40, 145–6, 178, 229, 247–53, 258–67
Farne Islands, Northumberland, 109, 195
fate, 56, 68, 75, 109, 116–17, 127, 132–4, 149, 152
Faversham, Kent, 40
feasting, 78, 113
feathers, 4, 121–3
feet, 21n, 30, 32, 47, 104, 131, 143, 159, 211, 236n
Felix of Crowland: *Vita Guthlaci*, 190, 202, 210
fens, fenland, 195, 210–11, 227, 279
fern pasture, 259
fighting, *see* combat
finches, 273, 276
Finn, king of the Frisians, 168
Finnsburg Fragment, 108
Finnsburh Episode, 168
fire, fires, 7, 56, 63, 81–2, 114, 162, 222
fish, fishing, 2, 4, 14–15, 20n, 21–2, 24, 36n, 37–40, 42–3, 49, 56, 59–60, 63, 82, 89, 131, 138, 140, 142–3, 145, 147, 151–2, 226–7, 279–80, 282
fish ponds, 147
fishing eagles, 122
Flateyjarbók, 170–71
fledglings, 105
flies, 231, 234, 247–50
flight, flying, 15, 39n, 76, 104n, 108, 109n, 143, 146–7, 211, 221–2, 249
Flood, the, 116, 195n
flounders, 279
flowers, 142, 225
foals, 147, 262
folklore, 67, 127, 170, 173, 253

food, 3–4, 14–15, 21–2, 43, 49–51, 106–10, 180, 212, 219–21, 259, 282
fords, 183–5, 196, 237, 239, 248–9, 262, 264, 267–9, 274–7, 280
forecasts, 132, 139
foreheads, 152, 162
forests, 56, 128–9, 176, 197–8, 207–8, 222–7, 261–2, 268–9
fortifications, 182, 186–9
fortresses, 165, 216
Fosse Way, 266
fossils, fossilisation, 247, 255
fowls, fowling, 2, 4, 21, 30n, 43–4, 46n, 272–3, 277–8
foxes, 270–1, 280
Francia, Franks, Frankish, 40, 42n, 50–1, 101, 166
Franks casket, 195
Freya, goddess, 47
Freyr, god, 71, 163–72
Frisia, Frisians, Frisian, 50, 168–9
frogs, 147, 233n, 278–9
frost, 214–15
fruits, 136–7, 142, 251
Fulda, monastery of, 84
funerals, funerary, 7, 36n, 157, 165–9, 190
fur, furs, 20–1, 24
furniture, 94–102, 110–12, 151, 174

gadflies, 249–50, 278
Gaia, *see* Lovelock, James
Galicia, Spain, 153
Ganymede, 155
gardens, 151–2
garnets, 13, 34
Gaul, 29, 48
Geatland, Geats, 78
geese, 14–15, 48n, 147, 272–3, 276
Geiseric, king of the Vandals and Alans, 152–7
Gelimer, king of the Vandals and Alans, 152–5, 174–5
gender, 111–12, 180
generosity, 75, 79, 196
Genesis, 122, 194
Genesis, book of, 110n
geometry, 29, 60–2
Gepids, 159
Germany, Germans, Germanic, 8–11, 16–19, 26–9, 47–50, 59, 73, 76, 78–9, 84, 87–8, 101, 106, 131, 134–5, 149, 151–75, 213–14, 233
ghosts, 124
giants, 104, 194, 215, 254
gibbets, 274
Gibraltar, straits of, 153
gifts, gift-giving, 64, 68–9, 78–9, 96, 263, 279
Gildas, 195
Gillingham, Kent, 31

Index

glass, 23
Gloucestershire, 263–9, 253–82
gnats, 231, 234, 251, 278
Gnomic Verses, see Maxims I and *Maxims II*
goats, 14, 25n, 49n, 131, 146–7, 249, 257, 259–62, 265–6
goblins, 254
Gök stone (Sö, 327), 89–90
gold, 11, 13, 17, 25, 40, 69, 74, 76, 78–84, 100–3, 113–14, 124, 142–5, 148–9, 162, 164–5, 168, 172–4, 216, 221, 236n, 263, 280
Goliath, 193
Gorgons, 40
goshawks, 272–4
Gospels of Wulfila, 160
Goths, Gothic, 153, 157–73
Gotland, Sweden, 94, 158
grain, 136–7, 251
Grand Basilica, Hippo, 157
grapes, 39
grasshoppers, 143
grassland, 247–8
Grave, 561 Birka, Uppland (Sweden)
graves, 16, 24–5, 28–39, 46, 50, 62, 81–2, 94, 111, 192, 199, 203
Great Heathen Army, 188
Great Palace, Istanbul (Constantinople), 38
Greece, Greeks, Greek, 21–2, 39, 40n, 50, 73n, 84, 134–5, 145, 157, 218, 232
greed, 38–9, 74–5, 78–81, 91–3
green, 123, 208, 212
Gregory the Great, pope, 225
  Moralia in Iob, 144
Grendel(s), 11, 73–5, 78–80, 109, 113–14, 116, 118n, 120, 121n, 123–5, 128, 130, 178, 179n, 195–7, 201–3, 212–15, 219, 254
Greuthungi, 162–3, 173
greyhounds, 48n
griffins, 14, 22, 27, 36, 38n, 48, 51
Grímnismál, 96–7, 110n, 111, 126–8
groves, 156, 210n, 221–3
Gullinbursti, 165, 170–2
Gunnars þáttr helmings, 170
Gunthamund, king of the Vandals and Alans, 153–5, 158
Guthlac A/B 205, 209–13
Guthlac, saint, 190, 195, 202–3, 209–13, 220
Guðrúnarkviða I 126

habitats, 192–3, 209, 212–13, 221, 237–45, 247–8, 271–2, 282
hackle weirs, 280
Hæðcyn, 115n, 128
Hagia Sophia, Istanbul (Constantinople), 100
hagiography, 11, 73n, 188–9, 193, 201–2, 203, 205, 211
Hákon the Good, king of Norway, 57

Hallfreðr Óttarsson, 65
halls, 67, 74, 96, 107–8, 110, 112, 113–14, 116–18, 120, 121n, 124–5, 127, 163–4, 172, 194–5, 212–14
Hamðismál, 57, 71
Hamwic, 265–6
hanging bowls, 40
Haraldr Hárfagri, 126–7
hares, 21, 23–4, 27, 40n, 48, 51, 268
harnesses, *see* equestrian equipment
harts, 267, 270, 277
harvest, 4, 135–7, 144–5, 168–9
Hasding Vandals, 153, 157, 160–3, 166, 170–3
Hauksbók, 163–4
Hávamál, 87–8
hawks, 42–4, 46n, 48–51, 122, 267, 272–8, 280–1
headlands, 213–14, 266n, 267
heads, 14, 19, 24, 25–7, 31–2, 34n, 36, 42–3, 60n, 68, 102, 131, 215, 266, 267n
heath, 59n, 108n, 185, 268
heathen burials, 191, 211
heathendom, heathens, heathenism, 68, 76, 151–75, 176, 178–9, 191, 193–4, 206–21, 254, 266
Heathobards, 213
heaven, 42n, 49n, 108, 113–14, 121, 155, 167–8, 195n, 211–12, 216–18, 222
Hebrew, 84
hedges, 268, 277n, 281
heifers, 264
Heimdallr, 69–70
heirlooms, 64, 74, 80, 168
Heiðrekr, king, 162–4, 171
Hel, 67
Helena, saint, 165–6
Helgakviða Hjǫrvarðssonar, 59–60, 70, 171–2
Helgakviða Hundingsbana I 57
Helgakviða Hundingsbana II 71
helmet plaques, 38
helmets, 1, 16, 38, 40, 104–5, 162, 168, 171, 177–8
Hengest and Horsa, 199
Hengest's Hill, 186, 191, 199–201
hens, 272–3
Heorot, 7, 10, 74, 78, 107–8, 114–18, 123–4, 128–9, 157, 194–5, 201, 212–15, 227
Hera, *see* Juno
Hercules, 146, 155
herd, herding, 239, 259, 262
Herebeald, 115, 128–30
Heremod, 74–5, 79
hermitages, 205, 210, 213–15
heroes, heroism, 55, 67–8, 73–4, 77–9, 89, 95n, 97n, 109, 110n, 118, 124, 169–70, 209–21
heroic literature, 17, 78–9, 89, 131, 162, 172–3, 190, 193–4, 195–8, 201–3, 210

Index

herons, 272, 277–8
herringbone, 59, 64–5
herrings, 279–80
hidden knowledge, 9–10, 79, 85–6
hides, 264
Hildebrandslied, 157–8
Hilderic, king of the Vandals and Alans, 152–8
hill forts, 190, 194, 200, 266
hills, 182–7, 190–1, 199–200, 209, 233–4, 240–4, 249–51, 261, 263–4, 267–8, 271–2, 274–7, 280–1
hilts, 56–7, 59–66, 72–5, 79–81, 90n, 91, 93, 124–5
hinds, 267, 270, 280
Hingsdon Down, Devon, 199
Hingston Down, Cornwall, 199
Hippo, Algeria, 153, 157, 169
hippogriffs, 36
Historiska Museet, Stockholm, Sweden, 62
Hliðskjálf, 98, 110
hoards, hoarding
Hollingbourne, Kent, 28
Holy Spirit, 98
Holy Trinity, 154–55
Homer: *Iliad*, 176n
homilies, 214, 218
Hon Hoard, Norway, 65
honey, 135–8, 144, 146–7, 245–6, 251, 278
Horace, poet, 155
horn, horns, 1, 4, 14, 38, 39–40, 87, 147
horse crofts, 262
horses, 13–15, 20–7, 31–2, 36, 39–40, 43, 45–51, 78, 96–7, 98n, 112, 131, 133–4, 139–40, 147, 199, 249, 253, 258, 260, 262–3, 265–8, 280
horseback, *see* equestrianism
hostility, 22, 116, 147, 211, 214n, 215
Hǫðr, god, 165
hounds, 24, 25n, 27–32, 39–40, 43–4, 46–51, 260, 268–9
Hoxne, Suffolk, 24–5
Hoxne bracelets, 24–6
Hrefna Wudu, 115, 128–9
Hrefnes Holt, 115, 123–4, 128–9
Hrethel, 115n, 128–9
Hrómundar þáttr halta, 126
Hrothgar, 74–5, 78–80, 91–3, 94n, 212–13, 215
Hrothulf, 115n, 116
Húsdrápa, 165, 168
Huginn and Muninn, 9, 96, 104, 110, 126
humanoids, 7, 254
humans, 1–12, 13n, 15, 18, 24–7, 31, 39, 42n, 51, 53, 76–7, 79–80, 86, 95, 99, 106–11, 135, 138–41, 145, 148, 151, 192–8, 203, 205–28, 229, 245, 247–51, 282
Humber, river, 194, 237
Huns, 162, 166, 167

hundred (administrative unit), 250, 266–7
Huneric, king of the Vandals, 153–5, 171
Hungary, 47, 101–2
hunt, hunters, hunting, 3–4, 8, 12–52, 131–2, 147, 152, 174, 253, 258, 267–71
hunting dogs, 13, 27, 48n, 260, 262, 268
husbandry, 4, 10, 12, 132, 135, 137, 151, 229–30, 247–8, 252, 258–67
Hwicce, 267
hybrids, hybridisation, 1, 14, 22
Hygelac, 115n, 123, 128–30, 198
Hylas, 155
Hyndluljóð, 171–3

ibexes, 25n
ice, 66, 215
Iceland, Icelanders, Icelandic, 54–6, 97n, 100–1, 104n, 106–7, 109–12, 118, 162, 165, 197
iconography, 13–52, 91, 98–9, 103n, 104, 177
ideology, 18, 161
idols, idolatry, 193, 208, 216
illness, 86–7, 132, 147
Indo-European, 118, 121
Ine, king of Wessex, 259
Ing, god, 11, 166, 168–70
Ingvi-freyr, *see* Ing
inheritance, 90–1
insects, 15, 229–52, 278–9
interlace, 14, 42–3, 60n
invasion, 18–19, 129–30, 151, 157, 173–4, 195, 206
invertebrates, 229–52, 278–9
Iona, Scotland, 207n
Ireland, Irish, 97, 103–4
iridescence, 121–3
iron, 58–9, 61, 64, 66, 74, 77, 168,
Iron Age, 39, 177, 194, 200, 266, 280n
Isaiah, book of, 205, 209, 222
Isidore of Seville: *Etymologiae siue Origines*, 13–24, 27n, 42, 144
Islam, Islamic, 21, 45, 51, 101
islands, 138, 153, 184, 186, 195, 231, 251, 267, 272, 274
Isle of Eigg, Scotland, 61
Isle of Wight, 40, 274
Íslendingabók, 126n
Israel, Israelites, 216
Italy, Italians, Italian, 39, 49, 149, 153–4, 156, 160
ivory, 147–8

jackdaws, 274–5
Jason, 160
javelins, *see* spears
jays, 275
Jerome, saint, 49n, 110n, 225
Jerusalem, 165, 216, 218, 223
Jesus, *see* Christ

Index

jewellery, 13, 23, 63, 68
John the Evangelist, 40
Jǫrmungandr, 67–9
Jove, *see* Jupiter
Judaism, 3
Judeo-Christian, 6, 228
judicial proceedings, 11, 191
Judith, 63, 122
Juno, goddess, 98, 160
Jupiter, god, 27, 169
Justice, 164, 191
Justinian, emperor, 154, 174
Jutes, 50
Jutland, Denmark, 157

Kent, Kentish, 17, 25, 30, 31, 34, 42–3, 48, 199, 259–61
kestrels, 274–5
kids, 146, 265
kingfishers, 276
Kirklevington cross-shaft, North Yorkshire, 104
kites, 257, 273–4
Kjølstad, Norway, 62
Knútr the Great, king of Denmark, England, and Norway, 68, 80
Konungsbók, *see Codex Regius*
Kormáks saga, 59
Krefeld Gellep, North Rhein-Westphalia, Germany, 39

Lacnunga, 86–7
Lactantius: *De Ave Phoenice*, 221–3
lakes, 215, 247
lambs, 98–99, 264–5
lampreys, 279
Landnámabók, 110n, 126
landscape, 11–12, 108n, 176–282
Langobards, 18
lard, 147
larks, 273–4
larvae, 249
Lastingham, North Yorkshire, 209–10
law codes, 48, 259
Laxdœla saga, 165
learning, 81, 132, 141–4, 148–50
leather, 4, 14, 32
Lebanon, 51
Leda, 155
leeches, 247
Lejre, Denmark, 94–112
leopards, 25n, 152
letters, 24, 73–4, 80–93, 167–70
Lévi-Strauss, Claude, 18, 78n
Libya, 21, 154, 174
lice, 233–4, 257, 278
life cycles, 106, 108, 118, 229, 247
lightning, 66, 76
liminality, 11, 189, 194

Lincolnshire fens, 210
Lindisfarne, Northumberland, 76, 207, 209, 254
Linnaeus, Carl, 3
lions, 10, 14, 25, 27, 40, 46, 104n, 131, 141, 145, 147–9, 151, 156, 199
liturgical calendar, 133–4
livestock, *see* cattle
lizards, 15
locus amoenus, 206, 211–12, 215
locusts, 233
logic, 144, 148–9, 181
Loki, god, 67
Lombards, Lombardy, Lombardic, 101–02
Londinium, *see* London
London, 38, 109–10, 275
Long Marston, Yorkshire, 32–3
Long Wittenham, Berkshire, 32–3
Longinus, 102–3
louse-berries, 257
Lovelock, James, 6–7
lozenges, 61–64
Luddington, Avon valley, Warwickshire, 265
Lullingstone, Kent, 40
Luxorious of Carthage
 Latin Anthology, 151–75
 Liber epigrammaton, 151
lynxes, 269
lyres, 175

Mabinogion, 109
magic, 5, 18, 71, 84–6, 97, 111, 177, 193–4
magpies, 152, 231, 273–6
Maiestas domini, 98–104
Maldon, battle of, 181n
Malverns, 261
mankind, *see* humans
Mannerupskat, Mannerup, Denmark, 101
mantic practices, 134–5, 149
manure, 248
manuscript illustrations, 40, 95n, 98n, 119n
manuscripts, 21, 40, 42, 50, 55, 63n, 80–7, 95n, 100, 103n, 104, 131–50, 159–60, 163, 168, 187
marble, 173
Marcomanni, 84
mare, 199, 263
Mars, 17, 151, 155–7, 170–1, 173
marsh harriers, 274
marshes, 194–7, 200–1, 231, 234, 237n, 263, 265, 279–80
Marsyas, 155
martens, 270–1
Martial
 Epigrams, 151–2
 Liber spectaculorum, 156
masks, 18, 26, 198
masonry, 156, 173, 194, 223, 226–7

Index

maturity, 98, 105–8, 112, 267
Maxentius, emperor, 165–6
Maxims I 87n, 254
Maxims II 76–7, 88, 190, 195, 254
meat, 47, 49, 159, 219, 264
medals, 98
Medea, 155
Medicina de quadrupedibus, 131
medicine, medication, 13, 133–5
Mediterranean, 46, 49, 131–4, 148, 153, 157, 159
meeting places, 250
memorial stones, 88–91
memorialisation, 157, 169–75, 182, 189, 190–4, 200–1
memory, 64, 84–5, 96, 110, 193, 196, 199
merchants, 136–7, 153
Mercia, 267
Mercury, god, 14, 17
meres, 73, 79, 108, 184, 195–7, 212–15, 227, 237n, 238–9, 243, 247, 251, 254, 261–2, 268, 270–81
Mermedonia, Mermedonians, 178–9, 218–21
Merovingia, Merovingians, Merovingian, 36, 39n, 47–8
Mesopotamia, 110n, 134, 215–20
metalwork, metalworking, 13–19, 22–3, 32, 37–8, 42–5, 48–51, 53–72
 chip-carved, 20
 relief cast, 26, 29
meteorology, 132–3, 136–9, 141–2, 147
mice, 14–15, 147–8, 152, 270–1, 276
Middle English, 6–7, 231
Middle Welsh, 123
Midgard serpent, *see* Jǫrmungandr
midges, 244–5, 278
Midlands, 237, 257, 259, 272
Migration Age, 18, 26–7, 96n, 101–2, 166
Miles Christi, 210
military, militaria, 22n, 24, 26–9, 38, 50, 152–3, 176–204, 199
milk, 49n, 137, 142, 264
Milvian Bridge, battle of the, 195n
mines, mining, 69, 101
minnows, 279
Mirkwood, 197
missionaries, 160, 205–7
mistletoe, 165
mnemonics, 13n, 169–70
monasteries, 84, 132, 209–10, 280
monkeys, 152
monks, 5, 49, 279
monsters, 4, 11, 74, 117, 123–5, 140, 177–8, 191, 194–203, 213–15, 253–6
Montepagano, Italy, 39–41
months, 133, 139–41, 144–5, 249
monuments, monumentality, 54, 90–1, 182, 188–94
Moors, 157, 174

moors, 200–1, 231, 234, 237n
morality, 79–80, 91–2, 191, 195, 197, 202, 206–7, 209–10, 220
Morrigan, 97n
mortality, 7, 116, 140, 171, 191
mosaic, 22, 43–5, 49, 100
mosquitoes, 251
moths, 15
mounds, 1, 14–16, 38, 42–4, 47–9, 77, 104, 122, 182–3, 186, 190–6, 210–11, 233–4, 255
mountains, 156, 183–5, 201, 202n, 207–10
mules, 263
murder, 78–9, 155, 219
myrmecology, 144

nanny goats, 265
natural disasters, 138
Near East, 148
Nebuchadnezzar, king, 216–20
Nemean lion, 156
Neolithic tombs, 192, 254
Nerthus, god/dess, 170
nests, 107n, 221–3, 234
Netley Marsh, Hampshire, 196
nets, 20, 22n, 30n, 267
New Forest, 262
niello, 94, 100
night, 106–7, 116, 124, 166–8
nightingales, 277
Nine Herbs Charm, 68n, 86–8
nits, 257
Níðhǫggr, 67, 69
Njáls saga, 97
Njǫrðr, god, 170
Noah, 110n, 116
Norman Conquest, 139, 276
Normans, Normandy, 226n, 267–8
Northumbria, 76, 127, 207n, 209
Norway, Norwegians, Norwegian, 9, 61–2, 63, 69, 88
Numidia, 153
numismatics, 98–101
Nydam Bog, 99n
Nydam Style, 26

oak (tree), 274
oceans, 42n, 194–6
Odin, *see* Óðinn
Odysseus, 176
Óláfr Haraldsson, king of Norway, 57
Old High German, 157–8, 160, 170–1
omens, 105, 108, 113–30, 139
Ongentheow, 128, 198
onomastics, 182–7, 229–82
Oppian of Apamea: *Cynegetica*, 20–1, 30n, 46n
orchards, 246–7
Orderic Vitalis: *Historia Ecclesiastica*, 226n

291

ornithology, *see* birds
Oseberg ship, 69
Oseberg tapestry, 62
ospreys, 42
Ostrogoths, Ostrogothic, 59, 153–4, 159–60, 162–3
Oswald, saint and king of Northumbria, 195, 207n, 209
Óttar svarti: *Hǫfuðlausn*, 56–8, 64
otters, 131, 256, 263, 270
Óðinn, god, 16–18, 47, 58, 63, 66n, 68, 87–8, 94–112, 117, 121–3, 126, 163–5, 172–4
Outremer, 51
Ovid
  Amores, 155
  Metamorphoses, 156
owls, 98, 277
oxen, 49n, 147, 262, 264–6
Oxfordshire, 278–9

pagans, paganism, 8–9, 17–20, 40, 49, 84–5, 94–112, 127–8, 155–6, 161–70, 178–9, 193–4, 205–28, 236, 266, 275
panthers, 25
parasites, 233–4, 257
parchment, 137
parks, 174, 200
pastoral (genre), 155–7, 168–70
pastoralism, 12, 229–30, 247–51
Pater Noster, 80–1, 86
paws, 24, 30–2, 46
peace, 132, 135–7, 142, 144, 212
peacocks, 14, 98
Peada, king of Mercia, 210
peafowl, 277
Penda, king of Mercia, 210
Persia, Persians, Persian, 45, 46n, 174
Petersen Type D, 61
Petersen Type H, 61–2
Phoenix, 221–2, 225–6
phoenixes, 10, 131, 221–2
Physiologus, 131, 144
pigeons, 276
pigs, 3, 14, 49, 137–8, 151–75, 253, 259–63, 266–7, 269, 280
pigsties, 261–2
pike (fish), 37, 279–80
pillars, 221, 224–5
Pioneer helmet, 162
pits, 89, 91n, 256–7, 269, 274–5, 280
place-names, 158n, 176–204, 229–82
plague, 49, 74, 208
plaice, 279–80
plants, plantlife, 2–3, 7, 222–7, 280
Pliny the Elder: *Naturalis Historia*, 13–14, 27n, 36–9
ploughs, ploughing, 147, 264
plovers, 277–8
Poe, Edgar Allen, 105, 108

poison, 57, 68, 220
ponds, 147, 276
pools, 194–5, 251, 279–80
porpoises, 280
portents, *see* omens
Praxeis, 218
predators, 22, 30, 32, 40n, 46n, 48, 107, 122n, 178–80, 197, 202–3, 269
Procopius: *Wars of Justinian*, 157, 159, 173–5
prognostics, prognostication, 131–50
prophecy, 97, 104–5, 111–30, 131–50
puppies, 152, 171
pyres, 165–6, 168

quadrupeds, 14, 25n, 27, 34, 36, 51, 138–9, 147
quoit brooches, 24–5, 29–31

rabbits, 131
raids, raiding, 76, 100, 116, 128, 160, 168
rain, 147, 208
rams, 25n, 264
Ramsund stone (Sö, 101), 89
raptors, 1, 14, 18, 22, 25n, 43–5, 47, 49, 102n, 107n, 177, 198
rats, 15
Ravenna, Italy, 153
ravens, 9–10, 15n, 17, 94–130, 149, 179, 178–9, 192, 273–5, 274–6
ravine, 265, 274
realism, 46, 95n, 97–98, 110
Regin, 78, 81, 89
Reginsmál, 104–5
Regius Psalter, 140
relief-cast, *see* metalwork
reliquaries, 68
reptiles, 53n, 139–41, 195–6, 278–9
Revelatio Esdrae, 135–9, 142–5
Rhineland, 23
rhinoceroses, 255
riddles, 7, 84n, 144, 159, 163–4
Rígsþula, 69
Ringmere, battle of, 108n
rings, 69, 77, 169
ritual, 1, 18, 107, 177, 266
rivers, riverine, 141–3, 160–1, 183–4, 187–9, 194–7, 200, 226–7, 236, 237n, 249, 262–3, 279–81
rivets, 32, 66
robins, 277–8
roe deer, 15n, 270, 281
Roman script, 80–1
Romanisation, 155–6, 160
Romano-British, 15, 50, 200, 206–7
Romano-Celtic, 104
Rome, Romans, Roman, 13–50, 98–104, 151–75, 178n, 190, 194, 207, 220–1
rooks, 108, 128n, 256, 272–3, 275n
roosting, 106

roots, 2, 87, 214–15, 222–3
Ruin, The, 194n
ruins, 194, 220–1
Rune Poem, Icelandic, 81–3, 90–3
Rune Poem, Old English, 81–3, 169
rune stones, 68, 88–91
runes, runic inscriptions, 15n, 68, 73–93, 169–70

sagas, 16–17, 54–9, 64–6, 69–71, 78–9, 88–9, 96–7, 104, 126, 162–3, 165, 177–8, 197
St Mary Bourne, Basingstoke, 31
St Peter's, Gloucester, 264
saints, 15n, 49n, 51, 165, 187, 190, 193–4, 195n, 202, 211, 218, 226, 275
saints' lives, *see* hagiography
Salin's Style I and II 16–20, 32–51
sandpipers, 277
Sardinia, 153
Sarre, Kent, 32–3
Sarre brooch, 30–1
Sassanids, Sasanian, 44–5
Satan, 211n, 220
scabbards, 29, 66
scales, 60–1
scavenging, scavengers, 105–7, 179, 274
scorpions, 131
sculpture, 13, 38, 78, 94–100, 111
Scyld Scefing, 124
Scyldings, 107, 124–5, 168
sea, seas, 6, 13, 22, 31, 123, 136, 138, 142, 147, 152, 157, 174, 271
sea hawks, 42
Seafarer, The, 122, 195, 215
seagulls, 272–3
seals, 271
seasons, seasonality, 135n, 136–7, 144, 208
seeds, 140
serpents, 15, 24, 36–9, 43, 51, 53–93, 102n, 131, 147–8, 177, 196, 255–6, 278–9
settlements, 182–6, 220–1, 235, 246, 256, 276, 281
shamans, shamanism, 1, 18–19, 97, 110n, 177
shape-shifters, shape-shifting, 4, 18, 53, 71, 177
sheep, 3, 49, 131, 135–40, 144, 248, 253, 260, 262–66, 280
sheepdogs, 48
shield bosses, 16n, 36, 47
shield mounts, 36, 38
shields, 36, 38, 49, 197–8, 263
ships, 13n, 69, 113–14, 124, 136, 140, 225n
shoulders, 1, 24, 29, 30, 32, 47, 96, 97, 98n, 103–4, 126, 152
shoulder clasps, 47
shrew mice, 271
Shropshire, 234
Sicily, 153
Sigemund, 73, 77

Sigurd, 88–91
Sigvatr Þórðarson: *Vikingarvísur*, 57–8, 66
Siling Vandals, 158
silk, 148, 174
silver, 27, 29, 30, 34, 36, 38n, 61, 94, 96, 98–101
skaldic poetry, skalds, 17–18, 55–60, 65–7, 71–2, 126
Skírnismál, 70–1
sky, 13, 22, 31, 76, 119, 127
slavery, slaves, 21, 265
Sleipnir, 112
snails, 247, 279
snakes, *see* serpents
snipes, 272–3, 276–7
Snorri Sturluson
  Gylfaginning, 96–8, 78, 103, 110–11, 126, 163–5
  Heimskringla, 96, 104
  Skáldskaparmál, 63, 66–8, 70
  Ynglingasaga, 96
Soliloques, Old English, 221–8
Solomon and Saturn I 80–1, 86, 92
sorcerers, 193
Sösdala Style, 26
souls, 40–2, 110n, 152, 155, 223
South Saxons, 193, 208
Spain, 153, 158n, 160–1
Spangenhelme, 39–41
sparrows, 273
spears, 1, 22n, 38n, 46n, 63–4, 87, 103, 122, 129, 152, 166, 219, 236
spiders, 278
spirituality, 5, 79, 81, 108, 195, 202, 207–8, 210
spoliation, 173
Spong Hill, Norfolk, 28–9
sprats, 279
spring, 135–7, 144–5
springs, 271–2, 275–8, 281
stags, 21, 23–24, 25n, 38, 40, 49n, 51, 215, 267
stakes, 266, 267n
stallions, 147, 199, 263, 266, 280
standards, 24, 27, 100, 166, 212
standing stones, 182, 190
stone, stones, 13n, 63, 68, 77–8, 88–93, 104, 156, 173, 182, 186, 190, 193, 213, 226–7, 234n
storms, 136, 144–5
Strabo, 21
strap ends, 27–8, 32–4, 38
streams, 183–4, 236, 247, 250, 262, 267, 279
structuralism, 118
studfolds, 253, 262
sturgeons, 280
Sturlubók, 126
subterranean, 69, 76, 88, 213
summer, 135–7, 144, 225, 259

293

sun, sunshine, 114, 116–17, 121, 125–6, 128, 141–5, 149, 167, 222
supernatural, 7, 18, 22, 110, 118, 182–3, 186, 191, 193–4, 197, 203
superstition, 161, 208
Sussex, 208
Sutton Hoo, Suffolk, 14–16, 38, 42–9, 162
Sven Estridesen, king of Denmark, 100
swallows, 273
swallowing, 67, 70
swans, 272
Sweden, Swedes, Swedish, 88–91, 94, 115n, 127, 236
swifts, 273–4
swine, *see* pigs
swine-herds, 259–62
swine-pasture, 259
swords, 1, 7, 38n, 46n, 53–72, 74–5, 77, 113, 120–1, 124–5, 162–3, 168, 215, 263
symbols, symbolism, 3, 10–12, 19, 22, 24–5, 27n, 45–7, 65–70, 76, 90–1, 97–105, 110n, 113–50, 164, 178–81, 194–202, 213
Symeon of Durham, 187
  Historia Dunelmensis Ecclesiae, 226
Synesius of Cyrene, 21
Syria, 51, 134

Tabarka, Tunisia, 204
Tacitus, Cornelius: *Germania*, 161–2, 165, 170–1
tails, 1, 15, 25, 30–1, 46, 60
Taliesin, Book of, 123
talking animals, 4, 127, 129, 146–7
taxonomy, 53, 70–1, 131
teeth, 30, 145, 165
temples, 36n, 221, 223
Temple of Jerusalem, 223
territory, 106–9
Tervingi, 162–3, 173
textiles, 14, 137
theft, 76, 79
Theoderic the Great, king of the Ostrogoths, 59, 154
thorn (tree), 251, 257, 274
Thrasamund, king of the Vandals and Alans, 153–5, 159
threshing, 139–40
thrones, 94–112
thrushes, 273, 276
thunder, 139–41, 144
timber, 213, 223–5
tit-mouse, 276
toads, 278–9
topography, 176–204, 229–82
toponymy, *see* place names
Torslunda, Sweden, 1
torture, 67–8, 221
Tower of London, 109–10
towns, 72, 220–1, 225–6, 266, 280n

trade, trading, 29, 100–1, 264–5
Trælnes, Norway, 61
traps, 20–2, 51, 236
treachery, 146–7
treasure, 7, 73–83, 90–3, 101, 254–5
trees, 2–3, 7, 67, 87, 104n, 140, 142, 167, 174, 185, 188–9, 197–9, 206, 210n, 212, 214–16, 222–7, 237, 246–7, 257–9, 269n, 274, 280
tribute, 100–1, 153
triumph, *see* victory
trolls, 197
trout, 279
tumuli, *see* mounds
Tunisia, 11, 104, 153, 157
turtle-doves, 276
tusks, 14, 20–21n, 148
Twyford, Berkshire, 63

Þiðreks saga, 59, 78
Þjóðólfr of Hvinir: *Haustlǫng*, 168–9
Þóbjorn hornklofi: *Haraldskvæði*, 126
Þormóðr Kolbrúnarskáld: *Þorgeirsdrápa*, 71

Úlfr Uggason: *Húsdrápa*, 165, 168
uncanny, 67, 109
underground, *see* subterranean
underwater, 120, 121n, 214
urbanism, urbanity, 190, 215–21

Valentinian III, emperor, 153
Valhalla, *see* Valhǫll
Valhǫll, 112, 164
Valkyries, 70, 131, 143
valleys, 183, 187, 245, 249, 251, 264, 274, 277, 280–1
Valsgärde, Sweden, 63
Vandals, Vandalic, 10–11, 44–5, 151–75
Vang, Oppland, Norway, 61
Vanir, 170
Várpalóta, Hungary, 101–2
Västerljung stone (Sö40), 89, 91n
Ved Moss, Norway, 61
vegetation, *see* plantlife
Vehmaa, Lahdinko, Finland, 60
vellum, 5
Vendel, Vendels, 1, 19
Vendel Mound One, 104
Vendsyssel, Jutland, Denmark, 157
venom, 21, 59, 86–7
Venus, goddess, 151, 155, 156–7, 171, 173–4
veterinary medicine, 134
victory, 22, 24, 50–1, 74, 80–1, 117–18, 187, 193, 195n, 197, 199, 203, 209–21
Vik, Iceland, 107
Viking Age, 54–6, 88, 94, 97–8, 100–1
Vikings, 16–20, 46, 53–112, 121–2, 162–6, 177–8, 181, 188, 191–4
villas, 43, 45, 49, 152, 173, 175

Index

vine scroll, 39, 45
violence, 105–6, 109, 112, 154, 174–5, 177, 174–204, 216, 219–20
vipers, 60–1, 65
Virgil: *Aeneid*, 155, 214
Visigoths, Visigothic, 38n, 154, 159–62
Visio Sancti Pauli, 214
visions, 110, 166–7
Vita Gregorii Magni, 127–8
Vita Sancti Wilfrithi, 187, 193
vocalisation, 119, 130
voles, 271
Vǫlsunga saga, 78, 88–9
Vǫluspá 67

wagtails, 273
walls, 77, 165, 194, 214, 220–1, 223, 225
wands, 65–6
Wanderer, The, 194–5, 215
Wansdyke, 193
war, warfare, 13n, 20, 22, 110, 132, 153, 165–9, 176–204
warriors, 1, 38, 46–7, 71, 77–9, 104–5, 110, 112n, 113–14, 118, 124, 128–9, 162, 166, 171, 177–8, 193, 196–205, 216, 258, 263
wasteland, *see* wilderness
water, 69, 120, 121n, 174, 194–7, 200, 202, 209, 214–15, 219, 226–7, 237, 247–8, 271–2, 274–5, 279
water-crossings, 202, 248–9
wax, 137, 245–6
wealth, 9, 69–70, 74–5, 79–80, 83, 90–3, 132, 147, 264–5
weapons, 1, 7, 22n, 36, 38–9, 46n, 49, 53–72, 74–5, 77, 87, 103, 113, 120–2, 124–5, 129, 152, 162–3, 166, 168, 180, 197–8, 214–15, 219, 236, 263
weasels, 271
weather, weather forecasting, 132–45, 149–50
weeds, 140
weevils, 235, 248, 251–2
weirs, 280
Weser, river, 27
wethers, 264–5
wetlands, 183–4, 186, 188–9, 194–7, 272
whales, 14, 195

whetstones, 66
white, 121, 147, 167, 263
white-tailed eagles, 122
Widsith, 158–9, 166
wildcats, 270–1
wilderness, 11, 109, 177, 194–203, 205–15, 217–28, 254, 258
Wilfrid, saint, 187, 193
wills, 263
wind, 140
wings, 32, 34–5, 38–9, 42n, 45, 50, 53n, 95, 103, 109–10, 112n, 227, 232
Wint Hill, Somerset, 23
winter, 27n, 107, 109–10, 135–7, 144–5, 225
witches, 112n, 193
Wið Færstice, 193
Woden, god, 17–18
Woden's Barrow, 192–3
wolf hunting, 50, 271
wolves, 1, 18, 43, 46–8, 112, 127, 172, 177–9, 198, 216, 258, 269–71, 280–2
women, 50, 94, 97, 99, 111, 136, 147–8
Wonders of the East, 131, 141, 143–4, 148, 236n
wood, 14, 24, 56, 213–14, 223–6
woodcocks, 276–7, 280
woodland clearings, 198–9, 237, 249, 251, 255–6
woodpeckers, 273, 276, 278, 280–1
woods, woodland, 46n, 115, 128, 185–6, 188–9, 196–201, 210, 214–15, 221–7, 237, 245–7, 249–51, 255–62, 267–81
woodsmen, 224–6
wool, 49, 131, 264–5
worms, 176
wounds, 56–8, 65, 71, 87, 152, 168
wrens, 257, 272–3, 276

Xenophon, 21

yellowhammers, 273, 277
Yggdrasill, 67
Yngvi, *see* Ing
York, North Yorkshire, 226

Zeus, 98–100
zoomorphism, 14

ANGLO-SAXON STUDIES

Volume 1: The Dramatic Liturgy of Anglo-Saxon England,
M. Bradford Bedingfield

Volume 2: The Art of the Anglo-Saxon Goldsmith: Fine Metalwork in Anglo-Saxon England: its Practice and Practitioners,
Elizabeth Coatsworth and Michael Pinder

Volume 3: The Ruler Portraits of Anglo-Saxon England, *Catherine E. Karkov*

Volume 4: Dying and Death in Later Anglo-Saxon England, *Victoria Thompson*

Volume 5: Landscapes of Monastic Foundation: The Establishment of Religious Houses in East Anglia, *c.* 650–1200, *Tim Pestell*

Volume 6: Pastoral Care in Late Anglo-Saxon England,
edited by Francesca Tinti

Volume 7: Episcopal Culture in Late Anglo-Saxon England,
Mary Frances Giandrea

Volume 8: Elves in Anglo-Saxon England: Matters of Belief, Health, Gender and Identity, *Alaric Hall*

Volume 9: Feasting the Dead: Food and Drink in Anglo-Saxon Burial Rituals,
Christina Lee

Volume 10: Anglo-Saxon Button Brooches: Typology, Genealogy, Chronology,
Seiichi Suzuki

Volume 11: Wasperton: A Roman, British and Anglo-Saxon Community in Central England, *edited by Martin Carver with Catherine Hills and Jonathan Scheschkewitz*

Volume 12: A Companion to Bede, *George Hardin Brown*

Volume 13: Trees in Anglo-Saxon England: Literature, Lore and Landscape,
Della Hooke

Volume 14: The Homiletic Writings of Archbishop Wulfstan,
Joyce Tally Lionarons

Volume 15: The Archaeology of the East Anglian Conversion, *Richard Hoggett*

Volume 16: The Old English Version of Bede's *Historia Ecclesiastica*,
Sharon M. Rowley

Volume 17: Writing Power in Anglo-Saxon England: Texts, Hierarchies, Economies, *Catherine A. M. Clarke*

Volume 18: Cognitive Approaches to Old English Poetry, *Antonina Harbus*

Volume 19: Environment, Society and Landscape in Early Medieval England: Time and Topography, *Tom Williamson*

Volume 20: Honour, Exchange and Violence in *Beowulf*, *Peter S. Baker*

Volume 21: *John the Baptist's Prayer* or *The Descent into Hell* from the Exeter Book: Text, Translation and Critical Study, *M.R. Rambaran-Olm*

Volume 22: Food, Eating and Identity in Early Medieval England, *Allen J. Frantzen*

Volume 23: Capital and Corporal Punishment in Anglo-Saxon England, *edited by Jay Paul Gates and Nicole Marafioti*

Volume 24: The Dating of *Beowulf*: A Reassessment, *edited by Leonard Neidorf*

Volume 25: The Cruciform Brooch and Anglo-Saxon England, *Toby F. Martin*

Volume 26: Trees in the Religions of Early Medieval England, *Michael D. J. Bintley*

Volume 27: The Peterborough Version of the Anglo-Saxon Chronicle: Rewriting Post-Conquest History, *Malasree Home*

Volume 28: The Anglo-Saxon Chancery: The History, Language and Production of Anglo-Saxon Charters from Alfred to Edgar, *Ben Snook*

Volume 29: Representing Beasts in Early Medieval England and Scandinavia, *edited by Michael D.J. Bintley and Thomas J.T. Williams*

Volume 30: Direct Speech in *Beowulf* and Other Old English Narrative Poems, *Elise Louviot*

Volume 31: Old English Philology: Studies in Honour of R.D. Fulk, *edited by Leonard Neidorf, Rafael J. Pascual and Tom Shippey*

Volume 32: 'Charms', Liturgies, and Secret Rites in Early Medieval England, *Ciaran Arthur*